Education and the State in Tsarist Russia

PATRICK L. ALSTON

1969
STANFORD UNIVERSITY PRESS
STANFORD, CALIFORNIA

Stanford University Press
Stanford, California
© 1969 by the Board of Trustees of the
Leland Stanford Junior University
Printed in the United States of America
L.C. 68–26775

To the Memory of

GEORGE V. LANTZEFF

*who introduced me to the dry delights
of administrative history*

Preface

> *But of all the things which I have mentioned that which*
> *most contributes to the permanence of constitutions is the*
> *adaptation of education to the form of government, and yet*
> *in our own day this principle is universally neglected.*
> ARISTOTLE, Politics

Among the first of many peoples to take instruction in modern civilization from its Western teachers, the Russians were among the few to keep their political independence throughout the nervous period of cultural dependence on better-educated powers. From the introduction of state schooling at the beginning of the eighteenth century until the resolution of its most acute crisis at the beginning of the twentieth, tsarist statesmen promoted education as part of a political effort at reform from above in a country too ignorant to be renewed from below and too tough to be reorganized from outside.

From the French Revolution on, earnest young products of tsarist schools fondled assorted theories, which generations of alumni raised on government stipends strove to realize, looking to the abrupt and, if necessary, bloody regeneration of the country through direct union of the state-educated with the state-neglected. Professional scholars, most of them employees of the central educational bureaucracy, were skeptical of shortcuts to Aristotle's "good life." If Russia's western neighbors were able to emerge refreshed from successive plunges into violence more dynamic and better organized than before, this was partly owing, in their opinion, to a centuries-old educational tradition that Russia lacked. "Our European schoolmistress," a university professor advised Alexander III after his father's assassination by student youth, "threatens to destroy us by arousing a passion in us for self-expression before inculcating in us academic discipline." Maintenance of ignorance for security reasons was equally hazardous. Education, the Minister of Finance advised the son of Alexander III on the eve of war in Asia and civil strife at home, foments social revolution, but popular ignorance loses wars.

Torn by mounting foreign pressures and growing social unrest, the tsarist state experimented with a wide variety of academic devices. As generations swiftly passed, its central system of general education, particularly at the secondary level, assumed a heavy responsibility for harmonizing the ambivalent demands of the modernization process—the state's ballooning need for disciplined intelligence and society's insatiable appetite for self-determination. Under the prevailing rules of tsarist politics the field of general education became a stormy sector of the broad struggle between bureaucratic absolutism and local control of local affairs. For a half-century the educated class in and out of government fought to decide whether the empire would adopt bureaucratic or public direction of national enlightenment. By the end of the nineteenth century, partisans on both sides were convinced that control of the general educational schools—whether lodged in central, local, or professional authorities—would shape in the long run the empire's social and political form.

On the brink of exposure to the unprecedented hazards of mass industrial war, tsarist Russia in 1914 was still in many obvious ways the least educated of the great powers. Humiliation and pride had already encouraged it to go further than others in the elaboration of central academic levers commanding social change. Other nations flaunted more sophisticated intellectual equipment. Few had explored in as much depth the interfaces of international, national, local, and personal stakes in schools. None had accumulated as much hard practical experience in the uses and abuses of a centralized educational system as a mechanism for controlling social development. *Education and the State in Tsarist Russia* examines that experience.

The governing concept of the book—the organization of education as a device to guide social change—grew initially out of my experience as an exchange student from the University of California to the University of Leningrad in 1958–59. For that opportunity I am indebted primarily to Professor Charles Jelavich. Viewed from the trenches of a student dormitory, the Soviet Union struck me less as a fresh idea than a secondhand machine. The peculiar feel of the Soviet bureaucracy led me to its origins in tsarist modes. The Ford Foundation enabled me to pursue the subject further at the Helsinki Slavic library, and it was there that I found the documents which led me to concentrate on the educational bureaucracy. Over the years, graduate colleges in Berkeley and Iowa paid most of my modest photoduplication and typing bills. Professor Nicholas Riasanovsky encouraged the work in its beginnings and Professor Cyril Black its completion. Toward the end, Coe College provided an ideal working base. My wife spent hours improving the clarity of the manuscript. In transliterating, I placed readability ahead of consistency. All dates are those in use at the time. The interpretation is mine. I am not wedded to it for better or for worse; it simply makes the most sense to me out of the documents I found.

P.L.A.

Contents

PART ONE

The State's Initiative
1700–1875

Chapter One

The Centralizing Tradition: Education as State Enlightenment, 1700–1855

The kingdoms of this world have their periods of rise and fall, and in every period the structure of government must be compatible with the educational level of the citizens upon which the state rests. Whenever the form of government falls below or rises above that level, the state will be shaken by greater or lesser convulsions. In general this is what explains the political upheavals which in ancient times and in our own days changed the course of governments. This also explains the failures which often accompany the most beneficent political reforms when public education has not adequately prepared men's minds.

MICHAEL SPERANSKY, *1809*

Intermittent Efforts to Introduce State Schools, 1700–1800

In the first quarter of the nineteenth century, Alexander Pushkin surveyed the impact of Peter the Great's reign on Russian history and gave it the name of the Petrine revolution. As it issued from its creator's hands, the Petrine revolution was the accelerated Europeanization of tsardom under the leadership of the state. This required a major military operation. For as Peter expressed it, Sweden's occupation of the Baltic provinces "not only has robbed us of the necessary ports, but has drawn a thick curtain over our mind's eye, robbing us of even the joy of eyeing the outside world."[1] The first quarter of the eighteenth century was spent lifting the curtain. In the process it became clear that a further interest of the tsarist government was to observe the military and industrial technology of its neighbors. The official appetite for practical and useful things inevitably exposed Muscovite society to change. "Russia sailed into Europe like an advancing ship—to the thud of axes and the roar of cannon," the poet Pushkin remarked. "But the wars undertaken by Peter the Great were beneficent and fruitful. Successful national reform was the result of the battle of Poltava, and European enlightenment moored on the banks of the conquered Neva."[2]

Convinced that his subjects must learn from foreigners in order to compete with them, Peter began the educational campaign simultaneously with the military. At the beginning of his reign the Slavonic-Greek-Latin Academy was the sole source of civic training. Its circumscribed spirit precluded it from introducing secular learning. What the country needs, the Tsar notified the patriarch, is a school "from which people could go forth into church service, civilian service, and ready to wage war, to practice engineering and medical art."[3] Creation of a system of higher education capable of producing a comprehensive roster of trained personnel lay in the distant future. For the time being emergency measures had to do. In 1702 a proclamation distributed in Western Europe invited "useful artisans" to enter the tsar's service on generous terms. Simultaneously, the government sent young men abroad, particularly to England, to learn shipbuilding and seamanship.

With the help of Englishmen the first schools of secular science, "navigation schools," were opened in Moscow. A member of the Grand Embassy had inspected England's Royal Mathematical School in 1698 and recruited two recent graduates for the service of the tsar. The youths arrived in Russia the next year and in 1701 were appointed instructors, along with a resident Englishman, in the newly established Moscow School of Navigation and Mathematics. The Moscow school was the first institution of secular science in tsardom and the prototype for vocational training installations attached directly to army barracks, shipyards, and mine pits. A Soviet scholar of the period has observed: "The establishment in Russia of different types of schools stretched out over many years. But that practical tendency that characterized the first Russian schools of the Petrine period ... was the indisputable result of English influence."[4]

After the victory at Poltava the tsarist government passed from emergency war measures to rudimentary plans for reorganizing society. The battle-tested army became the primary agency of social stability and individual advancement. Initially, promotion to officer from the ranks was open to all, serfs and boyars. The civil bureaucracy was subjected to the same rules as the military, and its offices were thrown open to talent. In addition to making performance rather than ancestry the foundation of status, the Tsar was determined to force the nobility back into actual lifelong labor for the Crown. At the age of fifteen all noblemen were ordered to present themselves in the capital for assignment to the military or the civil service. In 1714 two decrees commanded the children of noblemen, officials, clerks, and scribes to obtain schooling from the age of twelve as a prerequisite to entering government employment. In the words of B. H. Sumner, education became "the first rung in the ladder of state service."[5]

Peter moved with characteristic energy to implement this program. Once the foundation of St. Petersburg was secure, the school of navigational sciences was moved from the Moscow to the Neva. In the new seat of administration it was transformed into a full-fledged naval academy. The academy was also utilized as the nation's first teachers college. In 1715 a ukase despatched two midshipmen to each province to teach "geometry and geography to young men from every class of people." Such was the origin of the so-called cipher schools.

With the whole force of the autocrat behind it, the experiment in vocational training for the provinces prospered briefly. In 1721 the cipher schools reached a peak, with 42 in operation. But it was a state operation without public support. In the towns the artisans won a reprieve when the government accepted their petition that book learning was useless for their station in life. Ultimate success of the venture rested with the privileged class. But from the start the gentry put up a determined resistance to the additional obligation of going to school. To encourage compliance the Tsar forbade noblemen to marry before completion of their scholastic service. As truancy continued, the authorities resorted to imprisonment, the knout, chains, and pursuit with horse and hounds to fill the classrooms with recruits from lower society. Between 1714 and 1722 only 93 pupils out of 1,389 completed the course. The rest, in the words of the official report, simply "ran away." In 1727 the nobility accounted for a meager 2.5 per cent of the two thousand pupils left in the system. Artisans contributed 4.5 per cent, petty officials 18 per cent, soldiers 20 per cent, and the clerical estate 45 per cent.[6]

The cause of public schooling was saved in the eighteenth century by the church. The sons of priests not only regularly supplied more than half the pupils for the secular schools, but as the state's establishments floundered, Petersburg turned directly to the ecclesiastical authorities. Tax relief and special privileges encouraged the monasteries to teach children at large, and a number of bishops were persuaded to provide free instruction for the sons of priests. Finally, in 1721 a new legal code reorganized the church. In addition to ensuring the state's control of religious affairs, the law required each diocese to maintain a school out of its own resources. By 1725 at least 46 episcopal schools were going concerns. The creation of a religious system hastened the decline of the secular enterprise. As the Holy Synod established more schools, it demanded that members of the clerical estate be transferred to its jurisdiction.* As a result, fourteen cipher schools shut down for lack of pupils. After 1723 the remaining ones were gradually transferred to the jurisdiction of the Holy Synod. From 1721 to 1786 the Orthodox church was responsible for providing what limited educational opportunity there was for the general population.

In 1721 the Treaty of Nystadt brought the Northern War to a close. There was now time to give final legislative form to the reconstruction of society. After a year of careful preparation the Table of Ranks was promulgated on January 24, 1722. Previously existing noble rank (*chin*), based on birth groups such as the Moscow nobility, town noblemen, and boyar sons, was abolished. Personal service was to replace pedigree. Hereditary titles of "prince," "count," and "baron" were to account for nothing as long as the bearers "serve neither us nor the fatherland." All unemployed noblemen were considered to belong to the general body of gentry. The only way to escape out of this mass into position, office, and status was up the bureaucratic ladder.

The fourteen levels of the Petrine hierarchy were divided into three parallel routes: military, civilian, and the purely titular. Military service was subdivided into infantry, guards, artillery, and naval branches. The central bureaucracy was reorganized into a number of administrative boards called "colleges," and the term "collegiate" assumed a prominent role among the titles signifying position on the civil Table of Ranks. However exalted their ancestry, "noble children are to enter the colleges from below. And namely: first Collegiate Junkers, if they are educated as witnessed by the college ... but if they are not schooled, and for lack of scholars must be employed, they are to become Titular Collegiate Junkers ... without rank." Rank was counted down from the top. Acquisition of the eighth rank, Collegiate Assessor, conferred hereditary nobility "with all its honors and advantages" on Russians and foreigners alike, "although previously of low birth and lacking a coat of arms." It was this provision of the law that prompted Pushkin to remark a cen-

---

* To direct the nobility toward the cipher schools, the Tsar forbade them to enter the Slavonic-Greek-Latin Academy on pain of shipment to the galleys of his new fleet. Katkov, p. v.

tury later, "*Pierre I est tout à la fois Robespierre et Napoléon (la révolution incarnée.)*"*

Realizing that without a system of education to support it the Table of Ranks would remain a façade on boyar ignorance, Peter the Great devoted the last years of his reign to broad organizational plans for lower, secondary, and higher schools. His own predilections were to build from the top down with the aid of Western institutions, and the idea of establishing an academy of sciences ripened throughout his reign. The Grand Embassy's visit to England, the correspondence with Leibniz and with Christian Wolff, and the visit of the Tsar to France in 1717 all contributed to the formulation of the charter that was ratified on January 22, 1724. The distinctive feature of the original design was the conjunction of a university and a school with an academy. Such a departure from European practice was necessary because of the lack of "regular schools, gymnasiums, and seminaries in which young people could begin to study and afterward assimilate the higher levels of the sciences."[7] The novel organization, it was hoped, would serve as the center of the state's pedagogical mission to the countryside.

The death of Peter early in 1725 removed his guiding hand, and the two functions of the academy became separated. Owing primarily to the activities of foreign scholars, research prospered. In contrast, the educational branches of the academy never flourished. The university depended on its secondary school for students; while in its first year (1726) the gymnasium admitted 120 pupils, in succeeding years the number steadily declined. In 1727, 74 students were corralled by enrolling the children of soldiers, artisans, and even serfs. The establishment of military academies for the nobility siphoned off the remaining gentry after 1730. The government strove to keep the university functioning by granting stipends, constructing a dormitory, and recruiting candidates from the seminaries. All such measures were to no avail, and the academic university ceased operation for the second time in 1753.

* W. Lednicki, *Pushkin's Bronze Horseman* (Berkeley, Calif., 1955), p. 65. The "educated Russian," Dostoevsky reminded a Moscow audience in 1880 in an address on Pushkin, "emerged suddenly at the beginning of the second century after the great Petrine reform, torn away from the people and the national roots and cast with our intellectual society ... ; for a century he has been a stranger in his own country, alienated from labor, without culture, raised like a convent girl within closed walls, fulfilling the strange and innumerable obligations attached to one or another of the fourteen classes into which educated Russian society has been divided." *Polnoe sobranie sochinenii* (St. Petersburg, 1895), XI, 457–58.

With the departure of Peter the Great, the revolution he set in motion shifted its course. He had placed the autocracy in charge of enlightening the nation and then imperiled his work by upsetting the traditional law of dynastic primogeniture in favor of appointment by the reigning monarch of his heir. He then died without naming his successor. The result was an interregnum of 40 years, during which a series of puppets nominally occupied the shaky throne. Its size and confidence swollen by the men of rank that the Petrine revolution had elevated to positions of authority, the gentry exploited each political opening. Step by step its members widened their rights and reduced their obligations at the expense of the peasantry and the Crown.

Restrictions on access to career-oriented schools inevitably accompanied the relaxation of service. The nobility took a major step toward the goal of monopolizing secular educational opportunity and the rank and status that lay beyond during the reign of Anna. In 1731 the widowed niece of Peter the Great established a military academy for noblemen in St. Petersburg. Sister institutions followed. One of the rights granted the pupils of the cadet corps was to become officers directly on graduation "without having been soldiers, sailors, or other lower ranks." The higher technical schools—the artillery, engineering and naval academies—were also reserved for the privileged class. Noblemen narrowed the social structure of state education and broadened its content. The defunct cipher schools had provided vocational instruction. The cadet corps, however, were only peripherally concerned with military science. Foreign language training, first German and later French, were uppermost, followed by heraldry, genealogy, dancing, and smatterings of "polite" subjects such as history, geography, jurisprudence, and philosophy. Military exercises were restricted to Saturdays so as "not to interfere with other sciences."[8]

Concentrating on refinement of manners and expansion of privileges, the nobility abandoned the academic grind to others. The foundation of a university and a gymnasium had been a part of the original Leibnizian design for the Academy of Sciences. But every effort to utilize the institution for advanced instruction had failed. For a time it also appeared as though the research facilities of the establishment would wither or at best remain a haven for peripatetic German scholars. Such was not to be the case. During the reign of Peter the Great's daughter, Elizabeth I, a native son and commoner captured the libraries, laboratories, and lecture halls for Russian interests. His name was Mikhail Lomonosov, and his life exemplified the vitality of the democratic potential of the Petrine revolution kept alive in state general educational institutions during the period of aristocratic ascendency. Denied the support of his family, Lomonosov was rescued by the state and sent to Germany at its expense to complete his education. At Marburg he studied philosophy, physics, and chemistry under Christian Wolff, the herald of the Enlightenment east of the Rhine. Returning home in 1741, he was appointed assistant professor at the academy in St. Petersburg.

Anxious for Russia to produce "her own Platos and quick-witted Newtons," Lomonosov inspired efforts to open a higher school in the old capital after a generation of frustration in the new. "I was the first to formulate the principles for the establishment of a university," he maintained. The financial and administrative organizer was Ivan Shuvalov, an aristocratic patron of Lomonosov, a correspondent with Voltaire, and a favorite of Empress Elizabeth. Encouraged by "the large number of domestic tutors supported by the Moscow nobility," he persuaded the daughter of Peter the Great to realize the scholastic dream of her father in full. Shuvalov's original plan called for opening the doors of science to nobles only, but the democratic views of Lomonosov prevailed. When Moscow University began operations in 1755, its three faculties of law, medicine, and philosophy accepted all social classes and estates. In the earliest days even a few serfs attended with the permission of their masters.

Drawing on his experience in St. Petersburg, Lomonosov emphasized the importance of gymnasiums for the success of university life. For higher learning without preparatory institutions, he observed, was "a plowed field without seed."[9] A gymnasium was accordingly opened in Moscow and another in Kazan. To render general education attractive to the privileged class, the government made a number of special arrangements. The Moscow school was divided into two branches, one for commoners and one for the gentry. In the aristocratic section a diluted academic course was offered, the emphasis being laid on conversational French, with time evenly divided between the Russian language and ballroom dancing. But even these concessions were not enough. The nobility were in the habit of putting their children into service as soon as possible, usually at the age of fifteen, so that they could begin accumulating seniority on the Table of Ranks. Such considerations were a major reason why parents were loath to have their sons attend a university.

To break down resistance to higher learning, the government allowed wellborn students to enroll in military regiments or civilian offices and receive credit for service while they studied. All these measures, however, failed to keep the gentry in school. From the 1750's to the 1770's hundreds of them matriculated, stayed for a year or two, and then departed for government employment. The situation was so depressing that the faculty council went on record with a formal protest: "Most of the students from the nobility exercise their right to withdraw whenever they like or matriculate in the university shortly before it is necessary for them to enter service.... On leaving the university, such persons can only defame it by their abysmal ignorance."[10]

State enlightenment fared better with the *raznochintsy,* the term applied to people of "assorted rank," such as townspeople who were exempt from the poll tax, burghers who were not members of a merchant guild or an artel, the sons of priests, foreigners, professional men, and free peasants (like Lomonosov) who had left the vocation of their fathers. Even though the curriculum of the plebeian division of the gymnasium was more rigorous, the poor had good reasons for enduring it. When a lowborn graduate of the gymnasium became a university student, he received a sword as a token of his ennoblement. When he acquired his academic degree, he also donned an officer's epaulettes. State general education became the cadet corps of the nonprivileged class. Of the 48 students in residence in 1764, only eight were noblemen. Forty were government stipendiaries. Of the state scholars, nineteen were the sons of soldiers, six the sons of priests, three the children of petty officials, two the children of teachers, and one the son of a serf. The noble students were often as destitute as their social inferiors. An undated daily report to the director of the university reads: "Nine noblemen and six *raznochintsy* absent from class for lack of shoes."[11]

The state university in Moscow failed for decades to furnish the autocracy with an official and professional class freed from the dilettantism of the self-educated gentry. The local gymnasium was not enough. Without an organized system of provincial secondary schools, the national center of learning lacked sufficient numbers of seriously motivated and adequately prepared students. In 1765 there was only one undergraduate in the faculty of law. Five years later the first two domestically trained jurists in Russian history were graduated. During the entire reign of

Catherine II only one physician passed the final examination for the medical degree. To increase enrollment the Empress issued rules making government office dependent on academic examinations, but the rules were ignored. Since the gentry could obtain preferment on easier terms through the military academies, the academic population failed to grow. At the end of the eighteenth century, as the university approached its fiftieth anniversary, there were still no more than 100 undergraduates preparing to furnish the forty million people of the realm with teachers, doctors, and administrators. Just as significant for the future was the fixed opinion among the upper classes that "scholars should come from below."

When Empress Elizabeth died, her nephew, a grandson of Peter the Great and Charles XII of Sweden, became tsar as Peter III. The last sovereign with an indisputable claim to Romanov blood reigned only six months, but within that time he formulated in two legislative acts significant social consequences of the Petrine revolution: the resurgence of the nobility and the deterioration of the church. Peter III began the extensive secularization of ecclesiastical property, and his wife continued the policy. The church was the only feasible institution for spreading the rudiments of civilization to the public at large. After 1762 it was too poor to expand its educational activities to the growing population. The most memorable procedure of Peter III's reign also influenced the structure of organized learning. On February 18, 1762, an imperial ukase released the nobility from compulsory duties to the state. In effect, the Manifesto of Liberation officially recognized that the Muscovite nobility of service had become a European noblesse of leisure. The proclamation explained that it had been necessary in the past to exercise force because of the "coarseness and ignorance" of the gentry. The notables were now invited to volunteer their services to the government as an expression of their maturity and refinement. Restricting itself to the pious admonition that "no one should presume to raise his children without the ministrations of science," the emancipation manifesto all but formally excused the landowners from serious educational concern.[12]

After humiliating the clergy and exalting the nobility, Peter III made the final mistake of antagonizing the palace guards. Among other insults, he threatened to replace them with a German bodyguard from his ancestral duchy of Holstein. His spouse, Catherine, was a full-blooded

German too, but she had adopted Russia and identified its interests with her own. In the summer of 1762 the guards removed the husband from the scene and set the wife on the throne.

The first decade of the new reign was a period of peril and adventure. The 33-year-old princess was a usurper and a foreigner. Informed opinion expected neither a lengthy nor a productive stewardship. But Catherine II had private resources. During her apprenticeship at the court of Elizabeth, the wife of Peter III had stocked her mind. "Eighteen years of tediousness and solitude," she recalled, caused her to read many books. The deceased daughter of Peter the Great had forbidden Voltaire as a topic of conversation. But "this evil man, who ridiculed everything and never went to church," was the new sovereign's spiritual director. His wit had supported her in the isolation of the bridal years, and his cool, bantering intelligence had shaped her own. With Voltaire guaranteeing her credit with educated European opinion, the Tsaritsa recovered the cultural initiative for the state, established her personal preceptorate over the nation's intellectual development, and maintained it for a quarter of a century, until the coming of the French Revolution.

Until the translation of enlightenment themes into mob action, the French-dominated cosmopolitan culture of the European upper classes streamed into tsardom under her aegis. The ideas that the *philosophes* were clarifying and popularizing—faith in science, in human reason, in natural human rights, and in progress—became part of the mental equipment of an alert and inquisitive section of the serf-owning class. Kliuchevsky observed that "under Peter, the officer aristocrats went abroad to learn artillery and navigational science, under Elizabeth, to study hair styles and eating habits; now they traveled westward to be initiated into the secrets of philosophy."[13]

From the 1760's onward, the civilizing process gave rise to increasingly sharp differences within the ruling class. In the outlying areas the rank-and-file landlords continued their brutish existence. At the other extreme, the provincial magnates and court aristocrats gradually melded with the glittering noblesse of Europe. With their palaces in Petersburg and Moscow and their estates larger than many Continental principalities, the great ones of the realm began to occupy Russia as a foreign power ruling over wild tribes. Suspended between the crude bumpkins and the elegant grandees was a mobile layer of officers, officials, squires, and men of assorted rank who were either employed in the capital cities or maintained contact with urban life on retirement from military and civilian service. This aggregate was Russia's functional "middle class." It was this social stratum that provided the reading public whose appetite created a market for ideas, books, plays, and periodicals in the 1760's. It soon became complex and plentiful enough to support the activities of Nikolai Novikov. From 1775 to 1789 his press, affiliated with the University of Moscow, turned out a greater number of books than had been produced in Russia since the invention of printing.

An informal community of people sympathetic to ideas arose. It came to be known as the *obshchestvo,* "society," or "the public." The expression of its values, reflections, and attitudes became known as "public opinion." What distinguished the reading public from the middling gentry official class as a whole was its attitude. The members of "society" were not merely literate, they were thoughtful. They not only mirrored the Petrine revolution, the genteel culture, the Catherinian preceptorate; they reflected upon the Western educational process and began to ponder its long-term implications for the nation, the people, and the regime.

An early exponent of public opinion was a bankrupt provincial nobleman, Aleksandr Radishchev. Through his mother's relatives, Radishchev obtained an appointment to the aristocratic page corps in St. Petersburg. In the late 1760's Catherine sent him with a group of students to Leipzig composing part of a program designed to provide a cadre of trained jurists for the reforms expected from her legislative commission. In Germany the state student came under the influence of the more radical *philosophes,* Helvetius, Raynal, and Rousseau. On his return to Russia, Radishchev entered the civil service and quietly worked his way up the Table of Ranks to Collector of Customs for the port of St. Petersburg. The government official spent his leisure time, as he later confessed, translating the ideals and rhetoric of the French Revolution into a garbled Russian prose styled after Lomonosov.*

* In the 1780's Radishchev was re-creating such sentiments as "Man is born into the world equal with all others. . . . If it is not within the power of the law to intercede for him, then a citizen enjoys a natural right of defense, of preservation, of welfare. For a citizen, on becoming obedient to the state, does not cease to be a man, whose first obligations originate in his nature." *Polnoe sobranie sochinenii* (Moscow, 1938), I, 278–79. In 1790 a state court condemned the Collector of Customs to death for publishing such views. The Empress commuted the sentence to ten years in Siberia, and Radishchev became the first of a long line of Russians banished because of their education by the government that educated them.

In time, the society represented by Radishchev became the nation's self-appointed conscience. The Voltairians of the 1770's became the Rosicrucians and Rousseauists of the 1790's, and their descendants became active revolutionaries. But the Catherinian public did not develop into an organized instrument for solving concrete problems. It was not itself the product of an educational tradition or the graduate of a system of higher schools; these did not exist. Its characteristic feature was dilettantism. It was at best an amateurishly educated class, produced by reading, travel, discussion, and the polite curricula of the aristocratic schools. Two generations later a systematically educated class with a broader social base would emerge on the initiative of the state. By this time self-educated society would have a tradition, a psyche, and even a martyrology of its own. Eventually, the newer, state-educated class would absorb the genteel public, but not before the prototype had time to impart its weaknesses and its charm to the successor—its enthusiasm for foreign philosophical methods of diagraming the universe, its sentimentality, and its distaste for methodical, routine, practical intellectual effort.

Aware of this deficiency in the Russian approach to learning, Catherine did not restrict her efforts to the mere refinement of manners. In collaboration with the theorist Ivan Betsky, she concentrated on the moral aspect of the educational process. Before Catherine's day the concept of education as the teaching of self-discipline (*vospitanie*) was associated with religion. In keeping with the secular bent of the Enlightenment, character formation now became a state concern. The governing educational document of the period maintained that "the reason, adorned and enlightened with the sciences, does not of itself produce a good and reliable citizen. In fact, in many cases harm can result if the child is not trained in virtue from its tenderest years ..., for the root of all vice and virtue is education (*vospitanie*)."[14]

Peter the Great was accused of conspiring to turn the Eastern Slavs into Dutchman. Diderot suggested raising the cultural level of Russia by importing Swiss. With the morals of the nobility uppermost in mind, Catherine II formulated an ethical standard that was frankly *bürgerlich*. This middle-class behavioral norm became the lodestar of tsarist educational policy. Catherine's grandson, Alexander I, romanticized it. Another grandson, Nicholas I, militarized it. And in the 1860's Count Dimitri Tolstoy, a critic and admirer of the Catherinian system, would create the state's most ambitious educational device around the concept of discipline. In the second half of the eighteenth century, the Russian government lacked the means of creating and sustaining a comprehensive system for transforming recalcitrant subjects into responsible citizens. But a limited start was made on a segment of the upper classes. The boarding school (literally, character-building home, *vospitatelnyi dom*) became as fashionable in the northern forests as in the West. Homes for four- and five-year-old males were opened at aristocratic schools in the 1760's.[15]

The Empress reserved her warmest pedagogical zeal for her own neglected sex. In the mid-1760's a boarding school for young gentlewomen and a day school for middle-class girls were opened at the Smolny monastery in St. Petersburg. The combined institute was one of the Continent's earliest ventures into lay education for women. The Empress spoke of the pupils as her grandchildren and retained a direct hand in the running of the school. As other academies modeled on Smolny were established, they were organized into a special department, named after its first patroness, Princess Marie, the wife of Crown Prince Paul. Starting with the schools of Empress Marie, female instruction assumed an aristocratic-eleemosynary character. Like ecclesiastical training, it remained separated from the mainstream of subsequent state enterprise.

Catherine the Great was not only the initiator of institutionalized character training for the aristocracy; she was also the first Russian monarch to devote attention to the systematic education of the rulers themselves. For assistance she appealed to Europe's men of letters. D'Alembert declined an invitation to become the tutor of Alexander I. A Swiss philosopher, Frédéric-César de La Harpe, accepted. This ardent republican opened the mind of the boy autocrat to French-Revolutionary approaches toward national enlightenment.*

In the first decade of her reign Catherine II exploited what opportunities were available for organizing the education of Russia's ruling class. The peasant mass, however, was fatally neglected. The sovereign herself remained sensitive to the need for introducing the prerequisites of civilized life into the outlying villages and back country communes. From the 1760's to the 1780's the rough drafts of her many scholastic schemes contained provisions for offering elementary opportunities to the coun-

---

* When he became tsar, Alexander wrote to "citizen La Harpe, former member of the Swiss directory," that he would strive to prove himself "worthy to have been your pupil." Nicholas, Grand Duke of Russia, *L'Empereur Alexandre I*, I, 331.

tryside. For a moment, a first step seemed possible in connection with the legislative commission. In 1770 a subcommittee on schools devised a plan, based on the Prussian model, for establishing obligatory instruction for all male peasants. The localities would pay the expenses and the clergy would furnish the teachers. The program was minimal but not impractical, and it came from the people themselves. Nevertheless, it was filed away and forgotten.* In the ensuing decades the rural masses sank out of the ranks of the educable. The "orphans" of the seventeenth century became the "dark people" of the nineteenth. For the duration of the St. Petersburg period the majority of the nation remained impervious to enlightenment, whether from official or public sources.

By the end of the first decade of her reign Catherine II was learning what every autocrat after her experienced, that it was easier to expand the empire than to enlighten it. The conduct of foreign affairs afforded less frustration and quicker results. After forty years of hesitation and indecision the march of Slavic armies toward Constantinople and Berlin was resumed. By the end of her long sway, Russia stood as firmly on the Black Sea as on the Baltic, and Poland had disappeared. In the early 1770's the strains of the Polish-Turkish imbroglio emphasized the need for firmer control of the countryside. Since the emancipation of the nobility, the peasantry had been increasingly restless, and repeated outbreaks hampered the collection of the taxes and recruits indispensable for diplomacy and war. But the major shock needed to cow the gentry into accepting a reform of local government came when Emelian Pugachev, a cossack army deserter, raised the standard of rebellion in the south. Famine and artillery dispersed his wild hordes in the vicinity of Moscow, and Pugachev was drawn and quartered in Red Square. Before he died he is reported to have said: "I am not the real raven. I am but the fledgling. The real raven is still flying in the sky." *Pugachevshchina* passed into the language as the term for Armageddon, an elemental upheaval that would one day sweep away the old order.

Pugachev's execution was followed by a decade of strenuous cooperation between the monarchy and the privileged class. The unwieldy satrapies of Peter I were reduced to some 50 more manageable provinces (*guberniia*), which were themselves subdivided into ten to a dozen districts (*uezdy*). The districts and the provinces were equipped with compli-

---

* For a comment on the project a century later see below, pp. 102–3.

cated mechanisms for administering justice, collecting taxes, maintaining security, and promoting welfare. Their administrative apparatus relied heavily on the participation of local estates acting in separated capacities. As one penetrated downward toward the people, administration became more distant from a systematic educational process. For since the disappearance of Peter the Great's cipher schools, there was no state schooling in the provincial towns.

In the late 1770's Catherine turned her attention once more to this deficiency. She had Diderot's assurance that the conjuncture of Europe's educational development with Russia's lack of it made the moment "most opportune" for devising "a universal system of education" for her realm. In Europe the human spirit was "off on a spree." Whereas "the appetite for true science" was everywhere being aroused and knowledge of every kind was being carried "to new heights of perfection," the Empress of Russia had "no ancient institutions cluttering her view. She enjoys a vast field, a space cleared of all obstacles upon which she can build at will. I do not flatter her. I speak sincerely when I assure her that from this point of view her position is better than ours."[16]

By this time, however, Catherine's thoughts were not aimed at raising up a rival, academically prepared official class to offset the gentry, but at simply improving the middle level of government in the reorganized countryside. Seventy years had passed since the first effort to upgrade provincial life with organized learning. If the second effort was to succeed, the tactics of Peter the Great would have to be revised. There should be no compulsion; the syllabus should be general-educational rather than vocational and the schools should be public, i.e., based on local support. The newly fashioned political units would provide the administrative framework with ultimate authority in the hands of the provincial governors. The clerical academies would provide the necessary teachers. For detailed planning the Empress did not appeal to her philosopher friends but hired the services of a professional pedagogue and administrator.

By 1780 the Tsarina had found a military ally and cultural confidant in Joseph II, the aggressively enlightened sovereign of the Habsburg domains. At a meeting arranged to discuss joint operations against Turkey, the Emperor explained to the Empress how the Austrian government was successfully adapting the Prussian system of public schools to the special requirements of a polyglot state. He personally recommended the services of Theodore Iankovich de Mirevo "as a man already expert in the development of popular education, versed in the Russian language, and professing the Orthodox faith." The versatile Serb, who had recently introduced elementary schools for the Slavic population in Hungary, accepted the Tsaritsa's offer of employment.

In 1782 a ukase announced the formation of a Commission for the Establishment of Public Schools. German professors from the Academy of Sciences acted as consultants under the presidency of Petr Zavadovsky, a nobleman of rank. As the work progressed, the commission was converted into the Supreme School Administration, with Zavadovsky as chairman of the board. This body served as the nucleus for the future Ministry of Education. The professional experts on the Zavadovsky committee recommended the adoption of the Austro-Prussian model. The actual work of writing an educational statute and preparing teaching materials was entrusted to de Mirevo. During the next four years he translated the better part of 27 German textbooks and teaching manuals to accompany his legislative arrangements. His emphasis was secular and academic. Materials were prepared for teaching geometry, mechanics, drawing, writing, Russian, natural history, geography, and history. The instructional aids were ready simultaneously with the charter in 1786. From the perspective of the twentieth century, Paul Miliukov considered the Austrian Serb "the real creator of the first Russian general-educational school."[17] The beginnings were simple enough. Impoverished seminarians memorized the *Methodenbücher* in translation and then led the children of petty gentry, local officials, and soldiers in learning the prescribed lessons by rote.

The Statute of 1786 proposed opening a two-year "minor school" in every district seat and a four-year "major school" in every provincial capital. Public reception was restrained. In 1790 a town council sent the following petition to the governor of the province: "Schools are not necessary for the children of merchants and craftsmen. Therefore, we do not intend to send our children to school. We have no desire to support the schools and we see no value in them for us."[18] But despite the widespread apathy the enterprise proved workable. Within a decade every province of European Russia north of the Kuban boasted a major school, and by the end of the century half of the empire's 500 largest urban centers supported at least a minor school. This number was achieved by including already existing institutions of the Baltic and Polish provinces, as well as foreign and private schools in the larger cities. In 1800 the network had grown to 315 establishments, employing 790 teachers and supplying basic instruction to 19,915 pupils, including 1,784 girls. At about this same time (1807) the schools of the Holy Synod, dating from 1721, were responsible for 24,167 children. The population of the empire in 1800 has been estimated at forty million. Russia, then, entered the nineteenth century with less than .5 per cent of its school-age population under instruction. But the difficult first step had been taken two long generations after the abortive start with vocational schools in 1716.

The "people's schools," as Catherine's foundations were called, marked a victory for the state over the efforts of the aristocracy to monopolize organized educational opportunity. In 1760 Ivan Shuvalov had proposed a general secondary system for the gentry alone. The major schools, however, quickly became social blenders. In the province of Petersburg in 1801, 16 per cent of the 4,136 pupils were gentry, the rest commoners. In Novgorod in 1803 only 13 per cent of the 507 pupils were wellborn. A study made of 38 major schools in 1801 revealed that children of hereditary and personal nobility accounted for one-third of the pupils, with the other two-thirds distributed among the lower classes: common citizens 14 per cent, merchants 12 per cent, soldiers 11 per cent, serfs 11 per cent, clerks 8 per cent, state peasants 5 per cent, and clergy 2 per cent.*

Parents seldom left their children in the schools for the duration of the course. An official report of 1789 declared that the curriculum of the major schools surpassed the needs of the population. Literacy was sufficient for the lower government jobs of clerk, copier, and scribe. As a result, "pupils in the second class usually do not wish to continue their studies in the third form." Of the 1,432 youths who entered the schools of the province of Archangel between 1786 and 1803, only 52 earned an exit diploma. The experience of the northern province was repeated across the land. Appearing in this early period as the reflection of a serious gap between the cultural ambitions of the political leadership and the limited employment opportunities open to the nonprivileged population, the problem of dropping out of school would remain to plague the regime, culminating in the crisis of the cook's circular a century later.

Catherine's son, Paul, succeeded his mother in 1796. For decades she had kept him off the throne and confined in virtual house arrest. Coming

---

* Miliukov, "Shkola," pp. 759–60; Miliukov estimated that women made up 7 per cent of the student population of the empire at the end of the eighteenth century.

at last into his inheritance, the 42-year-old monarch reacted against his mother's closest counselors and then against the nobility as a whole. His immediate impulse was revenge for years of humiliation, but his more statesmanlike goal was to terminate the privileged status of the nobles by forcing them back into obligatory service to the state. "When the Empress was alive," Count Komorovsky observed, "we were always in evening clothes, going either to the theater or to a social affair. Now, from morning till night, we were on the parade ground, being ordered about like recruits." By the end of 1800 Paul's tyranny had turned against his family, threatening Crown Prince Alexander and placing the dynasty in jeopardy. The outcome was his murder at the hands of noble officers.

The Creation of the Central Educational Apparatus, 1800–1825

The eighteenth century passed into Russian consciousness as the period when the ruling class placed itself "in a direct pupil relationship to Western education."* During this period of "school exercises" in civilization, several types of formal learning were institutionalized. By the late 1780's prospects glimmered for synthesizing technical training, enlightenment, and civic discipline into a comprehensive educational program capable of harmonizing central authority with the public appetite for self-expression. At this moment, however, before the Russian students of the West had time to digest the European Enlightenment, the European Revolution, dramatized by the French, intervened. It was to the credit of the tsarist state, and guaranteed its formal pedagogical initiative for decades to come, that in the immediate wake of the French Revolution influential men in its service were convinced that it was time for the country to pass from spasmodic curiosity to a comprehensive program of centrally organized schooling. The initiator of the program to preclude Pugachev by means of Condorcet was the dreamful pupil of La Harpe who became autocrat of all the Russias at the age of 23.

The character of Alexander I was plastic. The memory of his tacit consent to parricide and the erratic course of the contest with Napoleon turned him toward the supernatural with advancing years. But by his early education he was a child of the Enlightenment. His tutor had intro-

---

* A. N. Pypin, *Istoriia russkoi literatury* (St. Petersburg, 1899), IV, 189. Pypin's fellow professor, K. D. Kavelin, remarked: "...we dawdle lazily through the various classrooms history has led us through and do nothing to advance from the school desk into real life" (p. 1055). (His metaphor referred to the West, which is a "classroom" where the Russians now learn enlightenment, later revolution, and later nihilism.)

duced him at the age of twelve to the writings of Locke, Gibbon, Radishchev's model Mably, and Rousseau. To the end of his days the Tsar remained emotionally attached to the saving graces of reason, equality, liberty, law, and education. As Crown Prince, Alexander had consorted with a cosmopolitan quartet that included the Polish patriot Prince Adam Czartoryski and the "Jacobin," Count Paul Stroganov. The Emperor's "friends" shared his condescending attitude toward the courtiers of his grandmother's day and his contempt for the native nobility. "What is this nobility?" Stroganov burst out at a conference with the Tsar at the beginning of the new reign. "In our country the nobility is composed of a horde of people who became gentlemen through service, who received no education.... It is the most ignorant class, the most debauched and the stuffiest."[19] During the first years of the reign the four friends acted as the Tsar's closest advisers, forming the *comité secret,* or, as Alexander called them, his committee of public safety. With the help of these consultants the monarch undertook the task of reorganizing the central government.

Like many of their contemporaries, the young friends of the Tsar's intimate circle were Anglophiles. But their ideas for remodeling Russia were inspired less by British practices than by the *esprit de système* of enlightened Continental despotism, in particular by the administrative absolutism of the "organizer of the Revolution," Napoleon Bonaparte. The central bureaucracy and the national school system are generally considered to date from the secret committee's initiatives and plans. That the two appeared together was no accident but an essential part of the design. La Harpe argued for establishing a ministry of education without waiting for administrative reform, but the admirers of Napoleon placed great value on education as part of a general reorganization of the state. A manifesto of September 8, 1802, replaced the governing boards of Peter the Great with a battery of eight executive agencies. The ministries of war, naval affairs, foreign affairs, interior, finance, justice, commerce, and "enlightenment"* appeared in outline. A decade later the Statute of June

---

* In the midst of the discussion whether the prospective central office of education should be named "Ministry of National Enlightment" (*Ministerstvo Narodnago Prosveshcheniia*) or "Ministry of National Instruction" (*Ministerstvo Narodnago Obrazovaniia*), Count Kochubei remarked that the term "enlightenment" to designate the state's pedagogical mission "would have a bad effect in view of the widespread feeling that it is dangerous to shed too much light." *Stroganov,* II, 226. After the publication of Konstantin Ushinsky's *Chelovek kak predmet vospitaniia* (1868–69; see below, pp. 88–89), *vospitanie* began to replace *prosveshchenie* as the preferred term for the general learning process. Later, Marxist

25, 1811, endowed the new offices with the basic structure that they kept until their subordination to a prime ministership after the Revolution of 1905. The Alexandrian remodeling of the center implemented Catherine II's remodeling of local government. The Empress had supported her provincial design with a public network of locally financed schools. Her grandson's central apparatus would depend on state schools more solidly financed by the imperial treasury.

The secret committee included devotees of the latest pedagogical views. Several members had lived in Paris after the fall of the Bastille and were partisans of the republican approach to education. The tutor of Count Stroganov had helped the Marquis de Condorcet draft the school bill presented to the National Assembly in 1792. The committee adapted two basic principles from the program of the French Revolution: the concept of a "unified school," one all-embracing system of state schools, cross-connected for ease of transfer, open to all citizens without restriction; and the "democratic ladder," the arrangement of all levels of instruction in an unbroken series, with advancement from lower to secondary to higher stages, based on academic performance rather than ability to pay.[20]

When the Ministry of National Enlightenment was established as part of the Bonapartization program of 1802, Count Petr Zavadovsky became its first director. Working closely with the German scholars of the Academy of Sciences, the aging courtier imbued the new department with a liking for German academic models and invited the initative of the local gentry. The youthful planners of the secret committee were impatient with the "grandfathers" of the eighteenth century. They also expressed hostility toward the "German" emphasis on academic refinement at the expense of "French" concern for social breadth. Viktor Kochubei remarked to Mikhail Speransky, "We do not need universities, especially universities on the German model, when there is no one to study at them, but primary and secondary schools.... The [French] system of lycées is the best that Russia can adopt."[21]

On January 24, 1803, the "provisional rules for national enlightenment"

pamphleteers adopted the cover name of "pupils" (*ucheniki*) for themselves and used the term "enlighteners" (*prosvetiteli*) to belittle the liberals of the great reform tradition. See V. I. Lenin, "Ot kakogo nasledstva my otkazyvaemsia." When Lenin's group came to power, they dropped "enlightenment" for "instruction." in the name of the central office for state schools. Russian Communists like the term *vospitanie* and acknowledge Ushinsky's influence. See below p. 249.

appeared, the product of a compromise between the "German party" of the old supreme school administration and the "French party" of the secret committee. Expanding on the organization of 1786, the guidelines of 1803 projected a secondary school in every provincial capital and an improved elementary school in every provincial and district seat, the network to be supported by state funds. The opening paragraph of the grand design announced categorically that "national enlightenment in the Russian Empire is a *special function of the state.*"[22] Tsardom would reap the benefits without enduring the agony of the French experience. By anticipating public demands for culture and progress, the educational bureaucracy would render popular upheaval unnecessary. To facilitate the exercise of central authority, the provinces were grouped into six educational districts, and six members of the central school administration were appointed curators to represent area interests in St. Petersburg.[23] At the local level each district would be placed under the supervision of a territorial university as soon as one was established.

Two of the original curatorships encircled national minorities, and these territories received separate regulations. In 1803 a special law was applied to the Vilna educational district, which included provinces of Lithuania and White Russia. While adopting the existing Polish organization, the Vilna Statute attempted to eliminate Polish influence from the curriculum. The region included the Jewish pale, and a decree of December 9, 1804, admitted Jewish youth to all levels of Russian schools, including the universities, without restrictions. It also allowed Jewish communities to maintain confessional schools at their own expense. In addition to the western provinces, the Baltic area received special treatment. It was organized into the educational district of Dorpat and eventually received its own charter, tailored to the dominant German culture of the ruling class. In 1810 the Russians annexed Georgia and Finland. The ancient Orthodox country in Transcaucasia became the nucleus for the educational district of the Caucasus, with its headquarters in Tiflis. When Finland became an autonomous grand duchy with the tsar as its grand duke, the Protestant-Lutheran nation maintained its own separate school system, including what became the University of Helsinki.

In 1804 the charters for Great Russian schools and all higher institutions began to appear. With varying degrees of difficulty the government laid the foundations for university life in the capital cities of the newly created school districts of St. Petersburg, Kharkov, Kazan, Dorpat, and Vilna.* In each of these except Kharkov and Kazan, there were existing institutions in which to mount the medical, physics-mathematics, and philosophical faculties. On November 5, the constitution for the secondary schools was published. It converted Catherine's major schools into four-year provincial schools and her minor schools into two-year improved-elementary district schools. Providing a finished program at each level, the curricula of both stages were utilitarian rather than academic. The courses of study were dovetailed, however, so as to provide continuous progression from lower through secondary to university instruction. Access to the "democratic ladder" was open to all elements of the population regardless of social, national, or religious origin. A recent authority on the comparative history of education has observed that the system of 1804 "was the first democratic *école unique* in Europe."[24] The legislators coordinated not only the academic structure of the schools but their management. The self-governing universities were at the apex of the administrative hierarchy. The institutions of higher learning supervised the provincial schools, which in turn were responsible for the district establishments.

Comprehensive as they appeared, the arrangements of 1803 and 1804 represented a substantial retreat from the initial vision. In its early enthusiasm the secret committee had thought of incorporating the different schools for different people into a single, coherent system. But the heterogeneous legacy of the eighteenth century, the *"tableau d'une bigarrure extrême,"* as Count Stroganov called it, could not be overcome. The academies for army officers, the private pensions for noblemen, the seminaries for priests, and the institutes for young ladies continued to develop separately. In the first year of Alexander's reign, while his advisers were seriously concerned with the peasant question, educational designs also

---

* Sergei Aksakov was a fourteen-year-old boy in Kazan in 1805. In his memoirs (*Sobranie sochinenii*, Moscow, 1955, II, 123–24) he described the mood that accompanied the "somewhat premature" advent of university life in a provincial town. "It is impossible to recall without a deep sense of satisfaction the passion for enlightenment and science that inspired the older boys of the gymnasium [when they learned that they had been chosen to become the first university students]. They all grew so thin and pale that the director was forced to take steps to restrain our enthusiasm. At night the inspector circulated through the dormitories, snuffing candles and hushing the boys who were reciting their lessons to one another under the blankets. The teachers, too, caught the infectious spirit and worked extra hours with the boys after class and on holidays. . . . So passed the first year after the opening of the university. Beautiful, golden days! A time of pure love for knowledge, a time of noble enthusiasm."

included the rural masses. Both La Harpe and Maximilian von Klinger, the director of the cadet corps, urged the extension of enlightenment to the villages.[25] When emancipation of the serfs proved impossible except in several minor ways, state instruction for the peasantry was discarded in favor of private, gentry, communal, and ecclesiastical enterprise. This meant its effective abandonment. The problem of creating a coherent and comprehensive instrument for guiding society would burden the old regime to the end of its days. At each period the state would concentrate its limited resources on controlling the key passes of educational opportunity, the strategic links between lower and secondary, secondary and higher schools.

During the respite in the struggle with Napoleon after 1807, while the army was busy annexing Finland and Bessarabia, the government turned its attention once more to domestic reform. In the ensuing period Michael Speransky, the son of a village priest, emerged as the dominant personality in the administration. As a protégé of the secret committee, he had been promoting the pedagogical function of the state since 1803. In his view, the autocracy itself should take the lead in preparing the people for responsible participation in government under law. From personal experience Speransky was aware of acute abuses in the central bureaucracy. Widespread ignorance was only one defect. Not only was it possible to be promoted up the fourteen-class society on the basis of family connection and longevity, but the existence of a purely ceremonial Table of Ranks enabled sycophants to enjoy prestige without responsibilities of any kind.

The ambitious educational program of 1804 had likewise gone awry. With the exception of the districts of Dorpat and Vilna, which were inhabited by Germans and Poles, the yearly reports of the Ministry of Education were disappointing. Lagging enrollments failed to justify the large expenditures for facilities. Most annoying of all, the nobility maintained its preference for foreign tutors and foreign schools. The government openly confessed that the lack of a "firm national educational system" was responsible for the chronic administrative weakness of the empire. The grand design of 1803 had included the provision that within five years of the establishment of the projected school system in a province, no one was to be admitted to local service "that required knowledge of jurisprudence without having completed the course of study of a public

or private school." Speransky was determined to apply this principle to
the central bureaucracy. He would stiffen the old Table of Ranks and
invigorate the new universities by linking the two anemic institutions
together. This he accomplished by abolishing ceremonial rank and by
promulgating the Education Act of 1809.[26]

The official title of the law of August 6, 1809, was "Rules for Promotion
in Rank in the Civil Service and for the Examinations in the Sciences
for Promotion to Collegiate Assessor and State Councillor." The rules
stipulated that before any official (*chinovnik*) could be promoted to the
eighth rank (*chin*) of Collegiate Assessor, which also conferred nobility,
or to the even higher fifth rank of State Councillor, he must serve the
designated number of years at the lower level, be recommended by his
superior, "and in the event of his not being able to produce a certificate
from a Russian university testifying to the successful study of sciences
appropriate to his branch of civil service must pass an examination in the
requisite knowledge." The actual testing was left in the hands of the
universities. The law conveniently provided for the release of officials
from work in the afternoons from May to October for the purpose of
attending courses preparing them for the state examinations.

The Education Act restored the Petrine bond between education and
state service. It also injected an underlying tension into the relations between the absolute state and the autonomous universities. The social
prestige of the universities came to rest on the civil service examinations.
The government would become increasingly loath to leave the key to the
fourteen-class society in the hands of an independent corporation. To the
extent that the universities did preserve a measure of self-rule, the state
would tend to compensate by tightening its grip on the preparatory gymnasiums.

"The Examination Act," Karamzin reported, "was everywhere greeted
with sarcastic ridicule."[27] Unable to attack the autocrat directly, the ruling class vented its irritation on Speransky. The first minister was accused of seeking to replace *cette noblesse vraiment noble* with Latin-bab-
bling officials recruited from the sons of priests and government clerks.
Within less than three years the break with Napoleon enabled the aristocracy to rid itself of the parvenu. Denounced as a secret French agent,
Speransky was banished from court, to the chagrin of the nobility, which
had hoped to see "the tyrant" hanged.[28] His odious act remained, in-
exorably shifting the weight of prestige and opportunity away from good

manners and family connections toward scholarship, academic competence, and disciplined learning.

After the Education Act, steps were taken to convert the provincial schools into gymnasiums exclusively concerned with university preparation. In 1811 the curator of the St. Petersburg district, Count Sergei Uvarov, introduced a Latin-oriented curriculum into the middle schools under his jurisdiction. By 1817 intensive courses in Latin were adopted throughout the empire. The major schools of 1786 and the provincial schools of 1804 had been locally oriented. Now, secondary institutions became funnels directing the flow of territorial talent toward the universities, toward rank in state service, and toward participation in capital society. Eventually both state and society would recognize them as the governing valve in the system of social stimulation control.

The dependence of a government career on formal scholarship not only modified the curriculum of the secondary schools but their social composition as well. Compared with polite breeding, general education was not only intellectually taxing but socially degrading. As long as promotion in rank was possible without it, the highborn avoided it. In vain Count Zavadovsky sent his own sons to the gymnasium in order to "raise general educational institutions in the public eye." In 1809 the Tsar complained officially of the gentry's lack of interest in academic schooling: "To our great sorrow we observe that the nobility, which is preferred above every other class, participates less than others in this useful undertaking."[29] In St. Petersburg the aversion of the notables for the arts and sciences was particularly slow to abate. As late as 1824 the pensions and academies of the capital gentry were instructing over 2,000 pupils, whereas the state gymnasiums were training 450 and the university 51.[30] The future, however, belonged to the academic schools. Although figures for this period are difficult to assess, it appears certain that by the end of Alexander's reign in 1825, when the master plan of 1803 was largely fulfilled and the nation possessed six universities and some 57 gymnasiums, the majority of the approximately 6,500 secondary pupils were members of the privileged class.

Drawn to higher education for the first time since the Petrine revolution began, the nobility immediately set about to impose class bias. The threatening international scene aided their efforts by prompting the government to seek the support of the peasants' masters. After the treaty of Tilsit, the authorities permitted the gentry to erect exclusive dormitories around the gymnasiums and universities. From this time on, the aristocratic hostel became a favorite device for promoting narrow class interests in general education. After Speransky's fall and the French invasion, discrimination became explicit. In 1813 a ukase of the tsar prohibited serfs from entering gymnasiums without special permission from the Ministry of Education. In 1819 the district of St. Petersburg introduced fees to discourage the poor from ascending the democratic ladder.

Aristocratic pensions, legal restrictions, and tuition taxes curbed the social scope of the statutes of 1804. Of more importance for the growing aristocratic bias of general education was the extension of the secondary course from four to seven years. Although this act was inspired by the desire to raise academic standards to European levels, the appearance of the seven-year gymnasium after 1812 had the effect of ignoring the democratic ladder. Even though the district school offered Latin for students intending to continue their studies, it no longer served as the official preparatory stage for secondary training. The unified school began to separate into two distinct compartments reflecting the social cleavage between rural gentry and urban commoners.

In Speransky's projects education was a bureaucratic device to prepare society for constitutional reform. His aristocratic opponents feared to awaken the public and welcomed the educational philosophy of the refugees from Napoleon gathered in St. Petersburg. First tacitly and then overtly, they agreed with Joseph de Maistre's warning to the court that the scholastic program of 1804 would lead to a revolt of the intellectuals, to a *"Pougatchev d'université."** In view of the steady erosion of the peace of Tilsit by Napoleonic threats to reconstruct an independent Poland, the court was in a defensive mood. In 1810 de Maistre's friend and confidant, Count Alexai Razumovsky, replaced the conciliatory Zavadovsky as Minister of Education.

Razumovsky's appointment coincided with the emergence into the public eye of Admiral Aleksandr Shishkov, a Gallophobe and spokesman for a "genuinely Russian" education based on Orthodoxy and Slavic rather than natural law and French. Born in the reign of Elizabeth Petrovna, Shishkov was a military bureaucrat by profession. By choice he was a man of letters who had won distinction as champion of old-Russian roots in the literary vocabulary. At the beginning of Alexander's reign the admiral withdrew from politics, muttering imprecations against the "Frenchified dandies" of the secret committee. Officially,

* See pp. 16 and 45.

however, he outlived them. In his old age, during the reform of the
schools touched off by the Decembrist rebellion, he would serve as Minister of Education. The turn in his official fortunes occurred when he
caught the Emperor's ear with a fiery lecture to high Petersburg society
on the need to educate the younger generation in the spirit of reverence
for the historic faith, love of country, and enthusiasm for the mother
tongue. The following year, as Napoleon began to move toward the
Russian frontier, the admiral was summoned to the Tsar. "I entered,"
Shiskov described the scene, "and he said to me: 'I read your oration on
patriotism. With feelings like that you can be useful to the fatherland. It
appears that war with France is unavoidable and it is necessary to mobilize recruits. I desire you to draft the manifesto.' "[31]

Shishkov's call to arms—a piece for Russian schoolboys to memorize—
heralded a new phase in state schooling. For a century, educated Russians had aped European modes. Napoleon broke the spell. The might of
his threat, the suddenness of his fall, and the wreckage of his house had a
touch of the supernatural. For souls already tuned to providential interest
in legitimate monarchy, the evidence for divine intervention was impressive.* With the miracle of 1812, even sophisticated Russians rediscovered
the enduring values of native achievements obscured by the Petrine revolution—the Slavic language, the Orthodox faith, and the autocracy. The
appreciation of the discovery marked a turning point in the attitude of
tsardom toward education. The victory over Europe's military-cultural
hegemony and over the forces of the French Revolution opened a deep
spring of proud conservatism within the ruling class. The attitude of
those in power toward schooling changed from a naïve spirit of experi-
menting with Western models to cautious use and jealous control. Educational goals became less European and more Russian. "We continued
to learn from our older brothers; we did not abjure the blessings of en-

---

* Reflecting in 1808 on Russia's chances of success in a showdown with Napoleonic
France, the Prussian reformer Freiherr vom Stein feared that a "thinly peopled country,
devoid of industry, will make but a feeble resistance, and a country ruled by a weak sen-
sual prince (intimidated by the failure of a number of schemes abandoned as lightly as
they were undertaken) through the agency of a stupid, awkward, corrupt and meddlesome
bureaucracy—a country where the great mass of the nation are slaves—such a country will
not long maintain the fight against civilized Europe." J. R. Seeley, *Life and Times of Stein*
(Leipzig, 1879), III, 115–16. Four years later Stein was in Moscow, where he witnessed
the "high degree of religious and national enthusiasm" evoked by the visit of Alexander I
to the threatened old capital in 1812. The enthusiasm for the tsar on the part of serfs and
nobles convinced him that Russia was not one of those artificial states (like Prussia) which
shatter after defeat, but "one of those great spiritual fabrics which are state and church and
family in one and which are well-nigh invincible even when barbarous, even when corrupt." *Ibid.*, pp. 125–26.

lightenment, but we acquired the right of criticism and independent judgment."[32]

Alexander I had always been susceptible to emotional impulses. Under the influence of events that seemed to defy rational explanation, he surrendered progressively to the charms of faith. The deterioration of his personality could not help but accelerate the trend that had already affected general education with the appointment of Razumovsky. In 1817 Education was combined with the Holy Synod into the joint Ministry of Education and Religious Affairs. Academic policy, like foreign policy, was to be inspired by Christian principles. In 1819 the new chief of the combined departments and president of a Bible society, Prince Aleksandr Golitsyn, substituted catechism lessons and scripture reading for ethics and civics in the gymnasiums. In 1821 Professor Aleksandr Galich, a favorite of Pushkin and the author of a scholarly two-volume history of philosophical systems, was expelled from St. Petersburg University by the curator on the charge that he "openly preferred paganism to Christianity, wanton philosophy to pure religion, the atheistic Kant to Christ, and Schelling to the Holy Spirit." In 1825 the curator of the University of Kazan informed the faculty that, instead of those "mad dreams of some Germans, ideas that arose out of the arrogance of the Lutheran reform and are falsely labeled philosophy ... we possess the healthy, true, unadorned philosophy that straightens and exercises the mind, in which our forefathers lived happily, faithful to God and the tsars, and in which the most outstanding men of our fatherland, the saints of our church, were educated and schooled."[33]

The Elaboration of Autocratic Controls, 1825–1855

"Quiet reigns everywhere. What else does Russia require?" asked Admiral Aleksandr Shishkov, appointed Minister of Education in 1824. The following year the news reached St. Petersburg that Alexander I had died suddenly in the south. The opening of his testament revealed that the heir apparent had abdicated all rights to the crown in favor of Paul's third son, Nicholas. Exploiting the confusion over the swearing of allegiance to the "accidental" tsar, a group of Westernized army officers attempted to replace the autocracy with a constitutional monarchy. The emancipation of the serfs figured prominently in the scheme, whereas the more imaginative conspirators contemplated the establishment of a republic. In the manifesto of July 13, 1826, announcing the death sentences meted out to the ringleaders, the government insisted that the "deadly *growth of semiknowledge,* this flight into fanciful extremes which begins in moral corruption and ends in total ruin, cannot be ascribed to enlightenment, but to the idleness of mind which is more dangerous than physical sloth and to the lack of disciplined intelligence."[34]

Pondering the fiasco of his generation and his class, Aleksandr Pushkin also laid the blame on the deficiencies of aristocratic schooling. Concerned in their youth solely with "military service, fashionable etiquette, and recreation," the conspirators had become infatuated on a sudden with Western liberal ideas. Blind to reality, they had been unable to appreciate the strength of the government, "based as it is on the power of things as they really are." In the West, the poet observed, political changes, even violent upheavals, came about only after lengthy intellectual preparation and social conditioning had rendered their success inevitable. In Russia, on the other hand, political notions sprang suddenly from the minds of the half-educated in the form of "bloody and insane ideas."[35]

Nicholas was the man for a cautious hour. By temperament and training a military engineer, he developed in his early years a special interest in the science of fortification and defense. As tsar he devoted his immense energy, granite will, and limited imagination to making his domain impregnable to the revolutionary forces of the modern world. This general policy was to be carried out within the country by a resolute combination of surveillance and instruction. It was characteristic of the Nicholaian system that the police were to educate the public and the schools to discipline them.

Nicholas lost no time setting in motion the machinery of domestic control. On June 25, 1826, the centrally organized *gendarmerie* was established as the Third Section of His Majesty's Own Chancery. The purpose of the Third Section was to provide the regime with political police. A corps of agents, informers, and uniformed officials collected information on "all happenings without exception," to alert the government to any "flight into fanciful extremes" on the part of educated society. To ensure long-range guidance of the mental and moral development of the educated class, a committee was established "to collate and equalize the schools and define their courses of study." The Minister of Education, Aleksandr Shishkov, was specifically instructed to introduce the "necessary uniformity" into teaching and discipline "without delay."[36]

In 1824 the 70-year-old Shishkov had accepted the direction of the schools with the conviction that "to teach the whole nation to read and write would do more harm than good." His skepticism corresponded perfectly with the educational philosophy of the chief of the newly established "higher police," Aleksandr Benkendorff, that the state "should not rush ahead with education too fast. Otherwise the people will become as knowledgeable as the monarchs and seek to curtail their power."[37]

The police chief's analysis touched the nerve of tsardom's dilemma. On the one hand, trained intelligence was vital for domestic prosperity and the preservation of tsardom's hard-won European leadership. On the other hand, the constitution of 1804 with its unified school and democratic ladder threatened the stability of the social order. The solution lay in rationing the learning process by class. "The education of the nation," Nicholas reminded Admiral Shishkov, "is one of the main supports of the welfare of the power entrusted to us by God." To ensure the school's correspondence with the "genuine" needs of the state, he continued, "it is necessary to adapt the course of studies and even the pedagogical methods to the probable future careers of the students. In this fashion each one will acquire the necessary general knowledge of the faith, the laws, and morality, as well as the more specialized knowledge that will enable him to improve his lot. For a person should not sink below his station, neither should he strive inordinately to rise above the condition to which he ordinarily has been assigned."[38]

Without waiting for the Shishkov committee to complete the revision of the basic law, the Tsar eliminated an anomaly inherited from the previous reign. A check revealed a number of serfs studying in the gymnasiums and universities. School officials complained of the corrupting influence of "undisciplined" peasant boys on the other children. In some cases parents refused to send their children to the "unruly" schools. The "successful" and "outstanding" serfs presented a special problem. Such students "grow accustomed to a way of life and to modes of thought incompatible with their social condition. The inevitable tensions become unbearable, and thus very often in their despair they surrender to disastrous dreams and vulgar passions."[39] On August 19, 1827, an imperial decree forbade the universities and gymnasiums to admit serfs. The servile population was restricted to parish, district, and industrial schools. The comprehensive school law appeared the following year.

Shishkov's statute of December 8, 1828, was carefully drafted to neutralize the revolutionary potential of Western education on Russian soil without sacrificing academic standards as had been done in the last years of Alexander's reign. The law formally preserved democratic access to general education for "the free estates." Social restrictions were imposed by means of departmental directives from Petersburg to the provinces. Ministerial circulars explained to local officials that the different types of school were specifically designed "to fit the needs of the social classes that will complete their training in them." The so-called parish elementary schools under the direction of the Holy Synod were for "peasants, craftsmen, and factory workers of the lower stations." The three-year "lower," i.e. improved elementary district schools, located in the provincial and district towns, served the children of "merchants, officers, and gentry." The district schools were also adapted to the needs of the urban lower classes, the so-called *meshchanstvo,* or petty service people, artisans, and tradesmen. The gymnasiums were organized "primarily for the sons of gentry and officials."

The constitution of 1828 remodeled general education as an agency for supplying the needs of the state for trained personnel without undermining the existing social order. But the Nicholaian system did not depend on administrative formulas alone to protect privilege from talent and ambition. Control rested ultimately on academic considerations. For a decade the spread of the classical curriculum and the extension of the secondary course from four to seven years had been weakening the democratic ladder of 1804. The program of 1828 introduced Greek into the gymnasium. This "strengthened the purely scientific and academic part"[40] of the school and confirmed the break between the programs of lower and secondary learning. The addition of a third year and the elimination of Latin completed the conversion of the district school to a terminal institution. In the reform commission Admiral Shishkov had pointed out that actually less than one per cent of the graduates of the district schools continued on to the university, demonstrating that the "democratic ladder" had been more provocative as an idea than practical as an instrument of social mobility. The gymnasiums, in turn, ceased to be "secondary" or "middle" schools in the sense of bridges between lower and higher stages. Instead, they became exclusively concerned with university preparation.

In 1833 the man who had introduced the classical gymnasium into the capital, Count Sergei Uvarov, was appointed Minister of Education. As a diplomat in the service of Alexander I, the new chief of public instruction had shared his sovereign's liberal emotions. As an official of Nicholas I, he was anxious to demonstrate that enlightenment could be used to inspire conservative loyalties. In his inaugural circular Uvarov reminded the curators of their "joint obligation to conduct the education of the nation in the combined spirit of orthodoxy, autocracy, and nationality." Professors and teachers were cautioned to labor as "worthy instruments of the government," and students were advised to display "the proper humility and obedience toward their superiors."[41]

Uvarov's credo inspired a tight reorganization. In 1835 district reform converted the loose professional structure of the schools into a centralized bureaucracy. Despite the protest of faculty who remembered the oppression of the 1820's, the universities were placed under the administrative authority of the curators. These officials now took up residence in the university cities. The gymnasiums were removed from the jurisdiction of the universities, the secondary directors were relieved of responsibility for lower schools, and all levels were placed under the district functionaries.[42] The curators not only controlled the employment of teachers and directors but also had the right to dismiss "unreliable" professors. The rectors and the deans of higher institutions remained elected as before, but the rights of the faculty council were sharply curtailed.

To enforce uniformity and standards, the curators exercised the office of inspection over the schools. District inspectors, often former military personnel and teaching staff members designated as such, kept a check on academic performance, student discipline, and the conformity of school authorities to the directives radiating from the curatorships and the ministry. The Emperor played the role of supreme inspector. Accompanied by the chief of gendarmes, he traveled unannounced through the land, bursting into schools to obliterate any sign of "arbitrary teaching through arbitrary books and manuals."[43] The semiofficial historian of Moscow University expressed the mood more elegantly. Whereas it was necessary for the state "to send gifted youths in search of knowledge to all the corners of enlightened Europe," it was equally necessary for the state to see to it that "they, like bees, suck only honey from the flowers of world enlightenment."[44]

The efficient operation of the state machinery depended on public cooperation. In the 1830's and 1840's, however, neither the upper nor the lower estates accepted their assigned fields of study and the attendant social roles. In 1828 the gymnasium had been designed as a scholarly institution, and the invitation to attend it had been extended to the gentry. The government, however, soon found itself up against the traditional resistance of the privileged class to submit to academic discipline. When forced to choose between scholastic standards and aristocratic bias, it compromised. The Minister of Education artfully observed that the noble youth, who by birth were "already destined to occupy the most important offices in the state," must be educated separately where possible. To further this end the government organized provincial cadet corps under a special department of military education. The gentry were also allowed to establish and support with their own funds special five-year gymnasiums. Here the imperial elite who were unable to patronize the military academies could at least escape the rigors of classical studies. This left time to pursue courses "closer to the educational needs of the upper classes." Offerings included French conversation, ballroom dancing, fencing, and horsemanship. The noblemen in the regular academic gymnasiums were protected from harmful integration with lower elements by being housed in exclusive dormitories, which by 1849 had been attached to 47 out of some 70 establishments.[45]

While the government was making concessions to the class bias of the nobility, the lower orders were showing increasing interest in advanced education. For them the classical school offered the most practical opportunity of escape out of the social depths into the light of European culture and civil rank. During the closing years of Alexander's reign, the membership of the gymnasiums grew very slowly. In 1825 there were only 7,682 pupils, compared with 5,569 in 1809, the year of the Examination Act. In the first decade of the reign of Nicholas I, however, enrollment doubled, reaching 15,476 in 1836. Although the nobility contributed three-fourths of the enrollment, the increase in absolute numbers sent increasing contingents of commoners on to the universities. "In view of the general trend of all classes toward higher education," the Ministry of Education began to reexamine admittance policies. "The canons of justice," it was officially admitted, must continue to be observed. Nevertheless, the authorities began to pay closer attention to "the social origins of our young candidates and their prospects for a future career." While the "ample development of trained intelligence" was obviously useful, it could also be dangerous if it did not bear "some relation to one's subsequent position in civil life." In view of the fact that "the passion of the young for superfluous knowledge, which will seldom find a successful practical application in later life, deceives the hopes of poor parents and the utopian expectations of their children," the Ministry of Education began to wonder publicly in 1840 whether "the uninhibited appetite for higher learning might not shake the civil order."[46]

After lengthy consultation with the districts, St. Petersburg developed a plan of action for stemming "the universal drive toward education." In 1845 tuition was raised "not so much to improve the financial condition of the schools as to restrain the drive for education within the bounds of social reality."[47] In addition to economic sanctions, the government appealed to local self-interest. The gymnasiums and universities were forbidden to accept urban taxpayers, the children of merchants and craftsmen, without certificates of release from their guilds and artels.[48] Since the poll tax was levied on a collective basis, any loss of members added to the fiscal burdens of the remainder. The local corporations could be counted on to resist departure of personnel. These measures, it was officially hoped, would encourage the "middle class" to confine its ambitions to the institutions especially created for its needs, namely, the three-year terminal district schools.

The restrictive policy of the 1840's visibly slowed the growth of higher education and hence of the educated class by shrinking the population of the gymnasiums. Between 1836 and 1848 university enrollment doubled, from 2,016 to 4,566. But the enrollment in the gymnasiums increased by only one-fifth, from 15,476 in 1836 to 18,911 in 1848. A quarter of a century later the universities contained only one thousand more students than in 1848. The constitution of 1828 formally admitted all free estates to higher education. The fundamental law was not changed, but ministerial directives qualified its force. The use of secret administrative orders to constrict the scope of state laws was an operational routine of the tsarist state. The Ministry of Education employed the device whenever it was driven on the defensive.

By the 1840's the government was concerned not only with restricting the size and composition of the educated class but with restraining its rebellious spirit. In the previous reign the empiricism and materialism derived from French rationalists and British utilitarians had seriously undermined faith in the theological foundations of tsardom's political and social order. Now, under Nicholas, a new generation drew on the metaphysicians of Germany to fill the vacuum left by the failure of the activists of reason, the Decembrists. They did so with ideological fantasies of limited application in a world of growing technical virtuosity but of intense emotional force and rare synthetic power. Revolutionary idealism, even Alexander Herzen's persuasive blending of Schelling with Saint-Simon, would have amounted to little more than "that mixture of Jacobinism and anarchism that can coalesce only in the brain of a Slav"[49] without the community spirit that established institutions afforded isolated individuals. In this case the agency that enabled thoughtful persons from different social orbits to become an independent, public force outside the gentry corporation, the merchant guild, the church, the army, and the civil service was the formative agency of the fourteen-class society itself, state education. "The most down-to-earth definition one can give of the intelligentsia," Herzen's most recent biographer has written, "is to say that they were the 'student youth' trained in the various establishments of the 'Ministry of National Enlightenment.' "[50]

The center of creative activity was the University of Moscow. It alone of the higher academic schools was of sufficient size, age, and prestige to develop a significant *esprit de corps*. It profited more than any other center of learning from the network of provincial gymnasiums. Through them it drew increasing numbers of young people from the lower gentry, *raznochintsy, meshchanstvo,* merchants, clergy, and even peasantry. As enrollment rose from 441 in 1836 to 871 in 1842 to the high of 1,329 in 1848, the proportion of commoners in residence fluctuated between 60 and 54 per cent and then leveled off at 57 per cent.[51]

Under the curatorship of Count Sergei Stroganov, the shared experiences of lecture hall, dormitory, and literary circle were allowed to mold both faculty and undergraduates into common "citizens of Russia." Social and sectional differences disappeared in the joint desire to wrest the intellectual leadership of the nation away from the official propagandists of Orthodoxy, autocracy, and nationality. In order to protect the faculty from the central bureaucracy, Stroganov fought a running battle with the Minister of Education. To strengthen the teaching staff he actively recruited professors trained in Germany. The most gifted lecturer of them all was Timofei Granovsky, who used his courses on medieval history to raise in a public forum and in affirmative Hegelian terms the questions posed by Catherine II: Is Russia European? Does her future course lie in continuing "the rational progress begun by Peter the Great," or in recovering the principles of "political paternalism and social fraternity" which allegedly inspired Muscovy before the innovations of Western education and state bureaucracy? Answering these questions, the university community and, following it, the educated public divided into at least two disputatious groups broadly identified as Slavophiles and Westernizers. It was on the fringes of the larger, occidentally attuned camp, among the philosophical idealists, utopian socialists, scientific positivists, and anarchists of the heart that the militant doctrinaires, the intelligentsia *par excellence,* began to emerge.

The herald of the radical trend within the educated class was Vissarion Belinsky. The son of an impoverished military surgeon, he was a classmate of the wealthy Herzen at the University of Moscow in the 1830's. His experience as a student convinced him that, "owing to the indefatigable solicitude of a wise government, education is proceeding rapidly."[52] Under the influence of the Left Hegelians and Herzen his faith in official enlightenment turned to acid criticism of the regime. In the early 1840's he announced that his god was negation and that his heroes were Luther, Voltaire, the Encyclopedists, the terrorists of the French Revolution, and other "destroyers of the old." In the West social philosophers were exchanging the individualistic rights of man for the socialistic brotherhood of men. "Sociality, sociality—or death!" became the young rebel's motto. "In effect, 'sociality' as Belinsky means it here," a recent investigator has observed, "might be approximately interpreted as a principle of humanitarian concern for the welfare (Belinsky would have said the enlightenment) of one's fellow-men."[53]

Belinsky's combination of mordant skepticism with boyish enthusiasm, of nihilism toward the past with faith in the future, became a permanent characteristic of the radical section of the educated class. His high moral tone appealed to the young. In an editorial to Gogol, the fatally ill critic provided the coming generation with its manifesto. "Russia sees her salvation," he announced, "not in mysticism, not in asceticism, not in pietism, but in the successes of civilization, enlightened education, and humanity. She does not need sermons. She has heard enough of them! She does not need prayers. She has recited them too long! What she needs is an awakening in the people of a sense of their own human dignity, which has for centuries been trampled in the dust. She needs rights and laws, not derived from the teaching of the church, but compatible with right reason and justice. And above all, she needs their strict enforcement."[54]

Belinsky's metamorphosis dramatized the danger that state education posed for tsardom even under maximum security conditions. By 1840 the system that had been fashioned to prepare "humble" and "obedient" candidates for the state administration was becoming the seedbed of opposition to the government. Within a decade the Slavophile Ivan Aksakov reluctantly reported that "there is not a single gymnasium *teacher,* not one district school teacher, who is not under the authority of the Russian West, who does not know Belinsky's letters to Gogol by heart, and is not educating the younger generation under their influence."[55]

As long as the spirit of rebellion was contained in the West, the propagation of "disastrous dreams and vulgar passions" was susceptible of regular controls. In 1848 a revolutionary storm blew up out of France, mixing the dust of republicanism with socialism and nationalism as it moved eastward, wrecking the diplomatic breastworks of the Nicholaian system. St. Petersburg and Moscow harbored no politically ambitious bourgeoisie. Serfdom prevented the rise of an excitable industrial proletariat. The peasantry was insensitive to any ideological call to arms. The national minorities, including the Poles, were quiet. The most unreliable sector of the population appeared to be the minute but noisome educated class. The Tsar concentrated his preventive police action on this group. The censorship became suffocating. Foreign travel was restricted to official business. A series of *ad hoc* emergency measures destroyed the symmetry and sense of the carefully composed educational laws of 1828 and 1835. Nicholas had disliked Latin from his youth, and ultraconservative court circles had long suspected Count Uvarov of retaining a secret affection for liberalism from his Alexandrian days. Nationalists had never liked the "German" gymnasium. Conservatives recalled that Greek and Latin had been the language of republicans and that the French revolutionaries had quoted Cicero and Plato. Badgered from all sides, Uvarov made way for Prince Platon Shirinsky-Shikhmatov, who boasted that he was but a blind tool of his emperor's will.

At the height of the revolutionary scare Nicholas considered abolishing the universities altogether. They were preserved, but under rigid control, with enrollment at each place restricted to 300 self-supported students (those without government stipends) outside the faculties of theology and law. The undergraduate population contracted by one-

fourth, from 4,016 in 1848 to 3,018 in 1850. Introducing this drastic measure, the government expressed the hope that "the children of the privileged classes, as heirs of the ancient order of knights, would seek military
in preference to civil service. To this end we are making it possible for
them to enter military educational institutions or to enlist directly in
the ranks of the army—*where a university education is not necessary.*"[56]
Further precautions were taken to protect the reduced contingents from
contamination. The study of the constitutional law of those European
powers "that had been shaken internally to their foundations by upris-
ings and riots" was excluded from the program of studies. The study of
philosophy was declared useless "in view of the scandalous development
of this science by contemporary German scholars." The teaching of logic
and psychology was allowed to continue after the subjects were entrusted
to the teachers of theology on orders to "reconcile" them with revealed
truth. The self-government of the faculties was curtailed in favor of rectors and deans appointed by the Ministry of Education.

Official reaction to the events of 1848 suspended outright the independent life of the universities. At the secondary level, it "shattered the
strict unity of the system" nurtured for seventeen years by Count Uvarov.[57] After the exodus of this conscientious classicist from office, the
curator of St. Petersburg recommended that from the fourth year the
gymnasium be divided into two branches, a practical terminal course
leading directly to employment and an academic program preparing
qualified, responsible students for the universities. In order to "meet the
needs of contemporary education" and to prepare candidates for "exact
and fundamental work in the mathematical and medical faculties," the
Ministry dropped Greek from all but a handful of schools, and in its
place it expanded the number of hours available for natural sciences.
It was within this emotionally charged political context that the pedagogical controversy, raging in Europe "since the Thirty Years War"
over whether "the ancients" or "the moderns" should direct general education, entered the Russian empire.

Despite alarms and dislocations in educated circles, the apparent im-
munity of tsardom from the revolutionary epidemic of 1848 convinced
Nicholas of the essential soundness of his regime. Several years later he
exerted a routine show of force in the Balkans to keep the Turks in line.
When the maneuver developed into a war with Great Britain and
France, he accepted the challenge with reluctance but without fear. In

many ways the allied armies were as obsolescent as the tsar's. But they came in steamships, built the first railroad in the Crimean peninsula, and laid the first telegraph cable under the Black Sea. Meanwhile, the effort to mobilize the Russian armies threatened the disruption of the countryside. The peasants deserted the manors in droves, and the lack of railroads made it impossible to defend the southern coast even from invaders operating at the end of long sea lines. Already discredited morally, the serf system was now revealed as an inadequate political base for guaranteeing the security of the realm. Early in 1855, as the strains of war were becoming acute, Nicholas I died. His death cleared the way for his son, Alexander II, to reach a settlement with Europe and to contemplate a fundamental reorganization of the empire.

Chapter Two

Official Liberalism: Education for Reform, 1855–1865

> *In the limitless intellectual chaos in which Russia is currently bogged down, there is only one life-saving current that carries us toward firm ground. And that is the public appetite for enlightenment. Every single Russian, whether rich or poor, cultured or ignorant, feels that the nation's first urgent daily need is for education. From this it follows that any measure tending in the slightest to restrict educational opportunity will arouse universal resentment and ensure public support for every protest against the government.*
>
> BORIS CHICHERIN, *1861*

Professional Autonomy for the Universities

Since the credibility of tsardom rested on the invincibility of the army, it was not surprising that the Crimean debacle raised doubts even in the most loyal and patriotic minds. As the naval base of Sevastopol fell to the Western allies in the autumn of 1855, a high official confided to his private journal: "Only now is it becoming apparent how awful the last 29 years have been for Russia. The administration is in chaos. Moral feeling has decayed. *Intellectual development has ceased*."[1] In March 1856 Great Britain concluded the war in exchange for neutralization of the Black Sea. Such an admission of weakness on the part of a power that had led the Continent militarily since 1812 drastically reduced its influence on international affairs. Peace gave the new tsar time to concentrate his authority on domestic affairs.

As Crown Prince, Alexander II had excited neither the hopes of the educated class nor the fears of the serf owners. Those who knew him personally noted his warmth and indecisiveness. His manifesto announcing the conclusion of the war referred to the need for "laws equally just for all." This hint he followed up with a warning to the nobility that it would be wiser for them to "destroy serfdom from above" than to wait for it to "destroy itself from below." In the face of this threat the conservative majority of squires clung more tightly to the rural status quo.

A minority, composed of those rendered more flexible by modest means and a university education, toyed with the Decembrist idea of erecting constitutionalism directly on feudal ruins. In effect, the gentry was neutralized and the initiative for change passed from provincial society to the central bureaucracy.

Progressive officials, those who favored guiding necessity, gravitated to the support of Grand Duke Constantine, the second son of Nicholas I. With his brother, the future Alexander II, Constantine had been educated under the supervision of the venerable literary colleague of Pushkin, Vasily Zhukovsky. Born in the reign of Catherine II, at the time when Iankovich de Mirevo was preparing the first general-educational statute in Russian history, the imperial tutor was a living link between the Catherinian enlightenment and the age of reform. Although Zhukovsky was never able to overcome Alexander II's suspicions about "progress," a word that the Emperor reportedly ordered banned from official correspondence,[2] he inspired the influential younger prince with his own predilection for guided "motion, the organized development, the modest, steady, peaceful progression that is life." Reform at the right time in the proper place, he advised Constantine in 1851, is the only effective safeguard against the storms currently punishing Western Europe, the destructive "revolution *forward*" and "the equally ruinous revolution *backward*."[3]

In 1857, at a time when it appeared to the "partisans of new ideas" that the "retrogrades" at court and the hack men-of-rank entrenched at subordinate levels of the civil service would succeed in stifling reform ("The bureaucrats," an educated official retrospectively complained, "are worse than the Poles and nihilists"[4]) Grand Duke Constantine, now head of the Naval Department, described the broad political vision and sharp fiscal cramps of official liberalism: "The extremely critical condition of our finances compels us to cut the current expenses of every department of government to the bone and sacrifice the future's rosy hopes in order to extricate ourselves from the present predicament. Public safety demands the rapid resolution of a number of vital problems, such as serfdom, minorities, justice, and police. The people must find redress for grievances. Official commands must be enforced and worthy goals achieved without resort to illegal means. At the same time we must develop new sources of national wealth on a gigantic scale if we are to raise Russia to the level of its neighbors and competitors. For we can no longer fool ourselves, but must candidly confess that we are weaker and poorer than the first-class powers. We are poorer not only in material means but in intellectual capacity; and we are especially short of trained administrators."[5]

Once again, as so often in the past, the reorganization of government depended for effectiveness on the reorganization of schools. This truth had been enunciated in the autumn of 1855 by A. S. Norov, the last head of public instruction appointed by Nicholas I: "If our enemies triumph over us, it is due solely to the superiority of their education."[6] Fortunately for the regime, this admission, wrung from a man who preferred close-order drill in the curricula to political economy, confirmed an official change of heart. Faithful to the instincts that had moved it sporadically since the Petrine revolution, tsardom responded to military challenge by assigning a high priority to formal learning. "It is particularly important to note the sequence of events," comments Franco Venturi, the historian of revolutionary populism. "Even before other aspects of Russia's social life were transformed, even before the fate of the peasants was decided and the organization of justice effected, a start was made to open up the universities."[7]

Without waiting for the war to end, the government took steps to revive academic life. The southern school districts, which had lain under a modified form of martial law, were returned to civilian control. Authoritarian curators were replaced by diplomatic men. The ban on the importation of scholarly materials without prior submission to the general censorship was removed. International law and the history of philosophy were welcomed back to the fellowship of medicine and mathematics. Administrative flexibility and the improvement of academic tone led to the renewal of the faculties. Veterans who had fled returned and fresh talents appeared.

International pressures dictated prompt development of the nation's education at all levels of achievement. Domestic conditions recommended caution. For at the very moment when quiet cultivation of adolescent competence became the state's first order of business, at a time when all the state universities and state gymnasiums together were graduating fewer than 400 students a year qualified to fill the 3,000 annual vacancies in the 80,000-man state bureaucracy, the most disruptive turbulence since the Decembrist revolt broke over the schools. This time the "saviors of the fatherland" were not cadet corps aristocrats but university students.

The trouble began with a gesture of hospitality. After restricting enrollment for a number of years, the government, as part of its reversal of
the countereducational policies of post-1848, lifted restrictions on admissions. Within four years the population of the universities increased by
almost 50 per cent, to 4,998 students in residence in 1859. To a later age
of mass instruction, such figures appear Lilliputian. At the time the influx strained existing facilities.

More upsetting than mass was the composition of the invasion. Numerous incoming candidates for degrees were non-nobles, the so-called
"black students,"* among whom predominated the impoverished, ill-
prepared, and ambitious sons of provincial government officials. The
newcomers were not housed with relatives or in gentry pensions. There
were no resident colleges to receive them and no state dormitories. They
settled down where they could in the corners of crowded rooms in the
gregarious slums of the university cities. Here in the cauldrons of empire
they organized themselves, often as fellow countrymen from the same
region, into cooperative kitchens and mutual aid societies. These served,
in turn, as nuclei for self-study circles—the basic molecules of public life.

The spontaneously generated student associations avoided the guidance of certified scholars. They sought, instead, the inspiration of journalists and philosophizers. "In these circumstances the orderly conduct of
university courses and lectures was at an end. Instead of pursuing serious
academic work, the students circulated in the original and in litho-
graphed translations the works of Feuerbach, Büchner, and Moleschott.
Since they took socialism and materialism as the last word of science,
the conservative circles disappeared and the radicals swept the field. If
such were conditions in Moscow University, the mood in St. Petersburg,
which stood under the direct influence of Chernyshevsky and company,
was even more critical. The same process repeated itself in the provinces."[8]

The contempt of the student youth for official liberalism, the modestly
budgeted modernizing effort of the ruling class, was labeled "nihilism."
The term was derived from the brash positivistic credo of Bazarov, the
medical student "counterpart of Pugachev," whose portrayal converted
the publication of Turgenev's *Fathers and Sons* in the early spring of
1862 into a literary event with political dimensions. "And if he [Bazarov]

---

* The term "black" for students who were not from the upper class appears in a letter
from Prince Dolgoruky. Venturi, p. 232.

is called a 'nihilist,' " the censor-ridden author confided to a friend, "one must read 'revolutionary.' "[9] Other thoughtful contemporaries were inclined to view the revolution against reform much as the previous generation had interpreted the Decembrist uprising—as the bizarre harvest of decades of intellectual drift and academic neglect. "Nihilism is nothing more or less than a degenerate form of scientific skepticism," Nikolai Pirogov, one of the most sympathetic and knowledgeable observers of student life wrote in 1863. "And I know," he continued, "that both faith and lack of faith in science came to us, together with science, from overseas."[10] A conscientious university professor and government official, who had climbed the state's educational ladder from serfdom to nobility, remarked: "Up to the present we have been living off borrowed mind. We have developed no native science except nihilism."[11]

In the midst of student enthusiasm for self-enlightenment, it was observed that the state experienced difficulty in recruiting bona fide graduates for teaching positions in provincial secondary schools.[12] Not only were the youth negligent in their search for regular employment outside the capitals; except for the medical candidates, they were slow to acquire degrees at all.[13] Neglecting their studies, they had more time for organizing their special interests. Curators like Pirogov in Kiev, Kovalevsky in Moscow, and Shcherbatov in St. Petersburg encouraged the trend toward public activity by receiving undergraduate delegations in their offices and responding sympathetically to their grievances. Other officials bristled in the presence of unauthorized spontaneity. Inevitably, the "schoolboy skeptics," as the Slavophiles called them, clashed with state authority.[14] The code of 1835 placed responsibility for maintaining undergraduate discipline in agents of the curator—the inspector and his assistants. The university police, designed to restrain drinking parties and literary rebellion in the days of Nicholas I, were inadequate in numbers and mentality to cope with the new, "scientifically" motivated dissent. After 1858 the inspectorate was relieved of its duties of surveillance beyond the walls; off campus, the students were no longer treated as wards of the educational bureaucracy, but were subjected to the same security regulations as the general citizens. At the time, the reduction of the inspectorate was looked upon as a victory for liberty over despotism. Its effect, however, was to remove the cushion between the student youth and the adult instruments of compulsion. Troops were summoned to dispel assemblies that diplomacy and tact might have good-humoredly dispersed. As organized self-study groups increased their influence within the student bodies as a whole, strictly intra-university interests gave way to political views. The running dialogue between students and administrators over dismal housing, putrid food, insipid lectures, and police brutality was seasoned with larger demands—independence for Poland, land and liberty for the peasants, a constituent assembly for the country at large.

By 1859 even the more sympathetic faculty members were becoming annoyed with the pretensions of the adolescent intelligentsia to national leadership.* In another year the royal patience had been worn thin, and the Tsar notified E. P. Kovalevsky, who had become Minister of Education in 1858, that further scandals would elicit reprisals. When Kovalevsky turned to St. Petersburg University for advice, he found the occupant of the chair of civil law, Konstantin Kavelin, propounding an engaging theory. Spontaneous student rallies—the *skhodki* where the Third Section smelled sedition—were folk habits of the Russian peasantry transferred to the bureaucratic setting of the Western school. Kovalevsky was taken with this idea, and at his request Kavelin composed a code for student life that allowed it to organize under faculty supervision. The document was no sooner completed in June of 1861 than the government signaled a reversal of policy by changing the top educational command.

Kovalevsky had been an uncertain tool of official liberalism. Through his diplomatic service in the Orient the new Minister of Education was associated in the public mind with the closed despotism of Japan.† Admiral Evfimy Putiatin owed his sudden elevation to the influence of the clerical-police faction at court. Prince Vasily Dolgoruky, the head of the Third Section, had undermined the Crown's confidence in Kovalevsky, and the saintly Metropolitan of Moscow, who opposed emancipation of the serfs on the grounds that the substitution of "theoretical progress" for immemorial custom would only stir the "false hopes and baser appe-

---

* "Russian society has given students a sense of their own importance which does not exist in any other country . . . ; the student is no longer a pupil but is becoming a master, a guide of society." Chicherin, quoted in Venturi, p. 225.

† Admiral Putiatin headed the Russian diplomatic mission to Japan during the Crimean War. Herzen inveighed against "our Japanese" Minister of Education. Herzen, XV, 164, 174.

tites of God's irremediably poor," recommended Putiatin to the Tsar as "a pious Christian gentleman." Grand Duke Constantine protested the appointment in vain.[15]

Acting under orders that originated in the Council of State and the Committee of Ministers to bring the undergraduates under control, Putiatin crushed Kavelin's scheme for encouraging the students' taste for public life in favor of a bureaucratic *coup de main*. Without warning or explanation, an annual 50-ruble tax was imposed on university enrollment. Simultaneously, the number of state stipendiaries and exemptions from fees was curtailed. The increase in educational costs was accompanied by circumscription of liberties. Henceforth, the meetings and organizations that since the war had become a tolerated feature of student life were explicitly forbidden. Anticipating resistance to both demands, the strategists of the Ministry of Education planned to forestall evasion by requiring the students to purchase matriculation booklets as evidence of registration. These contained, among other formalities, the new "Japanese" rules for deportment. It was explained that the individual's signature on the leaflet would constitute a contract with the administration to abstain from collective action.

It was the fiscal more than the disciplinary aspect of these innovations that aroused public concern. Since the days of Lomonosov the material level of student existence had scarcely improved. In St. Petersburg two-thirds of the 1,000 undergraduates were excused from fees for inability to pay in 1859. Pirogov, who knew conditions intimately at Dorpat and Kiev, noted in 1863 that the majority of those seeking a university education were the children of people with little influence in society; many of them scarcely had enough to eat. Heads of families in straitened circumstances might even welcome the ban on extracurricular activities, but the raising of tuition and the cancellation of scholarships blighted many a middle-class hope for membership in the fourteen-class society. The result was an outpouring of sentiment hostile to the Ministry. Gentry assemblies, military officers, and government bureaus collected funds to rescue the careers of the deserving poor. "A petty official in the Treasury or a clerk in Welfare gladly sacrifices a portion of his meager salary to the students' cause."[16]

The professors, too, whose counsel had not been solicited since June, were incensed by the bureaucracy's action. In agreement with society at large, they were more anxious to preserve democratic access than to foster communal folkways in the schools. In October one of their number, Boris Chicherin, extraordinary professor of civil law at Moscow and an aristocrat of means in direct communication with the court, warned the Petersburg authorities: "Experience shows that the poorest people work the hardest. They have to clear a path for themselves by strenuous effort. From their midst come the classroom teachers who are indispensable to all further progress. Out of their ranks come the mass of state officials, who, for all their cultural deficiencies, are the indispensable workhorses of the state. The children of poor officials will simply have no place to go if the doors of the university are closed to them."[17]

While Moscow's academicians were confining their displeasure to the inner circles of the regime, the students of St. Petersburg were roughing out new channels of communication. In October a series of rallies, strikes and boycotts against the administration suspended all academic life. When the curator succeeded in clearing the university courtyard, "white with the snowflakes of torn matriculation booklets," the demonstrators moved across the river into the heart of the city. Here they staged the first street demonstration in the capital since the Decembrist's impertinence in Senate Square. "When we appeared on the Nevsky Prospekt," a veteran recalled, "the French barbers came out of their shops and their faces lit up and they waved their arms cheerfully, shouting, 'Révolution! Révolution!'"[18]

After a final clash in November on St. Isaac's Square with a guards regiment, hundreds of students were arrested. Viewing this confrontation of elite soldiery and ragged undergraduates, Herzen announced that the torch of national liberation had passed from the aristocracy to the democracy. "This initiative belongs by rights to the students—*they alone are pure*. The idea of Russian citizenship has been bred in the universities."[19]

Stubborn student resistance to the administration's demands was confined to the capital. After some initial protests and disruptions elsewhere, highlighted in Kazan by a demonstration of solidarity with the peasantry and in Moscow by a sharp scuffle between gendarmes and students at the grave of the gifted teacher Granovsky, matriculation proceeded on schedule. Putiatin's fees were collected; his rules were enforced; lectures, laboratories, and seminars resumed. The restoration of order in the country at large convinced officials that victory could be theirs if the faculty closed ranks with the government. In a meeting with the St. Petersburg academic council, the curator, a cossack general, challenged the professors to choose "either the university or Russia."[20] The response to this unsavory option transformed the autumn's disciplinary "storm in a water glass" into a constitutional crisis.

Since the start of the semester's troubles, faculty members had been meeting regularly with one another in private homes. Under Kavelin's direction they now voted fifteen to fourteen not to support the administration against the students. To reinforce their protest against the bureaucracy's wrecking tactics Kavelin and four of his closest supporters resigned. They forthwith became the heroes of the hour to the liberal and democratic press. But given the constitutional structure of the universities as established in 1835, the refusal of the faculty to support the curator was tantamount to a mutiny inside the civil service. It was this unpublicized, procedural revolt rather than the students' dramatic defiance that prompted the government to close down all the universities in December. When the other schools complained that they were being punished for the sins of St. Petersburg, the Ministry pointed to the bright side. Salaries would continue and the suspension of teaching duties would leave more time for research.[21]

Scholarly concentration would be difficult. For around the academic anarchy swelled a rising sea of national uncertainties. After four years of preparation the manifesto of emancipation had been signed into law on February 19, 1861. The settlement it announced divided the agricultural resources of the nation into roughly equal portions between "30,000 noblemen" and "20 million peasants."[22] It then went on to bill the peasantry in perpetuity for the landlord's loss of income, labor, and land in the form of rents, taxes, and redemption payments. The crying injustice of these politically opportune terms drove elements of the educated class toward a final break with enlightened absolutism and liberal reform. While Herzen cried from London that the old slavery had given way to a new, anonymous pamphlets and leaflets began to circulate in the capitals. Addressed to young Russia, they summoned the peasantry to "take up axes" and seize "land and liberty" behind the leadership of the student youth. Secret societies, recruiting members from students dropping out of the state universities, were proliferating in the great centers of population. Their shabby emissaries were observed abroad seeking contact with the Russian émigrés of the Nicholaian era as well as with the reactivated Polish underground. Quite apart from the revolutionary ferment in the urban centers, the incidence of old-fashioned sedition in the barn-burning and pitchfork tradition of Pugachev was mounting in the rural areas. By 1862 radical propagandists, security officials, and newspapermen were viewing the scattered protests as a revolutionary crisis.[23]

Against this background, the Empress's reference to the disorder in the schools as *l'époque des troubles de l'université*—with its overtones of falling dynasties and civil war—was an understandable exaggeration.[24] It was also useful. For the sense of doom encouraged the Crown to end the time of academic troubles before greater trials could press home. The first step was to restore public confidence in the government. This was achieved by removing Admiral Putiatin. In January 1862 he was replaced by Aleksandr Golovnin, a long-time associate and personal confidant of Grand Duke Constantine. The new Minister of Education had worked closely with his royal patron during the latter's reorganization of the Naval Department. His appointment was viewed as a promise of liberal and efficient things to come. This initial impression was reinforced when he despatched Kavelin to Paris to study the scholastic procedures of Napoleon III.

Upon appointment to office, Golovnin was specifically charged with resolving the university question. Under his direction the Ministry took up the task of gathering and editing the material that had been accumulating since the war, as well as acquiring new opinions from foreign and domestic experts. The final decisions, however, were not left in his hands alone. Instead, they were entrusted to a special committee. This body included among its constituents both the Minister of Education and the Chief of the Third Section, as well as members of the Council of State. They deliberated under the presidency of Count Sergei Stroganov, a cavalry general with a grave sense of history, who enjoyed the complete confidence of the Imperial Family and was currently supervising the educational travels of the heir to the throne. Stroganov's principal claim to the trust of the academic community was his record as curator of the Moscow district during the period of official nationality, when he had defended the university's independence against St. Petersburg. Threading its way for eighteen months between the conflicting claims of national enlightenment and national security, the Stroganov commission conducted the most extensive investigation into the idea of a Russian university ever undertaken by the old regime. Much of the discussion was philosophical and much of the language technical. But the purpose throughout was practical—to draft a new statute for higher education that would ensure a solid official front in any future showdown with upstart social forces, be they professional or undergraduate.

The first question to be decided was whether the organization of higher learning ought to be maintained in its existing form. There was a line of thought popular in aristocratic and religious circles that recent events made it imperative to abolish the universities and, along with them, the very name and legal category of "student."[25] Responsibility for training the young could then be divided among a number of agencies for easier control. Scientific training could be parceled out to professional schools on the model of the military academies and the technological institute opened in St. Petersburg in 1831. The nation's modest liberal arts requirements might be satisfied at the municipal level. The city councils (dumas) could sponsor lecture series to be delivered by traveling scholars from the Academy of Sciences. The general public would be invited to slake its thirst for enlightenment alongside the local youths preparing themselves in a wholesome home environment for civil service examinations.

The universities, however, the alleged "hotbeds of nihilism," were currently proving themselves of inestimable value to the regime. "One must give the universities credit for preparing a whole generation to reject serfdom in their hearts, thus enabling the government to realize the greatest political act of Russian history—emancipation," Professor Ivan Andreevsky of St. Petersburg University reminded the authorities in a memorial written in 1862 in the middle of his duties as tutor of civil law to the Tsarevitch. "They also bred a generation that recognized the necessity for reform of the judicial system and the legal procedure and one that is ready and able to help the government transform the idea into action. And finally, they equipped an entire generation with the rational tools for broad, critical investigation of the historical, ethnographic, geographic, cultural, and economic foundations of our national life—in a word, they introduced all the branches of science for which both state and society have so desperate a need."[26]

Andreevsky's conviction that "the orderly development of the state as well as of society depends directly on the routine sovereignty of science" was broadly enough shared to ensure the preservation of the universities in the form devised by Peter the Great in the days of Leibniz: "an assembly of scholars gathered to instruct the younger generation in the most

advanced scientific wisdom of the day."[27] Within a decade the government would reaffirm its commitment to scholarship by opening two new
universities, at Odessa in 1865 and at Warsaw in 1869. In the same
period four separate vocational institutes were founded, one to promote
agriculture and three to train language teachers for the gymnasiums.

The decision to preserve the academic structure of the university raised
the question of administrative control. Russia's seats of learning were
rooted in the scholarly tradition of eighteenth-century Germany and the
bureaucratic format of Napoleonic France. The frequent intrusion of
officialdom into academic life since the days of Prince Golitsyn had generated a passion for autonomy. It came, then, as no surprise when the
faculties responded with exceptional unanimity to the solicitation of their
views. Allowing for a divergence of opinion on student discipline, they
asked that ultimate authority for all internal affairs be vested in a faculty
council composed of all regular teaching staff. Depending on the size of
the institution, this would entail an assembly of from 50 to 90 persons.
The constitution of 1863, for instance, provided the largest establishment,
the University of Moscow, with a regular staff of 88. This number included 39 professorships, 18 extraordinary professorships, and 31 docent
positions. The faculty council would, in turn, elect its own executive officers and judicial arm. It would also choose its own fellows.

In tsardom any degree of self-government was experimental. But reform was in the air, and some adventurous souls were ready to go beyond
administrative independence toward regional self-determination. The
suggestion was seriously put forward that each university be granted its
own individual charter, allowing it to develop a local character. The central ministry would be reduced to approving budgets and coordinating
standards. In time the state institutions would become territorial schools.
Academic federalism derived considerable support from the outlying
western provinces of the Baltic and the Ukraine, where the cultural
predominance of Greater Russia was resented by the local educated class.

Few scholars from any section, however, warmed to Nikolai Pirogov's
formula for professional independence. He proposed that the universities
free themselves completely from "the bureaucratic world, with its formalism, ranks, and privileges."[28] This would entail, he admitted, the loss
of a certain amount of prestige as long as the public continued to rank
government service and its attendant social status higher than the pursuit of knowledge. But the professors should be willing to make this

sacrifice. For it was inconceivable that the state could ever tolerate genuine academic freedom as long as philosophers and jurists, astronomers
and mathematicians, historians and economists, surgeons, chemists, and
biologists retained the same civil service status as police captains and
tax officials. "Science has its own hierarchy," Pirogov advised. In response
to the argument that official props were necessary for material support,
he offered the cold comfort of pure idealism: "Where the scientific spirit
reigns, there great things can be accomplished with meager means."[29]

Even if the professors were to renounce citizenship for themselves in
the fourteen-class society, should they retain control of admission for the
rest of the population? Since even liberal officials would be tempted to
interfere in the management of the schools as long as the acquisition of
a degree qualified recipients for the table of ranks, the thought of separation was attractive. If the faculties so desired, Golovnin was prepared to
sever the universities' connection with civil service rank altogether. The
fact remained, however, that academic life had begun to attract significant popular support only after Speransky's law had bound education to
state service and social advancement. In view of this fact, Chicherin
warned the Ministry that any attenuation of scholastic prerequisites for
state employment would drastically lower standards of national achievement at a time when Western Europe was raising them.[30]

As it picked its way through the maze of conflicting philosophies and
contrasting values, the Stroganov commission was guided by the circumstance that with each passing year tsardom became more dependent on
the coherence of its educated class to restrain the centrifugal tendencies
of its myriad tribes, creeds, races, and peoples. Despite the argument
that decentralization would allow experimentation and attract public
support, the commission was loath to subsidize cultural self-determination, racial nationalism, religious separatism, political federalism, or geographic secession in the schools. Even the supporters of federalism admitted that the underdeveloped character of provincial life would inevitably
lower the academic standards of locally oriented schools.[31] Accordingly,
the decision was firm to draft not several but one charter for all universities. Technical institutions and professional schools continued as before
to receive separate constitutions. Within the framework of a comprehensive statute the state was willing to grant a considerable degree of
self-government. Authority was accordingly restored to the professors in
the form familiar before 1835. The faculty council elected the rector and
the deans. In academic affairs the council no longer took orders from the

district curator, but dealt directly with the Ministry of Education. The faculties retained their positions in the Table of Ranks. Professors were granted an annual salary of 3,000 rubles a year, extraordinary professors 2,000, and docents 1,200. All obtained the pension rights attached to the civil service. They also remained the guardians of the quality of the central bureaucracy through continued responsibility for examinations, which conferred scholarly diplomas, academic degrees, official position, and social status. Detailed stipulations accorded regular graduates the right to enter the fourteen-class society at the twelfth-rank, advanced graduates at the tenth, masters of arts at the ninth, and doctors of philosophy at the ennobling eighth.

The university, in sum, was denied one attribute—regionalism. In return, it was granted three of the choicest gifts in the bestowal of the autocracy: academic freedom, professional self-government, and social authority. The maintenance of these favors would depend less on the precise language of the charter than on mutual self-restraint. "The crux of the matter is not the law," Pirogov commented, "for the law can always be circumvented, but the conscientious and responsible enforcement of the law." If the government assumed responsibilities, so did the professors. "An independent faculty means a group that assumes a moral responsibility before the government and the public for spreading science and enlightenment."[32] The professors would be expected to enlist as volunteers in the state's campaign against nihilism.

The government's acquiescence in the principal demands of the teachers enabled it to deal summarily with the students. The immediate cause of the trouble, the annual tax of 50 rubles (40 rubles outside the two capitals), was not removed. But the dearth of qualified candidates for state service, at a time when competing fields of public employment were expanding, encouraged an open purse. The poor continued as before to furnish the bulk of the student bodies. In the fall semester of 1875, 283 of the 1,259 students enrolled at Moscow University were government stipendiaries; 337 were exempted from fees, and 40 were allowed to defer payment until after graduation. Only 376 persons—roughly one-fourth—paid their bills when due. Of the remaining, the majority filed certificates of poverty, but were ineligible for aid because of unpromising academic records."[33] "The nihilist's best recruiting ground is amongst the poor students," the chief of internal security observed. "Their poverty is inconceivable."[34]

The enunciation of a democratic admissions policy returned the university question to its starting point—the organization of student life. It was on this issue that the academic world divided. In the hope that group activity would overcome the tendency of state schooling to produce "bureaucratic types" and instead engender "public types" fit for managing local affairs, Golovnin was prepared to realize Kavelin's project for legalizing collective student activity. In contrast to St. Petersburg, whose academic liberals favored what was sometimes called the "French" and sometimes the "English" principle of higher education and which in both instances implied an emphasis on civic training, Moscow University's "healthy conservatives" preferred the "German" accent on scholarship. The 33-year-old Boris Chicherin, Kavelin's prize pupil and personal friend, defined "healthy conservatism" as "strong authority enforcing liberal reforms." An expert on the history of local government, he was as devoted to the furtherance of public life in Russia as any other member of the "party of all thinking people." Within a few years he would follow Kavelin into academic retirement as a protest against what he considered government interference with faculty prerogatives.

In Chicherin's view the university had a single *raison d'être*—the production of "scholarly types." This function was too vital to the national interest to be infringed upon by any extraneous activity, however worthy in itself. Without the development of the mind there would be no public life or state life in Russia worthy of the name. Believing this, he led the opposition in the 1860's to any extension of official recognition or professional patronage to undergraduate organizations. Scholars, he feared, already labored at a disadvantage because of their ties with the Table of Ranks and the state administration. The introduction of an additional "public" theme would further dilute the already thin intellectual atmosphere. In the midst of political battles the students could best prepare themselves for the future service of the country "not by reading newspapers but by serious academic work."[35]

Chicherin's position was strengthened by the fact that the faculty advocates of student self-government had been compromised by the October days. "The constitution [of 1863] was based on our principles," one of their number recalled, "but A. V. Golovnin could not conceal from us the fact that in the higher spheres we were considered firebrands and the instigators of the student movement."[36] Shared by Count Stroganov and agreeable to Prince Dolgoruky, Chicherin's view prevailed. The fifth and final draft of the university bill consigned responsibility for the nonacademic behavior of students to the educational bureaucracy. The creation of a faculty court to deal with minor infractions resulted in no fundamental change. In effect, the state compartmentalized its pedagogical mission to society at the university level, making the faculty responsible for learning and the district curator for discipline. The struggle over student rights permanently scarred the academic community, wrecking careers and embittering personal relations. Years after the original dispute, Kavelin refused Chicherin's hand at the deathbed of a mutual friend.

And so, after eighteen months of intermittent labor, in the middle of domestic upheavals and foreign alarms, the Romanovs committed themselves to the continuation of university life. On June 18, 1863, the comprehensive statute was ratified, enabling the schools to open without incident in the fall. By this time the authorities were deep in legislative plans for organizing and controlling the opposite end of the educational spectrum—the pace and direction of basic instruction for the rural masses.

Multiple Administrative Arrangements
for Elementary Schools

Simply as an organizational chore, educating the peasants raised grave problems. At the university level tsardom was dealing with foreign but familiar pedagogical formulas and manageable cadres. At the rural elementary level it was grappling with the unknown. In addition, it was confronted by sheer numbers, millions of children, not packed into cities but scattered in villages, behind impassable roads over an area larger than Western Europe. The immensity of the task, the inadequacy of resources, and past neglect might well have paralyzed action altogether if certain individuals had not taken the initative. Among the first to act were landlords sympathetic to emancipation. Some of these began tutoring their peasants in anticipation of the day when the communes would assume more responsibility. The patriarchal benevolence of some landed aristocrats was overshadowed by the missionary spirit of another small group of volunteers, the university undergraduates. While their northern colleagues had been agitating the university question, the student youth of the southwest had been stirring the elementary question to life with the Sunday school movement.

To supplement the education of the working classes with Sunday

schools was a widespread practice in Germany. From there it passed to
the educational district of Riga, where it attracted the attention of Nikolai Pirogov, a professor of medicine at the provincial university. In 1858
Pirogov was appointed curator of the Kievan region; it was there, under
his protection, that a history professor, Platon Pavlov, convinced that "la
révolution par l'école" would do more for "semi-Asiatic" Russian society
than civil violence, inspired local university students to organize the first
Russian Sunday school, with the purpose of equipping illiterate working
adults with the basic tools of modern human eixstence—reading, writing, and numbers.[37] The impromptu undertaking exhibited a number
of advantages. The student teachers gave freely of their time, and the
local nobility loaned the facilities of one of their suburban day schools.
The adults who attended classes did so without compulsion, and the
enthusiasm of the venture drew public attention. Sunday witnessed
workers trooping toward the place of instruction, while from the opposite
direction a parade of urban notables, state, government, and municipal
officials, professors, and students came to observe the miracle of popular
enlightenment.[38] The venture spread—first to the neighboring towns of
Poltava and Chernigov, where secondary-school teachers and their advanced pupils replaced university volunteers, then northward, for its
greatest successes when Professor Pavlov moved to St. Petersburg. Within three years there were 500 literacy clinics in operation without a ruble's
expense to the state.

On the face of it the Sunday school movement was the answer to a
bankrupt nation's prayer. The appetite of the masses for learning was
being stimulated; the resistance of the backlands to books eroded. Then,
as suddenly as it began, the experiment in public spirit faltered as a result
of popular apathy and official suspicion. Unable to make specific charges
hold, the police insinuated that the students—protected by the Ministry
of Education—were spreading antigovernment propaganda under the
guise of teaching the masses. To protect the local venture from central
interference, Pirogov placed it under strict district control. The student
teachers were subordinated to a faculty adviser; instruction was limited
to basic grammar from an approved text, and an inspector regularly
made the rounds. This was not enough for the Third Section. Warning
that the state could not afford to leave to individuals the responsibility
for educating the people, Prince Dolgoruky advised the Crown to place
the movement under central surveillance. After engineering the removal
of both Pirogov and Kovalevsky from office, he succeeded in placing the

literacy campaign under the triple Argus of the Ministry of Education, the Holy Synod, and the Ministry of the Interior. In 1862, as part of that year's "revolutionary crisis," Professor Pavlov was arrested and the remaining Sunday schools shut down. For even before the government's action, the movement had been withering. Publicized enthusiasm for enlightening the people was one thing; the quiet grind of doing it was another. Even without police harassment, the students lost interest, the proprietors grumbled, the nobility sat on their hands. As yet, society was too weak and too disorganized to mount a national literacy campaign outside of an official framework.[39]

The adventure in educational populism did not pass without bringing into clearer perspective the dilemma facing the autocracy—either to risk enlightening the people or to risk leaving them in darkness. Secular schooling would inevitably induce habits associated with higher levels of consciousness—religious skepticism, individualism, the urge for national self-determination, a yearning for popular sovereignty, and the demand for social justice. Almost surely, it seemed to the guardians of domestic tranquillity that "too much light" would render the peasants as susceptible as the students to the "latest Western intellectual fashions." It was just as obvious, however, that emancipation without education would unravel the fabric of rural life and weaken the empire. For not only the regular revenues of the state but the surpluses necessary to accumulate and secure investment capital abroad rested on the backs and minds of the peasants.

Fortunately for the cause of popular instruction, emancipation was accompanied by a far-reaching departure in rural self-government—the *zemstvo* experiment. Created by statute in 1864, the zemstvos were representative assemblies organized at the district and provincial levels to bridge the gap between the government and the villages created by the abolition of the gentry's command over the serfs. Zemstvo members were elected through an all-class franchise weighted in favor of the large rural landowners at the expense of the peasantry and the towns. The district councils elected executive boards. These, in turn, hired the zemstvo "third element" of university and gymnasium graduates—doctors, lawyers, teachers, agronomists, statisticians, and engineers. The new institutions were introduced into the strictly Russian provinces of the empire. The borderlands, it was felt after the Polish revolt of 1863, could not be trusted with tools of local self-government.

From the beginning the state made it clear that the territorial assem-

blies it was creating were to have no national political significance. Their
powers of taxation were rigidly confined, and from Petersburg's point of
view there was no legitimate reason for the representatives of one province to communicate with those of another. In fact, any effort to do so
would be regarded as conspiratorial. "Zemstvo," however, was an old-
Russian term denoting the land and the people as distinct from the state.
The very word conjured up romanticized memories of the seventeenth-
century zemsky sobors, one of which had elected the first Romanov, the
grandfather of Peter the Great, to supreme power in 1613. Despite strenuous official counteraction, the aura of popular sovereignty and indige-
nous Muscovite constitutionalism clung to the local assemblies from the
moment of their conception until their flowering in the state duma after
the revolution of 1905.

As the zemstvos settled down to work, they gradually revealed themselves as "schools of public life" within the bureaucratic system. Formally
excluded from national politics, they shouldered responsibilty for a variety of "local economic needs." These included welfare, sanitation, poor
and famine relief, upkeep of roads, and encouragement of agriculture
and industry. Of its various undertakings, the one that provided the
various district and provincial deputies with a common sense of purpose
and a crusading spirit was public schooling. "The role of the educated
class in Russia," Turgenev reminded Herzen in 1862, "is to transmit
civilization to the people until they can decide for themselves what they
will repudiate and what they will accept. This is, essentially, a modest
role, although it continues the work of Peter the Great and Lomonosov,
and sets in motion a revolution."[40] The same Turgenev once referred to
the prospective idea of the zemstvos as a practical joke played on society
by the bureaucracy. Even with all its shortcomings, however, the constitution of 1864 provided the local educated class—gentry in the 1860's,
democratic in the 1890's—with a permanent, semipublic base from which
to contest the state bureaucracy for the leadership of rural Russia.

The creation of the zemstvos coincided with the reawakening of the
state's own interest in popular education. Blocked from realizing the
plans of La Harpe and the secret committee for abolishing serfdom and
instructing the masses, the grandsons of Catherine the Great had confined the government's pedagogical mission in the countryside to several
minor forays. The most important of these were activities of the Holy
Synod and the Ministry of State Domains. Together, these two depart-

ments offered a minimal program of religious instruction and domestic handicrafts in some 7,000 ill-equipped and poorly staffed schools to approximately 200,000 children annually out of a total school-age population approaching 15 million. These figures indicate that by mid-century some advance had been made since the days when fewer than 25,000 pupils were under instruction in the parish schools of the Orthodox church. Measured against Western progress for the same period, however, the level of national intelligence was declining at an accelerating rate of speed. The turning point came with the Sunday school movement and the reorganization of rural government. Within the context of events, which not only expressed but guaranteed the interest of society in popular enlightenment, the Ministry of Education, in order to assure the state's commanding position, came forward with the first serious program for organizing a national elementary educational system in Russian history—the Public School Statute of July 14, 1864. Subsequent progress, while not spectacular, was at least measurable. By the end of Alexander II's reign, the first comprehensive census of rural schooling revealed that in the 60 provinces of European Russia, 1,140,915 pupils (four-fifths of them males) were attending 22,770 elementary schools. Most of these establishments were under the joint or separate jurisdiction of the Ministry of Education, the zemstvo assemblies, and the Holy Synod.

This complex administrative structure was no whim of state. From the outset St. Petersburg recognized that education for the millions of "sheepskinned peasants in their warm and dirty hovels, with their chronic indigestion and their deep-seated abhorrence of anything suggestive of civic responsibility or social initiative,"[41] was too vast a project for any single department of government. The autocracy's first concern was to isolate the rural masses from the student intelligentsia. It then sought to ensure its control over the mental development of the peasantry by balancing off legitimate interests. Accordingly, the law of July 14 created the district school boards. Composed of representatives of the Ministry of Education, the Holy Synod, and the zemstvos, with a permanent observer from the provincial governor's office to advise on security affairs, and directly subordinate to the district curators, the district boards provided an administrative device useful not only for coordinating and advancing but for restraining the spread of knowledge in the countryside. They also furnished a fixed arena within which the partisans of ecclesiastical traditionalism, bureaucratic Westernism, and gentry paternalism could struggle among themselves for the minds and loyalties of the people they had all neglected for centuries.

During the discussions of the zemstvo statute the gentry had urged that the district assemblies be given complete responsibility for rural education. The peasantry, so their argument went, had always been under the guidance of the local nobility and the state had never injected itself into this area.[42] The party of official liberalism, however, was anxious to establish direct contact with the emancipated masses. As a result, the zemstvos were made responsible for financial support of the schools, and the Ministry of Education assumed control of teacher education and academic standards. Fortified by this clear and favorable division of labor, Aleksandr Golovnin henceforth devoted the power of his office to gathering all elementary establishments under the purview of the school boards. To support his campaign he publicized the fact that although other departments lacked the interest, the experience, and the professional skills to conduct adequate training programs, the state treasury expended twice as much money on their inferior schools as on those that fell within the scope of the educational charter of 1864. Administrative diffusion, Golovnin warned the Council of State in 1865, deprived the Russian Empire of the educational coherence "that in other countries does so much to reduce social tensions and inspire a strong unifying national spirit."[43] As a result of this appeal, the Ministry was permitted to absorb several minor systems for the first time since 1842, when it had acquired jurisdiction over the confessional schools of the Jewish pale. The new acquisitions included scattered outposts belonging to the Ministry of State Domains and the Office of Nomadic Tribes. But Golovnin's principal purpose was to capture the largest prize—the more than 3,800 parish schools of the Orthodox church in the sensitive southwest area.

It was at this juncture that the drive of official liberalism toward administrative consolidation of rural enlightenment ran athwart the political problems of the empire. These had become intensely acute in the western borderlands since 1860, as the agitation of Polish gentry and Catholic clergy fired historic resistance into open insurrection. Claiming the frontiers given by "God and history," the Warsaw patriots showered sparks of unrest as far as Vilna and Kiev at a time when nihilism and emancipation were harassing St. Petersburg flank and rear. General

Mikhail Muravev hastened westward armed with extraordinary powers. Seeing him off at the train station, the Empress implored, "At least save Lithuania for us."[44]

In its response to the rebellion, tsardom did not rest content with military pacification. It sought to homogenize the area culturally as well. Like the Sunday school movement, the Polish revolt speeded up the state's efforts. Using his authority as military governor of the northwestern provinces to strengthen the local peasantry in Russian language and Orthodox faith, General Muravev opened 389 village schools with treasury funds. Agencies of imperial unity, these emergency institutions were brought under Golovnin's district school boards as soon as these were organized. In the southwest the situation was more complicated. In the middle Dnieper basin, where history had deposited a Polish gentry and a Jewish middle class, the local clergy had taken the lead and were operating with their own funds the largest Orthodox elementary system in the empire. Conducted by village priests, the parish schools concentrated on moral tradition. To security-conscious officials they appeared better suited than zemstvo or state schools to nourish "unity of spirit" among the eastern Slavs. They might also better immunize Little Russians, White Russians, Great Russians, and others against such "foreign influences" as Catholicism, separatism, and socialism. Golovnin sought to annex them in the name of "unity of command."

Golovnin's offensive threatened Count Dmitri Tolstoy. An ardent administrator with a scholar's interest in the past, Tolstoy earned a doctorate from the University of Leipzig in 1864 with a monograph on *Le catholicisme romain en Russie*.[45] Relieved from duty in the Ministry of Education when Golovnin replaced Putiatin, Tolstoy was appointed Ober-Procurator of the Holy Synod in the summer of 1865 to organize the cultural defense of tsardom's western frontier. The personal rivalry between the two statesmen grew out of different assessments of the country's priorities. Tolstoy saw in education a device for strengthening the unity of the empire; Golovnin considered it an opportunity for encouraging public initiative. In his defense of the southwestern status quo, Tolstoy suggested that the transfer of the parish schools from synodal to ministerial jurisdiction would be interpreted as a vote of no-confidence in the local clergy, with disastrous consequences for morale. Besides, he continued, the coexistence of 3,869 parish schools in an area with 51 state schools might provide "useful competition" between departments of state. Hopefully, the Ministry of Education would be inspired to expansion and the Holy Synod to higher quality. As for the threat of "clericalism" raised by some liberals, if advanced European countries dared to use Roman Catholic priests in primary education, what had Russia to fear from its national clergy? Finally, arguing that "unity of spirit" was a more potent formula for social cohesion than mere "unity of command," Tolstoy struck a note that would carry him far in the service of the tsars.[46]

The debate in the Committee of Ministers in the early spring of 1866 over administrative arrangements for rural enlightenment in the southwest territory was the opening skirmish between the two official Westernizing camps which would grapple in the decades ahead to give liberal and public or nationalist and state direction to general education. Their major test of strength would come in the field of secondary reform.

Potential Public Status for Secondary Schools

From its beginnings tsardom had anchored itself in rural Russia and drawn its service class from the landed proprietors. Now, as former serf and former master faced uncertain futures, the autocracy turned toward the towns. Deriving its format from resident gentry and local officials, the educable urban class was not only overwhelmingly loyal to the regime, it was also anxious to assume a more responsible role in local affairs. "What this country needs most," Chicherin noted in the midst of the university disorders of 1861, "is for society to enjoy a high degree of participation. Local initiative is indispensable for life. Without it we will always remain in the very condition that plunged us into the disasters of the Crimean War."[47] In some 50 metropolitan centers of the empire, state agencies for organizing regional talent were already in existence— the gymnasiums. Narrowly redefined as realschulen rather than classical schools after the European Revolutions of 1848, they were designed to cast the middle estate of lower gentry and upper townsmen into types fitting the administrative and professional slots of the Nicholaian system. In an era anticipating reorganizing of provincial life along more independent, representative lines, their social bias, administrative restrictions, and vocational curricula needed revising. " 'To make us human beings,' this is what not one of our realschulen do, since they strive to transform us *from early childhood* into merchants, soldiers, sailors, priests, and lawyers,"[48] Pirogov commented on the eve of reform.

The prospective shift of provincial politics toward local control of local affairs created a domestic climate favorable to decentralization and democratization of the schools. The flurry of ideas for enriching their content and broadening their goals came from abroad. Since the Petrine revolution, tsarist educators—"now striving after German, now after Napoleonic models"—had aped changing foreign fashions; and their emergence as the "saviors of the fatherland" after the Crimean War coincided with the climactic phase of a prolonged European contest over pedagogical values. From the Italian Renaissance through the French Revolution to the Romantic Era, through all the gyrations of thought and turbulence of feeling which separated one generation from another, classical humanism—despite "Montaigne, Bacon, and Rousseau"—had continued to provide Europe with its governing educational ideal. Things were different, but tastes were the same. Whether his place of residence was London, Paris, Vienna, or Berlin, the educated man was "a gentleman and a scholar" bred on the literature of Greece and Rome.[49]

By the mid-nineteenth century, however, there was a growing sense of discontinuity. The break could be traced, in large measure, to the progress of the mind. Science as such was no longer primarily a philosophical adventure. Knowledge was becoming increasingly specialized and more rigorously applied. The inventive reason was now in harness as a workhorse for economics and politics. The resultant technology was spreading prosperity, democracy, and militarism across the northern hemisphere; and as trade, industry, and arms developed into marvels of ingenuity, profit, and power, they fed the demand for a more direct, businesslike approach to education. The whole network of learning from the elementary level to the universities came under critical review. The attack concentrated on the most strategic point—the secondary schools.[50]

The pedagogical argument turned on whether practical or literary disciplines were the soundest guarantee of progress in the age of iron and steam. In organizational terms the question was whether the classical gymnasium, with its concentration on the "everlasting accomplishments of the human spirit," or the realschule, with its emphasis on "the laws that govern nature and affairs," should set a nation's tone. "Why is there so much discussion," Pirogov asked in 1861, "why are governments and leading persons of all educated nations analyzing, weighing, and reckoning at such length the advantages and disadvantages of a classical or a real direction in the academic program of the school, if they are not seeking in one or the other a firm principle for guiding the future course of the whole society?"[51]

In countries where schools were older than states, the controversy between classicism and realism was a conflict between vigorous and articulate social interests. Behind the tumult, which continued unabated until the First World War, over the relative importance of literary or scientific studies for the nation as a whole, government officials, professional educators, and school-going citizens were defending or attacking the traditional credentials committee for verifying social status, the Latin- and Greek-oriented university preparatory school. In the commercial and manufacturing centers of the West, where "the progressive division of labor by which both science and government prosper" was a growing reality, the controversy between humanists and realists pitted the entrepreneurial and artisan classes against the scholastic establishment. The main social support for conventional secondary schooling in England, France, and Germany came from a growing number of affluent families. The children were apt to be "*sans aptitude pour les belles-lettres*," and the parents were anxious to be rid of the "rubbish of Latin and Greek." But all wanted to obtain the "social stamp" conferred by a classical education.[52]

In tsardom the classical-realist debate dominated secondary school reform until the Revolution of 1905. The language used in official circulars, professional meetings, scholarly articles, and polemical tracts drew on European terminology, and contestants drew support for their "practical" or "cultural" stance from European examples. But the task in Russia was not to revise but to *create* a national educational tradition.[53] The lack of one had long been etched on the public consciousness by a literary tag. In the days of the Decembrists, Eugene Onegin epitomized the dilettantism of the nobility:

> "We all pick up our education in bits and pieces,
> Something and somehow."

A decade later Belinsky transferred Pushkin's characterization of the aristocracy to the democratic intelligentsia: "We are all self-taught geniuses; we know everything without having studied anything; we acquired everything without shedding a drop of blood but only for our own amusement and sport. In a word, 'We all pick up bits and pieces, Something and somehow.' "[54] Reviewing the scene since Belinsky, Niko-

lai Pirogov concluded with affectionate irony: "We Russians are fortu-
nate in at least this respect, that our intellectual fashions, like the governors of Podolia, never last for long. We Russians, we are not like the
Hebrews and the Western peoples: *we have no educational tradition.*
'We all pick up bits and pieces, Something and somehow.' "[55]

Whether scientific or classical, tsardom's instructional apparatus was
still too new and unsure of itself for social allegiances to have been
formed. During the Crimean war the University of Kazan housed only
four students majoring in the natural sciences. In the immediate postwar
years the University of St. Petersburg produced one graduate from its
liberal arts faculty. Mikhail Katkov complained that the readers of
his newspapers—the local leaders of provincial society—could scarcely
pronounce the terms gymnasium, realgymnasium, realschule correctly,
much less define their special functions. This outburst was more than
just another instance of the Moscow editor's celebrated spleen. It was a
fact of provincial life, officially verified. At the same time that Katkov
was making his unkind assessment, the curator of a populous educational
district was reporting to St. Petersburg, "Even though it has been put to
them in detail with a clear explanation of the differences between classical and real gymnasiums, people, when asked, are at a loss how to answer
the question. Some citizens for no reason whatever want classical programs; others for equally fatuous reasons want modern curricula." All
families were agreed on one point: "the state secondary school established in their locality should grant graduates the right to enter the university."[56]

Public interest in secondary school reform remained focused on legal
rights. Until the 1890's at least, high state officials, rather than public and
professional men, led the "battle"—as Katkov called it—to replace "bits
and pieces" with firm guidance and comprehensive planning. Latin
versus German and Greek versus zoology in the university preparatory
curriculum was fought out within the Petersburg bureaucracy. For 40
years the inner ruling circle, the Crown's closest official and unofficial advisers—ministers, generals, admirals, police chiefs, grand dukes, tsare-
vitches—argued ostensibly over whether students without Greek should
be admitted to the universities. The issue on everyone's tongue was not
pedagogical but administrative—the political thrust of secondary reform: whether state officials responsible only to themselves and their
immediate superiors, or state officials deliberately sensitive to public

opinion, were to shape the empire's long-range social goals. Specifically, should the reorganized general secondary schools be endowed with rigid bureaucratic form, the better to serve as bastions of state power and state standards in the underdeveloped countryside, or should they be allowed to assume a flexible, locally responsive air, to become, in effect, enclaves of public life, constitutionally sensitive to parental, professional, municipal, regional desires, inevitably nurturing imperial society's slow crawl away from central control?

In any event, whether general education took an ancient or a modern turn, whether it went back to the classical direction of 1828 or settled on the real impulse of 1849, or divided and followed separate tracks toward the universities and the special institutes of higher learning, academic careerism, with its traditional concern for admission to the Table of Ranks, was now too narrowly focused. Exclusive commitment to education for imperial service would hamper development of the organs of urban and rural self-government, which were in the process of being either created or refurbished. To be successful, emancipation and its related great reforms of local government would need to attract trained personnel oriented toward regional and community concerns, and should be able to function efficiently outside the paramilitary organization of the central bureaucracy. To fill this need for public as distinct from state servants, tsardom needed a public as distinct from a state philosophy of education. The formulator was Nikolai Pirogov, "the first of us to regard the problem of education with philosophical breadth, and to see in it not just a question of school discipline, didactics, or rules for physical training, but the ultimate concern of the human spirit—'the vital question.'"[57]

In the 1830's the government of Nicholas I had sent Pirogov to the West to complete his medical training. Following in the footsteps of Lomonosov, he prepared himself in Germany for the service of Russia. The Crimean conflict found him a professor of surgery at the University of Dorpat. From there he volunteered for the front, where his organization of the medical corps brought him international renown. In the first summer following the war he published an article entitled "Vital Questions." Describing mid-nineteenth-century Europe as an "intensely practical" place in which "moral man" no longer felt at home, and mid-nineteenth-century Russia as "life in a dress uniform ... a starched shirt ... a suit of iron armor ...," the essay challenged the reader: "subject every instant to moral freedom ... force yourself into battle with yourself and those around you."[58]

The tone of the sermon was reminiscent of Belinsky, whom Pirogov admired, and its appearance "shattered a decade of slavish silence." But "Vital Questions" was more than a manifesto of personal liberation from European materialism and Russian bureaucracy. It also presented a program for national revival through a unified and comprehensive system of general education, available to both sexes, open to all classes of society, responsive to Russia's peculiar national and varying local needs, and based on careful consideration of both the latest European science and enduring European values. Such views were not necessarily new. Catherine II had promoted schooling for women, the democratic ladder was reminiscent of the grand design of 1803, and Belinsky had been rabid on the need for social justice and individual dignity. What aroused public interest and professional excitement was the fact that such sentiments were no longer confined to historical archives and literary circles but enjoyed the support of the government. For "Vital Questions" appeared in *Sea Chronicle,* the official journal of Grand Duke Constantine's Naval Department, under the editorship of Aleksandr Golovnin.[59] "Our newspapers flourish by republishing excerpts from *Sea Chronicle*," a Minister of the Interior observed.[60] Both liberal and democratic periodicals used this device for circumventing the censor to publicize their own lengthy glosses on Pirogov's original message. The outburst of critical activity launched a pedagogical literature of sometimes high professional competence. By the 1890's these independent writings would visibly influence the organization of state schools.

For "Vital Questions" Pirogov was appointed curator of the educational region of Odessa, where he worked to prepare the transformation of the local *lycée* into a university that might attract southern Slavs from the neighboring Balkans. In 1858 his liberal admirers in the Petersburg bureaucracy had him promoted to the third most important post in the provincial hierarchy, the curatorship of Kiev. Here he presided over the beginnings of the Sunday school movement, and in the face of opposition from "persecutors of enlightenment," who favored replacing "the salutory birch" with even more efficacious "blows to the face," he advised the pedagogical councils of the Ukraine to dispense with corporal punishment as "residual routine ... devoid of pedagogical significance." By insisting on detailed reports, he cut the "arbitrary violence" of directors and inspectors by 90 per cent within a year.[61]

While the "old soldier" was busy in the southwest translating humane ideals into bureaucratic procedures, one of his most ambitious projects was receiving serious attention in the capital—the emancipation of women through educational reform. The nation's girls, he insisted, should be trained "not to become soldiers, bureaucrats, and ministers of state," as some radical feminists were advocating; neither should they be patronized as "empty-headed dolls," as at present; but they should be challenged academically as intelligent human beings. Even Norov had been sympathetic to the idea of doing more in this direction. "Up to the present," he admitted, "the vast system of education in Russia has only been concerned with one-half of the population, namely the males."[62]

But despite its good intentions, the Ministry of Education had little money to spare. And so the statute for women's gymnasiums and progymnasiums that it prepared invited the local gentry, municipal dumas, zemstvos, and private benefactors to assume the burdens of financial support. It retained for itself responsibility for inspection of academic standards and teacher certification. What treasury funds were available were concentrated on planting outposts of Russian culture among the national minorities, particularly in the more highly civilized, politically sensitive western areas. Uncertain budgets and the difficulties of recruiting qualified staff plagued women's education throughout the remainder of the imperial era. Offsetting these disadvantages was the fact that the fiscal modesty of the operation and its closeness to community support stimulated rapid growth. By the end of Alexander II's reign, the 76 girls' gymnasiums operating under the jurisdiction of the Ministry of Education, together with the 27 schools of the Empress Marie, were comparable in numbers of associated students with the much more handsomely financed male secondary schools.

When the clerical-police alliance reached for control of the Ministry of National Enlightenment in 1861, improvement of women's training was one of the few signs of progress toward reconstruction of secondary schools. Golovnin's appointment revived hopes for far-reaching revisions in general education for men. For his refusal to maintain "secret police surveillance" over the student body when the Polish unrest was spreading, Admiral Putiatin removed Pirogov from his provincial post in the spring of 1861. Early in 1862 Golovnin recalled him to the state's service as special consultant. In the essays, articles, and memoranda of this final period of his official career he pushed two of his favorite themes—the need for administrative decentralization and academic flexibility. State enlightenment, he warned, would never serve national interests well without active local support, whereas too rigid a distinction between traditional and modern, cultural and scientific, classical and real disciplines would tend to prolong into emancipated Russia the caste divisions and social resentments that had stifled the growth of a productive middle-class civilization since the Petrine reforms.

Pirogov's conciliatory presence on the academic committee of the Ministry of Education was sorely needed as the bureaucracy moved with increasing difficulty toward drafting an acceptable educational bill. By 1862 the classical-realist dispute was no longer a "narrow pedagogical issue" but had become "a full-blown question of social philosophy."[63] As such, it served the argumentative national press, which had increased from 25 to almost 200 Russian-language periodicals alone since the war, as a shrill device for the dissemination of political views. The Ministry of the Interior, which allowed "the most contradictory currents of opinion to circulate up to a point" while "immediately stopping those that transgress the limits of political, social, and moral tolerance," divided "the world of independent views" into four major trends: liberal-cosmopolitan, democratic-socialist, Westernizing nationalist, and xenophobic Slavophile. These, in turn, were loosely organized behind the editorial command of a half-dozen "colorful" newspaper publishers working out of two capitals.[64] Moscow was the seat of nationalist opinion with both pro- and anti-Western overtones. Ivan Aksakov's Slavophile paper, *Day,* deplored the Europeanization of Russian schools. Mikhail Katkov, on the other hand, whose "strong voice" drew a tsar's praise for having "awakened Russian national feeling" and a tsar's blame for meddling in governmental affairs, devoted his *Moscow News* (its printing plant leased directly from the University of Moscow and indirectly from the Ministry of Education) to promoting the view that only the full Latin-Greek curriculum could rescue the state schools and Russian society from intellectual decay and moral ruin.[65]

St. Petersburg was the center of what was officially described as "doctrinaire" and "cosmopolitan" opinions. Included within these views were the publishing ventures of Katkov's ideological and business rival, Andrei Kraevsky. In the 1840's the two editors had frequented the same avant-garde literary circles orbiting the University of Moscow. By the 1860's, they had become bitter personal foes. For two decades their newspaper feuds helped widen the differences of approach and emphasis among the Westernizers into two mutually suspicious camps, "liberal" and "nationalist." Katkov feared the indecisiveness of the central government. Kraevsky feared its oppression. A staunch advocate of local self-government, the Petersburg editor greeted the establishment of the zemstvo assemblies as "the realization of a 200-year-old dream." His applause for the libertarian impulses of the great reforms built the circulation of the *St. Petersburg News* to an unprecedented 10,000 (over three times the outlay of Herzen's London *Bell* at the peak of its muffled popularity) before he left it to establish a newspaper that carried Pirogov's by-line on education. This avowedly independent undertaking served frequently as the organ of official liberalism. In keeping with this position, Kraevsky rejected the Latin-Greek "Katkovian" gymnasium as needlessly imitative and formalistic. Instead, he lent his patronage to the realgymnasium, which, with its deemphasis of the ancient languages and its greater attention to modern languages and natural sciences, was attracting increasing support from both official and public sectors of the educated class.

But even the realgymnasium, with its retention of Latin as a tool rather than a cultural subject, smacked too much of aristocracy for St. Petersburg's democratic press. Its principal representatives were *Contemporary,* the journal founded by Pushkin, revived by Belinsky, and converted into the voice of peasant socialism by Nikolai Chernyshevsky, and *Russian Word,* a product of the postwar period, which the critical talents of Dmitri Pisarev elevated to national significance. These two organs— "the voices of the younger generation"—preferred the applied science approach of realschulen. In the summer of 1862, however, both journals were suspended on the charge of abetting "that tendency to materialism, to nihilism, and particularly to extreme socialism ... on the part of the half-educated who already have a hankering for forbidden fruit."[66] The chief contributors were arrested and the best known of them, Chernyshevsky, the son of a village priest, was banished to Siberia on trumped-up charges. While awaiting transportation east he was allowed to write and publish (to Kavelin's horror) a socialist novel that became the "nihilists' sacred scripture."[67] The lesser known Pisarev was imprisoned in the capital for drafting a manifesto that referred to the autocracy as a "stinking corpse" ripe for instant burial. Pisarev also confessed that after a paper brilliance, which masked a "sheeplike treading of the gymnasium routine," his experience as a student at the University of St. Petersburg had "transformed him into an active constituent of the democratic *raznochintsy*."[68] Nevertheless, "by origin and by law" he remained the privileged son of a provincial nobleman. On the personal petition of his widowed mother to the Tsar, he was permitted to continue publishing articles for her support on such "nonpolitical" matters as educational reform.

From solitary confinement in the Alexis dungeon of the Fortress of Saints Peter and Paul, near the place where Peter the Great had sacrificed his son to the vision of a remodeled Russia, the 25-year-old enemy of the state composed perceptive pedagogical essays. Classical studies he dismissed as doomed "unless the Moscow publicists succeed in coming up with some kind of artificial respiration for their perishing sympathies." He flayed the Petersburg authorities for failing "to rehabilitate physical labor," a necessary first step in the prisoner's opinion to prepare the populace for the "inevitable advent of Western industrialism." In time, however, "as surely as the horse drags the cart," Europe would pull Russia toward "real" schooling based on scientific principles.[69]

Under the impact of public argument, the secondary schools became identified with political goals—European classicism, with the assertion of central authority; the realgymnasium, with local control of local affairs; and "real" schooling, with utilitarian democracy. As academic programs became identified with ideologies, the temperature of debate spiraled. In its review of public opinion trends of 1864, the Ministry of the Interior noted with alarm "the especially intense, even violent struggle over the system of secondary schools."[70]

These publicized differences amplified the uncertainty within the academic committee charged with responsibility for drafting a new constitution for secondary schools. The majority supported Pirogov's view that "only lack of material means, not social prejudices, can justify vocational training for a child before his fourteenth year."[71] Most also agreed with the period's most prestigious pedagogue that division of the secondary program was essential, to avoid the "bits and pieces" approach that plagued national practice and to allow young, growing, undisciplined minds to concentrate on mastery of a few, broad, time-tested fields, and so prepare them "for the reception of all possible kinds of truths, moral as well as scientific."[72] The majority also shared Pirogov's uncertainty of what subjects should predominate in the general educational schools. For although Pirogov himself, in agreement with "the experience of centuries," ascribed a "high educational force exclusively to intensive study of the ancient languages, one's native tongue, history, and mathematics," he emphasized again and again that the teacher was more important than the subject and the goal "to become a human being" more important than any means; and he was not at all ready to force his views on the Russian public, which, he admitted, might find "modern languages and natural sciences" as fully educational for their children as "ancient languages and mathematics."[73]

As for Pirogov's engaging vision of a more sophisticated version of the *école unique* of 1803—of one integrated system, from the two-class village schoolhouse to the universities, rounded off at each level, with academically distinct real and classical branches interrelated for ease of cross transference as a child's talents surfaced or his economic condition improved, organized "so that every school can serve as the threshold of another"—these "rosy hopes" had to be indefinitely postponed for lack of funds, teachers, tradition, public support, and official sympathy.[74]

The difficulty of fashioning nebulous ideas into institutions, with distribution of hours and legal rights, which had to be spelled out, prolonged the business of revision through four drafts. Even journals friendly toward official liberalism became impatient. *Spark* pictured the educational "horse of progress" in 1863 as a crawfish with its tail tied to a standard labeled "Forward!" fixed in the sand.[75] Finally, in its fifth edition, the new constitution for seven-year gymnasiums and four-year progymnasiums was published on November 19, 1864.

Its appearance did not quell the controversy. Katkov found the new charter "confused by the struggle that produced it." Even Pirogov had reservations about its ability to please all parties. On admissions policy, at least, the legislators achieved clear accord. An early draft declared that "Inasmuch as education is the main basis of the state and the source of its welfare, the profits of education ought to be enjoyed by all persons, without distinction of sex or social origin."[76] The substance of this proposition was incorporated into the final text as Paragraph 23: "The gymnasiums and progymnasiums are for the education of children of all conditions without social or religious distinction." In this form social democracy remained a part of the fundamental code of tsardom's educational law until the destruction of the regime in the First World War.[77]

In the area of administration the constitution of 1864 reversed the trend of 30 years. It entrusted district curators with a wide range of deci-

sions previously referred to St. Petersburg. In imitation of the recently
enacted university charter, it declared the pedagogical councils the re-
pository of ultimate authority within the individual schools. The director was no longer the commander of the staff but a colleague. As the
chairman of the council he was subject to majority rule. Bureaucratic
absolutism, Pirogov noted with approval, was officially rejected in favor
of collegiate responsibility.

Conditions of service were also improved. Previously, teachers were in
the habit of working above the norm of twelve class hours a week without receiving extra pay. The statute of 1864 kept the norm at twelve hours
but introduced payment at the rate of 60 rubles a year for every hour a
week taught beyond that level. The staff was also divided into two categories, regular and temporary. Regulars were paid from state funds,
temporary personnel from local sources such as students' fees. The qualifications for both types remained the same—a university degree and a
teaching certificate. The latter was acquired by state examination upon
completion of specified courses in pedagogy. Regular staff were appointed by the district on the recommendation of the director. As members of
the civil service they enjoyed its privileges and pension rights. Temporary teachers were hired and dismissed at the director's discretion.

Before 1864 instructors were paid on a sliding scale according to the
subjects taught and the geographic location of the school.[78] Golovnin
abolished the wage differential between lower and upper division and
raised modern language teachers to the general norm. Catechists and
manual arts instructors continued as before to receive less pay. Hardship
benefits for towns in the interior were abolished, but the higher pay scale
for the border areas continued in force. A regular system of raises was
also introduced, based on a twelve-hour teaching load.

1st year	750 rubles	16th year	1,250 rubles
6th year	900 rubles	21st year	1,500 rubles
11th year	1,050 rubles		

The regular teachers could not live on their base pay. The schools could
not function with the staff instructing only twelve hours a week. As a
result, it was common practice for a regular staff member to earn half of
his income as a temporary employee on hourly pay.

On the questions of social democracy, decentralization, and orderly
employment procedures, the secondary constitution was clear enough.
On the hotly contested issue of academic principles it was deliberately

vague, leaving "to time and experience" the final decision on which type of general schooling would constitute the national standard. The very name "realschule" was avoided as smacking of nihilism on one hand and vocational training with its taint of social inferiority on the other. The sense of the document, however, was to confirm both traditional and modern programs of study as equally "educational." In keeping with this arrangement, the central authorities limited themselves to mathematical guidelines. According to a directive of the Council of State, half of the country's 76 secondary schools were to offer the academic program of realgymnasiums; the remaining were to be evenly divided between so-called general schools, which were in fact realschulen, and classical gymnasiums.[79] Only graduates of the full Latin-Greek course would be allowed direct access to the universities. Within the guidelines the local communities were free to petition the Minister of Education to convert existing institutions into the type they preferred. Pirogov doubted whether the public would support for long a general educational school—no matter how modern its curriculum—whose graduates were barred from the universities. He had urged ease of transfer; the new statute made it easier to change the academic structure of the school than to move a pupil from one type to another. Despite some misgivings and considerable confusion, the educated class welcomed the new legislation as an invitation to share with the state responsibility for social development.

Chapter Three

Bureaucratic Nationalism: Education versus Revolution, 1865–1875

The whole of this education question is not one between classical schools and modern, between Greek or Latin and technics: it is a battle between industry and idleness, seriousness and frivolity; and, unfortunately, our history has been such that numbers are on the side of frivolity.
DMITRI TOLSTOY, *Minister of Education, 1866–80*

Intensification of the Search for a National Educational Ideal

By the tenth anniversary of the Peace of Paris, tsardom had recovered as much as it ever would from the immediate effects of the Crimean War. The serfs had been freed, the borderlands secured, the administrative, judicial, and educational props of feudal empire torn out and rearranged. "In many respects our times are more important than the period of Petrovian reforms," Konstantin Ushinsky wrote in the liberal St. Petersburg newspaper, *Voice*. "Then, our energetic genius applied pressure to force the people into activity; now public forces, awakening to freedom, demand scope for activity.... Then, for intelligence, education, brains, and brawn, we had to send for German philosophers, German generals, German engineers, and even German craftsmen; now, with the help of its own people alone, the Russian government is building the academies, universities, gymnasiums, elementary schools, navy, armed forces, and finances... which our survival demands."[1]

The sum of effective revisions was perhaps greater than the Petrine Revolution itself. And yet the trial-and-error expediency of the process, the tendency to respond to crises rather than to anticipate them, the simultaneous currents of reaction and reform, imparted a sense of drift to affairs. Transformations were accomplished without disturbing the superstructure of absolutism, but also without regenerating it. Given the structure of the regime, only the tsar could lead, and Alexander II was more likely to apologize for change than to take credit for it. The resultant mood puzzled the Minister of the Interior. "The government," he remarked in 1861, "has yet to clarify its own features."[2]

Events, however, were hardening tsardom's resolve. When the Polish reach for independence in 1863 raised the specter of separatism on the part of myriad nationalities imprisoned in the empire, Russians of every station and type rallied to throne and altar. Katkov displaced Herzen as spokesman for the Russian soul. Social concerns temporarily receded before patriotism's rising tide. The Poles by taking up arms, Leroy-Beaulieu observed, "retarded for ten or fifteen years the maturation of the revolutionary seeds already sown in the schools and universities."[3] Within months of the final pacification of Poland, another stroke of violence consolidated national feeling still more. On April 4, 1866, as the Tsar was promenading near the summer gardens, a young man attempted to shoot him. The attack misfired. Despite the assailant's protestation that he was "pure Russian," the police and the public remained convinced that he was a foreigner, probably a Pole. Fresh from his victories in Poland, General Muravev was placed in charge of a special committee to investigate the background and ramifications of the crime. Under his direction committee members dug to find connections between the assassination attempt, the Warsaw underground, the international socialist conspiracy, and liberals within the Petersburg bureaucracy.

This broad line of research paid surprising dividends. The prisoner stood revealed as indeed a Russian, Dmitri Karakozov. By origin an impoverished nobleman, he had become by education the personification of nihilism as it degenerated from the boyish literary skepticism of Bazarov and Pisarev toward the homicidal mania of Nechaev and *The Possessed*. Expelled from the University of Kazan for participating in the disturbances of 1861, he was later dropped from Moscow University for nonpayment of fees. Papers in his possession led to the arrest of some 35 members of a clandestine circle, composed mostly of persons identified as "students" by their passports. Despite evidence that the assault was not the product of a mature conspiracy but "the hare-brained act of an unbalanced schoolboy," Karakozov was hanged and his comrades exiled to Siberia.

The discovery of the purely Russian roots of the crime turned educated and ignorant alike against the students. In Moscow troops inter-vened to protect undergraduates from loyalist mobs. Konstantin Kave-lin, the "firebrand of 1861," advised the Tsar to purge "materialistically inclined" textbooks and teachers.[4] His honor stained by his failure to protect the sovereign from attack, Prince Dolgoruky resigned. He need not have, for the Muravev commission did not charge the Third Section with dereliction of duty. It implied, rather, that lack of firm leadership on the part of the Ministry of Education had permitted the widespread infection of the student bodies with the "plague of socialism."[5] Katkov narrowed Muravev's attack down to personalities. To the academic community Aleksandr Golovnin might appear as the personification of *Spark*'s caricature of the "liberal" as "tightrope-walker between 'da' and 'nyet,'" a "bureaucrat from head to toes," deft at "wavering to all sides in search of the prudent middle."[6] But in the more rugged vocabulary of Katkov's camp, the Minister of Education, who favored "home rule" for students and Poles, was nothing less than "le chef principal du radi-calisme révolutionnaire russe."[7] As Katkov was painting Golovnin as Herzen in uniform, Dmitri Tolstoy was challenging him in the Com-mittee of Ministers. The Ober-Procurator of the Holy Synod delivered his most elaborate defense of the Orthodox church—"protector and pre-server of pure Russian folk principles"—together with his claim for the Orthodox clergy of an "indisputable primacy" in rural education, on the morning after Karakozov's attack and won the full approval of the Tsar.[8]

Golovnin's position had already been undermined by the failure of Grand Duke Constantine to effect a peaceful settlement of the Polish question. The Karakozov affair, with its hint of subversive threads run-ning from Petersburg to Warsaw, completed his ruin. Simultaneously, it crowned the fortunes of his two arch rivals, the Westernizers who had distinguished themselves as Great Russian Orthodox nationalists during the recent strains. In the past a conciliatory government had found it necessary to curb Mikhail Katkov's zeal on behalf of "true Russian feeling." After April the Fourth he was admitted to the imperial pres-ence and given assurance of supreme sympathy and august support. Henceforth in his self-appointed role as chief propagandist for the in-divisibility of the Russian empire, he functioned no longer as a "volun-teer militiaman" but as the "mouthpiece of the state."[9] Higher confidence was extended to the Ober-Procurator of the Holy Synod. Within ten days of the attempt on his life, Alexander II summoned Golovnin, and "in his habitual soft manner" thanked him for his services. "But the present time demands a different system of administration for the Ministry, *different principles,* and more energy. I have named Count Tolstoy in your place."[10]

Ten years earlier Alexander II had rejected Norov's recommendation that all schools except the military be concentrated in the Ministry of Education to prevent "diffusion of the spiritual resources of the people."[11] With Tolstoy's role as Minister and Ober-Procurator, plus his commanding presence on the Supreme Council of Women's Education, the old regime came as close as it ever would to centralizing the administration of state enlightenment. This time, unlike that after 1812, the secular and ecclesiastical offices were not combined. "Unity of spirit" subsumed "unity of command." Looking back, the friends of public initiative would interpret Tolstoy's rise negatively as part of the government's overall campaign to halt the libertarian tendencies of the great reforms. The ruler who appointed him, however, did so in the hope that he would seize the initiative in the schools as part of a positive, long-range program to strengthen the unity of the empire.

For the next two decades, Westernizing nationalists—except for one brief interruption—led tsardom's search for an educational solution to the problem of control of social change. In the early 1870's their leaders, Tolstoy and Katkov, carried the state's pedagogical initiative to a peak of resoluteness and rigidity. Along the way the Petersburg statesman and the Moscow editor made themselves the most hated public figures of their day. The intensity of the animosities they aroused (the amiable historian and rector of Moscow University, Sergei Soloviev, could not "imagine a more odious figure"[12] than the Minister of Education) was due not only to their uncompromising principles but to their self-defeating personalities. Each man was, in Bismarck's phrase, *ein guter Hasser.* The very vigor with which they went about their mission of imposing "German pedagogy in a French uniform" on the educated class alienated men who shared their concern, but not their militant approach, for the very real problem of the country's lack of educational tradition. Worse, they drove from office some of the most gifted educators of the period, men whose services the nation could ill afford to lose in the best of times. For both Katkov and Tolstoy were afflicted with an inflated sense of their own importance. Both viewed themselves as "saviors of the fatherland," fighting in heroic isolation, uncertainly backed by a wavering tsar, against an array of lax officials all too ready to give in to the selfish whims of a frivolous society. And yet with all their egoism and conceit, both Alexander II and Alexander III found them sincerely devoted to Russia, to the autocracy, and to European standards of education. Unlike so many other highly placed advisers, they contemplated no dilution of the central power, no loosening of unity for the empire, no lowering of intellectual goals. And thus, while personally hard to bear, and despite the widespread feeling that Katkov and Tolstoy were two of the chief spoilers of the public promise of the great reforms and therefore a national disaster on the order of the Crimean War, they remained treasured servants of the monarchy for more than 20 years.[13]

For all its outward strength, the alliance between the journalist and the bureaucrat was not without severe internal strains—friction between the aristocratic man of action and the self-made man of words. Sprung from impoverished origins, Katkov was proud of his position as an independent publicist, dueling with the censor and driving ministers of state from office. He considered the bureaucracy the seat of inertia, formalism, careerism, and routine, and supported the concept of public initiative as a stimulant to state enlightenment. He sustained his convictions by founding his own school, the Lycée of the Tsarevitch Nicholas, and covered its annual deficits of 12,000–15,000 rubles out of his personal funds.[14] Formulating his ideas on education in his own study, and overwhelmed by the persuasiveness of his own prose, honed on the Latin classics, he could not understand what took Tolstoy so long to transform an editorial into law. At one time he spread the word among his friends that but for him Tolstoy would sell out to the liberal opposition to save his job. Meanwhile even those who agreed with Tolstoy on the necessity of a firm hand were appalled by the speed with which Tolstoy moved and privately hoped that the 43-year-old "neck-breaker" would "grow old soon."[15] Distrustful of journalists, Tolstoy welcomed Katkov as a useful, sometimes irritating, ally. Katkov's view of himself as the mastermind behind the educational crusade allowed the Minister–Ober-Procurator to portray himself as a moderate when tactics demanded. His manner toward the "Thunderer" was tinged with the indulgence of the professional politician for the volunteer worker. The two were harnessed together by their belief that rigorous enforcement of tested European educational standards was the best means for providing the disorderly empire with the disciplined educated class that might just hold it together as it plunged toward the scientific-industrial future, for which its dallying with "bits and pieces" of the European heritage had so poorly prepared it; thus the former professor and the future policeman labored together for twenty years, "sparing nothing to subjugate the young Scythian rebels to the yoke of the Latins and the Greeks."[16]

The starting point of Tolstoy's critique of official policy was hardly original. Bureaucratic nationalists went back with official liberals to 1828 —to the educational reform that Granovsky had eulogized in terms Tolstoy would echo as marking the "passage from the exclusive and harmful supremacy of foreign ideas to a system based on a deep understanding of the Russian people and their needs."[17] A decade before Tolstoy, Granovsky had taken the government to task for disrupting after 1848 the efforts begun by Shishkov and Uvarov to implant serious pre-university training when they insisted, against the personal predilections of Nicholas I, that Russian schooling needed Greek as well as Latin.[18] Five years before Tolstoy's emergence as champion of Greek, Pirogov had joined Granovsky in pointing out the futility of Latin without Greek in a general curriculum.[19] Visiting the Black Sea provinces on the first of his many inspection trips around the country as Minister of Education, Tolstoy noted with an enthusiasm his audience did not share that here "Greek enlightenment"—the "origin," as Pirogov called it, of "our faith and our education"—had touched down and was still visible "in the stones."[20] Historically, it had guided the development of the Russian mind. Dare Russia lag behind Western Europe in making it the starting point of any serious national educational concern?

Tolstoy also shared the liberal view that with the "pseudo-conservative" measures of 1849, as Kavelin called them, the government itself had unwittingly laid the ground for student revolt. In Moscow, both Latin and Greek had been classified as "special" rather than "general" subjects; in Kazan, Greek had been considered no more educational than Arabic, Persian, Turkish, Mongolian, and Manchurian; in Orenburg, Tartar had been listed as a general requirement, Latin as optional. Curricular anarchy and abdication to "local needs" had deprived the young of indoctrination in a universal hierarchy of time-tested cultural values. That was not all the government had done. By placing arbitrary limits on the number of students admitted to the liberal arts faculties of the universities, Uvarov's successor had steered an unduly large number of young men toward medicine and science. Lacking preparation for independent intellectual work, they "picked up bits and pieces" of philosophy and biology and fell prey to the pseudo-science of nihilism. Kavelin reminded the Tsar after the first nihilist attack on his life that, for all their rhetorical devotion to "science," the nihilists, including their ideological leader, Chernyshevsky, were notoriously ignorant of elementary scientific principles and procedures. When he began dissecting society, Bazarov had not gone beyond dissecting frogs.

It was when they left off analyzing past failures and began proposing cures for educational distemper that the nationalist and liberal proponents of classical direction parted company. The official liberal position after Karakozov, formulated by Kavelin and refined and presented to the Tsar by General Dmitri Miliutin, the Minister of War, maintained that the revolt of the younger generation against all forms of established authority was the product of educational uncertainty and bureaucratic oppression; that more freedom and opportunity would attract the young idealists back to the service of the fatherland.[21] Tolstoy disagreed with the second half of this prescription for neutralizing nihilism. "From the time of Peter the Great to the present day," he observed, "parents have been accustomed to look upon education as nothing more than a means to get boys into the service of the State, civil or military, as soon as possible. And the less they have to learn, the better they like it! I once asked Alexander II if he wished to do something that would earn him the gratitude of every mamma and papa in Russia. He jumped at the suggestion. 'But how?' 'Let examinations in future be confined to reading, writing, and the four rules of arithmetic!' "[22] The state had wavered and backtracked in the past; it must impose its will in the future. The government, in Katkov's phrase, must govern. And the places to start were the state universities before they could become schools for assassins. Katkov turned rabid on the statute of 1863. To him it came to represent a retreat on the part of the government, the surrender of responsible majorities to radical minorities. Tolstoy was in less of a hurry to change the 1863 university law. Despite the autonomy of the faculty councils, the professors remained civil servants. Those who could not comply with ministerial policy could resign their positions in the Table of Ranks like any other unhappy official. In the years ahead, he had little trouble harvesting the resignations of professors, even rectors, who disagreed with him.

The students were another matter. Considering them cadets training to become servants of the state, Tolstoy did not hesitate to impose on them

a kind of martial law, camouflaging the whip with more government
stipends. For despite the slanders of his enemies Tolstoy agreed with
Chicherin, whose resignation he accepted, on the necessity of state aid to
the "deserving" poor. But he refused to "subsidize sedition." Pirogov
observed that the universities were the "barometers of society." If the
weather outside was turbulent, the universities would anticipate the
storm. But it was pointless to break the barometer in a blizzard. Tolstoy,
again like Chicherin, conceived of the university in a way Pirogov considered naïve—as the temple of science—and Tolstoy intended to keep
it that way, a sanctuary of teaching and research, removed from the con-
troversies in the newspapers and the strife in the streets.[23] To this end
stricter rules governing student conduct were issued in 1867. The police
were instructed to report student delinquents to university authorities,
and they in turn were to inform the police of any student acts that might
raise doubts of political and moral reliability. Tolstoy's new rules forbade
the students to organize public entertainments in order to raise funds for
their impoverished colleagues. Funds raised by outsiders were not to be
given directly to the students but to the university officials for distribution
to those in "genuine need" and "worthy of support."

Tolstoy did not have to be reminded by Pirogov that stricter regulations of student life were at best external measures compelling order but
not equipping the students for serious study. This could be achieved only
at the secondary level. Tolstoy's "fundamental idea was perfectly just," a
veteran nihilist sourly observed, "that thoroughly to 'purify' the universities he must go first to the fountain-head and purify the gymnasiums,
from which they draw their yearly tribute of students."[24] The conditions
prevailing when he assumed office convinced Tolstoy that the imposition
of uniform academic standards across the length and breadth of the empire in the general educational schools, the restoration of Russia to the
academic principles of 1828—to "the mainstream of educational enlightenment, to the route tested by the experience of centuries, along which the
peoples who lead the scientific development of the world have not only
traveled for centuries but continue to advance"[25]—would require the
most forceful kind of state action after decades of drift, confusion, abrupt
reversals, and neglect. Paradoxically the "liberal" statute of 1864 allowed
him considerable discretion. The flexibility that had been built into it at
Pirogov's behest to allow public influence on the question of whether
general education should assume a classical or a real direction laid the system open to his intervention.

To put the statute of 1864 into action within the guidelines set by the Council of State, Golovnin had committed the Ministry of Education to a five-year plan. By 1870 the country would have 20 gymnasiums and one progymnasium that would not offer any classical languages; 20 gymnasiums and one progymnasium that would offer both Greek and Latin; and 40 gymnasiums and one progymnasium that would offer Latin alone. The new budget of 1,808,000 rubles for these schools still fell 36,000 rubles below the state's annual expenditure on its universities. The delay in carrying out the reform was necessary because of the shortage of teachers of Greek. In face of the delay, there was much confusion, compounded by the abrupt change of ministers. As a result, people were following, as they had since 1849, "the demands of life rather than the commands of statutes," and students with Latin only were being let into the universities.[26] Such had been the liberal idea—to allow "time and experience" to resolve the classical-realist controversy. True to form, the public showed little interest in academic subtleties. In addition, Tolstoy discovered that the district curators, responding to local opinion, were stalling the establishment of the full classical curricula by neglecting to use the funds allotted them to hire teachers of Greek from neighboring Slavic countries. As Katkov observed, the hopes of "reactionaries" (in the sense that they wanted to go back from 1864 to 1849 rather than to 1828) were being realized. As soon as parents grasped that high school graduates with Latin only would be refused admittance to the universities, they would not demand Greek in the curriculum of the local school but its elimination as a prerequisite, and once Greek was out, Latin would follow. Pressure was already building to make Latin optional. When this happened, the effort begun in 1828 to overcome "bits and pieces" would be nullified. Tolstoy, however, had inherited Golovnin's authority to convert classical to real and real to classical gymnasiums and was fulfilling the stipulations of Golovnin's statute of 1864 when he recruited teachers of Greek from Galicia to hasten the day when only students with both Greek and Latin would enter the universities. On this point he was realizing the will of the Tsar, and obstruction, as Katkov reminded his opponents, was sedition.

Encouraged by Pirogov to "avoid a one-sided approach to progress," Golovnin had sought consensus preparatory to framing the statute of 1864. To the proponents of state initiative his efforts to reconcile differences of opinion and to involve a broad spectrum of society in academic policy was grubbing for "popularity"—an odious word in Dmitri Tolstoy's vocabulary. Eschewing "ignorant" and "superficial" views, Tolstoy relied on Katkov to hammer public opinion into line. In a series of lead editorials in the *Moscow News* between 1864 and 1871, Katkov lectured his fellow countrymen that they were the "children of Europe," that in science they were still the "pupils of England, France, and Germany," that it was not enough to build more but necessary to build better schools, that the secret of Europe's world supremacy was the "incorporation of their historic spirit in their schools," and that the classical school was the "mother of science." Obviously the quickest way out of "subjugation to Europe" was to follow Europe's road.[27] Katkov's argument was not popular. Subscriptions to his newspapers declined. Katkov insisted that the gentry that had resisted emancipation (the same gentry that according to Kavelin had taught the younger generation the spirit of nihilistic resistance to the government by resisting reform) was the core of the "reaction" against higher educational standards. Provincial resistance convinced Tolstoy and Katkov of the necessity for ruthless central action.

Determined, in Katkov's words, "to exclude the compromises" which exposed the constitution of 1864 "to the shifting winds of public opinion," Tolstoy sought a "clear, guiding idea" abroad. In 1862 Golovnin had sent Kavelin to gather ideas from France. Since then the Austro-Prussian war had altered the balance of cultural power. Ordering the district curators to assemble statistics on the operation of both lower and secondary urban schools since the Crimean War, Tolstoy traveled westward himself to investigate the academic institutions of the most dynamic state in Europe, Bismarck's Prussia. Upon his return he edited the district reports in the light of his Prussian experiences, and in 1869 he announced his three-point program for reorganizing state enlightenment and "clarifying the ambiguities" of 1864.

First, Tolstoy made clear, the government would concentrate its limited resources at the most crucial phase of the formal learning process —the secondary school. Within a decade, for the first time since its educational initiative began, the state was spending more on general secondary schools than on the universities.[28] Second, the intermediate stage of study would be divided into two branches—an academic and a practical. Each type would receive its own constitution. On the one hand, there would be a distinct and separate realschule for the express purpose of preparing local talent for local affairs. On the other, there would be the classical gymnasium. Uniting intellectual skills with moral training, it

would be the exclusive agency for funneling provincial talent toward the universities and the state administration. The gymnasium would be a European school on Russian soil, an institution capable of supplying the nation's most pressing social need—"an aristocracy of intellect, an aristocracy of knowledge, an aristocracy of work."[29] Finally, the Europeanization deemed necessary for disciplining and refining the national character would be enforced through strict centralization. With this announcement Tolstoy unveiled the outlines of his system for culturally guaranteeing the state's control over the development of the new service class.

The Tolstoy System

The Minister of Education's program to impose bureaucratic enlightenment on a society anxious to emancipate itself from the state bureaucracy aroused strenuous resistance throughout the educated class. Prominent members of the academic community, from the historian Sergei Soloviev to the chemist Dmitri Mendeleev, were bitter critics of Tolstoy's personality and his educational philosophy.[30] Educators who agreed with Tolstoy that the classical curriculum could simplify the task of returning to "serious, strictly academic work" a generation of students infected with "superficial attitudes toward the intellectual, moral, and social questions of the day" were opposed to his abrupt and defiant methods, in particular the reintroduction of Greek as a prerequisite for university schooling "by a single stroke of the pen" without "preparing the public for the reception of such a major reform."[31] The chief of the security police placed much of the blame for the alienation of the younger generation from the government on his friend, the Minister of Education.[32] The student intelligentsia denounced Tolstoy as the "man of fate ... brought forward by the reckless reactionary party after the Polish rebellion ... entrusted with plenary powers for the purification of the schools of the empire from social heresy and political discontent." The student revolutionaries pursued him with poisoned daggers, pistols, and bombs.[33]

A few years earlier the spokesman for professional opposition to Tolstoy would have been Nikolai Pirogov. But after being relieved of his duties and deprived of his pension by Tolstoy, he had withdrawn to his estate and devoted himself to medicine. He remained a close observer of the educational scene. His comments on "our classical Minister, whom the humanities have not made more humane," were confided to friends. To them he expressed his displeasure with Tolstoy for exchanging the "pseudo-realism" of 1849 for the "pseudo-classicism" of 1871—both false, because in both instances political motives rather than pedagogical considerations shaped curricula.*

Pirogov's role of theoretician for a public as distinct from a bureaucratic system of education passed to an acknowledged disciple, who eventually surpassed him in influence and fame, Konstantin Ushinsky. As a student at the University of Moscow in the "golden forties," Ushinsky had brushed with Herzen and Belinsky. Practical employment disciplined his imagination. He lectured on jurisprudence in the provinces until the reaction to 1848 cost him his job. Years of hardship followed, which undermined his health. Only after the war was he able to return to pedagogy, first as an inspector of classes at Smolny Institute for Girls and then as editor of the *Journal of the Ministry of Education*. During the late 1850's he became acquainted with experimental approaches to learning that were being made abroad, especially in the United States of America. Inspired by foreign novelties and the humane philosophizing of Pirogov, he conceived the ambition to free Russian educational theory in general, and the classical-realist dispute in particular, from the fixed positions of political controversy, and to relate education instead to the mobile findings of psychology, physiology, comparative social science, and the historically conditioned, peculiar but changing circumstances of national life.

Ushinsky's first efforts to apply his empirical method to a concrete problem took the form of an article on "The Psychic and Educative Significance of Work." The essay's sociological approach to ethical questions offended conservative circles. For a time Ushinsky's future looked bleak and the chances slim that he would ever have the opportunity to convert his ideas into a major scientific treatise. Then a kind fate intervened. The controversial educator had attracted the attention of the Empress during his years at Smolny Institute. And it was she who made available grants-in-aid to enable him to travel and study extensively abroad. With the help of government grants, two volumes of his pro-

---

* Pirogov, pp. 608–9. In 1861 Chicherin remarked that "military problems are simply technical problems, but at the present time educational problems have become *political* questions. This cannot be emphasized too strongly" (Chicherin, *Vospominaniia,* p. 38; original italics). In the 1920's Kizevetter wrote that the Tolstoy system was hated "because its goals were political rather than educational" (Kizevetter, p. 99).

jected three-volume study, *Man as Educable Subject: An Outline of Pedagogical Anthropology,* appeared in the years just prior to his death at the age of 46 in 1870. Over the next 30 years the *Anthropology* passed through eleven editions. Gradually weaning the classroom teachers away from bureaucratic formalism and ideology, it prepared them for the acceptance of a professional educational ideal sensitive to universally validated propositions and the changing conditions of national life.

Like Pirogov, Katkov, and Tolstoy, Ushinsky's starting point for criticism of Russian education was its lack of a historical tradition and the need for creating one to guide the social development of the nation.[34] Again, like the classicists, he was out to raise the quality of Russian science and Russian morals, and like them he was committed to the priority of moral over utilitarian direction up to the university, where, it was assumed, the adolescent should be ready to launch out into the deep of critical, cautious thinking on his own. Ushinsky said that no one questioned the superiority of general education to special training. The question was how best to shape general education as a moral force. At this point Russia's pioneer in comparative education departed both from Pirogov, whom he admired, and Katkov and Tolstoy, whom he outflanked. Like Pirogov, he recognized the importance of public involvement in the school. Russia, he insisted, had had enough of educational systems imposed by bureaucratic fiat from above. It was time for the state to recognize and encourage the creative energy of society. Education was too complex a subject for a few to decide. Even Pirogov had been unable to give a clear answer to the classical-realist dispute. The resolution of this crucial question demanded the broadest possible participation, including the people themselves. Ushinsky shared Turgenev's view that the ultimate choices rested with the masses. As for European models, they should not be mechanically translated into Russian, as Tolstoy and Katkov were doing and much as Iankovich de Mirevo had done a century before. Rather, Western models should be carefully studied to separate their national from their universal features, and these latter should be adapted selectively to Russia's own time and place.

By rejecting Europe's "final solution," which Russian classicists accepted, Ushinsky moved the classical-realist debate off dead center.[35] Examining the unique historical conditions that had made classical humanism at one time a liberating force in Europe, he emphasized how much had changed since the sixteenth century. In an essay on Pirogov he doubted whether Greek and Latin were still the best subjects for opening the nineteenth-century child's mind to the pursuit of moral and scientific truths. To strengthen his case he drew attention to Western European impatience with the old ways. If in too much of a hurry to swallow traditional classicism whole, Russia might find itself stuck with a foreign model at the moment of its abandonment by its creators. As for Greek and Latin immunizing the young against nihilism, "are the proponents of classicism deceiving us or themselves?" The Greeks and the Romans were outrageously materialistic in the worst sense. "You have only to recall the views of their poets and philosophers on slavery, on women, on religion, on the soul."[36] In place of the Katkov-Pirogov formula, Ushinsky recommended organizing general education for both terminal and university-bound youths around the mother tongue, modern foreign languages, and natural sciences. "At the present time we do not need Hellenists and Latinists. We need people active in state and public service, factory workers, machinists, industrial managers, agricultural specialists, and other *real people*."[37]

This was a program for the future. Where are the teachers, the textbooks, the programs, Katkov asked, for presenting Russian, German, French, zoology, biology, and other "real" subjects as general educational subjects to Russian adolescents in 1870? The universities did not even have modern-language departments for training teachers and preparing course materials. It may be possible, as Ushinsky and those who welcomed him into the official liberal camp suggested (Kraevsky's *Voice* carried his views), to find a substitute pedagogical method for developing the type of maturity that the pursuit of science at the highest level demands, Katkov conceded. The Moscow "fanatic of Greek and Latin" anticipated that some day, when the groundwork had been well laid, mathematics might profitably replace ancient literature as the high school fundamental.[38] "The fact remains, however, that at the present time there exists no other means."[39] Under the pressure of controversy Tolstoy also revealed his pragmatism. "Discipline" rather than "Greek versus technics" became the issue in his mind. The important thing was for the state to establish a firm, time-tested policy and stick to it. This exchange, not personal but substantive, between Ushinsky and the Minister of Education was the closest that real and classical sides came to dialogue. It revealed the possibility of agreement on a serious program for a unified general educational school if the administrative issue could be subordinated to the pedagogical. This state of affairs would be reached after 1905.*

Konstantin Ushinsky was the most effective opponent to appear during the formative decade of the Tolstoy system. By 1870, official liberals were shifting from Pirogov's European classicism toward Ushinsky's national realism. His overwhelming influence, transcending the chronological framework of the old regime, lay far ahead.† In the immediate present the burden of vocal opposition was assumed by the press, for the publication of Tolstoy's three-point plan for consolidating state enlightenment around the secondary school brought to a climax the newspaper war between Moscow and the Petersburg journalists who had escaped the censor's scythe after Karakozov. By 1869 the northern liberals had driven Katkov on the defensive with the charge that classicism was a police measure—stiff daily gymnastics in Latin and Greek grammar to keep the younger generation from thinking for themselves. Suggestions were made of how the mind-deadening exercises might be made even more effective—such as by having the boys conjugate verbs rhythmically in unison.[40] The savagery of the attack and public willingness to accept it at face value forced Katkov to divert his energy to explaining that Tolstoy's plans did not aim at the "expulsion" of natural sciences from the schools. In fact, "to accelerate scholarly and pedagogical activity in the field of the natural sciences" Tolstoy had established the first Conference of Natural Scientists in St. Petersburg. He subsidized the second Moscow Conference in 1869 with Ministry funds, and personally welcomed the delegates, praising their role in the schools.[41] In the summer of 1870 the drawn-out diplomatic contest between Prussia and France broke into war, and the passions raised in Russia by the conflict were promptly transferred to the educational field. Kraevsky's *Voice* and the *St. Petersburg News* linked the preservation of the second French empire with the defense of domestic liberty. Defeat of Prussia, it was hoped, might undermine Tolstoy's plan to Prussianize the schools.[42] Forgotten for the moment were Kavelin's strictures on French education: "Centralization, control, rigid progress, uniforms—all these strikingly familiar things are here. It seems that in all this we impiously aped the French, and the results, understandably enough, are the same. The

* Dmitri Miliutin moved from a firm to a soft position on classicism between 1866 and 1871. Contrast Zaimchkovskii, pp. 323ff with *Obzor MNP,* 523ff.
† See p. 249.

similarity of French historical forms to ours simply appalls me. I explain this by our sympathy for Napoleonic institutions and the dreadful influence on us of French civilization. May the powers above keep us from the same final end as the French."[43]

To keep Russia "from the same final end as the French" the Minister of Education prevailed on the Ministry of the Interior to restrict public discussion. Tolstoy's reach was long. The charges brought against the publishers of *The Almanac for 1871* included criticism of the government's anti-Polish policy in the northwest territory and criticism of the classical system of education. On order of the Committee of Ministers, 920 copies of the 950 published were destroyed.[44] With public opinion muzzled, the center of resistance shifted to the highest official level, where a special office was formed out of the Council of State to examine the educational bill. Its fifteen members included the future Alexander III, the Ministers of War, Finance, and Education, Aleksandr Golovnin, and, "in view of the importance of the matter for the vital interests of the fatherland," the chairman of the empire's supreme deliberative body, Grand Duke Constantine. The committee members hostile to Tolstoy looked for leadership to General Miliutin, Minister of War.

The career of Dmitri Miliutin illustrated Chicherin's maxim that the progress of the nation rests on the ambitions of the poor. Born the son of an impoverished nobleman in 1816, he ascended the military Table of Ranks to the summit, was created a count for his services in the Russo-Turkish conflict, and lived to hear himself honored at the first all-Russian congress on pedagogical psychology, which was organized by the military department of education in the midst of the Revolution of 1905. As a professor in the cadet academy after the Crimean War, Miliutin had been impressed by Pirogov's attack on early specialization in the schools. Upon appointment as Minister of War in 1861, he worked closely with Aleksandr Golovnin to remodel the five military academies and expand them into a system of 23 academic gymnasiums under their own department of education within the defense ministry.[45] He also invited women to attend the army's medical schools after Tolstoy had refused them admission to the universities on the grounds that most of the "crop-headed" applicants were already known to the police as nihilists.

These reforms were simple accomplishments compared with Miliutin's most ambitious scheme. For centuries the tsarist armies had relied on serf levees for their manpower. Emancipation made it necessary to devise new means of recruitment. From the beginning of his administration Miliutin favored introducing the Prussian system of universal military service and a relatively small professional army, backed by a large, truly national reserve. Only partial readjustments could be made until the outcome of the Franco-Prussian War made everything German—"from helmets to school systems"—irresistible. By this time the slow pace of army reform locked step with the drawn-out reconstruction of the secondary school. As a result, two of the most fundamental pieces of legislation governing the life of the country till 1914 were brought together in the public mind by being debated simultaneously in the Council of State—the Military Statute, which became law on January 1, 1874, and the Tolstoy system, which took legal form between 1871 and 1874. The conjunction of the two measures, the antagonism of the two men, the sight of the Minister of Education attacking Miliutin's military program and the Minister of War attacking Tolstoy's plans, the obvious eagerness of both to borrow from Prussia in order to strengthen the country against its new and mighty neighbor, Bismarck's Reich, served to impress on the public the degree to which national enlightenment, social modernization, and international security were interdependent.

Pondering the relationship between military and educational needs, General Miliutin came to the conclusion that the Russians should make one major change in the Prussian system. Because of the empire's reliance on trained intelligence as well as on peasant arms, and in view of the serious lack of the former and the relative abundance of the latter, the military draft should be utilized not merely to fill the ranks but to keep the population in school.[46] Tolstoy objected. For one thing, he insisted, knowledge ought to be pursued for its own sake, not out of aversion for army life. For another, special favors to the educated class would overstimulate its already exorbitant sense of self-importance.

He offered a suggestion guaranteed to make him more unpopular than ever: the maximum reduction in military service should be granted for completion of the gymnasium's sixth year. Even Tolstoy's critics had to admit that this would clear out of the system those "useless for science" who stayed in school in order to further reduce the time of required army service.[47] The Council of State supported the Ministry of War. It declared Miliutin's progressive exemptions for educational advancement "a powerful instrument for the spread of enlightenment."[48] The Tsar concurred, and in the final bill the regular seven-year term of enlistment was reduced for educated draftees. A primary school certificate reduced the training period to four years, a district school diploma to three. Secondary graduates served for two years and university students for six months. All of these periods were further shortened for volunteers. In addition, the army provided illiterate recruits with primary education. In this manner, it is estimated, more than a million and a half persons were introduced to reading and writing between 1874 and 1891.[49]

It was as the rising champion of public enlightenment that Dmitri Miliutin counterattacked the Minister of Education in the early summer of 1871. In place of Tolstoy's bifurcated secondary school, he recommended the introduction of a single general educational high school with classical and modern branches. All students would take Latin. Greek scholars would advance to the history-philology faculties and realists could enter the physics-mathematics and medical colleges of the universities. In this opening skirmish the special office of the Council of State supported Tolstoy nine to six, and the debate moved to the full Council. In the general assembly the opposition mustered its full strength. In the final tally it voted 29 to 19 to reject academic elitism. "It is manifestly unfair," declared the majority opinion, "to exclude from the university, the temple of comprehensive science, precisely those young people who specialize in the study of science and to admit only those who are proficient in dead languages."[50] In his defense the Minister of Education stressed the importance of following the Western lead. From his own research he produced figures to show that "wherever the sciences flourish, both natural and medical," only the gymnasium with a full classical course was designated a *Gelehrtenschule* and only the graduates of scholarly schools were eligible to enter the universities. The admission of realists would provide a high and a low road to the top. The entire effort to establish and maintain time-tested European practices would be undermined.

Unpopular as it was, Tolstoy's plea for rigid standards of access to the higher schools could not have been better timed for maximum emotional effect. Not far from where the Council of State was discussing his proposals, the Ministry of Justice and the security police were staging the first political trial in Russian history to be given full coverage in the newspapers. The government's purpose was to shock the public out of its sympathy with the student revolutionaries. In the dock were the followers of Sergei Nechaev, a primary school teacher and part-time student of the University of Moscow. Nechaev himself was still at large, having fled to the West following the murder of a companion. The police had stumbled on his confederates in the so-called Russian section of the World Revolutionary Alliance during their investigation of the suspiciously well-organized university disorders of 1869. The active core of the 152 persons arrested were university students and high school graduates. The public was shocked by their contempt for enlightenment and the educated class. To many thoughtful persons their defiant fanaticism appeared as part of a general pattern of dissolution. One had only to recall the collapse of the second French empire, the excesses of the Paris commune, and the theme of Darwin's recently published *Descent of Man* to be convinced that politics, society, and science were racing one another downhill. The overall effect was unusually favorable to a minister of state with a clearly defined program for taking the younger generation in hand. On July 30 the Tsar ratified the foundation of the Tolstoy system, the statute for gymnasiums and progymnasiums. Until the end of the imperial regime the statute of 1871 would remain the central operating device of the state's scholastic machinery for directing social change. Its pledge of equal access to opportunity for all social classes, minority races, and religious creeds would be violated but not revoked. Its academic program would be revised. Its rigid administrative propositions and its monopoly of university entrance rights would survive unchanged.[51]

The constitution of 1871 increased the number of hours devoted to classical subjects, although the amount still fell below the German norm. To enable the students to master the increased material, the seventh class was lengthened to two years and subsequently divided into distinct seventh and eighth forms. This extension had the effect of differentiating academic from practical education even more, since the realschule retained a fundamental course of six years. Even more significant for the social development of the gymnasium was the addition of a preparatory class for children between eight and ten years old. Tolstoy's purpose was to provide a more systematic, uniform, and controlled preparation for secondary study than the training that private tutors supplied. Established to raise standards, the preparatory class would eventually become the principal avenue through which the urban public would infiltrate the academic school and loosen its bureaucratic structure.

The extended debate over the elite gymnasium delayed consideration of "a separate institution for average talents." Tolstoy utilized the time for another trip abroad to study the lower and middle polytechnicums of Germany. During the winter he explained his concepts to the special office of the Council of State. The curriculum of the realschule would not be restricted to commercial and industrial subjects, but would include sufficient cultural and scientific background to prepare select pupils for advanced training. The first four years would, in fact, offer the same program as the progymnasium except for the substitution of modern for ancient languages. Specialization would begin in the final three years. The fifth and sixth forms would divide into two branches, a general educational and a terminal business course. The extra seventh year, open only to the graduates of the general section, would offer three alternative programs—general, mechanical, and chemical. Again, only the graduates of the general course could advance to the agricultural, mining, engineering, and veterinary colleges.

Fully aware of the cool reception given any secondary school whose graduates were not admitted to the universities, Tolstoy sought public support by other means. Zemstvos, estates of the realm, public organizations, and private persons contributing substantial financial support to an institution were given the right to elect an honorary curator with a seat on the pedagogical council. The council, in turn, was free to organize the last three years of the course of studies to meet local needs. For its part, the Ministry of Education undertook to open 50 new schools and make stipends available to train the necessary teachers of chemistry, mechanics, and accounting. Despite these attractive offerings, the special office rejected Tolstoy's draft bill nine to six. In the full Council of State the majority once more rallied behind General Miliutin's proposal for a general gymnasium. Again supporting his minister against the weight of official and professional opinion, the Tsar ratified the statute for real schools on May 15. The realschule statute of 1872 fixed bifurcation of general education on the empire until 1917.[52]

The charter for real schools brought to a close the first stage of Tolstoy's design: specific institutions for what he considered the differing needs of state and society. In his circulars to the districts and in his addresses to local officials the Minister of Education urged provincial Russia to assimilate the realschulen, to adapt their programs to their particular needs, to assume responsibility for their maintenance and support—in a word, to make them "public" schools. The gymnasium, on the contrary, he regarded as the exclusive property of the state. As the official matrix of Russia's future scientists and administrators, it must be preserved intact as it came from the lawgiver's hand. The integrity of its principles and the uniformity of its standards guaranteed the quality of the modernization process. Every phase of its operation must be protected against the accidents of place and the erosion of time. Noting with pleasure that several curators had drawn up lesson plans for their districts, Tolstoy prepared a master study plan for the whole empire. A circular of November 12, 1866, requested the provinces to provide St. Petersburg with copies of all hourly schedules currently in use. After six years of editorial work, uniform lesson plans controlling the emphasis and sequence of all subjects were issued on July 31, 1872.[53]

Scholarly standards could hardly be maintained without adequate testing. In his first year in office Tolstoy called the attention of the local authorities to complaints from the universities of the influx of "academically weak" students and warned them not to indulge in "irrelevant softness" when grading pupils. He also instructed the pedagogical councils not to allow anyone to repeat the same year's course more than once. Thirty years later this order still impressed teachers and families alike as an example of "bureaucratic despotism." On December 8, 1872, uniform rules for entrance, passing, and exit examinations were published, bringing to a conclusion the second stage of Tolstoy's interlocking design: central control of academic life.[54] The third and final phase was even more ambitious and irritating.

Tolstoy's predecessor had recognized moral training as a primary responsibility of family and home. In keeping with the principles of official liberalism and Pirogov's concept of public education, Golovnin had restricted school authorities to a supporting, supplementary role. This, however, was before Karakozov, the Nechaev trial, and the campaign "to the people" revealed the advanced stage of young Russia's alienation from the regime. "Nihilism is a disease," Tolstoy once remarked. "It is the moral cancer of our time. You can no more stamp it out or abolish it than the Hebrew leprosy, but the one and the other may be reduced to comparative harmlessness."[55] As Minister of the Interior in the 1880's, he would reduce the revolutionary movement to comparative harmlessness by energetic police action. In the 1870's he sought to neutralize it by combining discipline with learning in the state schools.

To unite the "scientific educational with the moral educative task"[56]

Tolstoy relied on both academic and administrative devices. In his repli-
cation to a hostile State Council he argued that "the distinction between
ancient languages and every other means of preparing for advanced scientific education is a choice not only between serious and superficial
study but an option for moral or materialistic development of the whole
society."* In a directive on examinations the Minister of Education advised the curators that "laxness in the evaluation of academic achievement has a thoroughly corrupting influence on the young, encouraging
superficiality and conceit."[57] Formal requirements, however, were not as
efficacious as personal contact. In the end only the classroom teachers
could be the active apostles of the state's moral mission to the coming
generation. Restricting pedagogy to intellectual skills "leads to a weakening of the moral influence of the teacher on the student."[58]

Petty functionaries to supervise behavior were already familiar. The
statute of 1828 had created the post of prefect of discipline without speci-
fying its educational level. Because of the abuse inflicted on ignorant
beadles by playful students, Golovnin had insisted that prefects have the
same professional qualifications as teachers. Such a demand was impos-

---

* *Obzor MNP*, p. 250. In *Anna Karenina*, written in the 1870's, Leo Tolstoy made Anna's
husband a spokesman for Dmitri Tolstoy's educational philosophy:
" 'It seems to me,' said Karenin, 'that only a people with a higher development can in-
fluence another people.'
" 'But that is precisely the question,' Pestsov broke in. '... The English, the French, the
Germans—which has reached the highest stage of development?' ...
" 'It seems to me that influence is always on the side of genuine education,' Karenin said
... 'and the marks of genuine education are known.'
" 'But are they fully known?' put in Kosnyshev. 'Today only pure classical education is
recognized as genuine education, but we see a savage struggle on the issue ... I had a classical education myself, but I am having difficulty taking a position in this controversy. I do
not see overwhelming reasons for preferring classical sciences to real.'
" 'The natural sciences have as much pedagogical value,' Pestsov broke in. 'Take astron-
omy, take botany, zoology with its system of general laws.'
" 'I cannot fully agree with you,' Karenin said. 'It seems to me that it is impossible not
to admit that the very process of studying the forms of languages exerts an especially salutary influence on one's spiritual development. Besides, it is impossible to deny that the
influence of classical writers is eminently moral, while the teaching of natural science is,
unfortunately, associated with those destructive and false doctrines which poison our
times.' ...
" 'But,' said Kosnyshev, 'one cannot help agreeing that it is difficult to define all the benefits and weaknesses of either branch of study, and the question which to prefer over the
other would not have been resolved so quickly and so decisively if classical education had
not been endowed with moral, let me speak frankly, with antinihilistic virtue ... If it
had not been for classicism's presumed antinihilistic quality we would have studied the
question more closely ... we would have given breathing space to both systems. But now
we know that these little pills of classical education possess antinihilistic curative powers
and we boldly prescribe them to our patients ... But what if they don't possess curative
powers?' " *Sobranie sochinenii* (Moscow, 1958), VIII, 425–27.

sible to fulfill, and by 1870 the districts were complaining to St. Petersburg of the shortage of competent personnel. Tolstoy's solution was to make the teachers themselves responsible for character training as well as academic instruction. Simultaneously with the promulgation of the new statute for gymnasiums, he ordered directors to appoint a teacher as counselor to each of the school's eight classes. The duties of the class counselor (*nastavnik*) included development of a personal interest in each one of his charges and maintenance of contact with the pupil's other teachers and with his family. The intimate knowledge of the student's character acquired in this way was ultimately assessed as part of the Maturity Examination, a name applied to the battery of written and oral tests that were the equivalent of the German *Abitur* and the French *Baccalauréat*. It determined whether a youth would obtain the Certificate of Maturity—the coveted passport to the university. A joint commission from the curator's office and the local university composed the academic questions. The state relied on the class counselor to evaluate the maturity of the candidate's social, moral, and political attitudes.*

Counselors received extra pay, and ministerial regulations explicitly favored the appointment of classical instructors to the posts. Before 1905 80 per cent of the directors of gymnasiums and more than half the inspectors were themselves classics men. The filling of the counselorships with ancient-language teachers made them a praetorian guard of the administration within the pedagogical councils. In the decades ahead the intramural aristocracy of directors, inspectors, and class counselors could be relied upon to defend the Tolstoy system against every inducement to change.

After 1871 the majority of the teachers in both the gymnasiums and the realschulen remained petty officials of the educational bureaucracy.† To become a social force in their own right, they would have to acquire an independent intellectual foundation, organize or at least communicate with one another, and make their economic position less dependent

---

* *Sbornik ras. MNP* (1872), No. 245; *ibid.* (1873), No. 263. Despite their different rights, the graduates of both gymnasiums and realschulen were referred to in Russian literally as "abiturients." *SMS,* I, Prilozhenie, p. 52.

† The St. Petersburg Historical-Philological Institute and Gymnasium, founded by Tolstoy in 1867, became the principal training center for secondary class teachers. Lists of graduates who became teachers, inspectors, and directors can be found in the three-volume memorial, *Pamiatnaia knizhka imperatorskago s-peterburgskago istoriko-filologicheskago instituta i gimnazii pri onom* (St. Petersburg, 1887, 1892, 1902). With an enrollment of around 200 students, the institute graduated about twelve language teachers a year, a sufficient number to supply vacancies during the pre-1905 period. *Otchet MNP,* 1890, p. 46.

on the director. Throughout the remainder of the century it was difficult for the rank-and-file instructors to accomplish any of these goals. The state allowed pedagogical associations only at the primary level in connection with the zemstvos, and even here only under the auspices of the provincial governors. The work of the pioneers, Pirogov and Ushinsky, for a public and professional educational ideal exerted a strong humanizing influence on individual teachers. But the empirical basis for education as a distinct discipline had yet to be created and imported into the country. This would occur in the 1890's. Until then, and until international shocks and domestic upheavals cracked the authoritarian structure of the old regime, the emancipation of the teachers from the bureaucracy and their emergence as a professional class on the order of the university professors would be delayed.

The regulation of the school still left the home beyond the reach of the authorities. It would be of little use to "conduct the guidance of youth in the spirit of religious truth, respect for the rights of property, and preservation of the basic principles of the social order"[59] if what was laboriously woven under official auspices was carelessly or deliberately unraveled by the social environment. As more students from the towns entered the academic schools, the problem became acute, for urban pupils lived at home or with relatives rather than in pensions with the academic staff. In order to extend the power of his office over day students, Tolstoy issued empire-wide rules of deportment for pupils of gymnasiums and progymnasiums on April 27, 1874.[60] The regulations were badly received. Like their Western counterparts, the Russian middle class accepted military regimentation in the classrooms and dormitories. Tolstoy's 100 pages of instructions extended iron discipline into the streets, public places, and private quarters. The stipulations requiring teachers and students alike to participate periodically in the rituals of the Orthodox church was an affront to both religious and nonreligious minorities. Even more bitterly resented was the school's assumption of extramural "surveillance."

Surveillance meant that inspectors, class counselors, and prefects must see to it that pupils went directly home from school, lived in approved housing, were off the streets before curfew, and did not visit parks, libraries, theaters, and lecture halls without permission. The very word "surveillance"—*nadzor*—carried odious implications. It was the term used to describe the watch that the security police kept over suspicious elements, such as student agitators banished from the capital cities to the provincial towns. Society found surveillance a calculated insult, daily evidence that the government considered the educated class inherently disloyal. Thus, while completing the architecture of the Tolstoy system, the 1874 rules of deportment contributed more than any other single feature, including classicism and bifurcation, to convert the "scholarly European school" of official intent into the "bureaucratic police school" of public resentment.[61]

Auxiliary Components of the Tolstoy System

The preparations for the secondary statutes focused attention on a pattern of enrollment Pirogov had commented on in 1860. Time and again, it was noticed, the three-year lower district school of a town would be sparsely filled with pupils while the first four years of the local gymnasium would be overcrowded. Suspecting that lower-class families were using the first four years of the eight-year school as a terminal facility, Tolstoy appointed an official of the Ministry and editor of the journal *Teacher* to investigate and recommend a solution. N. K. Vessel discovered that "not only those who have in mind a complete scientific education enter our gymnasiums. There are also a large number of youths whose parents are simply not satisfied with the district school. Such persons would like to provide their children with an education higher than elementary, less strictly scientific, and better adapted to the immediate aims of life than the program offered in the gymnasiums."[62]

To correct the misuse of expensive and sophisticated facilities, Vessel suggested adapting the eight-year Prussian *Bürgerschule* to the metropolitan areas. Such an undertaking would require a firm local base for financing. Fortunately, one of the last of the great reforms was on the verge of realization. For almost a decade reconstruction of the archaic municipal machinery of Catherine II had been inching its way through editorial commissions. The final result, the statute of June 16, 1870, granted limited self-government to the cities and the towns at a time when an enterprising industrial and financial bourgeoisie was being stirred to life by rapid railroad construction. A franchise weighted in their favor elected a municipal duma. The assembly, in turn, chose an executive board and a mayor. These arrangements provided ample support for a much higher-grade public school system than in rural, even zemstvo, districts. The town councils were also apt to be more conservative than some of the zemstvo assemblies and could be allowed a freer hand in local education. Tolstoy took full advantage of this situation in drawing up the law of May 31, 1872, which governed the conversion of the district schools of 1828 into redesignated urban schools of 1872.[63]

Designed to receive seven-year-old children without previous instruction or tutoring, the urban school offered a six-year course of advanced primary education. The program could be grouped into one, two, three, or four classes to fit local needs. One teacher taught all the subjects of a given class. Separated administratively as well as geographically from the rural elementary schools, the town institutions represented an ambitious form of basic instruction. At a time when one or two years of training were beyond reach for the overwhelming mass of the peasantry, the program of the urban school of 1872 was officially recognized as the minimum desirable for all social classes. In his original design Tolstoy allowed the graduates of the lower schools to transfer directly into the third year's course of either the gymnasium or the realschule. This arrangement, first suggested by Pirogov, would have restored the base of the democratic ladder. The State Council objected and a compromise permitted pupils with good records to enter the first year of either secondary institution at the end of their fourth year of lower instruction. Neither Tolstoy nor the Council of State made any effort at this time to realize Pirogov's recommendation that the lower urban schools be linked up with the village primary schools.

When he turned his attention from the towns to the countryside, Tolstoy retained the basic impulses and principles of his educational philosophy: his displeasure at the government's wavering initiative, his admiration for Germany, where academic precocity had paid off in political supremacy, his use of religion as a stabilizing force, and his aspiration to see Russia adopt Europe's tested scholastic standards. In his historical researches Tolstoy returned often to the eighteenth century—the age of enlightened despotism—and he prepared a study of lasting value (published in German) of Catherine II's organization of provincial schools.[64] Much as he admired Catherine's initiative in urban education, he scored the failure of her legislative commission's subcommittee on schools to realize its Prussian plan for the Russian countryside. "The subcommittee's plan for the creation of a network of rural schools was as progressive then as it is now.... It is easy to imagine what benefits the government would have derived from a century's head start on compulsory instruction. By now, almost all the Russian people would be literate, like the population of Germany; and the general level of education throughout the country would be a great deal higher, with corresponding benefits for all sectors of national life, cultural as well as material."[65]

Both liberals and reactionaries objected to Tolstoy's proposal "for achieving universal education" on the grounds that "compulsory elementary instruction" would violate local rights. In the face of this combined opposition to a proposal that tsardom would not take seriously until after 1905, Tolstoy had to limit his initiative to the creation of the office of state inspector of primary schools. The functions of the new official were to represent the Ministry of Education's interests on the district school boards, maintain uniform standards, curb regional deviations, purge unreliable teachers, and press the zemstvo assemblies into appropriating funds for building, maintaining, and staffing village schools. Even under the best of conditions there was friction between the state inspector and local authorities. Tolstoy made it clear that the inspector's presence on the school board guaranteed the Minister of Education the last word on policy. For the inspector was the only member of the board who could appeal decisions to St. Petersburg. Within a few years Tolstoy, like Golovnin before him, was forced to retreat for reasons of state security. Since the exhilarating days of the Sunday school movement and the academic time of troubles, the younger generation had dreamed of following Herzen's injunction, delivered in 1861, to leave the oppressed environs of "official learning" and, as "exiles of science," carry the social revolutionary gospel directly "to the people." For a decade thereafter the self-study circles were preoccupied with developing a coherent doctrine and a network of personal contacts. At length, in the early 1870's Russian populism (*narodnichestvo*) came of age, erupting as an organized campaign of considerable scope and nonviolent fervor. In 1873 and 1874 several thousand university students, together with those who had dropped out or were expelled and those returned from abroad, poured out of the cities into the forests and steppes to rescue the people, the *narod,* from the indignities of the patrimonial Russian past and the debasement of the industrial European future by persuading them to embrace an anarchical agrarian communism rooted in the existing peasant commune.

Tsardom's police bureaucracy had difficulty distinguishing between liberal and socialist, populist and nihilist, legal and illegal, educational and violent strains of opposition. Student teachers were as suspect as student rioters, and populism's educational crusade to the peasantry readily collapsed under a wave of arrests facilitated by village hostility toward urban missionaries. Repression turned contemplative students toward intensive study of long-range social and economic trends and the militant toward terror. These were later developments. In the immediate present the naïve, propagandistic phase of the social revolutionary movement frightened the government into modifying its educational policy. For years the nobility had been pleading for an enlarged role in peasant schooling. Now at last, against Tolstoy's advice, the Tsar yielded to gentry pressure. The revised constitution for public instruction issued in 1874 declared marshals of nobility *ex officio* presidents of provincial and district school boards, thus redressing the balance between central power and local initiative which had been upset five years before. The mandate that the marshals received was to protect rural learning "from the sedition and corruption" emanating from the university towns. To tighten the antisubversive net securely, the church schools were placed under the reorganized school boards.

The record of one of Tolstoy's earliest appointees demonstrated that a conscientious "bureaucrat" could work modest wonders within the existing power structure. A secondary school teacher of mathematics and physics, Ilya Ulyanov (the father of Lenin) climbed the educational service ladder to the rank of nobleman and on the way laid the foundations for civilizing the upper Volga. In 1869 he was appointed the first state inspector of schools for the polyracial province of Simbirsk in the educational region of Kazan. When he arrived in the territory, expenditures for education were running at the rate of 3.7 kopeks annually per child. Only six of the area's 276 primary teachers in the 50 schools were academically qualified. In addition to lack of facilities, the disappointing results attained from the use of Russian as the language of the classroom for the predominantly Finno-Ugrian population fostered the illusion that the minorities were incapable of standard achievement. Ulyanov converted a centuries-old backlog of neglect into a permanent investment within fifteen years. Native dialects were introduced as instructional languages; local curricula were enriched with agronomy and crafts, and state funds were obtained for a teachers' seminary. By the time death removed him from his post in 1886, this subordinate officer within the Tolstoy system had wrung sufficient funds from local zemstvos to open 400 additional schools.[66]

PART TWO

The Crisis of Monolithic Control
1875–1905

Chapter Four

Conflicting Pressures on the Authoritarian School, 1875–1895

The younger generation which was growing to manhood in the wake of the great reforms needed a firm guiding hand but not a calloused one. In order to restrain the excessive enthusiasm of the student youth, to guide their energies and transform them into useful and responsible builders of the future, rigid system alone was not enough. A measure of compassion was necessary. Unfortunately the direction of scholastic affairs during the reform period was less than benevolent. The controlling authority made matters worse by arming itself with a novel academic system and new constitutions for secondary schools which lacked the support of public opinion.

GENERAL LORIS-MELIKOV, *1880*

Official Repudiation of the Tolstoy System, 1875–1881

Twenty years after the fall of its Black Sea bastion to British arms, tsardom had recovered much of its foreign prestige and internal equilibrium. St. Petersburg's notice to Berlin that their alliance was not to be turned against France stabilized eastern Europe and lowered martial temperatures along Russia's western frontier. Peace, in turn, would allow the government to get on with the most urgent business at hand now that the countryside and the army had been reorganized. Top priorities were railroads and schools—two means to knit the scattered population of the realm into a coherent whole.

As if to underline the importance of the growth of physical and intellectual communications, Dmitri Tolstoy conducted a tour of the southern educational districts in 1875. Along the Pontic coast the abuse that had been his portion from the older, academically oriented educated class in the northern capitals was briefly drowned out by the plaudits of the commercial elements in the booming provincial towns. For his creation of the realschule with Treasury funds, his transformation of the county district schools into urban schools, and his invitation to the Jews to utilize state institutions, a number of municipal dumas and merchant guilds welcomed him as the man who had brought enlightenment to the steppes.* But even as the Minister of Education was being cheered in the Ukraine, the southern Slavs were once more rising against their Turkish masters. The revolt in the mountains of Herzegovina in 1875 set in motion an avalanche of events that would shortly bring Europe to the brink of general war, the Russian empire to the edge of anarchy, and its most irritating institutional component, the Tolstoy system, to the point of official repudiation.

At the outset St. Petersburg was reluctant to involve itself directly in the Balkan conflict. The second thoughts of statesmen could not dampen the enthusiasm of journalists anxious to project tsardom into the role of liberator of southern Slavs. At length, in the spring of 1877, formal hostilities began. After early successes, Russian fortunes turned. To save its gains, tsardom submitted its case to the great powers assembled at Berlin. The connection between foreign relations and state schooling was immediate, and well understood. The Tolstoy system had been inspired at a moment when Russian statesmen were impressed by Prussia but not yet overwhelmed by Germany. As admiration for a smaller power turned to fear before a giant, the intellectual atmosphere changed. The widespread bitterness at Bismarck's role at the Congress of Berlin worked itself out against the most accessible symbol of presumed foreign dominance over domestic affairs—the Tolstoy system.[1]

Germanophobia would not have been so corrosive of the educational establishment if, at the same time, patriotic fears had not been confirmed by the sudden upsurge of revolutionary populism. In this instance, as in international affairs, the government's indecisiveness paved the way for disaster. At the outbreak of hostilities in the Balkans, St. Petersburg

* A testimonial dinner in Kherson climaxed Dmitri Tolstoy's inspection of the Odessan district in October 1875. On this occasion the mayor of the city assured him that the "history of Russian education will dedicate its best pages to recording your administration. It remains for us simply to admire you and to thank you for all you have already accomplished and in particular for your enlightened readiness to make our city happy by opening a realschule in Kherson." In his reply Tolstoy paid his respects to public initiative that spent money: "Several years ago I found in Kherson only one boys' gymnasium and one private girls' school; now you have a gymnasium and progymnasium and a teachers' seminary, and today, at the request of the zemstvo and municipality I promised my cooperation in the establishment in Kherson of a realschule. Thanks to the enlightened initiative of society the entire province is covered with village schools.... It is proper for me, as the official representative of the school department, to take this occasion to express my heartfelt thanks to this enlightened public and to its representatives for sparing neither personal labor nor material resources on behalf of the development of education in this region." *ZMNP*, December 1875, pp. 128–29.

had reason to believe that it had suppressed sedition in the rear. By 1877, 1,611 socialist agitators had been arrested, for the most part young men from the middle class of lower nobility and townsmen "who had passed through school and university to become the most active and sensitive portion of the intelligentsia."[2] Irritated by pleas for clemency, the Ministry of Justice moved to eradicate public sympathy with the student rebels by exposing them to open trial. Several spectacles were staged; the greatest and the last, the trial of the 193, unfolded between October 1877 and January 1878 against the background of growing disenchantment with the war. The trial of the 193 closed with an attempt on the life of the police commandant of St. Petersburg. In February the governor of Kharkov was slain, and in March an attempt was made on the life of the head of the security police. The assault on the central authority culminated on April 7, 1879, when a former student and teacher unloaded a revolver at the Tsar.

The attack on the Tsar hastened the dissolution of the revolutionary party into factions, and by the fall of 1879 the militants completed the formation of a disciplined terrorist cadre, the People's Will, within the parent body. These dedicated assassins were obsessed with the fear that commercialization of agriculture would destroy their chosen framework for communism, the peasant commune. Power must be snatched at once from the state bureaucracy before it could be surrendered to the capitalists. Convinced in their haste that the most effective way to achieve their ends was to "fire at the center," the executive committee of the secret society formally condemned Alexander II to death toward the end of the year.

As terror increased, public backing for oppositional forces assumed alarming forms. A jury's acquittal of the would-be assassin of the police chief of St. Petersburg was openly applauded. A direct appeal to society from the Throne for cooperation in the "struggle against subversive ideas" elicited counterdemands. After lecturing the government on the major causes of unrest, which included "the nature of secondary and higher educational institutions," one zemstvo assembly voiced the thoughts of many by naming "freedom of speech and press, freedom of opinion, and free science" as the best means for mobilizing public sympathy for the government.[3] Such counsels of moderation were ignored. By the summer of 1879 an official investigating commission was alerting the Tsar to "the apathy of almost all of the more or less educated portion of the population toward the government's current struggle, with a relatively small number of plotters striving to undermine the basic conditions of state, civil, and public order. Most people are upset, but act as though they are awaiting the outcome of the struggle; they are not engaging in the struggle, and they are not rallying to the support of the government."[4]

As the government dallied, the Minister of Education hewed to a consistently hard line. In Dmitri Tolstoy's view, to compromise was to cease to govern, and to cease to govern was to cease to educate. His great fear was not resistance. Opposition, for him, was a sign that the bureaucracy was forcing a backward society to live up to European standards. What Tolstoy feared was that under mounting pressure the Tsar would surrender the educational initiative to local forces and their allies in the central bureaucracy. "No matter how much money the government spends," he warned the hesitant monarch, "no matter how much energy it exerts, no matter how perfectly it designs the curricula and trains the teaching staffs, the moment the schools waver from their academic principles they are likely to start training a younger generation that is devoid of character, lacking firm moral principles, confused, and dissolute. Unable either to command or to obey, such specimens will render ill service to throne and fatherland."[5]

The personality of the ruler was not the only factor complicating the realization of Tolstoy's cast-iron pedagogical vision. For political and economic reasons the civil bureaucracy had been forced to share responsibility for civilizing the peasantry with the church and the gentry. What was even more exasperating to Tolstoy, the university councils, despite periodic undergraduate unrest, had been able to preserve the autonomy granted them by a grateful government in 1863. Only at the secondary level of instruction had Tolstoy as Minister of Education enjoyed a free hand. For the past decade he had been exploiting it to the full in order to convert the college preparatory school into a bulwark of administrative absolutism. He could now use the gymnasium as a model and a base from which to expand the influence of his office and the sway of his ideas—European academic tradition, social democracy, and bureaucratic centralism—outward over the realschulen at the expense of local initiative, downward over the village schools in competition with the church, and upward to the seats of scientific learning against the wishes of academic liberals.

As the students spawned terrorist cadres and the police spread their nets, the minister of national enlightenment labored on in his office with a pistol in the drawer to make the school system a more refined instrument for stimulating society while controlling it. After 1875 a series of directives applied to the realschulen the operating rules for gymnasiums. The administrative distinction between state preparatory and public terminal schools disappeared. Internal procedures were also tightened. In his instruction of 1871 creating the office of class counselor, Tolstoy had stressed informality and spontaneity. In the hope that "free and unfettered intercourse between students and advisers" would inject vitality into teaching, he pointedly refrained from spelling out duties in detail. By 1877 he could contain his legislative mania no longer. In August he issued general rules regulating precisely the adviser's role within the school and his relations with the family.[6]

The penetration of the urban revolutionary movement into the countryside convinced Tolstoy that his original position, taken against Golovnin after Poland, that simple parish priests made the state's best rural schoolmasters, was no longer tenable. In the 1870's he became an enthusiastic advocate of special pedagogical training for village teachers. If anything, he now insisted, primary teachers needed more careful preparation than their secondary and university counterparts. Because of the crudeness of the material with which they had to work, they had to be better teachers. Reversing his argument of 1866, he pointed out to his skeptical colleagues that even Catholic countries were replacing local clergy with certified civilians in country schools. Between 1871 and 1879 Tolstoy used state funds to establish 50 teachers' seminaries. Of this number, 23 were placed "more for political than for pedagogical purposes," as he explained, in the borderlands of empire. This left only 27 normal schools in the Russian heartland. In the face of increased agitation he wanted to open at least one seminary in every province and several in the more populous areas. By now security officials and ecclesiastical leaders had strengthened their alliance, and Tolstoy found himself defending his creations. In vain he cited their security record. In eight years the schools had produced only three politically unreliable graduates.[7] Those who were skeptical of state enlightenment in the countryside were not impressed.

Tolstoy's failure to acquire more funds for his teachers' seminaries was the first solid indication that a grand coalition of liberal and reactionary interests threatened his grip on the Ministry of Education. To protect himself from the Right he moved more quickly toward answering Katkov's demand for an end to the autonomy of the universities. Personally, Tolstoy was more interested in bringing the civil service examinations given by the university faculties under ministerial control. Aware of his isolation, he broached the question cautiously. First, he requested the professors themselves to suggest revisions to the university statute of 1863. Only after their refusal he put together a commission of Katkov's friends, conservative academicians and central officials, to draft a bill. The resulting project converted the administrative officers of the university from elected deputies into appointed officials. The rectors were to be named by the Ministry, the deans of faculties and colleges by the district curators. The curators would be given broader powers to police the students. The Ministry would appoint special commissions to supervise the state service tests. Tolstoy delayed presenting his proposals to the Council of State until February 6, 1880. Only at this late date did he feel sure of a sympathetic hearing. The day before, an agent of the People's Will had dynamited the Winter Palace. The eruption literally rocked the ground under the autocracy. After such an obvious display of impotence in the capital, the government would have to take stronger countermeasures at once in order to reestablish its authority in the nation. The Minister of Education had some reason to believe that he was more indispensable than ever. And yet within weeks the one high official who over the years had despised "popularity" would be sacrificed to public opinion.

Within a week of the bombing of his St. Petersburg residence, Alexander II established a supreme commission with extraordinary powers to coordinate the activities of rival departments of state and provincial authorities. General Mikhail Loris-Melikov was appointed chairman of the extraordinary commission and became, in effect, military dictator of the country. Avoiding party labels in order to rally as much support as possible, Loris-Melikov was nevertheless closely associated with Dmitri Miliutin and Grand Duke Constantine. Katkov was in despair. Loris-Melikov's conceptions, he complained, represented the constitutionalist views of Kraevsky's *Voice*. The supreme executive commission, he scoffed, was a "dictatorship of the heart."[8]

The General did, indeed, contemplate measures that would afford the educated class a sense of representation at the national level. Even the faintest gesture in this direction was certain to arouse resistance throughout the court, the aristocracy, the church, and the bureaucracy. To realize such an idea would require time and broad support. Loris-Melikov acquired both by attacking the most unpopular man in the country, the Minister of Education. The Tolstoy system, he reported to the Emperor, had been imposed on the educated class against its will. "As a result the mass of young people, resentful as they were of the demands made upon them, met not with criticism but with sympathy from family and society. Leaving their scientific preparation unfinished, unaccustomed to routine work, and not trained for any practical venture, they abandoned school for life. Seeking an arena for action outside the law, they swelled the ranks of those attracted by false social doctrines."[9]

The alienation described by Loris-Melikov was exhibited in the life of one of the principal organizers of the People's Will. As a pupil Aleksandr Mikhailov had been irritated by the gymnasium's "German spirit." Utilizing his school time to absorb the literature of agrarian socialism, he formed a self-study circle among his comrades. Subsequently, the group circulated propaganda booklets among the working people until dispersed by the police. In the autumn of 1875 the budding populist came up from the provinces to St. Petersburg. Once in the capital he decided to study in the technological institute rather than in the university as a form of protest against Tolstoy. Before the semester was over, he was expelled for participating in a student demonstration. Disgusted by society's preference for "the next step on the career ladder" to civic spirit, he joined the revolutionary movement. At the conference in 1879, where the students created a central terrorist authority, Mikhailov singled out "the substitution of the dead languages for living service in the schools" as the most reactionary step undertaken by Alexander II. The harm from it had nullified the benefits of the early years of his reign.[10]

The hostility of the extremists toward the Tolstoy system was shared not only by Westernizing liberals but by Slavophiles. Disturbed by the sharp increase of university enrollments after 1875, cultural conservatives warned that it was "positively harmful in Russia to arouse by artificial means the desire to pursue higher education."[11] Tolstoy's isolation was complete. In April, Loris-Melikov recommended his removal. "Changes in the administrative personnel of the Ministry of Education," he assured the Tsar, "will meet with the enthusiastic response of all Russia."[12] With this indictment the educational history of the great reform period came full circle. Tolstoy had replaced Golovnin after an improvised attempt on the life of the sovereign. At that time Golovnin's liberal education policy had been blamed for indirectly encouraging dissent among the student youth. Fourteen years later a more highly organized assassination effort inspired the argument that Tolstoy's absolutist policy had driven the student youth to organized rebellion. On April 24, 1880, Tolstoy resigned as Minister of Education and Ober-Procurator of the Holy Synod. Following tsarist practice, he was elevated to the Council of State to await further developments.

When Tolstoy was dismissed, education in the Russian empire was still primarily an agency of state, more responsive to political will than to public desires. Its course depended closely upon the balance of power within the highest ruling circles. Tolstoy's exit was interpreted as a forecast of more cooperation between the central authorities and the organs of self-government in the provinces and cities. The Petersburg *Voice* expressed educated public opinion when it greeted the news with praise for the Tsar as the threefold liberator, who had emancipated the peasants from the gentry, the Bulgars from the Turks, and society from Dmitri Tolstoy.[13] The most volatile sector of the educated community, the university students, received the dismissal of the "scourge of Russia" as an olive branch. The People's Will was counting heavily on the support of the undergraduates to create an atmosphere of popular upheaval in the capital to camouflage the small number of those actively bent on assassination. After Tolstoy's abrupt departure on the eve of his bid to shorten the leash on science, the terrorists found it impossible to attract significant student support.[14]

As the months passed and autumn darkened into winter and winter brightened into spring, political life showed additional signs of returning to normal. When the mood of emergency passed, the supreme executive commission was abolished, and it was as ordinary Minister of the Interior that Loris-Melikov was closing the police net around the conspirators while drafting a plan (misnamed a constitution by alarmists and wishful thinkers) for enlarging the voice of the educated public in national affairs. Against the advice of the Crown Prince, the Emperor affixed his signature to a manifesto granting zemstvos and selected municipal dumas representation in the Council of State. The date was March 1, 1881. Later in the day remnants of the People's Will cut Alexander II in half with a homemade bomb. The murder, which was to have toppled bureaucratic centralism, brought its last robust practitioner, Alexander III, to power.

Reaffirmation and Revision of the
Tolstoy System, 1881–1887

The violent death of the Tsar-Emancipator completed a change that had set in with the Turkish war—a disposition on the part of educated Russians in positions of authority away from sentiment toward realism, away from a vague longing to be absorbed into European civilization, toward determination to assert themselves. As part of the trend toward sobriety, the enthusiasm for education as cultural enlightment receded in favor of spreading useful technical skills and bolstering traditional moral values.

The fervor of bureaucratic nationalism was sustained by observation of the immediate past. From the perspective of twenty years the great reforms seemed to have wrenched the social structure out of its protective shell without visibly improving its competitive capacity. Cultural substitutes for economic progress, conservative circles complained, had proved themselves not only artificial but dangerous. Liberals and radicals might denounce the Tolstoy system as formalistic and reactionary, but the official records showed it multiplying the opportunities for secular and scientific learning precisely among the lower classes and minority groups.* At the same time, its academic programs and disciplinary rules had visibly failed to inspire the students with loyalty to the regime. Tolstoy's protagonist, Loris-Melikov, sincere patriots believed, had inflicted even cruder harm. At a moment when the country was isolated abroad, the General had rewarded student terrorism with constitutional concessions, thereby all but inviting the final catastrophe. In sum, the Westernizers—whether "enlightened" or "liberal"—had manifestly failed to modernize the country without jeopardizing its security.

After March First and the assassination of the Tsar, Russian nationalists were convinced that their hour had struck. Their immediate task

---

* Between 1864 and 1875 the number of boys in gymnasiums increased from 28,202 to 51,097, the number of girls from 4,335 to 27,470. Between 1864 and 1875 the percentage of privileged youths in the gymnasiums dropped from 70 to 52.8 per cent, whereas the portion of townsmen rose from a fifth to a third. For Tolstoy's cordial relations with the Jewish communities of the Odessan region and his encouragement of Jewish attendance at state schools, see *ZMNP*, November 1875, pp. 63ff, and *ibid.*, December 1875, pp. 130ff.

was to restore the authority of absolutism. An inspirational model for reconstruction was close at hand. Patriotic memories were still fresh of peasant recruits under noble officers (both unspoiled by academic learning) struggling for Christian orthodoxy and Slavonic brotherhood against commercial Europe's heathen lackeys. Why could not the collective purpose and sacrificial spirit of wartime be transferred to civil affairs? All that was needed was a sovereign, absolute in practice as well as in theory. As if by divine providence, such a ruler was at hand.

Alexander III was close to the ideal character type sought by the Tolstoy system. Unimaginative and pedestrian, conscientious and upright, short on vision but long on industry and common sense, secure in his religious assumptions and sensitive to the country's immediate interests, the 36-year-old autocrat dedicated his comparatively short reign of fourteen years to restoring the prestige of autocracy at home and abroad. Already as crown prince he had voiced his disapproval of the hesitant way his father conducted the government. Once in command he settled the unfinished diplomatic business of the previous reign by restoring good relations with Germany. Accepting for the time being, at least, the official liberals' position on foreign affairs, he broke with them over the issue of representative government. The "constitution" of March First was rescinded and resignations from office accepted from Loris-Melikov, Dmitri Miliutin, and Grand Duke Constantine.

As the advocates of public participation in government withdrew, several outspoken absolutists, all of whom had been prominent in education for years, emerged as captains of the ruling Russian party. The first of the bureaucratic nationalists to recover his voice was Mikhail Katkov. Once the threat of restraints on central authority was past, he reasserted his role as gadfly of the administration and conscience of the nation. If Katkov was the most articulate spokesman of post-assassination nationalism, its most influential agent was Konstantin Pobedonostsev. While a professor of civil law at Moscow University, he had formed close social and intellectual ties with the editor of the *Moscow News*. As tutor to the Crown Prince he had become Alexander III's most trusted confidant as well as mentor to the new heir, the future Nicholas II. Pobedonostsev presently utilized his position as Ober-Procurator of the Holy Synod to recruit trustworthy personnel for the supreme echelons of power. His most decisive stroke, prudently delayed for some months, was to bring his predecessor as civil head of the church back into government. Apprehension swept the country as telegrams arrived from the north with word that Dmitri Tolstoy was returning to high office.* Notified of his selection as Minister of the Interior, the former head of schools mentioned as a likely disability his unpopularity. "That circumstance," Alexander III replied, "does not bother me."[15]

As chief of internal security from 1882 until his death in 1889, Dmitri Tolstoy manipulated the most comprehensive instruments of imperial authority. He had established his reputation and developed his techniques for social organization in the field of education. He now transferred the governing principle of bureaucratic centralism to the country at large. Although he remained skeptical of the productive capacity of the nobility as a class, after the assassination of Alexander II he went along with the official effort to attract Privilege into service by extending legal and economic favors to the gentry. Tolstoy's initiatives in the social and political sphere were supported in the economic field by two professors, Bunge and Vyshnegradsky, who as Ministers of Finance prepared the way for the influx of industrial investment by balancing the state budget and hardening the ruble into an internationally respected currency.

Not since the days of Alexander I's secret committee had there been such unanimity of thought and compatibility of feeling among independent and opinionated advisers to the Crown as among the half-dozen experienced educators who now guided the internal development of the empire. Intellectuals and scholars in their own right, they were not impressed by professors and journalists as such. Sobered by responsibility, they sought the possible. Administering a backward nation with global ambitions, they attracted the animosity of every segment of the population, from reactionary court circles to incipient Marxists. At the same time, most thoughtful men feared that the local initiative and professional autonomy encouraged by the great reforms would wither under

---

* "I still have a vivid picture in my mind of that event so long ago. I was sixteen at the time, a student in the sixth grade of the Orenburg Gymnasium. It was a warm May evening. The town boulevard along the winding banks of the Ural River was crowded with strollers. Suddenly the news spread along the boulevard of a telegram just received announcing the appointment of Tolstoy as Minister of Internal Affairs. Everyone remembered the name of the former Minister of Education all too well. The people, who had been strolling along the avenue, gathered in small knots. I saw troubled faces everywhere, and from all sides one and the same phrase recurred: 'Tolstoy—this means reaction.' The boulevard quickly emptied. I saw the people with gray and elderly faces shake their heads as they trudged home." Kizevetter, p. 125.

their hands. If this happened, the age-old cleavage between state and society would be widened and the central government isolated from the educated class, which alone could transform bureaucratic impulses into genuine public life.

The educational policy of the bureaucratic centralists was a direct extension of their cautious philosophy of power; and to implement their program for consolidating the structure of the empire, the Tolstoy system was restored. It was not restored, however, in its original form. In order to convert the explicitly "European" mechanism of the 1870's into the explicitly "Russian" mechanism of the 1880's, changes were in order. The modifying architect was none other than the conservative "nihilist"[16] whom Loris-Melikov had chosen to replace Tolstoy as head of the Holy Synod. Contemptuous of the educated class as "the great herd of intellect," suspicious of liberal reformers as mere "adepts of scholasticism," and scornful of social revolutionaries as "the doctrinaires of science,"[17] Konstantin Pobedonostsev opposed Tolstoy's educational design of 1871–74. He did so on the grounds that it unduly whetted the appetite for higher education among the lower classes and minority groups and was, in consequence, more conducive to unrest than stability. In his view, state schooling, which facilitated upward mobility and mixing of races by imposing uniform, international, and relatively high academic standards, ought to be replaced by more down-to-earth instruction favoring the Great Russian Orthodox believers among the peoples of the realm and the privileged caste among its social orders.

As Minister of Education to oversee this transition, Pobedonostsev recommended an adaptable official with a quarter-century's experience in school administration at provincial and central levels. In the previous reign Ivan Delianov had served both Golovnin and Tolstoy with equal punctilio. Under the latter he had become an expert on administrative technicalities. But whereas Tolstoy had raised the central office of public instruction to a position of unprecedented authority, Delianov's nomination confirmed its subordination to the Holy Synod and the Ministry of the Interior.

As official faith in enlightenment dimmed, the Ministry of Education both expanded and narrowed the scope of the Tolstoy system. As a former professor, Pobedonostsev was partial toward the autonomy of the universities. Tolstoy, however, persuaded the Tsar that as long as the civil-service examinations were administered by professors the state should exert more direct control over the universities. Accordingly, the constitutional revisions that he had been on the point of introducing in 1880 were imposed in 1884. After a precarious life of 21 years, faculty self-government passed from the scene, until restored 21 years later, in 1905.

Even as the educational bureaucracy tightened its hold on higher learning, primary responsibility for the alleviation of mass ignorance slipped from its jurisdiction. As the first step in his campaign to bring the entire area of elementary education under the auspices of religion, Pobedonostsev had the church schools removed from the competence of the secular school boards in 1881. What state funds were available were henceforth channeled largely through his office to the parish schools. Conservative zemstvos welcomed ecclesiastical instruction as a cheap method of providing the restless and overcrowded villages with a little learning without too much light. In answer to critics Pobedonostsev pointed out that, whereas the local priests had obvious deficiencies as pedagogues, they were still less alien to the peasants than the urban intelligentsia, the rural gentry, or Petersburg officials.

In the central areas of the empire, where the authority of the government rested on belief in the Orthodox religion, fealty to divine right monarchy, and membership in the Great Russian tribe, the Tolstoy system was restored as an agency of conservation. In the frontier provinces, where blood ties were non-Russian and religious affiliations non-Orthodox or non-Christian, it was presently introduced as an agency of change. Here its purpose was dynamic—to draw the younger generation away from the folkways of their fathers and make them adopted Russians.* For despite the difference between Pobedonostsev's nativistic approach to education and Tolstoy's cosmopolitanism, the two statesmen agreed on the need for absorbing the minorities through the schools. The unification of Italy and Germany and the liberation struggle of the southern Slavs were proof enough of the explosive potential of the idea that every lingual community had a right to nationhood.

After the lessons of 1878 and 1881, the nationalist party was more

---

* From Turkestan, where the academic program of the urban schools was simplified and sharpened as a tool of Russification (*Otchet MNP*, 1886, pp. 294–95), an official reported that the native children became "so accustomed to the conditions of Russian life and the school [the Urban School of 1872] that they seldom on their own initiative request contact with their relatives; and when their relatives and parents come for them, they do not express any special joy and go unwillingly on vacation." *Otchet MNP*, 1885, p. 212. Unlike the urban school, the gymnasium was not a significant Russifier of the native population in Turkestan. Of the 277 classical students in the area in 1886, only thirteen were Moslems; of the 279 in 1891, only nine were Moslems, and sixteen were Jews.

convinced than ever that as long as the Romanov realm remained a loose assembly of different languages, disparate cultures, and conflicting creeds, held to the Muscovite core by physical compulsion, it would be insecure. In the western areas the minorities question was further exacerbated by the condition of the Catholic Poles, the Protestant Germans, and the Protestant Finns. All three peoples enjoyed a more highly developed urban life than their Russian masters. By their mere physical presence in cities these western peoples were closer to the cultural opportunities of social advancement than the vast majority of their Orthodox neighbors. The Polish schools had been under severe pressure since 1863. Now the measures that had been taken against rebels were applied to the loyal. In 1886 the German secondary schools of the Baltic region were made Russian-speaking and placed under the Petersburg Ministry of Education. In 1893 the German university in Dorpat was closed and then reopened as the Russian university of Yurev. As a result of this reorganization, the number of students dropped from 1,000 in 1890 to 268 by 1900. The Finnish establishments were also threatened; before they could be absorbed into the Tolstoy system, Russification was extended in a negative manner to the southern frontier. In 1897 St. Petersburg authorities shut down the Armenian schools in the Caucasus.

The integration of the ethnic minorities was a territorial process undertaken primarily for security reasons. Representing the physical expansion of the Tolstoy system into previously exempted lands, it touched all stages of learning. The advance, of course, was bitterly contested by the affected provincials, who were forced to experience European education as an instrument of Russian imperialism. Uniform state schools, they realized, were a more deadly threat to their unique traditions than military occupation, and they felt lasting resentments. But important as Russification became as an irritant by 1900, it was still on the periphery of the educational scene in the 1880's. During the immediate decade after the assassination of the Tsar-Emancipator, the principal challenge to central control came from a different direction. As part of the broad urbanization process, stimulated by emancipation and the great reforms, a completely unorganized, totally leaderless movement emerged from below. Its participants were lower-class Orthodox and non-Christians scarcely familiar with the fine points of legal statutes and mostly indifferent to the nuances of curricula. Their aim was not to decentralize the administration or to liberalize the program of studies or to humanize the discipline, but simply to occupy the most accessible classrooms on their own terms.

The signs of squatter activity were duly recorded by local authorities. In the early 1880's provincial officials complained to St. Petersburg that "children rendered unfit for gymnasiums by the social condition of their parents" were filtering into the schools. Some district curators were of a mind that "parents living by hand labor" were ill-equipped to prepare their children properly for entrance into upper-level institutions. Poverty constrained them to transfer their children at the first opportunity to terminal facilities or to take them out of school altogether in order to place them in private employment or lower government service. Other officials were disturbed by the disciplinary problems created by the presence of large numbers of peasants in the schools. In order to attend classes regularly, rural children had to leave their homes and live for the greater part of the year in distant towns where, "freed from supervision before they were able to guide themselves, they became contemptuous not only of their parents but of all authority."[18]

In the metropolitan centers of the western territories the proletarianization of the academic schools was further complicated by the nationalities issue in its most intractable form. Since the partitioning of Poland had brought the Jews under the dominion of the Romanovs, their presence had posed a peculiar challenge to the Orthodox state. Unlike other captive nations, the Hebraic peoples harbored no vision of political independence until Zionism's spread at the turn of the century. Like the Poles, the Germans, and the Finns, they were on the whole more civilized than the bulk of their Slavic neighbors. Legal restrictions on their mobility had intensified their attraction for town life, so that by the final quarter of the nineteenth century they were the most highly urbanized ethnic group in the empire. As of 1870, 93 per cent of them still lived within the original pale of settlement defined by Catherine II. Within its bounds, comprising some fifteen western and southwestern provinces, they accounted for 11 per cent of the population. Outside the pale they represented but one-third of one per cent of the population of the empire. Within the educational regions of Vilna, Warsaw, Riga, Odessa, Kharkov, and Kiev, they made up a significant proportion of the urban population. Such cities as Grodno, Kovno, Minsk, Vitebsk, and Vilna, each of which hosted a state gymnasium, were in effect Jewish enclaves.

As a result of this concentration, the non-Christian minority, which made up but three per cent of the total population of the realm, was at least 90 per cent urban at a time when Russia as a whole was still 90 per cent rural. In consequence of this imbalance, approximately one-fourth of the urban subjects of Alexander III were Jews. More than any racial, religious, or historic propensities, demography gave them an advantage over their Christian neighbors, especially the aristocrats, when it came to utilizing the educational opportunities provided by the state. "Imagine the peculiarity of a government," Prince Nicholas Volkonsky, a landowner of Riazan, complained, "which so laid out its school system that it serves townspeople preponderantly, while in the western region the majority of the urban population is Jewish, up to 90 per cent in some places. Their broad-scale education on state funds is at the expense of the basic population."[19] The vast majority of the Russian nobility were small proprietors. For such persons the education of a large family threatened financial ruin. Either the children had to be boarded or the family itself moved into town. For the Jews, on the other hand, the first rung on the ladder of civil or professional ascent was conveniently attained by attendance at the local gymnasium as day students, living at home, however humble.

During the first half of the nineteenth century the central government had sought to break down the exclusiveness of the Jewish communities in the western territories by opening the Russian schools to their members. But for decades the non-Christians had resisted official efforts at absorption. With the great reforms, younger Jews exhibited a growing impatience with the restrictions placed upon them by their elders and looked to state instruction as the most direct means of liberation from the ghetto. For the legal privileges that St. Petersburg attached to higher education were most attractive to persons curbed by both secular and religious restraints. In 1861 permission to live outside the pale had been extended to holders of higher academic degrees and in 1879 to all university graduates. It was hardly surprising that an increasing number of young men took advantage of the official machinery of racial and religious emancipation. In 1881, 8,200 Jewish boys accounted for 12 per cent of all the students in the gymnasiums and progymnasiums. In the western and southwestern educational regions the ratio was much higher, in Vilna 27 per cent and in Odessa 35 per cent.

Although enjoying comparatively easy access to state education by living in towns, the Jews had not escaped poverty. And now, as the indigent exchanged religious tradition for secular enlightenment, they became rootless besides. Understandably enough, the government, which had contributed so much to an uncertain state of mind by mixing educational advantages with racial discrimination, was concerned. Some officials noted with gratification that government schools had produced a number of Jewish scholars, technicians, physicians, and artists, whose "purity of morals, high respect for learning, absolute sobriety, thrift, and constant activity" were of immeasurable benefit to society. Others observed, however, that the open access which was a basic principle of the original Tolstoy system was permitting migration into the academic network of "masses of students from the lower strata of the Jewish population without means of subsistence and devoid of religious beliefs." District authorities experienced this influx "from the marketplace and from the streets" as a disciplinary problem. Noting that non-Christian children gave the teachers twice as much trouble as the Christian, the curator of the Kharkov region ascribed the high incidence of insubordination to family circumstances. The parents of most of the Jewish pupils either were occupied with petty commerce or lacked a fixed occupation. "Deprived for the most part of domestic supervision, the children of such parents bring their habits of lack of restraint and incorrigibility into the schools."[20]

Whether Christian or Jewish, some of the plebeian scholars overcame the handicaps of home environment, completed the full eight-year course of classical studies, and acquired their Certificate of Maturity. Most, however, displayed little concern for the elaborate structure of the Tolstoy system. They simply used the university preparatory as terminal schools, departing, usually after the end of the fourth year, when their immediate goal was accomplished or their funds exhausted. In consequence, the rate of pupils leaving before graduation was consistently high. An independent study made in 1905 estimated that between 1872 and 1904, an average of 67.1 per cent of those entering the elite institutions left prematurely.* An official analysis related the high incidence of

* Antonov, pp. 307–20. Antonov based his study on the annual reports (*Otchet MNP*) of the Ministry of Education. He studied eleven school districts, but did not include western and eastern Siberia and the Caucasus. According to his calculations, the student population of the academic schools averaged 60,000 between 1872 and 1879 and 70,000 between 1890 and 1903. Between 1872 and 1903 an average of 11,300 boys entered the first year of study, a maximum of 8,757 and a minimum of 5,243 dropped out every year for an annual

drop-out directly to the influx of pupils "placed by domestic circumstances in conditions unfavorable to scholarly pursuits."[21] Far from being displeased at the early departure of democratic aspirants from academic life, authorities welcomed the exodus as a prerequisite to scholastic quality. "It is impossible not to approve of the egress from the gymnasiums and progymnasiums of the children of lower-class people," the Ministry observed. "For to the extent that the preparatory institutions are freed from persons falling into them by accident, they will more easily reach their goal of giving the remainder a serious general education as well as preparing them for the universities."[22]

Although the contemporary intelligentsia did not discuss the issue and historians have ignored it, both officials and the public were well aware that one of the principal reasons for the large influx of lower-class elements into the academic schools and the subsequent high rate at which they departed before graduation was the shortage of more suitable facilities. For in the last quarter of the nineteenth century the state's instructional apparatus still suffered the original Petrine distortion of having been built from the top down. As of January 1, 1887, there were 5,000 more pupils in the 175 gymnasiums and 70 progymnasiums (70,921) than in the 104 realschulen (21,040) and the 354 district and urban schools (44,163) combined. Pupils belonging to the lower classes and inferior estates, the Ministry of Education noted, "do not remain for long in the gymnasiums. As soon as schools with a shorter course are opened in the towns, most of the children of insufficient social means attend them."[23] This being the case, efforts were made to regulate the flow of pupils by drawing the economically restricted away from academic toward practical instruction. This was done in some places by transforming "troublesome" gymnasiums into vocational schools. More important results were achieved by reorganizing, expanding, and adding to the subordinate sections of the Tolstoy system.

Back in the late 1860's Dmitri Tolstoy had designed the realschule with the weak student in mind. From the second through the fifth year, students failing languages or mathematics or both in the gymnasiums

---

average of 7,582. Comparing the number of those finishing the gymnasiums with those entering, Antonov found that between 1872 and 1904 a maximum of 45.5 per cent and a minimum of 22.5 per cent of entering students graduated, whereas a maximum of 77.5 per cent and a minimum of 46.4 per cent, for an average of 67.1 per cent of entering students, dropped out. Antonov also calculated the cost to the state of those dropping out. As of 1890 the state was spending 175 rubles to educate one gymnasium pupil for one year. The amount it "lost" on students dropping out ranged from a high of 8,757,000 rubles to a low of 5,243,000 rubles, for an average of 7,582,000 rubles annually.

were encouraged to transfer to the equivalent grade in the terminal secondary school. "Owing to the realschulen, with their specialized sections beginning with the fifth year, even average talents will receive a useful direction," Tolstoy informed the districts. "It can be further assumed," he continued, "that with the smooth functioning of the total educational system not one talent will be lost to the country or turn out harmful to society."[24] The thoughtful design of the Minister of Education had made little impression over the years on the school-going public. His carefully designed realschule became known in popular parlance as "the trash can" of the gymnasium.

Tolstoy's successor feared that the realschule of 1872 with its emphasis on "general education of a practical nature" was offering too much enlightenment to persons who would be better off with strictly vocational training. To serve the country's developing industry and to curb at least one source of radicalism, Delianov proposed transforming the real into technical schools. The Council of State still contained a sufficient number of liberals from the previous reign to defeat this proposition. Instead, a revised statute for the controversial institution was devised which abolished its professional sections and increased the number of hours devoted to general subjects. After 1888 all realschulen were standardized with six grades, and a preparatory class was added. This loosened their contact with the urban schools but brought them closer to the gymnasiums.[25]

The Ministry's reluctance to narrow down the realschule cleared the way for the acceptance of the "general scheme of education" which had been elaborated by the future Minister of Finance, Vyshnegradsky, in 1884. The resulting statute of March 7, 1888, established a system of vocational schools under the Ministry of Education.[26] Previously, such agencies had been attached as needed to the appropriate departments of state. Now the desired facilities were organized at three levels. By the end of the reign of Alexander III there were four middle technical schools training 1,433 twelve- to sixteen-year-olds as assistant engineers and 48 lower technical schools giving instruction to 4,080. An indefinite number of elementary craft and industrial schools were also opened. The four-year course of the middle technical school was designed so as to receive pupils departing from different classes of the realschule. Specialization could be relied upon to ease some of the pressure on academic standards. The best permanent dikes to control the expensive and disruptive flood of misplaced persons in and out of the more sophisticated schools were the lower components of the Tolstoy system. Under Delianov's administration a trend became visible toward a more rational distribution of pupils throughout the various layers of schools. By 1899 the urban schools finally contained more pupils than the college preparatory institutions. This gain was partly due to an officially induced reduction of gymnasium enrollments. There was also considerable central and local support for speedier development of the municipal schools.[27]

Institutional modifications and orderly expansion took time. Meanwhile, the authorities searched for an immediate remedy to the mass assault on the intellectual schools. Waiting for students to drop out on their own seemed a wasteful use of people and facilities. A better course of action might be to admit only those candidates likely to complete the course. In specific terms, the best method for purging the gymnasiums of marginal pupils would be to restrict the entrance of children from the social layers that contributed most heavily to the drop-out population. Such action, if initiated from St. Petersburg, would inevitably raise the charge that the government was against education as such. Not surprisingly, therefore, St. Petersburg first left the question to the local authorities. Shortly after the restoration of the Tolstoy system, the individual school districts began restricting enrollments on their own initiative. The subtlest device was to raise academic standards; and in 1885 the schools imposed stricter control on pupils' daily work, higher qualifications for incoming pupils, closer supervision of promotions from one grade to the next, and more stringent demands in Russian language for non-Russian pupils. Almost immediately these measures exerted a noticeable effect. In 1885, 320 fewer boys dropped out of the gymnasiums than in 1884 and in 1886, 568 fewer than in the previous year. Recording these signs of progress, St. Petersburg congratulated the districts for ridding themselves of those not seriously committed to official goals and for concentrating on those who were "more reliable and appreciative of the schools in which they were being trained."*

---

* *Otchet MNP,* 1886, p. 82. On April 28, 1881, the Ministry of Education allowed pupils who received unsatisfactory marks in the written part of the maturity examination to take the oral examination, with the final decision based on both exercises. The district curators were soon complaining that because of the leniency of the 1881 rule there was a "slackening of pupil effort," and as a result the proportion of pupils passing the final test declined from 96.5 per cent in 1880 to 89.2 per cent in 1885 (*Otchet MNP,* 1885, pp. 81–82). St. Petersburg then introduced an oral and written examination at the end of the fourth year, with the injunction to let no one into the fifth year who had not acquired the capacity for work" (*ibid.,* pp. 68–69).

The official most deeply disturbed by what he considered structural flaws in the Tolstoy system was the Ober-Procurator of the Holy Synod. In the 1870's Konstantin Pobedonostsev had deplored the tendency of the gymnasiums to stimulate a "fallacious trend toward higher education." In the 1880's he felt his worst fears confirmed by the steep drop-out rate of lower-class elements from the academic schools and the large proportion of Jews registering in the same institutions. This closest adviser of Alexander III on cultural matters had always considered the presence of the Jews a special threat to the integrity of the regime. On no account ought these spiritual aliens be allowed unrestricted use of state agencies as elevators to the influential free professions or key posts in the imperial bureaucracy.

On the question of advancing the Orthodox poor scholastically, Pobedonostsev was motivated less by religious prejudices than by pedagogical views. If the state educated the downtrodden without alleviating their poverty, it ran the risk of converting the resigned into desperados. "To develop a person intellectually and then not give him the opportunity to practice what he has learned is to commit him to a form of moral self-torture that will eventually force him to seek improper outlets for his talents and energies. And in exactly the same vein—to begin a person's education and then to abandon him along the way to chance, which is almost never favorable, is to destroy him.... In specific terms, what this means is that we ought not to admit to university preparatory training children who lack the means to complete it or for whom we do not have a definite career in mind. And even if we have a professional goal in mind, we ought not to admit them if we lack the rubles necessary to carry their education through to its proper end."[28]

Tight money seemed to require a tight society, and one had only to review the history of the late Emperor to document the hazards of promoting enlightenment in a sluggish economy. In the spring of 1887 the Ministers of Education, Interior, and Finance held a series of meetings with the Ober-Procurator of the Holy Synod. Their immediate purpose was to formulate plans for preserving the integrity of the Tolstoy system's academic core while strengthening its Russian character. Their ultimate goal was political—to ensure the stability of the regime by more stringent regulations on applications to membership in the administrative and professional classes. Their willingness to defy public opinion on such a sensitive issue was an expression of their growing confidence in their ability to master the perplexities of tsardom's post-feudal pre-industrial age.[29] Out of the discussions between church and school, police and finance, came a proposal to exclude outright from the gymnasiums all but the privileged and proprietary classes. Acting on its own, the Ministry of Education immediately instructed its underlings not to admit to academic life "children of people occupying somewhat reprehensible professions." The Tsar rejected such crude discrimination as untimely and impractical. He ordered Delianov to find more subtle deterrents to those people whose "home conditions made them unsuitable for secondary education." Convening again, the committee of ministers had recourse to economic means, raising tuition in the secondary schools and elevating university lecture fees above the 50-ruble norm that had touched off the uproar in 1861.

The central authorities also scrutinized the preparatory classes. Their position within the gymnasium structure was peculiar. In order to conserve Treasury funds, the statute of 1871 had left their development in the hands of local officials. Because the introductory year was financed to a great extent by tuition payments, directors and pedagogical councils encouraged large enrollments. Most of the pupils entering the preparatory class would drop out; meanwhile, the added money they brought in provided funds for extra services at the more advanced and less populated levels of instruction. A financial boon to the schools, the preparatory class was also advantageous to the urban poor. Once enrolled in such a course, a boy could pass into the gymnasium proper without the entrance examination required of the sons of gentry and officials who had been tutored at home. In these ways the introductory form served as the main channel for the democratization of the elite schools. Although Tolstoy's purpose in creating the pre-Latin class had been to raise academic standards, the influx of lower-class, short-term students had the reverse effect. Observing that one-third of the 10,000 boys in the beginners' classes belonged to the very lowest strata of peasantry and craftsmen, the government cut off state funds for their support, thereby raising local tuition rates.[30]

St. Petersburg's attack on the preparatory classes aroused a great deal of resistance on the part of the schools, which were anxious to maintain a source of income independent of the Ministry. The furor over the classes was mild compared with the public reaction to the state's boldest effort to reduce the drop-out rate of the gymnasiums. On June 18, 1887, the Minister of Education published a circular that would haunt tsardom beyond the grave. The document began by directing the provinces to admit to university preparatory schools "only those children whose guardians can guarantee the proper domestic supervision and the necessary accommodations for scholarly pursuits." But then, as if fearful that the local authorities might not understand the intentions of the central government, Delianov spelled out in detail official motivation. Rigid observation of the above rule, he informed the districts, "will free the gymnasiums and progymnasiums from children of coachmen, menials, cooks, washerwomen, small shopkeepers, and the like. For, excepting occasionally gifted children, it is completely unwarranted for the children of such people to leave their position in life."[31] The June instruction became known as the cook's circular, and its tone and intent aroused public resentment against the regime of Alexander III as no other act of his reign. For the first time since the emancipation of the serfs, the state was resorting to outright social discrimination in the field of learning. The order was illegal, for it violated the clear text of the statute of 1871, which guaranteed access to the classrooms for all orders and estates.[32] It appeared to document not only "official lawlessness" but official hostility to national enlightenment. And as Chicherin had warned the government in 1861, a policy of discrimination would unite all sectors of society against it. Forty years after the publication of the offensive circular, Professor Kizevetter could still hear his uncle, a peripatetic Petersburg lawyer, describing the mood of the country in the summer of 1887. "In every railway carriage in which I traveled, everyone with one voice was crying out against this accursed letter and denouncing the name of Delianov in the most derogatory terms."*

* Kizevetter, p. 95. The Sunday edition of the *New York Times* carried the following despatch from Russia on October 2, 1887, p. 11: "RUSSIA'S SCHOOL POLICY CHANGES ANNOUNCED AS A BLOW TO NIHILISM. Peasants' Sons Not to Be Admitted to the Higher Institutions—Trade Schools for Their Benefit. St. Petersburg, Sept. 5. With great political insight and characteristic courage, Count Tolstoi, Minister of the Interior and *de facto* Premier, has just struck the most mortal blow which has been aimed at Nihilism since its origin some three-and-twenty years ago. A remarkable Ministerial circular was issued a few days since, restricting in a very considerable measure the accessions to the higher schools, gymnasia and universities." After distinguishing between the responsible "malcontents" who were "mostly people of wealth and of social and even official position who have tangible and material interests in the country that are being injuriously affected by the defective administration of the Government" and the revolutionists recruited "almost exclusively from [the] class of ex-students—men without a profession or regular means of livelihood," the *Times* correspondent went on to describe the "Nihilists" as "mere professional agitators who have nothing but their worthless lives to stake, and who resemble the carpetbag politician—

Centrifugal Tendencies within the Educational Bureaucracy, 1887–1895

The Minister of Education was credited with the first public relations blunder—the cook's circular. The curators of the border provinces were responsible for the second. It was, in fact, against Delianov's wish that edicts were published in July 1887 placing quotas on persons of Jewish origin in the gymnasiums and universities, limiting them to 10 per cent of the total student body within the pale of settlement, to 5 per cent outside of it, and to 3 per cent in the cities of St. Petersburg and Moscow.[33] The *numerus clausus* and the cook's circular constituted the central contraction policy of 1887. The policy's emotional effects are familiar enough to students of Russian history. The Jewish quotas are cited as typical examples of late nineteenth-century Christian-nationalist anti-Semitism. The cook's circular is cited as evidence of the reactionary character of tsardom after 1881. From the record a more revealing picture emerges.

In the school year 1886–87 there were 70,921 pupils in the 241 gymnasiums and progymnasiums of the Russian empire. In the autumn of 1887 this number had declined by 9,190, to 61,731. Over the next two years the population of the schools was reduced by another 2,990, until the smallest enrollment between the regicide of 1881 and the Revolution of 1905 was reached in the autumn of 1889, when 58,741 boys pursued courses in the state's preparatory schools. Thus, between 1886–87 and 1889–90 the elite secondary student bodies were reduced by 12,180—a loss of 17 per cent. With the opening of the fall semester in 1890, total enrollment increased for the first time since 1886. Although small—there were only 493 more pupils in the classical schools of the fifteen school districts in 1890 than in 1889—this resumption of growth signalized the end of recession and the renewal of expansion.[34]

The three-year decrement of 1887–1888–1889 was accomplished by reducing the number of incoming pupils. When the imperial gymnasiums opened in 1886, there were 15,008 entrants. In the September following Delianov's June circular, they admitted only 6,773; that is, they reduced admissions by 55 per cent. Given the normal pattern of increasing annual enrollments, this shrinkage meant that some 8,500 children who

---

minus even the carpetbag." In conclusion, the *Times* man pointed out the seriousness of the spread of Nihilism in Poland and the concern of the Russian government for the security of the area in the event of a war with Austria.

would have entered the academic core of the Tolstoy system at this time were kept from doing so by government action. The very next year, however, in the autumn of 1888, the same schools admitted 5,646 more students than the year of the cook's circular—an increment of 84 per cent in new registrations, which brought total entering enrollment to 12,419, only 2,589 less than in 1886, the last year before central intervention.

The reduction of beginners was the operating valve of the central contraction. In the fall of 1886, pupils coming into the gymnasiums and progymnasiums for the first time accounted for 21.2 per cent of the total student body. In the immediate wake of the cook's circular and the Jewish quotas, they accounted for only 9.5 per cent of overall enrollment. From 1888 onward the volume of entrants grew steadily, until by the end of the reign of Alexander III in 1894 the classical population was up 4,122 from the nadir of 1889.

The decline of the academic student bodies was accompanied by a reduction in the number of schools. There were 70 progymnasiums in 1887, but by 1894 they numbered 58.[35] During the same interval the gymnasiums declined from 176 to 166. The vacated premises were used as real, urban, and technical schools. Those institutions that remained seats of classical study contained fewer pupils. For years the government had allowed local authorities to open parallel sections with a combination of tuition funds and treasury aid when the number of pupils exceeded 50 in the original class. It was, of course, less expensive to overload existing facilities than to construct new buildings. As the volume of parallel classes declined, from 406 in 1886 to 278 within four years, it was hoped that the ampler space and quieter atmosphere would improve the quality of instruction. The relief was temporary. Even before the death of Alexander III, the Ministry once again allowed the schools to open parallel classes with local funds; and their number increased rapidly to 565 on the eve of the Revolution of 1905.[36]

The central authorities were not interested in decreasing merely the number of students but in decreasing specific categories. The initial cut fell heavily on the nonprivileged classes of both town and country. In the school year 1886–87, 25,388 urban commoners had been pursuing university preparatory studies. By 1888–89 this municipal contingent was reduced by 5,411, to 19,997, a loss of 21 per cent as a direct result of St. Petersburg's instructions to the regions. The small component of persons legally classified as peasants was also visibly affected. Before 1887 there had been 5,363 of them in the gymnasiums. Delianov reduced their numbers by 28 per cent, leaving only 3,779 within the network of the academic schools in 1888. In its simplified classification system the Ministry of Education included both Orthodox Russian and Jewish youths within the category of "townspeople." Scrutiny of the available records reveals that 2,233 of the 5,411 middle-class pupils eliminated from the gymnasiums were non-Christians. In other words, the Jewish quotas accounted for 43 per cent of the drop in urban components. This double-edged policy of discrimination—directed against an ethnic minority and a social class—increased the proportion of Orthodox in the schools by 5 per cent and the proportion of privileged in the schools by over 6 per cent at the expense of both Christian and non-Christian townsmen.

The statements of district and central authorities indicate that the contraction of 1887 was primarily an attempt to deal with a phenomenon that increasingly perplexes freedom-loving school administrators in the most advanced countries of the world—the drop-out problem.* In tsardom the failure of adolescents to finish the course was clearly related to the use of the academic schools by lower-class families that had neither the means nor the intention of permitting their children to complete the eight-year university preparatory program. Delianov's insulting letter was subsequently followed by modest but verifiable improvements on the educational scene. Local policies had already achieved some lessening of the drop-out rate in the years prior to central intervention. After the cook's circular the volume of premature departures declined still further. By 1890, 3,226 fewer pupils quit before graduation than in 1886. This staunching action was not a mere statistical illusion brought about by shrinkage of the number of people in the system. For the volume of those dropping out declined even more than the total population of the schools. During the year 1887–88, 17.8 per cent of the student body left before finishing, and in 1890, 15 per cent. During the steepest phase of the central contraction, between 1886 and 1890, total pupil population in the imperial gymnasiums and progymnasiums fell 17 per cent. During the same period the number of those dropping out declined 22 per cent.[37]

In their reports to the capital, eight educational regions supplied more detailed information than the others on premature student departures

---

* "Drop-out" was officially recognized as a national problem in the United States some 75 years after the tsarist experience with the adoption of Public Law 452 of the 88th Congress, "The Economic Opportunity Act of 1964" (78 Stat. 508).

for the two years 1885 and 1890. The curatorships in question distinguished between four types of departures: pupils leaving one school in order to transfer to another; those leaving in order to seek employment; those departing for family reasons; and those forced out by academic failure. The eight district reports not only reveal a more sophisticated approach to the drop-out problem; they enabled the authorities to gauge the effect of the central contraction policy on students departing for reasons of inadequate scholarship. After 1887 "flunking out" definitely declined. The sharpest drop was registered in Warsaw, where the share of academic failures fell from 23 per cent to 9.4 per cent of all premature departures. In this instance the strictures on lower-class children and minority groups were implemented by tighter requirements in the Russian language introduced locally before the cook's circular. The other educational region where the proportion of those "worthless for science" among those dropping out declined steeply was the Caucasus. In 1885 failures made up 19 per cent of the total exits. In 1890, the first year for which detailed information is available after 1887, students leaving school because of lack of success in their studies made up 8.8 per cent of all premature departures. Other districts followed the trend set by Warsaw and the Caucasus but to a lesser degree.[38]

The lowering of the drop-out rate in the empire was only one indication that the screening of applicants was improving the schools. There was also another piece of evidence available. The ultimate test of the gymnasiums as agencies worthy of the expenditure of state funds was not the volume of boys entering but the number leaving with Maturity Certificates. After 1887 the volume of graduates steadily increased, from 1,857 in the spring of 1886 to 3,383 in the spring of 1888, until by 1890 the gymnasiums produced 822 more graduates than in 1886, an increase of 22 per cent at a time when the overall population of the schools declined 17 per cent.[39]

Whereas the avowed purpose of the cook's circular was to restrict the entrance of the lower orders into the gymnasiums in order to preserve high academic standards, the maintenance of these standards was threatened by the continuing pressure of both gentry-official and democratic-minority elements to dilute the academic curriculum. By 1889 the provinces were voicing their concern to the capital that the latent hostility of the school-going public was turning into a direct attack on the classical program. The declining confidence of the teachers in the continuity of the program of studies and the expectation of the pupils that the hours devoted to Latin and Greek would be reduced or eliminated altogether were undermining morale. "Since the planting of the European school on Russian soil in the reign of the tsar-emancipator," the curator for Petersburg complained in 1889, "there has been no year during the last two decades more unfortunate for our gymnasiums than the present one."[40] Technically, the question of the secondary schools, as Tolstoy had cast it, turned on two subjects in the curriculum. On the surface the point at issue between the partisans of state and the devotees of public enlightenment was whether Greek and Latin ought to be indispensable prerequisites for entering the universities. But for all the pedagogical arguments for or against, the two language requirements were only the pretext of the underlying contest between the bureaucracy and the public for control of education, and through it of the future of Russian politics. The status of the ancient languages in the secondary program as a *sine qua non* of social advancement became the index of the state's actual power to mold the middle estate into an obedient service class. Any reduction of philological traditionalism would be more than a pedagogical adjustment. It would be tacit recognition of the strength of local society to maintain enclaves of public life within the bureaucratic structure of the regime.

As the feeling mounted in the provinces that something must be done to stabilize the curriculum, the Ministry of Education set up an investigating committee under an assistant Minister of Education. Recruited for the most part from language teachers, the assignment of the so-called small Volkonsky commission was to review the present method and range of teaching the ancient languages and to recommend changes. At the end of its studies, the group made several recommendations. Among the most important were the suggestions that less emphasis be placed on grammar, that more time be devoted to reading the ancient authors, and that the study of linguistic structure be eliminated after the sixth year. Pointedly, the committee did not recommend reducing the number of hours devoted weekly to the two tongues. No one wanted to open the question of hours, for this could lead into a review of the entire general educational question. It was Pobedonostsev who opened the question of distribution of class hours by gaining the Tsar's assent to intensified catechism in the secular schools.

The increase in the hours devoted to religion in the gymnasiums led to the formation of the large Volkonsky commission. This body included several curators, members of the Council of Ministers, educational officials, university professors, directors, and teachers. Guided by Delianov's instructions to preserve but simplify the classical curriculum, the committee recommended reducing the time devoted to Latin from 49 to 46 hours a week and Greek from 36 to 35. Meanwhile, the Council of State had taken up the business. Populated as it was by ex-officials friendly to the modern bias in education, it produced a plan that would have reduced Latin from 49 to 36 hours a week. Explaining that concentration was the pedagogical essence of the Tolstoy system, Delianov rejected the proposal of the empire's supreme deliberative body. The conflict between the Ministry and the Council of State was resolved by compromise. On July 20, 1890, new lesson plans appeared that reduced Latin from 49 to 42 hours and Greek from 36 to 33.[41] Even in the face of this moderate action, Delianov warned that the new schedules thinned classicism to the breaking point. The issue was clear. Either the state would have to regain control of entrance to the gymnasiums, admitting only academically qualified students, or yield to the public a voice in curriculum and academic standards as well.

The modification of the academic program amidst the furor over the cook's circular was one symptom of slipping monolithic control. Another was the failure of the contraction of 1887 to rout the laggards out of the gymnasiums and into the realschulen. Throughout the three-year period of sharpest fluctuation in the population of the university preparatory schools, both the enrollment and the social composition of the realschulen remained remarkably steady except for a noticeable influx of boys from the gentry-official class into the real schools of the Moscow area.

The central contraction policy of 1887 was the autocracy's most determined effort to manipulate the academic machinery since Admiral Putiatin's abortive coup in 1861. The effort to restrain the march of the poor and the deprived on the elite classrooms tested administrative absolutism in a sensitive area, at the contact points between the circuits of central and provincial authority. Contemporary opinion focused on the presumably nationwide impact of the government's bias for Orthodoxy and aristocracy in the European school. Imperial results, however, were merely the sum of separate provincial actions; and the two together gave a practical demonstration of the working effectiveness of the Tolstoy system's centralized structure. The ability of St. Petersburg to guide social development rested, in the end, on strict and prompt compliance of regional authorities to the controlling ministry. Under Nicholas I, barracks discipline had been the rule. Count Stroganov's limited defense of the Moscow school district against St. Petersburg had been an exception, based on personal ties to the royal family. Pirogov's career in the Ukraine had dramatized the value of provincial antecedents to central reform. His patron, Aleksandr Golovnin, had permanently injected vitality into the curatorships both by improving conditions of employment and by selecting district heads out of the ranks of experienced educators rather than from highly connected persons from the military and civil service.[42] Although Tolstoy emphasized conformity (the curator of Odessa assured him that his only desire was to be "the exact executor of superior designs"[43]), he had continued the practice of placing qualified men in provincial positions of authority.

The most illustrious of his appointments was the scion of impoverished Ukrainian gentry. Kirill Yanovsky had begun his career in education as the heir of Pirogov in a provincial district school.[44] The professionalization of district administration by the appointment of officials like him assumed special importance after 1881. For with its expulsion from the heights of executive power, official liberalism took refuge in the outlying areas. Between 1880 and 1882 four Ministers of Education succeeded one another in rapid succession, each registering the political direction of the moment. In the midst of this uncertainty at the top, regional levels remained relatively stable. Yanovsky, for instance, took up his post in the Caucasus in 1873 and retained it for 29 years, until his death in 1902. Hopes for less compulsion and more cooperation in state schooling depended on the capacity of provincial officials to adapt central directives to local needs. Between 1886 and 1894 the Caucasus did not follow the imperial pattern of decline in enrollment, but actually increased the size of its academic population. It also registered a slight rise in democratic content during the period of sharpest discrimination. Finally, it registered a rise in minority elements during the stress on Russification. Other districts, notably Riga and Kharkov, also diverged in significant ways.

The reactions of Yanovsky and his fellow curators to the central contraction policy are contained in the annual reports published somewhat haphazardly by the Minister of Education. By unraveling and coordinating this material, it is possible to clarify the sectional handling of cook's circular and Jewish quotas and to assess the vitality of local initiative within the educational hierarchy at a time when Pobedonostsev and Tolstoy were seeking to reverse the decentralizing tendencies set loose by the great reforms.

By the fourth quarter of the nineteenth century the Russian empire was divided into fifteen educational districts with uniform administrative procedures but of varying ethnic complexity, social pattern, and size.[45] Five Asian districts—Orenburg, West Siberia, East Siberia, Turkestan, and the Amur-Pacific coastal area—accounted for less than 6 per cent of the total enrollment in the gymnasiums and progymnasiums. Of these five frontier units of jurisdiction only Orenburg was organized as a regular educational region on the European Russian pattern. With a gymnasium population of less than 2,000, it alone accounted for half of the university preparatory population east of the Urals. Of the ten European districts, four—Moscow, St. Petersburg, Kiev, and Warsaw—were of comparatively equal student population—between 10,000 and 8,500. Together they accounted for 52 per cent of all the gymnasium pupils in the empire. These four major regions were followed by two middle-sized administrative units—Kharkov and Odessa—which, with their enrollments of between 6,000 and 7,000 apiece, together accounted for almost 19 per cent of total enrollment. The four minor European districts—Vilna, Riga, Kazan, and the Caucasus—were also comparable in size. With enrollments of less than 5,000, each contained between 5 and 6 per cent of the nation's preparatory scholars. Combined, they accounted for 23 per cent of all candidates for the Maturity Certificate.

During the brief operational phase of the central contraction (the three years from 1887 through 1889) the population of the academic schools throughout the empire shrank 17 per cent. Two districts, Kharkov and Warsaw, reduced their enrollment significantly more than the imperial average, and four districts, Orenburg, Petersburg, the Caucasus, and Riga, reduced theirs markedly less. Kharkov came down 20 per cent, Riga less than 10. Across the land new enrollments were cut back 55 per cent in 1887 relative to 1886 and increased 84 per cent in 1888 relative to 1887. The immediate response of individual curatorships to the Ministry's directives ranged from a 60 per cent reduction in St. Petersburg to a 23 per cent reduction in Riga. The following year the 6 per cent increase of incoming pupils in Riga contrasted with 300 per cent increases in Vilna, Warsaw, and Orenburg.

The cook's circular was expressly directed against the influx of townspeople into the academic schools. In the empire as a whole on the eve of the imperial policy, "townsmen" made up 35 per cent of the enrollment of the university preparatory schools. By 1894 their share had been reduced to 31 per cent. In 1886 two districts, Odessa and Riga, were more democratic than the empire as a whole and five districts were less. In Odessa more than 50 per cent of gymnasium pupils belonged to the urban class, whereas in the Caucasus less than 30 per cent were townsmen. In response to the central command to keep "sons of cooks and washerwomen" out of the academic schools, Odessan authorities reduced their urban student population by more than 13 per cent. At the same time the authorities in Kharkov increased the percentage of townsmen in their academic schools by almost 3 per cent.[46]

The reduction of commoners automatically raised the proportion of the privileged in the European schools. But here again the districts exhibited a variety of responses. Whereas in Odessa nobility and officials increased more than 13 per cent, their proportion of the student population in the Caucasus declined 2 per cent. In Warsaw the aristocratic trend was anti-Polish. Seventy per cent of the pupils who left the gymnasiums and progymnasiums of the Warsaw school district in 1890 for academic reasons owed their failure to difficulties with the Russian language.[47] Supplementing social discrimination with ethnic-religious bias, the central bureaucracy increased the proportion of Russian Orthodox in the gymnasiums by 5 per cent. District responses to the central policy of Russification of the European schools varied from Odessa, where the Orthodox Christian component expanded by more than 12 per cent, to Kharkov, where it fell off by more than 2 per cent. There were also modifications of central Jewish quotas in the provinces. While Odessa was cutting the percentage of Jews by more than 17 per cent, the Caucasus and Kazan made insignificant reductions, and Kharkov more than held the line.[48]

Analysis of district participation in the central contraction of 1887 thus reveals rather wide divergencies both in degree and timing of action. Whether major, middling, or minor, the educational regions responded in no uniform way to central direction except one—they all abandoned the policy quickly. After the death of Alexander III in 1894, officials ceased paying even lip service to the spirit of 1887. Clearly the fulfillment of St. Petersburg's commands by the provinces could not be taken for granted. Several districts, in fact, went directly against the trend of state instructions. There is further evidence that local authorities on their own initiative purged the central contraction policy of its repulsive social bias.

Between January 1, 1887, and January 1, 1889, the student population of the gymnasiums declined by 11,149. This loss was divided among the various social classes. Sons of clergy accounted for 5.4 per cent of the reduction, Christian peasantry for 13.4 per cent, Jewish townsmen for 20 per cent, Christian townsmen for 28 per cent, and the nobility official estate for 28 per cent. If the Jewish town population is kept distinct from the Christian, the contraction can be seen falling with equal force on the nobility and townsmen. In 1887 alone, 4,402 sons of the privileged classes were removed from the academic rolls. Between 1887 and 1889 the number of Christian townsmen declined by 3,178 (the number of Jews by 2,233) and the number of gentry officials by even more—3,233. Repelled by the crude phrasing of the cook's circular, the public concluded that the Ministry of Education was more interested in social reaction than in academic progress. Closer study of results, however, brings to light a fundamental difference of approach between St. Petersburg, where policies were formulated on paper, and the provinces, where they were actually carried out. The districts laid more emphasis on the academic goals than on the social biases of the central policy. Local authorities used the cook's circular to rid themselves of academic deadwood—aristocratic as well as plebeian, Orthodox as well as non-Christian. Even in the aftermath of 1881 the higher levels of government could not turn the educational apparatus on and off at will as in the days of Nicholas I. As the state educated the people, it made itself more complex and had to rely increasingly on its subordinate officials. As these became more professional, they became less bureaucratic. The variety and direction of district responses to the central contraction policy of 1887 indicate that the Ministry of Education was becoming sophisticated enough to develop independent life in the provinces. State education was showing signs of becoming a public agency.

Chapter Five

The Official Thaw of Academic Formalism, 1895–1905

For some time now, teachers and parents of students in the gymnasiums and realschulen have been decrying the deficiencies of these institutions. They are disturbed by the following symptoms: by the secondary school's estrangement from the family and its bureaucratic character, which introduces a dry formalism and sterility into teaching and places teachers and students in false relationships; by the neglect of the individual personality of the students and the neglect of moral and physical training; by specialization at too early an age, which commits children to one particular kind of occupation before their natural talents and inclinations have been revealed; by the daily overload of abstractions imposed on pupils, especially the younger ones; by the confusion of programs filled with superfluous demands; by neglect of Russian language, Russian history, and Russian literature, as well as by the pupils' ignorance of the contemporary world (these two failings robbing the school of a vital, national character); by the mis-emphasis on ancient languages and improper teaching of them, so that the aim of classical education, despite the large number of hours spent on it, is not attained; by the lack of mental maturity, which prevents secondary school graduates from doing successful university work; by the insufficient preparation of realschule graduates for advanced study in specialized institutes.

NIKOLAI BOGOLEPOV, *Minister
of Education, 1899*

Mounting Pressures for Change, 1895–1899

The stirring to life of local initiative in the Russian empire between 1890 and 1905 was celebrated at the time as the Public Movement.[1] Throughout the period, educated society was committed to emancipation from the state bureaucracy. Within the educational world, the awakening of initiative expressed itself as professional irritation with bureaucratic routine and personal dissatisfaction with the habit of assenting simply on authority. The ensuing revolt against scholastic formalism eventually touched every phase of academic life. At the university level

it renewed interest in the development of a scientific approach to pedagogy, a field that had lain practically fallow since Ushinsky's early passage from the scene. Among government officials and academic personnel it inspired support for channeling considerably more Treasury funds
into elementary and vocational schools in order to redress at last the
long-standing imbalance from concentration of state resources on the
education of the few to the neglect of the many. In 1890 it was pointed
out that the Ministry of Education was spending over 9 million rubles
to educate 71,522 youths in the gymnasiums and universities of the empire, but only 2.2 million rubles on the training of 20,218 young men in
its technical schools. Observing this emphasis on intellectual training,
Professor A. Kireev advised the government to multiply the lagging
vocational facilities tenfold. Such a program would help drain off the
weaker pupils from the academic schools.[2]

Even more significant for the future course of state enlightenment
was the view of Nikolai Bogolepov. A popular professor of Roman law
at Moscow University, he was the last rector to be chosen by his colleagues according to the charter of 1863. Subsequently he served as
curator of the Moscow district before becoming Delianov's successor as
Minister of Education. Speaking in terms reminiscent of Kochubei's
advice to Alexander I, Bogolepov as early as 1893 felt that the empire
needed schools for the masses even more than it needed universities.[3]
The task, however, of educating the peasantry could only be accomplished by an adept and willing professional class.

For a decade after 1890 the official agency for producing such a class,
the Tolstoy system, remained structurally unchanged. Concurrently, the
society upon which it depended for recruits began to stir from within.
In the late 1880's district reaction to the central contraction policy, combined with the government's modification of the classical regime, revealed the gathering strength of educated opinion. In the early 1890's
domestic catastrophe exposed the weakness of the bureaucracy and the
nation's need for public initiative. As the magnitude of the famine and
cholera epidemics of 1891–93 threatened to collapse the state machinery
for relief, direct aid to the countryside was organized by zemstvo gentry, municipal employees, and student volunteers. In 1894 the death of
Alexander III aroused further hopes in liberal, socialist, and professional
circles that the "leaden coffin lid" might be lifted from the spontaneous
energies of the population. The resurgence of public spirit was promptly
registered in the schools. In 1895, while the Ministry of Education was

still officially committed to the restrictive principles of 1887,[4] gymnasium enrollment jumped by more than 3,500 pupils over the previous year.

On the surface the accession of Nicholas II was the smoothest since the Romanovs were elected to the throne, and considerable pains were taken to preserve the façade of continuity between father and son. Pobedonostsev stayed on in the Holy Synod, a post he would occupy until 1905. His period of active intervention was over, and in the years ahead his counsel in the face of rising difficulties was invariably the same, namely, to do nothing at all. Delianov remained in the Ministry of Education. Discredited by the cook's circular, he appeared to many to have no other function but to liquidate whatever public and federalist tendencies were left from the era of great reforms. Dmitri Tolstoy had been dead for several years. But his reputation for reaction had passed to his chief assistant, Viacheslav Plehve, whom none other than Loris-Melikov had chosen to direct the police department after the absorption of the internal security forces into the Ministry of the Interior. Of Lithuanian family, a graduate in law of the University of St. Petersburg, and a zealous Russifier, he was already attracting supporters from among conservative gentry and traditionalists in the civil service as the future leader of bureaucratic nationalism.

Plehve's rival for the favor of the Tsar was another holdover from the previous regime. After establishing his reputation in railroad management, Sergei Witte had been appointed Minister of Finance in 1892. During his ten years in office he directed the investment of more than two-thirds of the state's annual expenditures into the internal improvement of the country, the highest proportion for any period between 1861 and 1917.[5] The subordination of agrarian interest to industrial, the priority of economic growth over political control, the preference for experiment at home to adventurism abroad—these characteristics of his policies between 1892 and 1902 became identified as the Witte system. By the turn of the century its creator was the most universally unpopular man in the country since Dmitri Tolstoy, and for many of the same reasons. For Witte in the 1890's, like Tolstoy in the 1870's, represented the Petrine tradition of enlightened despotism with its contempt for the nobility as parasites, its indifference toward the intelligentsia as irrelevant, and its criticism of the bureaucracy as slack and ill-trained.

Like the Tolstoy system, the Witte system depended for its initiative on the tsar, but for its realization on the educated class. By the end of the century the population of the towns, growing faster than the population as a whole, had doubled, from 8.1 million in 1860 to 16.7 million by 1900, increasing the empire's urban mass from 10.6 per cent to 13 per cent of the whole. Urbanization, combined with the impetus given to schooling at all levels but particularly at the secondary, generated a sizable stockpile of trained persons opposed to socialist radicalism and suspicious of political liberalism, but prepared to challenge the supremacy of the state bureaucracy and demand more freedom of action for qualified personnel in public, academic, and business life, as well as in government service.[6] The Minister of Finance himself represented a not uncommon type of university graduate (Odessa, 1871), devoted to the monarchy but more sensitive to the global environment than Slavophilic nationalists, loyal to the Orthodox faith but aware of the international importance of the Jews, and anxious to apply his liberal education to practical concerns without interference from either radicals or bureaucrats.[7]

By the mid-1890's a considerable number of the country's high school and college graduates were dissatisfied with the abstract, legalistic, administrative approaches of the previous reign to the nation's perennial problems. They were likewise determined to be up to date, businesslike, and realistic. Political pragmatism at the turn of the century meant broadening the scope of educated participation in government. No matter how accomplished and conscientious, the individual could do little in isolation. To amplify his impact beyond his professional specialty, he would have to organize and create an independent sector of Russian life capable of dealing with the civil service on morally equal and socially competitive terms.

In a land where freedom of assembly was meticulously circumscribed and political associations outlawed, the active and the concerned joined professional groupings. The oldest learned organization in the country, the Imperial Free Economic Society, which had been chartered by Catherine II, offered a broad appeal. Its location in St. Petersburg provided resident and visiting experts from a variety of callings with a permanent platform for exchanging views on a wide range of controversial subjects.[8] Another learned group was the Pirogov Society of Russian Doctors. Founded in 1885, it provided the medical fraternity with a service that the more tightly controlled pedagogical estate lacked, an organizational arena. Graduates of the gymnasiums, realschulen, and institutes of higher learning who desired to maintain continuous working contact with their comrades of student days joined the committees on literacy. Based in St.

Petersburg and Moscow, these groups supplied needy rural and urban areas with pedagogical information, library supplies, and limited instruction. While doing so, they also prepared hundreds of interested people for the anticipated day of passing from popular enlightenment to public leadership.[9]

In the meantime, the rapid increase of railroad trackage was making domestic travel easier. As cross-country communication became more convenient, the professional conferences allowed by the government became more popular. Technical talk invariably turned political, if for no other reason than that little could be accomplished in science, agriculture, or industry without the participation or permission of the state bureaucracy. In 1896 two memorable meetings, held under the patronage of the Minister of the Interior—the all-Russian commercial-industrial congress and the all-Russian congress on technical education—brought together hundreds of specialists from all parts of the country. The general sessions, in particular, served as pre-parliamentary forums, where the conflicting, overlapping, and mutual interests of the educated class could at least be aired from a public platform before a nationwide audience. It was at the congress on technical education that Kirill Yanovsky attacked the formalism of the general educational system.[10]

Two years later Anton Chekhov furnished the public with its sharpest image of the schoolmaster type produced by bureaucratic centralism. "The Man in the Instrument Case" (*Chelovek v futliare*) was Belikov, instructor of Greek in the gymnasium of a provincial town, who even in fine weather went about in a warm coat and galoshes, with an umbrella. "His umbrella was carried in a case, and his watch was in a case of gray suede, and when he took out his penknife to sharpen a pencil, even the knife was in a little case. His face also appeared in a case, since he always hid it behind his turned-up collar. He always wore dark glasses and an undervest, and stopped his ears with cotton wool; when he got into a carriage he ordered the top raised. In essence, with this man an unremitting and insurmountable tendency could be observed to surround himself with a shell, to create for himself, so to speak, a protective package, which would isolate him and protect him from external influences. Reality disturbed him, frightened him, kept him in a continual state of anxiety; and perhaps to justify his diffidence, his abhorrence of actuality, he was always praising the past and things that never were. The classical languages that he taught were for him like the galoshes and umbrella with which he hid himself from real life.... Belikov even tried to hide his thoughts in a case. For him the only clear statements were circulars and newspaper articles prohibiting something. When a circular forbade the students to be on the streets after nine in the evening, or if some article or other forbade carnal love, this was for him something clear, precise. It was forbidden—and that was the end of it."[11]

But even as the artist composed his comic lines, the classrooms were filling with another kind of pedagogue. The new breed had been nourished on the works of Pirogov and Ushinsky, and kept abreast of contemporary movements at home and abroad through two progressive journals, *Russian School* and *Educational Messenger,* both of which began publication in 1890.[12] The teachers who drew strength and cohesion from these literary sources sought ways to mediate the continuing friction between the school, with its insistence on the subordination of the child to a general order, and the family, with its pride in individual accomplishment. Instead of "intruding into the family circle as an alien force," they treated the classroom as a society in miniature and the child as the reflection of the fears and hopes of the nation at large. Within this context, teaching could be organized as a dialogue between two subjects, the pupil growing to maturity and the teacher learning from the child, rather than as a chain of command in which troops of adolescents were drilled in encyclopedic knowledge and uncritical obedience.[13]

Increasingly troubled by the hostility of the public toward the gymnasiums and realschulen, curators, directors, and teachers regretfully admitted that in the past, informal person-to-person contacts between themselves and pupils' families had generally proved superficial or embarrassing. Looking ahead, they were not yet ready to support direct representation of parents and guardians in the pedagogical councils. Even progressive teachers were hesitant on that score. They feared that in a conflict most parents would side with state authority. Discussions on ways of attracting public support for the schools invariably turned to the post of honorary curator. The constitution of 1871 had given to local groups and private persons contributing substantial sums to a school the right to elect an honorary curator to audit the expenditure of donated funds. Some teachers were anxious to have the office extended so that the honorary curator would not only supervise fiscal affairs but undertake some of the general supervisory duties currently reserved to the state inspector. District officials were understandably dubious about the proposition, since any encroachment on the inspector's power would inevitably weaken their own. They dismissed such proposals as beyond their competence. If local zemstvos, dumas, gentry, or merchants wanted more power on the pedagogical councils of local schools, it was up to them to petition the government themselves.

When the topic moved from public inspection of finances and discipline to public interference in the academic program, administrators and classroom teachers closed ranks. In the considerable number of secondary schools that received substantial amounts of aid from local sources the staffs already felt themselves dependent enough on society. Organized public influence should be directly connected with and restricted to material support. As for public meddling in education as such, the curator of the Moscow district formulated the view popular with the profession: "We are not competent to judge the form that social organization should take. We can judge only one aspect, namely, that public influence should not exceed its bounds, that the academic and educational side of the matter should remain, as before, in the hands of professional pedagogues."[14]

Throughout the 1890's and early 1900's, administrators and teachers maintained a united front against any interference on the part of the community in the academic program. When they considered the internal administration of the school, the latent conflict between superiors and subordinates surfaced. For his own position, the director was dependent upon nomination by the district, with the confirmation of St. Petersburg. As enunciated in the charters of 1871 and 1872, his chief duties included supervising both academic instruction and moral training, presiding over the pedagogical council and the financial committee, maintaining the physical plant, and faithfully executing all orders from above. As a state official he guarded the autocracy's interest in the secondary schools. It was his duty to evaluate the staff from the political point of view. His directives, issued to implement ministerial and district circulars, demanded unquestioning obedience. The teachers were at his mercy. For he recommended the hiring of regular staff to the district and recommended dismissal for incompetence. He had total discretion over the employment of hourly personnel as well as assignment of extra hours and duties with extra pay to the regular staff.

By the final decade of the century, the teachers viewed the director's appointive power as a barrier to any serious effort "to raise their moral and professional position in the eyes of the public and the pupils."[15] As they became more conscious of their dignity, they looked to the district for protection. The idea became more popular among them that the power to appoint, dismiss, and transfer ought to be vested in the curators, with the directors reduced to consultants. In all their activity, professional and social, the instructors preferred answering to the district alone.

The director was not only an executive officer, he was also a pedagogue who, until 1905, invariably taught the classics. As the local agent of the state bureaucracy he was independent of the classroom teachers. As a classroom teacher himself, he was their colleague. His efforts to guide the teaching and to improve upon it could not be based simply on orders, but were dependent on his prestige with the staff. By the end of the nineteenth century an effort on the director's part to dictate pedagogical formulas might still intimidate the weak. It would only arouse the antipathy of the strong teachers, those most respected by the students. "Recognition of the authority of the director as pedagogue can only be freely given, and depends to a large extent on his personal qualities, his learning, and his experience."[16] With the refinement of classroom skills, the bureaucratic routine of an earlier age became intolerable.[17]

There had been a time when the low cultural level of the teachers justified administrative formalism. But as they became more competent, they became restive. To emancipate themselves from the "kingdom of deadening paper work,"[18] they looked to the pedagogical council. As defined by the statutes of 1871 and 1872, this body gave the teachers an audible voice within the school. Practice, however, had impaired the council's competence. Even routine parental petitions on such matters as whether to allow an ill child to repeat a class were passed up to the curator's office for decision. Whereas the directors appreciated the advantages of a collective façade to protect them from the regional bureaucracy, the teachers were interested in genuine autonomy. For them, the director represented absolutism and the council the principle of representative government. With a strong council the director would become "the guardian of the law instead of the law."[19]

Divided on staff organization, directors and teachers united on pupil control. Together they challenged the existing method for measuring student achievement. The Ministry of Education had established throughout the empire the so-called numbers system (*ballovaia sistema*) for grading. Under its comprehensive rules the first twenty minutes of every class hour in the gymnasiums and realschulen were given over to testing orally the individual's knowledge of the lengthy home assignments. The teacher then graded the performance on a scale from one to five: five was excellent, four was good, three was satisfactory, two was inadequate, and one was unsatisfactory. The defenders of digital evaluation justified it as an attempt to rationalize measurement. A mechanical procedure, so the argument went, protected the student from personal bias. The numbers recorded under the immediate impression of the daily recitation were an official notation. They provided the statistical basis for the quarterly grades which were reported to the parents. The final grades at the end of the year were derived by simple arithmetic from the quarterly numbers and transmitted to the district. If a pupil was attaining mere twos, it was the parents' responsibility, not the school's, to provide remedial tutoring. The final grade determined whether a child would be admitted to the examination at the end of the school year, which alone determined passage to the next class. The numbers system also set up a strict record of excellence, a kind of junior Table of Ranks within the school. In conversations among teachers and pupils, a boy was identified as a "two" or a "three" or a "five." Seating in the classrooms was according to this rank, so that everyone knew everyone's place at all times within the scholastic hierarchy.

The students generally considered the numbers system a lesser evil than periodic examinations. Quarterly and final testing was more of a nervous strain than class performance; it was impossible to avoid and concentrated one's future in a few arbitrary acts. The mechanics of daily grading, on the other hand, were such that an astute child could play the game to his own advantage. In the classrooms crowded with from 50 to 60 persons, one's chances of being called frequently were greatly reduced. In classes that met only twice a week, a person was rarely disturbed more than once a quarter. After interrogation he could relax for weeks, even months. In their criticisms of the numbers system, teachers noted that pupils were adept at figuring out the pattern of call and calculating their own turns in advance. The statistical character of the evaluation further informed them of the exact effort required to attain the minimal passing grade of three. A damaging two could be balanced with a substantial four or two respectable threes. The authorities detected no significant public dissatisfaction with the existing procedure. It was simple and uncluttered. Parents were upset only when their children received low numbers. Defenders of the status quo pointed out that the strongest objection to revising the current procedure was that people were used to it and would resent a change to anything more sophisticated.

The attack on the formalistic measurement of achievement came not from outside but from within the school. In 1896 a number of educators at the second congress on technical education used the occasion to attack the numbers system for disrupting good relations between teachers and taught, the school and the family. It not only corrupted the pupils morally, but gave class work a purely formal character. On another occasion, the director of a provincial gymnasium accused the method of lessening the opportunity for a "vital dialogue" in the classroom.[20] It branded the learner in difficulty. The director of the Tula gymnasium accused his colleagues of "playing" the system. Teachers, he observed, used the noncommittal number three to avoid trouble. Critics further questioned the alleged objectivity of the device. No two instructors, it was pointed out, could agree on the exact meaning of the numbers on the scale, particularly the borderline between two and three, which determined whether a student could stay in school, or between three and four, which often determined whether he would actually advance to the institutes of higher learning. Analyzing the situation, advocates of greater flexibility insisted that the established method lumped a number of things without making necessary distinctions: general information, homework, degree of attention, and the mood of the teacher. In reality, the teacher was not a detached critic but "an arbitrary tyrant dispensing rewards and blows on inner feeling."[21]

The method also put the teachers under pressure. Either they adhered to strictly mathematical averages, ignoring attenuating circumstances and individual conditions, or they juggled the numbers to arrive at a more desirable average, thus running the risk of having to explain later to parents and authorities their flexible arithmetic. A final defect of the numbers system was that it shifted the burden of instruction from the classroom to the home. Within the school the procedure used up so much time that for a third of the class period most of the pupils sat idly by while the master grilled a few of their unlucky companions on the previous assignment. Thus, little time was left for explaining new ma-

terial to the class as a whole. In effect, the routine reduced the pedagogue to a mere quizzer. In consequence, he surrendered his teaching
function to the domestic tutor, the *repetitor* or crammer, often an impoverished university student or one who had not completed the course,
who drilled weak scholars for a ruble an hour.

As the twentieth century approached, several school districts experimented with liberalizing the grading procedure. The ultimate responsibility for determining a pupil's final mark rested by law with the pedagogical council. Although the teachers resented their decisions being
overruled by their colleagues, many directors favored the use of the
council as a device through which they could exert influence on a decision closely affecting relations between school and family. One provincial director suggested that commissions, composed of all the teachers
instructing a given class, assume responsibility for evaluating pupils. In
the sessions of these class committees the class counselor would be fully
informed of the reasons behind a boy's failure. He could then make a
detailed report to the parents concerned. As time went on, some authorities considered abolishing the numbers system altogether, as did the privately supported German gymnasium in 1897.[22] The members of the
Moscow Pedagogical Society, where professors from the university met
with secondary school teachers to discuss questions of joint interest, recommended caution. Ideally, the method of notation should be replaced
by written appraisals, Professor A. I. Kirpichnikov, dean of the historical-philological faculty of Moscow University, maintained. But, he concluded, it was impossible to abolish the system unless there were a
sweeping reorganization and expansion of the schools which would reduce the number of pupils in a given class.[23] Teachers, nevertheless,
favored the immediate abolition of daily and monthly scores. Instead,
the pedagogical council should determine a pupil's final grade "according to its inner conviction."[24]

Although deploring current practices, school officials insisted that it
was difficult to change the numbers system alone, since it was enmeshed
in a network of central rules, directives, and regulations that guided the
academic procedure of the school at every step, particularly the last. The
climactic function of the classical gymnasium was to administer the state
maturity examinations. Since these determined whether after eight years
of parental sacrifice and personal toil a young man would acquire the
prized maturity certificate, the government guarded the final rites of

acquisition with minute attention. The maturity, that is, the exit diploma and the tests leading up to it, incorporated the essence of academic formalism. In this instance, as with daily, quarterly, and annual ratings, criticism did not stem from the public. Parents actually tended to judge a school not by its standards but by the volume of pupils taking the exit examinations. Since more than 95 per cent of those admitted to the competition achieved success, the current method was popular as "an umbrella for the weak student" to get into the university. At century's end, the pedagogical council of a provincial gymnasium complained that "an ideal frame of mind is almost never observed among parents. Education as end in itself hardly interests them at all. They expect from it purely utilitarian ends, namely, the quickest and easiest acquisition of a certificate of maturity, and perhaps access to an institution of higher learning. For this reason, demanding teachers and academic subjects not bearing directly on furtherance of a career are extremely unpopular."[25]

Although some educators defended the value of the maturity examination as an opportunity for the individual "to express his personality apart from the mass," most agreed with the director of the Imperial Lycée of Tsarevitch Nicholas that the battery of written and oral tests assessed memory rather than stimulating intelligence and aroused fear rather than awakening the appetite for learning.[26] Skepticism toward the maturity examination developed over the years into feuding between the universities and the preparatory schools. Professors attacked the system for failing to keep the incompetent out of the higher schools.[27] To filter out marginal applicants, the rector of Moscow University suggested adding a qualifying examination. Teachers objected to this proposal on several grounds. It would place students in double jeopardy, once in the spring and again in the fall. Further, if the universities began excluding those with a rating of three, the schools would award more fours. A counterproposal, that the established procedure be replaced by a qualifying examination in the hands of a board of neutral teachers and university professors, would have been a return to the faculty examinations in use before 1871. It aroused little enthusiasm. Professors were reluctant to serve, and administrators recoiled before the logistic and security problems of transporting hundreds of excited adolescents to the major cities and housing them there for weeks. Many teachers, on the other hand, were openly skeptical of the competence of a committee composed of specialists who had never had classroom contact. How could it assess intellectual and moral qualities more accurately in a few minutes than the pedagogical council and the class counselors had over years of close association?[28]

The maturity examination did more than take the measure of the student; it also tested the school. Each year the district curator's advisory council, composed of professors and directors, drafted the written tests within the guidelines of the comprehensive rules of 1872. After the results were in from the schools, another committee, recruited this time solely from the scholarly community, reviewed the examinations subject by subject and school by school. After comparing the performance of one gymnasium with another and one year with the next, it published its findings and recommendations for restricted circulation within the educational hierarchy. On the basis of the Moscow regional review of 1890, for example, the gymnasium in the city of Riazan was officially denoted "the worst in the district."* Whatever its justification, such criticism aroused abiding resentment. The ensuing controversy over the maturity examination as an instrument of institutional quality control found the schools allied against the bureaucracy. The schools maintained that if the government wanted to check their performance, it should devise a means independent of the testing of students.

For their part, district officials accused the schools of adopting a "philanthropic" attitude toward grading. Curators laid greater weight on the written part of the examination, which could be subsequently reviewed.[29] The teaching staffs preferred to rely more heavily on the informal oral periods. They also opposed automatic district review of the written results together with the routine transmission of the protocol describing the oral examinations. Instead, they preferred a simple journal containing the reasons for a pupil's failure. The administration would then have detailed background material with which to fend off the objections of disappointed parents. The schools also desired to com-

---

* *Otchet o pis'mennykh ispytaniakh zrelosti, proizvedennykh v gimnaziiakh moskovskago uchebnago okruga,* 1890, p. 72. On March 31, 1884, the Ministry of Education provided 1,500 rubles to each district with a university to cover the costs of engaging professors to review the written maturity examinations (*Otchet MNP*, 1885, pp. 83–84). Representing the universities, district reviewers tended to apply higher standards than the examination committees, which represented the secondary schools. In 1895 the maturity candidates in the Moscow district wrote on the theme "Pushkin freed our literature from the spirit of imitation, which had dominated it since Lomonosov, and endowed it with originality." The schools considered 3 per cent of the 615 essays unsatisfactory; the university considered 15 per cent unsatisfactory.

pose their own questions. Although this procedure would weaken the value of the examination as a means of comparing one school with another, the Moscow region was ready to grant this much. The Petersburg ministry, however, insisted on district-wide examinations.

As the nineteenth century approached its close and the urbanization and industrialization of the country continued to nourish public initiative and professional self-esteem, criticism of certain aspects of the maturity examination became a demand for modifying the character of the exit diploma. Drawing on the writings of Nikolai Pirogov, the proponents of decentralization recommended doing away with the state rights attached to the exit diploma. In order to reassure those who feared that the separation of education and rank would weaken the school's ability to compete with domestic tutors and so threaten job security, the abolitionists observed that a simple certificate testifying to successful completion of the eight-year course of a gymnasium could constitute a prerequisite but not a right to a seat at the university. Defenders of the status quo continued to stress the close connection between the maturity examination and bureaucratic centralism.

By the end of the century an attack on the maturity examination was, in effect, an attack on the cornerstone of the Tolstoy system. For the most demanding hurdle of the exercise was the written translation from Russian into Latin and Greek. For a crucial moment the wheel of social transformation in the Russian empire turned on proficiency in archaic skills which had always eluded the many. Any weakening of the maturity system or any change in procedure or dilution of rights would weaken the interlocking foundations of scholastic formalism—European academic standards, institutional bifurcation and state control.[30]

Official Recognition of the Need for Reforms, 1899–1902

Before the provincial thaw could take on national dimensions, the liberation movement, of which antiformalism was a part, would have to crack the political defenses of the regime and force upon the central authorities the decision to reform the schools. By the end of the century prospects for change were brightening. Witte was at the height of his power, and his influence reached well into the Ministry of Education. When Delianov died in 1898, he was replaced by Professor Bogolepov, a man who stood closer to the Finance Minister's aggressive views on enlightenment than to the defensive thinking of the Holy Synod. The radical as well as the liberal intelligentsia denounced the appointee as a tool of Pobedonostsev. It made little difference to them that the Ober-Procurator went out of his way to deny responsibility for the nomination.* And indeed, the differences between the two were fundamental. Like Witte, Bogolepov was a champion of mass education. He was likewise anxious for secular authorities to recover the initiative from priests and bishops in popular instruction. When he took office, the state was still diverting the bulk of its funds for village instruction to the church. It was also spending twice as much annually on secondary as on primary schools. During his abortive term of office he reversed both of these trends.[31] Bogolepov's specialized knowledge of Roman civil law also strengthened his belief in authority. Although he had been a popular teacher of legal history at the University of Moscow, he would react forcefully against student disturbances.

Since the beginning of the reign of Nicholas III the university students had resumed their role as the harbingers of national catastrophe. In the 1860's their protests anticipated the distemper of the ethnic minorities and the restlessness of the peasants. In the 1890's their defiance forecast industrial strife. The very success of the Witte system exposed the country to the mysterious fluctuations of the international business cycle. A Western European monetary crisis in 1899 became a Russian industrial crisis by 1900 before sinking into the wartime depression of 1904. Against this depressing background, the students rioted early in 1899. The disturbances began innocently enough with a routine warning from the rector of St. Petersburg University that they should observe a routine ceremony with decorum. Their response was to strike. The rebellion spread southward and was finally quelled only when the government resorted to the extreme tactics of 1861, shutting down all the universities in the empire and the higher technical institutes in the capital cities.

It was Bogolepov's first trial under fire, and he responded in a way that destroyed public confidence in his tenure.† Anticipating more

---

* "Until his appointment, Bogolepoff was quite unknown to me, and afterwards we remained as strangers to each other. Indeed, he was, if anything, hostile and opposed to me" (Pobedonostsev, "Russia and Popular Education," p. 352).

† In 1898 Bogolepov was lauded: "In the select family of Russian Romanists, B. occupies one of the most prominent positions both as a scholar and as a teacher" (*Entsiklopedicheskii slovar*; St. Petersburg; Brockhaus-Efron, 1894, vol. 7, p. 171). In 1904 he was vilified as one of those who "received their preparatory training in politics at Moscow, under the auspices of Grand Duke Sergius. It is also known that the policy of the latter is that of unswerving reaction" (Miliukov, *Russia and Its Crisis*, p. 396).

trouble in the fall, he issued emergency rules for drafting into the army students expelled for insubordination. At the same time he issued instructions to the curators that those who could obtain assurance of readmittance from their schools would retain their deferred status.* This conciliatory gesture passed unnoticed. Meanwhile Dmitri Miliutin's replacement as Minister of War, General Petr Vannovsky, was "exhumed from the archives" and placed in charge of a special commission to investigate the causes of student unrest. The official review, as well as an independent study undertaken by a committee of professors, brought to light once more the unique social texture of the universities. Despite continuing public resentment at the cook's circular, the volume of destitute students remained high. In Moscow alone, half of the approximately 4,500 undergraduates had no visible means of support; nearly 2,000 were granted remission of tuition fees upon certification of their indigence, and some 900 were receiving state aid. On General Vannovsky's recommendation, the government made additional funds available for the construction of dormitories.[32]

Substandard living conditions were only an irritant. At the root of the trouble, the authorities were convinced, was the type of education received in the preparatory schools. On July 8, 1899, the Minister of Education issued a circular, less well known than the cook's circular, but more remarkable in its way.† With this document the state recognized the dissatisfaction "of teachers and parents" with the academic rigidity and moral sterility of the Tolstoy system. Bogolepov's admission concluded with a call to the districts to send delegates to a special reform commission to convene in St. Petersburg after the start of the new year. After a decade of intransigence the center was at last ready to listen to the provinces. As a precautionary measure a refurbished loyalty oath for the teaching staffs was added in August.[33]

For six months the outlying territories ruminated the issues raised by the July circular. The exercise was undertaken not only to clarify local thinking but to instruct the representatives that each area was empowered to send to the capital. The most exhaustive preparations were made in Moscow. Its size, the prestige of its university, and its historical importance as the seat of national self-sufficiency and provincial self-help conspired to make the old capital the most independent school district

---

* Temporary regulations for readmitting students expelled for participating in disorders were shaped into permanent rules on July 29, 1902 (*Sbornik ras. MNP,* 1902, No. 616).

† Quoted at length above, p. 140.

in the empire and its curator the most influential official after the Minister himself.

It was here that the Moscow Pedagogical Society of the Imperial University was established in 1898.[34] Nothing like it had existed in the country since Tolstoy had disbanded the St. Petersburg Pedagogical Society in 1879 for discussing nonpedagogical subjects and for admitting students to its deliberations.[35] The official purpose of the society was "to investigate scientifically questions of pedagogy and didactics, in their content, application, and history." In order to fulfill its practical function of preparing persons for the teaching profession, it was granted a number of state privileges. These included the right to hold public meetings, sponsor lectures, organize conferences and exhibits, publish a journal, and organize trips, laboratories, and libraries. But, most important for the immediate future, it was allowed "to develop relations with other persons interested in pedagogical subjects." Under this clause of its constitution, the Society became a meeting place for professors, secondary school teachers, school physicians, and educational writers. It thus enabled one of the most tightly controlled segments of the civil service, the teachers, to share in the movement toward public organization.

Nikolai Bogolepov's last act as curator of the Moscow region had been to obtain the government's approval of a charter for the Moscow Pedagogical Society. Eighteen months later his successor and admirer, P. A. Nekrasov, drew on the resources of the Society to organize the first full-scale conference of an educational region in Russian history. Meeting weekly from the end of September to the end of November 1899, the Moscow district conference marked a turning point in the development of the secondary teachers as a self-aware professional class. Representation at the congress was almost equally divided among university professors, gymnasium directors, and secondary teachers. Besides the 102 regular voting members, an additional 110 instructors, school doctors, and administrators furnished technical advice. The purpose of the assembly was to prepare the ground for the imperial conference to be convened in St. Petersburg at the beginning of the following year. Moscow would thus provide the guidelines for nationwide discussion of ways to eliminate the "shortcomings" of the Tolstoy system without a "sharp break" in continuity. To accomplish their appointed task of providing the central authorities with detailed plans, the members were broken down into five groups. Three special bodies focused their attention on various types of classical and realgymnasiums; a fourth concentrated on the realschule, and the last concentrated on a new type of comprehensive secondary school. Five additional subcommittees investigated the questions of equal concern to all: (1) physical education, (2) the function of the pedagogical council, (3) examinations and grading, (4) religious instruction, (5) vocational schools and the transfer to them of pupils from general educational establishments.[36]

While the editorial committees drafted precise schemes for improving the quality of the schools, the frontal attack on formalism took place in the general sessions attended by all the delegates. The curator and the directors remained firmly in charge of the official resolutions that issued from the general deliberations, but not of the preliminary debates. In these lively discussions the dissatisfaction and misgivings of the classroom teachers, which up till then had been confined within the pedagogical councils of the individual schools, broke into the open as regional and national concerns. Many of the positions taken by the pedagogues of the Moscow region would be echoed later at the top. The denunciation of the numbers system as bureaucratic oppression, the opinion that the abolition of the maturity certificate would seriously undermine the social prestige of the gymnasiums while the maturity examination should be simplified and curtailed—these views anticipated ministerial circulars. The most significant statement recorded at the Moscow meeting revealed how close the link was between political absolutism and educational formalism. The moral impotence of the schools, a bold teacher declared, the reason for their inability to influence the young, "lies in the lack of consciousness of human worth and the universal lack of pride flowing from the conditions of our public life."[37]

During the autumn of 1899 the district of Moscow recorded and amplified the voices of those directly engaged in classroom teaching. When the all-Russian commission gathered in St. Petersburg in January 1900, the views of the central bureaucracy predominated. Bogolepov was a classicist, and from the start he insisted that his purpose was not to change the academic structure of the Tolstoy system but to inject a new spirit of spontaneity into the arid formalism of the overcentralized school. Meeting until March 1900, the Bogolepov commission produced lengthy testimony on every aspect of educational reform but no substantial deviations from the consensus of the Moscow conference.

Protected by the Ministry of Finance from the upholders of the status quo in the Ministry of the Interior and the Holy Synod, Bogolepov did not wait for the legislative mills to convert the recommendations of Moscow and St. Petersburg into law. In the autumn of 1900 he began to decentralize the academic life of the schools on his own. His first concern was to rekindle the sparks of autonomy. In support of this purpose he urged the districts to revive the moribund organs of collective action. One such body was the financial council of the local school. Although legally entrusted with the day-to-day management of the budget, it seldom if ever met. Its decisions were usually made by the director alone, with staff signatures obtained informally between classes. Detrimental as it undoubtedly was to the cause of professional self-government, the atrophy of the fiscal committee was but a symptom of the ossification of the principal organ of representation, the pedagogical council. The statute of 1871 and related circulars charged the teaching staff, assembled under the chairmanship of the director, with ultimate responsibility for policy at the classroom level. "According to the exact sense of all these regulations," Bogolepov reminded the regions, "the pedagogical councils, either directly or through their subcommittees, can and must exert decisive influence on educational and disciplinary policy in the schools." As a matter of fact, they were either failing to fulfill their obligations or fulfilling them only perfunctorily. "The interests of the school," the Minister concluded, "emphatically demand revitalizing the activity of these institutions."[38]

Bogolepov's concern for local initiative went beyond moral support for collective decisions. Under his direction and in obvious response to provincial demands, the Ministry issued new regulations for evaluating student progress. The rules of 1900, which replaced the rules of 1872, kept the numbers system intact, but subordinated its mechanical calculations to the "conscientious" review of individual cases by the pedagogical council. Flexibility in grading was accompanied by personalizing of teaching. Since 1872 gymnasium instructors had been obliged to submit a detailed lesson plan to the pedagogical council—in effect, to the director—for approval at the beginning of each term. This procedure was supposed to guarantee that teachers would conduct their classes in close accord with the uniform programs established by St. Petersburg. Thus the students would be protected from what the Ministry described as "enthusiasm, blunders, and abuses"[39] of individual pedagogues.

Bogolepov did not share these fears. He informed the curators that, henceforth, the government programs were to serve as models rather than masters. They were not to be rigidly reproduced but adapted to local circumstances. The schools were even granted discretionary power to modify the state lesson plans as long as the principal goal of secondary education was attained. This goal was defined as the effort "not to cram the brains of pupils with as large a store of miscellaneous information as possible, but to teach the young to work deliberately, with clarity and persistence."[40] With increased freedom went the enlargement of duty. Granting more leeway to the judgment of the teachers, the Ministry placed directly upon them "the ultimate responsibility for the success of their pupils."[41] With his new liberty to adapt subject content to circumstances, an instructor could no longer maintain that his pedagogical obligation was discharged by mere faithful presentation of the material prescribed by St. Petersburg.

Delianov's successor also liberalized the core of the classical curriculum. Since 1890, schools had been under orders to restrict Latin and Greek composition to the minimum necessary to illustrate points of grammar. At the same time the maturity examinations continued to emphasize the translation of Russian passages into the ancient languages. It was not surprising, then, that this difficult exercise continued to dominate the class periods. Teachers quite naturally strove to prepare their pupils adequately for the tests leading to the exit diploma. Complaints from the provinces brought this anomaly to the attention of the ministry. As a result, the most drastic change in the comprehensive rules on examinations was the elimination of Latin and Greek composition. In a clarifying circular, Bogolepov instructed the schools to concentrate on ideas rather than grammar.[42]

Whatever plans Nikolai Bogolepov may have had for further loosening up the Tolstoy system were cut short by the resurgence of revolutionary terror. By 1900 opposition to the government was becoming both unruly and better organized. As expectations exceeded capacities, the educated class began to coalesce into militant cadres representing the principal ideological alternatives to tsarist absolutism—constitutional federalism, social democracy, and agrarian populism. Forced to compete with constitutional liberals and Marxists for the allegiance of the younger generation, the agrarian radicals formed the Socialist-Revolutionary Party. In February 1901 an expelled university student and member of the party shot and mortally wounded the Minister of Education for his part in drafting student strikers. The assassination was, as Witte observed, "the prelude to all the events that shook us between 1901 and 1905.[43] Indifferent to the dying man's condition, the public focused its attention on the choice of a successor.

On March 24, 1901, Petr Vannovsky, a retired army officer who had served as Minister of War for the entire reign of Alexander III, was named to fill the vacancy. Born in the reign of Alexander I, the old general was greeted with derision by radicals, with suspicion by liberals, and with perplexity by educators. While head of the war department, he had undone Dmitri Miliutin's efforts to broaden the academic scope of the military academies by reconverting them into vocational schools. On the other hand, his report on the disorders of 1899 had displayed understanding of the living conditions that impoverished students were forced to endure. In retrospect, his term of office marked the culmination of Sergei Witte's influence on general schooling. The imperial rescript announcing his appointment acknowledged "serious deficiencies" in the educational system and called on its new executive to undertake "a fundamental review and revision" of secondary schools.[44] Vannovsky himself appealed directly to the students to trust the government, to believe in its good intentions, and, by occupying their time with study rather than disturbances, to give the bureaucracy "the opportunity to dedicate our time and our talents to the reconstruction of the Russian school." From now on, he informed the districts, "the first, unswerving, and immutable obligation of the teaching staffs" will be "to introduce reason, love, and heartfelt concern" into the learning process.[45] The phrase "heartfelt concern" became the identifying tag for the brief but spirited regime.

Under Vannovsky's "dictatorship of the heart" the thaw of intellectual and moral formalism spread to institutional structure. He ended the twenty-year moratorium on new gymnasium construction, so that by 1904 ten additional academic schools brought the total number in the empire to 251 with 101,815 pupils. He was even more interested in expanding the terminal and lower components of the Tolstoy system. By 1905 there were 114,173 pupils in 755 urban schools. In the decade before 1895, only three new realschulen had been opened; in the next decade 51 were built. Simultaneously, their student population increased from 17,535 in 1895 to 51,502 by 1905. This expansion helped correct the chronic disproportion of secondary schools. In the reign of Alexander III the practical institutions had only a fourth as many pupils as the academic; by 1905 they had half as many. In addition, modern secondary schooling was being made more accessible and more attractive through a network of commercial schools designed by Vyshnegradsky and constructed by Witte. Since they were under the direction of the Ministry of Finance, they did not come under the Jewish quotas. They were popular not only with minorities but with teachers dissatisfied with the general institutions. By 1904 there were 68 commercial schools offering 18,269 boys and girls the equivalent of realschule training.

The annual expense of maintaining a child in school was the same for terminal and university preparatory institutions. Parents were understandably reluctant to spend the same amount of money without the prospects that the child might be some day admitted to the academic vestibule of the civil service. Both Witte and Vannovsky realized that unless realschulen and commercial schools were granted the state rights enjoyed by the gymnasiums—above all, the right of their graduates to enter the universities—they would never attract full public support. Unlike his predecessor, General Vannovsky was no friend of academic elitism. In fact, he intended, if at all possible, to bring the scattered sectors of secondary schooling closer together by harmonizing divergent curricula. To prepare for a "sweeping reform" of academic structure, he assembled a new commission composed of himself, the assistant Ministers of Education and Finance, the vice-president of the Academy of Sciences, the director of the Pedagogical Laboratory of Military-Educational Institutions, members of the Council of Ministers, curators of the school districts, and assorted academicians, university professors, directors of secondary schools, and teachers of gymnasiums and realschulen.

This group of experts began its deliberations at the end of May 1901. Since the preliminaries had already been done by the previous administration, the work advanced rapidly. As early as June 11 and June 18, supreme instructions from the Tsar ratified the conclusions of the Vannovsky commission. A week later these were announced to the school districts in two parts. First, the local authorities were apprised of a prospectus for a unified secondary school.[46] Second, they were notified that temporary revisions were to be introduced over a period of three years.[47] The first four years of the gymnasiums (in effect, the progymnasiums) were to be reorganized in September 1901; subsequent changes were to be implemented one class at a time until 1904. At that time the emergency program would end with the simultaneous graduations of the seventh and eighth forms, followed by the establishment in 1905 of a standard seven-year gymnasium. The reorganization of the realschule would also begin at once with the first two years and continue at the rate of one class a year until 1905, when a seventh year would be added. These staggered adjustments would presumably prepare the way for institutional unity by dovetailing the offerings of the gymnasiums and the realschulen.

According to the future plan for a unified school, Latin was to be introduced into the third year of the realschulen. Without waiting for the prospectus to be given final approval, the temporary revisions took immediate effect in the gymnasiums. Their drift was unmistakably against traditionalism. Already by the autumn of 1901 Latin was droppd from the first and second years of the gymnasium and Greek from the third and fourth. Reduction of the classical core left considerable time for increased concentration on contemporary subjects. The periods devoted to Russian language, geography, and the sciences were moderately increased. The subjects that gained the most were the modern European languages. The statute of 1871 had introduced one modern language into the gymnasium (French or German) in the second year, for a total of nineteen hours over the eight-year course. The curriculum revisions of 1890 had introduced a second modern language as an optional study from the second year. The revision of 1901 increased the hours devoted to the first modern language from 19 to 28 (as compared with 29 in the realschule).

Although popular, the extension of modern language training required some mutual adjustments. The supreme instructions published in June 1901 had not imposed upon the gymnasiums the obligation to offer a second modern language, but had left such action to local discretion.[48] In August the Ministry became more precise and insistent. Justifying its decision on "purely pedagogical grounds," it ordered the schools to introduce the second modern language into the periods left by the removal of Greek from the third and fourth years. Two weeks later it took an even stronger position. Encouraged by the passage of the prospectus for a unified high school through imperial review, it instructed local officials to offer courses in both German and French from the first year, so that pupils could choose their own field of emphasis.[49]

Lack of money, not lack of interest, threatened these designs. The proposed strengthening of modern languages added 340 rubles a year to the budget of the gymnasium, and the introduction of Latin added 228 rubles to the budget of the realschule. At the beginning of the summer, St. Petersburg was expecting the schools to cover the additional costs from local tuition fees. Local authorities objected strenuously, and by autumn the Ministry backed down. After reminding the districts to cut the salaries of teachers whose hours were reduced by the temporary revisions, it made funds available for the expanded programs.

Finding persons qualified to teach the additional subjects likewise induced the central government to accept change. As early as 1898 the shortage of French instructors had forced it to allow the localities to violate the all-male environment of the preparatory schools by hiring women for the first time. Applicants were to possess state certificates as domestic tutors in addition to having several years of experience. In each instance the district had to request permission of St. Petersburg before hiring. Even then the women were not employed full time, as regular staff members (this would have admitted them to the civil service), but only by the hour. In 1901 the regulations of 1898 were extended to cover recruiting of women as German and French language instructors. The increased emphasis on the natural sciences also created a shortage of teachers. To cover this scarcity, directors were permitted to use by the hour the requisite specialists from the local urban schools. Finally, when the schools complained of lack of space in which to teach the added courses, the ministry directed them to use the classrooms during the lunch period.

The central authorities gradually clarified the temporary revisions through correspondence with the districts. Meanwhile, the plan for a unified high school was delayed. In his original notification of June 23, 1901, to the school districts, Vannovsky carefully explained that the temporary revisions and the future plans were complementary. The one prepared the way for the other. St. Petersburg not only had drafted a careful synopsis for a homogeneous and comprehensive general educational secondary school; it had established "tentative timetables to facilitate the gradual realization within the space of three years of this projected type of unified secondary school." The districts were urged to report their recommendations and comments on the draft proposal back to the Ministry by November 1. Prompt reply, Vannovsky declared, would enable him to present the completed statute to the Council of State for final approval in the spring of 1902. Within a month (July 20, 1901), the Ministry warned that the realization of the unified plan could not yet be taken for granted. A second commission was to be formed at the start of 1902 in order to review the conclusions of the first.[50]

Granted a reprieve by the summoning of yet another deliberative body, the defenders of a compartmentalized school system launched their last counterattack against "the enemies of European education" in the winter of 1901–2. Once more they pointed out that Russia urgently required an elite "European school" to train the scientists, teachers, and administrators who alone could serve the demands of modern empire. The need for more technical training was no excuse for lowering the standards of the university preparatory schools, and the standards proposed by the Vannovsky Commission were even lower than those of republican France. The Russian bureaucracy was accused of being "ever prone to extreme conclusions based on the last word of science." The Germans, at least, had pondered for half a century before admitting realschule graduates to the university. The Russians were about to reverse the work of 30 years in ten weeks. Before they had "produced their own Lessings, Kants, Hegels, Goethes," they were ready to cut themselves off from direct contact with the original sources of Western culture. One thing appeared certain: even while the government was emasculating classical education by practically eliminating Greek and curtailing Latin, the maturity certificate, "the right to a government post and social position," would be maintained.[51]

In January 1902 the second Vannovsky commission met. By April it completed the project for a unified school and sent it to the Council of Ministers. In its final form Vannovsky's constitution not only eliminated bifurcation, it also eliminated the maturity certificate.* This most dangerous threat to the Tolstoy system since 1880 came at a time when the school question was becoming subordinated to the more insistent challenges posed by Japanese militarism, deepening industrial distress, and rumblings of Pugachev in the depressed countryside. It also occurred at a moment when the civil service was locked in a struggle over its

---

* In answer to a government questionnaire, 80 per cent of the Moscow professors favored admitting students from the realschulen to the universities. Of the 80 per cent, 13 per cent wanted them to have a full Latin course, 27 per cent a reduced course, and 39 per cent no course (SMS, VI).

composition, prompted by the desire of Witte and Vannovsky to bring it into closer contact with the accelerating tempo of national life.* This could be accomplished through a secondary school system which would embrace not only the gymnasiums and realschulen of the Ministry of Education but the commercial schools of the Ministry of Finance. By 1901 these, too, were ambitious of becoming full-fledged general educational establishments. If the graduates of these assorted institutions were admitted to the universities on an equal footing, the preponderance of the landed gentry in the bureaucracy would give way to more dynamic elements from the urban class, particularly its professional, commercial, and industrial members.

Deterioration of Discipline in the Schools, 1902–1904

Once again, as in 1881, political violence intervened to preserve the Tolstoy system. On April 2, 1902, a twenty-year-old student social-revolutionist fatally wounded the Minister of the Interior. The murdered official's replacement was Viacheslav Plehve, the Russifier of Finland's schools. The new guardian of domestic tranquillity had always been a stout supporter of gentry predominance. He was convinced that the landowning nobility, for all its deficiencies, was indispensable to state service. Committed to stabilization through separate schools for separate segments of society, he defended the formal structure of the Tolstoy system as revised by Pobedonostsev after 1881. Within a week of his appointment, General Vannovsky resigned as Minister of Education. The plan for a unified secondary school was shelved. To the relief of the gymnasium staffs, Plehve's ascendancy not only rescued the maturity certificate but reaffirmed the principle of academic elitism. Vannovsky had been giving serious consideration to admitting graduates of Witte's commercial schools to the universities on the strength of an abridged entrance examination. After April 2 any dilution of entrance requirements that would further democratize the student bodies of the higher schools was out of the question. Instead, St. Petersburg advised the districts to insist as before on the equivalent of the full maturity examination for commercial students seeking matriculation.[52]

Vannovsky's retirement ended the alliance between the Ministry of

---

* "It is probable that Witte intended to use the industrial classes as the civil service class" (V. I. Gurko, *Features and Figures of the Past*, Stanford, Calif., 1939, p. 203).

Education and the Ministry of Finance. The appointment of Vannovsky's successor, Grigorii von Sänger, a former professor at Warsaw University who had achieved a modest measure of fame by translating *Evgeny Onegin* into Latin, marked education's dependence on the Ministry of the Interior. The transposition occurred as Witte was becoming a political liability. In the south, peasant bands were ravaging estates. In the industrial centers, factory workers were protesting en masse the conditions of labor, and students were joining the strikes and demonstrations. It was not surprising, then, that the government brought an end to academic reform as quickly as possible in order to devote fuller attention to the problem of discipline in the schools. On June 10, 1902, an imperial rescript abruptly ended the era of "heartfelt concern": "A school that discharges youths with but a cursory knowledge, without relating that knowledge to moral and religious training, to the concept of duty, to discipline, and to respect for elders," the Tsar notified the nation, "is not only useless but often harmful, since such knowledge develops that self-will and conceit which is so destructive of everything.... Therefore," the autocrat concluded, "I demand that the school combine academic education with moral training in the spirit of faith, devotion to the Throne and the fatherland, and respect for the family. I also demand that, besides developing the young people intellectually and physically, the schools train them from the start in order and discipline."[53] To implement this program, a committee of directors of gymnasiums and realschulen was quickly assembled in St. Petersburg to work out details for stabilizing the temporary revisions of 1901. Its conclusions, published on July 20, 1902, solidified the structure of the gymnasiums and the realschulen until the First World War.[54]

The most popular change was the elimination of Greek from all but a handful of schools. It was retained in one gymnasium in each of the cities of St. Petersburg, Moscow, Warsaw, Kiev, Odessa, and Riga. Latin was eliminated from the first two years of gymnasiums without being added to the program of realschulen. Since the gymnasiums retained an eight-year course and the realschulen six, only the first two classes of each were coterminous. The reduction of classical studies released time for what was hopefully described as the "development of the whole man." This ambitious goal was to be reached through emphasis on modern languages, the sciences, gymnastics, military drill, athletic games, school excursions, and handicrafts.[55] It was rather late for the schools to retard the erosion of the cultural foundations of tsardom. As Professor Paul Miliukov, the historian of Russian culture and the future leader of the Constitutional Democratic Party in the state duma, suggested to an American lecture audience in 1903, "Nearly all of the Russian young people who have passed through the schools of Demetrius Tolstoy are socialistic. All the exertions of the school authorities, with all their system of minute police supervision and their teaching of politically indifferent subjects, have availed nothing; or, rather, this very system has contributed to produce results quite opposite to those desired."[56]

When these words were spoken, the revolutionary fever had already penetrated the secondary schools. In at least two dozen provincial gymnasiums the students were forming study circles "for giving utterance to the protest against the present obstacles to free thought and free study." Several organizations had started periodicals with the characteristic names of *Youth* and *Forward*. Scattered groups were banding together in the Kharkov alliance of undergraduates and the Kiev central branch of the united circles and organizations of the middle schools with the ultimate aim of founding an alliance for the whole of the country with its own all-Russian periodical. In May 1903 the Minister of the Interior informed the Minister of Education that in one of the cities of central Russia schoolboys had founded a "fighting branch" to conduct "active opposition to the detestable school regime."[57] Within the classrooms dissent became defiance. Classes refused to carry out assignments; individuals insulted and even attacked teachers who graded them below "three" on the numbers system.

The response of school authorities to the deterioration of discipline was mixed. At the classroom level, the teaching staffs blamed much of the trouble on the overcrowding of facilities. The resumption of physical expansion was hard put to keep up with increased enrollments, let alone relieve the backlog of twenty years. In 1900 the St. Petersburg region was training 10,272 pupils in 32 academic schools; five years later it had 12,489 in 34. In 1900 the Moscow area was instructing 11,937 pupils in 35 gymnasiums; by 1905 it had 15,861 in 41. As the population of the gymnasiums swelled from less than 60,000 following the cook's circular to more than 100,000 at the beginning of 1905, social democratization increased. From the beginning of the reign of Nicholas II to the outbreak of the Russo-Japanese war, the proportion of commoners in the university-preparatory schools rose from 44 to 59 per cent. The more conservative members of the pedagogical councils—directors, classics instructors, and class counselors—related the decline of order to mass inroads. Many looked back nostalgically to the days of Alexander III, when the classical colleges had been scholarly havens for "the civilized children of the privileged classes" rather than diploma mills for the off-spring of "the illiterate and the uncultured."[58] The force of this argument was diminished by the volume of privileged children who were openly rebellious. When a broader interpretation was needed to explain the universal scope of undergraduate discontent, officials sought help from the schools. In answer to a district questionnaire seeking the origins of pupil unrest, 74 pedagogical councils of the Moscow area blamed the newspapers, current literature, and the educated class in general for breaking down respect for authority in general and for nourishing a "negative and even hostile attitude toward the school."*

Not all educators agreed with this diagnosis. A significant number took Bogolepov's recommendation seriously that the schools ought to rely less on fear and more on persuasion. Convictions were strengthened by a four-year study made at one institution, which exposed the negligible results achieved by police methods.[59] Some teachers refused to take action against breaches of the peace. When questioned by officials, they excused their reluctance to enforce the rules of 1874 by referring to General Vannovsky's admonition to the teaching profession to extend "heartfelt concern" to the adolescents committed to their care.[60] Even in the face of hostility from above and harassment from below, some pedagogical councils continued to take into account not only the overt behavior of pupils but "their inner attitudes, their stage of development, the bad and good side of their characters, their personal traits, and their home environment."[61]

The central authorities likewise sought to restore order with a variety of tactics. A primary concern was to prevent students from drifting into political activity. To keep the weaker scholars occupied constructively

* *Ibid.* Visiting the Russian schools at the turn of the century, Bernard Pares reported that the "programme of Gymnasia has become easier in recent years. Greek is taught only in the top class; there is less Latin translation and no Latin composition. The Director believes in making boys work, whether they happen to find the subject interesting or not. His boys will not work unless they are compelled, and now, as everything is made too easy for them, they do nothing. This reacts upon discipline, which has undoubtedly declined since the days of Count Dmitry Tolstoy, 'who forced them to work' " (*Russia and Reform*, London, 1907, p. 213).

and the more capable away from subversive surroundings, they paid closer attention to channeling people to the "proper" schools. On orders from St. Petersburg, those dropping out of the realschulen and gymnasiums were guided toward the lower technical schools.[62] And whereas standards were slightly stiffened for ecclesiastical seminarians, an effort was made to attract different types of secondary graduates, including holders of maturity certificates, toward higher technical institutes.[63] For those persisting in their desire to enter a university, more careful screening was introduced. After 1902 a complete record of a student's conduct during his last three years in the gymnasium had to accompany his initial application. Where academic considerations were equal, admissions officers were advised to prefer "the graduates of those gymnasiums ... whose members contributed the least to the disorders in a given institution of higher learning in recent years."[64] Directors of gymnasiums were ordered not to admit to the maturity examinations students representing the more serious cases of insubordination. Such precautions, it was hoped, would keep "deliberately uncultured elements" out of the universities.[65]

Von Sänger's administration did not content itself with defensive measures. It also urged the schools to bridge the growing rift between faculty and students. Under siege, the central bureaucracy was brought to view the school not only as an agency of state compulsion but as a reflecting pool of social yearnings. In June 1903 the Ministry of Education reminded the teaching staffs that any injury suffered by a student at their hands, any injustice, particularly any insult "to the feeling of personal dignity which awakens in the young," could well warp an adolescent permanently, destroying once and for all his confidence in the established order, "whose image he sees mirrored in the schools where the state educates him."[66]

Along with this observation, St. Petersburg offered suggestions for touching the hearts and minds of the students on behalf of the government. A suggested innovation, which partially revived the academic thaw, was to have pupils write original essays on current national problems and discuss them in class. After composing his themes and hearing the comments of his comrades and teachers, so official reasoning went, "the student cannot help but realize what a great deal of work is required before reaching a decision on the more or less difficult public issues of the day." And finally, once again, as always in periods of self-criticism, the government sought to inject vitality into the office of student counselor. At the Moscow district conference in 1899, teachers had complained that the student adviser was often considered a "police spy."[67] The teachers were now urged to cultivate contact with the students outside the formal apparatus of the school. Once they had gained the confidence of the youth, they should seek to dispel the notion that respect for authority was bootlicking. When the opportunity presented itself, they should remind the students that "the feelings of the educated and the mature never boil over immediately into action but are subject to the control of conscience and reason."[68]

While the Ministry of Education was encouraging reason in the schools, the government was abandoning reason in its foreign policy. In the autumn of 1903, Witte was dismissed as Minister of Finance and elevated to the ceremonial office of Chairman of the Council of Ministers. His exit from power removed the last barrier to the ambitions of those who, encouraged by Plehve, were desirous of imparting to economic expansion on the Pacific an aggressive military character. Within less than six months Russia was at war with Japan. Internal security was immediately tightened. At the beginning of 1904, Plehve dispersed the congress on technical education for displaying "political tendencies." The zemstvo doctors, meeting later in the year for the ninth congress of the Pirogov Society, continued the process of converting educational problems into political questions. A joint session which brought together specialists on public hygiene, medical statistics, and children's diseases adopted a formal resolution that "since the principal reason for the abnormally high rate of children's mortality in Russia is the material insecurity and inadequate mental development of the population, this congress expresses its deep conviction that the successful struggle against this evil is possible only on the basis of broad social reforms."[69]

In the spring General Vladimir Glazov, the commandant of the military academy, was named Minister of Education and immediately espoused physical training and a greater expenditure of state and public funds as the principal means of overcoming the moral and physical deficiencies of the schools.* Meanwhile, Plehve impeded the efforts of

---

* In an interview appearing in the newspaper *Rus'*, March 17, 1905, Glazov declared: "The condition of our schools certainly needs correction, and, besides general reasons, our poverty plays a main role. As long as the school budget is but 43 million rubles, it is almost impossible to correct the problem."

the zemstvos to organize relief for soldiers and their families, until he was killed by a bomb. His replacement signaled a sharp reversal of policy. Prince Sviatopolk-Mirsky was an amiable aristocrat who hastened to promise the country that his administration would be devoted to restoring "public confidence." The ensuing "political spring" witnessed the rapid expansion of public activity, particularly on the part of the zemstvo assemblies, which began to organize a national opposition to the state bureaucracy. As the year wore on, continuing defeat in Asia isolated the government from nationalist support, from the gentry Tolstoy had favored in the 1880's and the industrialists Witte had protected in the 1890's. By the end of the year tsardom was approaching the point where it had been on the morning of March 1, 1881, contemplating some concession to society's appetite for representative government. Further educational development would depend on the outcome of the constitutional struggle.

Chapter Six

The Revolutionary Assault on
the Bureaucratic School, 1905–1906

We, the teachers of the secondary schools, cannot remain silent, especially now, when the blood of our children and former pupils is flowing in the Far East and on the streets of Russian cities while the whole country wearily awaits coming events. Joining the chorus of honest, thinking Russians, we, the teachers of the secondary schools, cannot but declare that the fate of the school is inextricable from the political reform that cannot be postponed.

MEMORANDUM OF 121 TEACHERS OF
THE MOSCOW DISTRICT SECONDARY
SCHOOLS, *February 13, 1905*

Local Initiatives

On January 9, 1905, a priest with contacts in both official and antigovernmental circles led a column of several thousand workers with their wives and children toward the Winter Palace to urge redress of outstanding grievances. As he and his pious horde trudged along, swinging aloft icons and pictures of the Emperor, intoning religious hymns and patriotic songs, they could think of themselves as coming to liberate the Father Tsar from the "German" bureaucracy. When the troops on guard fired on the petitioners, they converted the procession into Bloody Sunday. As the news of the massacre spread, it touched off the most elemental domestic turbulence in three hundred years. At the beginning of February an expelled student assassinated the Tsar's uncle, Grand Duke Sergei, who as military governor of Moscow had become the symbol of "standing firm." By the middle of the month the largest land battle of the Japanese war was on the point of forcing the Russians to evacuate Mukden. At a meeting of top officials called by the Tsar to discuss measures for "pacifying society," the Minister of Finance urged a statesmanlike gesture of reconciliation between rulers and subjects, if only to reassure Western investors whose credits were indispensable for carrying on the war. Isolated at home, dependent on foreign favor, the autocracy yielded its first formal concession of the year. On February 18 an imperial rescript announced the Emperor's intention to summon elected deputies of the people to participate in the preliminary discussion of legislative bills. For the next eight months, until mid-October, state and society would be at loggerheads over whether the prospective state duma would be a consultative palliative or a legislative remedy to the domestic crisis.

The summoning of an authentic parliament was the most urgent political demand the educated class made on the autocracy in the spring of 1905. Its clearest social demand was for genuinely public enlightenment. From Bloody Sunday onward, when the request for "measures to eliminate the ignorance of the Russian people"[1] was placed second only to the claim for a constituent assembly, innumerable resolutions asked for substantially the same thing. What society wanted was a unified public school system, the *école unique* of 1803, financed by the state but under local control. Applied to the universities, this entailed autonomy for faculty members and corporative rights for students. On the primary and lower or advanced primary plane it meant instruction in the native languages, toleration for non-Orthodox religions, and administrative authority vested in private or public bodies responsible to the community. For the institutions of higher learning as well as for the elementary schools, the transition from state to social control could take place within the framework of autocracy. Precedents and procedures were at hand. Freedom for the universities could be achieved by restoring the constitution of 1863 and abolishing the police inspectorate. Instruction of the urban and rural masses could be brought under territorial supervision by diverting Treasury funds from the Holy Synod to the zemstvo schools and by putting an end to Russification in the borderlands.

The emancipation of the secondary schools from the bureaucracy was another matter. It could hardly be accomplished without a readjustment of the political structure of the regime. As the "dearly beloved daughter of the Russian bureaucracy,"[2] the secondary school was the barometer of public life. In 1905–6 it was the index of just how far St. Petersburg would yield its formal cultural initiative to the educated class. Whereas the universities and primary schools attracted influential defenders within the political parties where the zemstvos, the municipal dumas, and the professors were heavily represented, the secondary school enjoyed no such patronage.[3] Not only were the gymnasiums and realschulen objects of public suspicion; their professional staffs did not want to emancipate themselves from the state bureaucracy only to become subject to the commercial interests dominant in the municipal dumas or the agrarian forces represented in the zemstvos.

Lacking champions in society, the secondary schools produced their own leaders. Students, parents, and teachers might differ among themselves on the details of reform, but they were united against their common enemy, the bureaucracy. All three groups were oppressed by the fear that in the larger struggle for constitutional government the battle to wrest control of the gymnasiums and realschulen from St. Petersburg might well be lost.* Realizing full well that the success of their venture depended on reconstruction of the national political framework, all three subscribed to the proposition that "it is absolutely essential for the salvation of Russian education to summon freely elected representatives of the whole people, without class, national, religious, or sexual distinctions, to participate in the legislative power and to control the actions of the administrative bureaucracy."[4] Also conscious that even under a constitutional regime the administrative structure of the Tolstoy system might remain unchanged, they exerted themselves to retain their identity as secondary teachers, parents, and pupils within the regiments of dissent.

The students were quick to join the "general liberation movement."[5] The first recorded strike of a Tolstoy gymnasium took place in St. Petersburg on January 11, two days after Bloody Sunday, when the students of the Larinsky school protested the beating given a comrade by a cossack. At Saratov in the educational region of Kazan boys and girls from the local high schools were prominent in the city-wide demonstrations of factory workers, zemstvo and municipal employees protesting the slaughter in St. Petersburg. By February, when strikes and disturbances were frequent throughout the country, students from the gymnasiums, realschulen, technical and normal schools were demonstrating everywhere. The arrest of a popular teacher, the expulsion of a comrade, rough handling by the police, an assault by Black Hundred gangs recruited from the anti-intellectual segments of the population, or simply the latent friction between races and creeds, sent the young people into the streets. Impromptu school disorders quickly fell into a pattern ritualized by a half-century of practice in the universities. After

---

* "In the immediate future the school has nothing to look forward to. School reform was not included among the reforms proposed by the ukase of December 12. It is still officially considered one of the less urgent problems of national life" (*Pravo*, No. 6, 1905, pp. 424–25).

a mass meeting in which speakers would hold the "police bureaucracy" responsible for "the blood flowing in the Far East and on the streets of Russian cities," a petition would be drafted for presentation to local school authorities.

Demands might vary slightly from place to place, but the schools were so much alike that grievances were similar. Across the land, parents, pupils, and teachers directed their venom against surveillance outside the school and obligatory attendance at religious functions as the two most intolerable features of the Tolstoy system. Restrictions on the rights of pupils to visit theaters, libraries, scientific institutions, and public lectures must be lifted as well. All forms of punishment that lowered the dignity or affected the health of pupils should be dispensed with. Parents were particularly interested in obtaining the right to select living quarters for their children and to be present in the pedagogical council when it discussed expulsion of their child. Pupils demanded the right to organize study groups, libraries, mutual aid funds, and honor courts, and the opportunity to discuss mutual concerns with the faculty and, on occasion, to publish their own periodicals. Both the families and the teaching staffs wanted the bureaucracy to stop taking reprisals against persons for their political convictions.[6]

Although such sweeping changes as these were beyond the capacity of local officials, they displayed some willingness to pass on requests to higher levels. Local police authorities were less tolerant. The upshot was violence and the first shedding of blood. Since the beginning of February, school officials in the provincial capital of Kursk, located in the educational region of Kharkov, noticed a growing unrest among the pupils in the city's half-dozen secondary schools. On February 10 and 11 the young people were allowed to express their grievances in a series of public meetings. Afterward they appeared satisfied with assurances that constructive suggestions within the competence of local authorities would be given consideration. Classes were resumed on February 12. At noon on that day the older boys left the classical gymnasium after the lunch period. Forming an orderly procession, they marched through the city past the various schools, which were still in session. As they moved along, they drew recruits from the other schools until their numbers reached more than a hundred. By this time the column had attracted a following of police officials, mounted guards, and Black Hundred toughs in civilian clothing. The procession was so peaceful that bystanders assumed that it was a delegation on its way to the railroad station to meet General Stessel, who was supposedly passing through Kursk on his way to St. Petersburg to report to the Emperor on the capitulation of Port Arthur. When the marchers halted in front of the first girls' gymnasium, "a police whistle sounded and an officer gave the command to attack. Whips and fists swinging, the cavalry and reservists hurled themselves on the students."[7] Rumor and report seeping through the censorship placed the number of injured children at 40, the slain at six.

Public opinion converted the bludgeoning at Kursk into the Bloody Sunday of the schools. The news of the outrage inspired sympathy demonstrations elsewhere among the young. Parents were horrified. Their fears for the safety of their children transformed them into a coherent pressure group for the first time in the history of the general educational schools. In one city after another mothers and fathers staged meetings to discuss measures for immediately restoring order as a prologue to permanent reforms.[8] Four days after Kursk the city of Minsk in the educational region of Vilna was shocked by a riot of its secondary pupils. Classes were suspended throughout the town pending a public meeting, which was held in the boys' gymnasium on February 17. Some 150 parents and guardians used the occasion to challenge the authority of local officials.[9] Over the vigorous objection of the director of the gymnasium, the elected spokesman of the parents read into the minutes a protest by the families against the bureaucratic school. The indictment singled out the *nadzor,* the surveillance of pupils outside the school according to the rules of 1874, as the major cause of the breakdown of mutual trust between students and teachers. The parents demanded that the director fire the petty police official whose job it was to supervise extramural behavior. When the director replied that such authorization could come only from St. Petersburg, the parents had to content themselves with a request to the director that he petition the Ministry of Education to abolish the external inspectorate. The meeting closed with a respectful telegram to the Ministry of Education, asking permission to postpone classes locally until the streets were safe.

In Ekaterinoslav, a provincial capital in the educational region of Odessa, parents placed the blame for manhandling schoolchildren on the central government. Its appeal to the population on February 18 to engage in "the struggle against subversion" was an invitation to anarchy.[10] The "dark masses," the parents complained, understood the

February rescript as a summons to attack the intelligentsia. For them the intellectual was the schoolboy, easily identifiable in his cap and uniform. Since the "simple people" could not distinguish between one pupil and another, all pupils were in danger of being attacked. After deploring student demonstrations as mere "playing at politics," Ekaterinoslav parents adjourned their meeting with a petition to the governor to use the police to protect the children from the mob.*

A month after the Kursk killings, the largest parental gathering of the spring was held in the city of Kharkov.[11] Searching for an explanation of why student disorders were no longer confined to the universities, "the mothers, fathers, and guardians of Kharkov" found it "in the existing pedagogical regime, which is simply an extension of the universal police-bureaucratic structure of the state." Reviewing the history of education since the great reforms, they accused the Ministry of Education of ignoring "the growth of public consciousness" and of paying only "mechanical lip service for the past five decades" to the vital problems of public education. As a result of being placed "in a hopeless professional environment," the teachers had lost all moral authority with the students. Since Kursk, the situation in the schools had taken a turn for the worse. Previously the "tyranny of the bureaucracy" had at least been limited to the psychological sphere, to the "mental and moral maiming of our children through the program of instruction." Now, however, parents could no longer be confident that their children would not be physically harmed by Black Hundred gangs instigated by secret agents and protected by the local police.

After criticizing the existing regime, Kharkov's families urged reconstruction of the Tolstoy system along lines capable of developing in the students "initiative, industry, and personal pride." The reformed schools should, of course, be accessible to all, regardless of social status, nationality, or religion. They ought to be greatly increased both "to satisfy the growing demand for secondary education and to improve the teaching now hampered by overcrowding." In the new school, responsibility for the fulfillment of religious obligations must be left entirely to the parents. Since surveillance lacked any "genuine pedagogical significance" and pursued "purely police goals," it should be done away with. The

---

* Agraev, p. 4. In Kazan the "ignorant masses" beat up both students and officials (*S-Peterburgskiia vedomosti*, 17 February 1905, p. 6). Some directors allowed gymnasium students to doff their uniforms for defense against hooligans (*ibid.*, 27 October 1905, p. 3).

purpose of general education was "the harmonious development of the physical, intellectual, and moral nature of man." Therefore, the reconditioned secondary system should be freed from political influences, "which the history of our schools has shown to paralyze the educational process." To ensure public control, parents ought to be given a "decisive voice in the pedagogical councils." Their association with the schools could be fruitful with proper organization. "Only freedom of assembly can make possible the development and activity of such groups." Acknowledging that the desired modifications of secondary instruction were possible "only in conjunction with a general reform of the political structure of the state," the Kharkov assembly concluded with a resolution that the Russian people be granted "freedom of speech, freedom of conscience, freedom of person, freedom of unions, freedom of assembly, and the participation in legislation and administration of their elected representatives."

The schoolchildren's revolt not only stimulated the parents to organized action; it also forced the schools to appeal to the families for help. Where local officials stood closer to the thinking of Pirogov than of Tolstoy, they confessed that not the gymnasium students but the general conditions of Russian life were responsible for the disorders. They also suggested as the first step toward the restoration of public confidence in the school that the central government renounce repressive measures against students once and for all. Enlightened provincial officialdom followed the pattern established at the end of February in the Black Sea city of Yalta.[12] There on February 23 a meeting was held in the town hall between parents and school officials to discuss the educational crisis. As a result of this conference a telegram was dispatched to the Ministry of the Interior denouncing the police brutality in Kursk. Arrangements were then made for another gathering of "parents and pedagogues" to discuss conditions in the secondary schools. This meeting was held in the boys' gymnasium on Sunday, February 27. There it was decided to elect a committee composed of six members from the teaching staffs of the various boys' and girls' secondary schools and six parents. The joint parent-teacher committee of twelve served as a mediator between the families and the pedagogical councils of the town. From that time until election day, March 2, a number of private conferences were held, together with vigorous pre-electoral campaigns. The most controversial of the many questions raised was whether the meetings of parents with school personnel were "public or not," and whether persons who did not enjoy the "rights of parents" nevertheless as citizens of the community could participate in the work of the schools. The question was decided in the negative. This decision was welcomed by school authorities, who preferred keeping cooperation with the public on as narrow a basis as possible.

The value of the parents as an instrument for restoring order in the schools was soon apparent to the Ministry. In March the curator of the St. Petersburg district, P. P. Izvolsky, brother of the Foreign Minister and future Ober-Procurator of the Holy Synod, was empowered to call a meeting of secondary school personnel as a preliminary step to permanently associating the parents in some formal way with the school. At the Izvolsky conference only a small minority of teachers favored unrestricted parental association. Making no secret of their fear of large groups, the majority preferred a small committee of delegates chosen according to social origin. The teachers were particularly dubious of the unwholesome effect on the schools of unlettered provincials. At the same time that it was eliciting the teachers' views, the Ministry of Education established a special committee under Izvolsky to draft a statute for parental organizations. It recommended that the parental groups should be organized by the director of the school and be kept small and under his control at all times. In other words, the parents' committees were to serve as an arm of the director for preserving order.[13]

As with the parents, the Kursk killings propelled the teachers toward collective action. On the day after the assault, faculty members of secondary-schools from the Moscow area urged their colleagues to join the liberation movement. The summons was transmitted to the educational regions through the pages of the constitutionalist journal *Pravo*: " 'So to live is no longer possible.' We the teachers of the secondary schools cannot acquiesce in the prevailing school order, with the bureaucratic-police school regime. Without academic freedom, without security in our own rights, we cannot train and educate the new generation condemned to the same lack of rights, to obedience to the same regime." The Moscow memorandum concluded with an appeal for representative government as the immediate prerequisite for reconstructing the school.[14]

The manifesto of February 13, 1905, the first of its kind in the history of the bureaucratic schools, stemmed from professional personnel associated with the Moscow pedagogical society. As early as 1899 the society had made a detailed study of the secondary school question in response to Bogolepov's July circular.[15] Besides liberalization of the curricula, it had recommended broadening the authority of teachers through the pedagogical council and a substantial pay raise to release them from economic dependence on the director. In March 1905 the Moscow organization issued an indictment of the educational establishment. It ascribed the current turmoil to the breakdown of rapport between faculty and students, and blamed the breakdown on the "police-bureaucratic" structure of the gymnasiums. The Tolstoy system not only excluded the public and the undergraduates from an active role in the learning process; it also interfered in their private lives and spread suspicion by encouraging spying among the boys. In its March report the pedagogical society welcomed the active interest of secondary pupils in current affairs. A calm and reasonable attitude toward student petitions, it suggested, could help break down the wall separating teachers from the taught. In the concluding resolution the group's more than 600 members, professors, teachers, doctors, parents, and journalists, pledged themselves to support constructive undergraduate demands. Excusing the students from responsibility for the "emotional agitation" and "misunderstandings" that had occurred, it condemned administrative reprisals and requested their immediate cessation as the first step toward restoring harmony between students and staff.[16] The Ministry of Education reacted to the unsolicited diagnosis with a severe reprimand. On the grounds that the Moscow organization had abandoned technical pedagogical discussion for politics and therefore violated its constitution, its operations were suspended.

The day was past when the bureaucracy could stifle public initiative with the stroke of a pen. Since the assassination of Plehve, society had been "seizing its rights" with increasing boldness. In the autumn of 1904 zemstvo assemblies had taken to organizing regional and national congresses in defiance of the government. Since the beginning of 1905 increasing numbers of townsmen were engaged in forming politically oriented professional unions at considerable risk to the individuals involved. "Indeed, with very few exceptions, the members of the various societies and unions were dependent on the state, the supreme command. They had only their service pay to live on, and when they placed their signatures on a resolution, they risked a great deal—they risked their livelihoods, their very bread."[17] By April the teachers were ready to join the rest of the professional class and organize. From April 11 to 13 educators from 30 provinces and the two capitals met in Moscow to draft a constitution.[18] The provinces were represented by 83 persons, St. Petersburg and Moscow by 58. (Eleven delegates gave no location.) Of the 152 delegates, 71 represented village and urban schools, 52 secondary institutions, and the remaining 29 various scholastic interests. By acclamation the congress advocated reform, from the village school to the university, along the lines of "freedom, democratization, and decentralization." It could not achieve unanimity, however, on the tactical activities of the group. Some delegates insisted on limiting the prospective organization to "purely professional tasks" in order to attract support from persons of all political parties and ideological persuasions. The majority disagreed. After lengthy debate the assembly recognized by a vote of 96 to 23 that "the all-Russian teachers' union ought to have professional and political functions."[19]

In St. Petersburg a union of teachers and supporters of primary schools, whose members were active in the creation of the all-Russian teachers' union, had already been formed. The militancy of the rural and elementary personnel with their double commitment to "political freedom" and "comprehensive socioeconomic reforms" alerted many Petersburg staff members to their own special concerns. The triumph of democracy might well level the schools. As a consequence, the secondary instructors in the capital diverged from the pattern of professional unions being molded out of almost every segment of the educated class. Unlike the university professors, primary teachers, secondary teachers in Moscow, zemstvo employees, lawyers, doctors, veterinarians, pharmacists, journalists, and accountants, they eschewed partisan political attachments as far as possible and concentrated on strictly professional tasks. Their first local union coalesced in St. Petersburg around the nucleus of a secret club that had come into existence the previous year. It was formed by 250 teachers who subscribed to the Moscow memorandum of February 13. Their own declaration appeared on May 1, 1905.*

The most persuasive essay in support of liberal education since Pirogov's Vital Questions, the Petersburg manifesto asserted that the purpose of schooling was to enable the individual to emancipate himself from police authority and develop personal initiative. Analyzing the problem

---

* *Pravo*, No. 17, 1905, pp. 1386–92. A translation of the manifesto is in Appendix B.

of guiding adolescents toward adulthood, the St. Petersburg pedagogues demanded that the school be responsive to society rather than subservient to the bureaucracy. This changing-of-the-guard was to be achieved through an informed public opinion and the flowering of professional competence rather than through subordination of the secondary school to local government. Distributed like its predecessor through the pages of *Pravo,* the May document concluded with a passionate appeal to secondary personnel to organize, both to overcome the isolation of the individual staff member and to "take away from the weak and inexperienced pupils the struggle for the school."

All-Russian Efforts

With the closing of the schools for the summer vacation, the direct agitation of pupils, parents, and teachers was suspended while the liberation movement spread in scope and deepened in intensity. In June mutiny aboard the cruiser *Potemkin* focused attention on the unrest of the armed forces. By August the government had agreed upon the terms that concluded the conflict with Japan. In an effort to divide the educated class from the masses and postpone the time when constitutional reorganizing might become necessary, autonomy was restored to the universities on August 27. This second major concession of the year made matters worse. Barred to the police, the lecture halls became enclaves for revolution. The professors soon abandoned the noisy classrooms; strike committees and the nascent councils (soviets) of workers' deputies took their place.

On October 7 the railway union struck in Moscow. The work stoppage spread to the entire rail network and beyond to the telegraph and telephone services. At first the strikers called for a constituent assembly, civil liberties, and an eight-hour working day. When results exceeded expectations, they raised the red flag, demanding a democratic republic and the arming of the people. Witte, back from America, where he had negotiated the peace with Japan, informed Nicholas II that he must either impose a military dictatorship or grant a constitution. A search was begun for a strong man. Meanwhile, on October 15 work commenced on a manifesto which would grant personal inviolability, freedom of conscience, speech, assembly, and union, as well as a state duma with limited but genuine legislative powers and some administrative control over the bureaucracy.

When the general strike was called in St. Petersburg on October 13, the students of the Larinsky gymnasium, who had responded with alacrity to Bloody Sunday, were the first of the city's secondary pupils to abandon their studies. Augmented by the first realschule, they marched about the city to the other schools singing the Marseillaise and calling the undergraduates out. By the next day all the gymnasiums in the city were closed. On October 17 the third and final concession of the year, Witte's manifesto, was published. Its appearance released a wave of jubilation and relief. A holiday mood swept the country. Sober editorials hailed the advent of liberty after centuries of despotism.[20] Schoolboys flew kites in front of police stations; water carriers abandoned their buckets; policemen polished their boots as never before.[21] Although regarded by most as but the first of many concessions to be won, the October manifesto accomplished the salvation of tsardom by dividing the social opposition to the bureaucracy. Absolutists were appalled by its radicalism; radicals were contemptuous of its conservatism. An influential if minor portion of the population was ready to accept it as a basis for peaceful reconstruction. This acceptance weakened the attack on the bureaucratic school.

In the spring, teachers, parents, and pupils had been united against the Tolstoy system. Now their differences surfaced. The parents moved toward cooperation with the directors to restore the normal routine in the schools as quickly as possible.* The teachers were increasingly embarrassed by the students. Inspired by the organizational rights granted university undergraduates, the secondary pupils strove in some places to seize control of the schools. Ignoring the objections of the St. Petersburg curator, the students of the Vvedensky gymnasium resolved "to elect elders from the older classes who will conduct the affairs of the gymnasium. Not recognizing the remains of the autocratic tsarist government, we do not recognize its henchmen, the heads of the gymnasium. We do not recognize expulsion or punishment unless approved by our central committee."[22] In the first realschule the students united with the faculty. On October 13 eight members of the pedagogical council supplemented their colleagues' decision to close the school in view of the general strike, with the resolution that "orderly classes are impossible

---

* Commenting on the "feverish temperature" of the schools in April 1906, the new Minister of Education, Aleksandr von Kaufmann, embraced both parents and students as "allies" (*S-Peterburgskiia vedomosti*, 6 April 1906, p. 2).

until the establishment of the rule of law in the country as a whole."[23] When the director called in police to keep the school open, the teachers forced his resignation. When the parents' assembly failed to support the inspector's bid for control, the faculty rallied behind the "progressive eight" and assumed direction of the school.

In the provinces the teachers likewise often found themselves caught between the students and the administration. In the Azov gymnasium the undergraduates used the pause that followed the October manifesto to frame a set of academic demands. When the director shelved their petition, the teachers banded together to force its consideration in the pedagogical council. The director then had the student requests denounced by the parents at a special meeting. The students' threat of a strike was averted when the pedagogical council voiced its approval of their suggestions. Rather than accept majority rule, the director shut down the school. In Pskov the teachers strove to restrain the students by accepting some of their demands, such as freer use of the library, and by rejecting others, such as student representation on the pedagogical council. In Libau the students rioted in defiance of both the director and the pedagogical council before letting themselves be mollified by a popular teacher.

At the end of October the pedagogical councils of the city of Kursk met in joint session. Analyzing student behavior, they found it perfectly understandable that the older boys were showing an interest in political questions at a time when all elements of society were in the grip of a "political tidal wave carrying the fatherland toward a new civil life based on the principles of freedom and law." This interest, in the teachers' view, inspired the pupils' enthusiasm for extreme political doctrines "in which they expect to find at once the most complete realization of their selfless dreams of universal well-being, but by which the objective relationship is destroyed toward the real condition of the state and the immutable general laws of national political evolution." Expressing understanding and even sympathy for the younger generation's "burst of passion," the teachers considered it their duty "to guide the political development" of the students "according to the word of science and conscience." Only friendly, informal pupil-teacher relations, the pedagogical councils of the city were convinced, could nourish mutual trust and prevent "the strikes, disturbances, and demonstrations that lead to a loss of precious class time and produce a state of sick, nervous excitement in the young people."[24] Through the introduction into the curriculum of a course in jurisprudence, the organization of lectures and class discussion of original papers on political themes, the Kursk teachers quieted the agitation and made possible the resumption of classes in November.

Looking beyond the restoration of discipline to basic school reform, faculty members organized themselves on a considerably larger scale than in the spring.[25] In Saratov the pedagogical councils had supported student demands against the directors. On October 14, 80 of the city's more than 200 teachers held a meeting, expressed opposition to the political strike, and drafted a statute for a strictly professional union. In Nizhni Novgorod groups combined, split, and proliferated until at the beginning of November a study circle combining oppositional elements of various pedagogical councils converted itself into a professional union. Uniting with members of the municipal government, the directors offered the teachers representation in a comprehensive organization. Whereas this offer failed to attract much attention, the union diminished its own allure by incorporating into its constitution support for direct political action. After the December strike movement subsided, the membership dropped from 117 to 99. In Kharkov the professional association grew out of three preliminary meetings of delegates from pedagogical councils throughout the city. Official hostility trimmed the organization's initial component of 160 to 97.

The provincial teachers who remained looked for national leadership to Moscow, where during the general political strike of October an organizational committee for the formation of the Moscow union of secondary school personnel was formed. To keep the question of secondary school reform from swamping in the heavy political seas, the organizers advertised a professional union with appeal for those willing to sign the Moscow memorandum of February 13, 1905. On October 21, 360 teachers gathered to launch the Moscow union. Its statute became a model for the provinces.[26]

According to its constitution the aims of the Moscow union were a "reorganization of all types of secondary schools on the principles of democracy and free access, to transform them from bureaucratic-administrative institutions into free and autonomous ones in direct contact with primary and higher schools." To achieve these ends the Muscovites proposed a six-point program. (1) Inside the classroom the teachers should exercise their own judgment in pedagogical and disciplinary matters rather than trying to reconcile contradictory circulars from the Ministry of Education. (2) Every effort should be made to bring the school into closer contact with pupils, parents, and public groups interested in education. (3) The authority of the pedagogical council should be expanded to include selection of administrative and teaching staff. (4) The members of the union should promote union resolutions in the pedagogical councils, adhere to the union program, and support one another by all means, including boycotts and strikes. (5) The union should enter into relations with all organizations pursuing the same aims. (6) The union should support morally and materially members made to suffer for their activity. It should finance a war chest and keep the progressive press informed of arbitrary administrative reprisals taken against teachers.

Soon after its formation the Moscow union clashed with the curator of the Moscow school district. Aleksandr Schwartz was disturbed by evidence that some directors and pedagogical councils were not only sympathizing with student dissenters but conniving with them. Information was reaching his office that students were violating discipline in the school with impunity, and participating in street demonstrations without reprisal. Directors were receiving unlawful petitions and permitting so-called delegates to be elected. They were even making classrooms available for meetings. In his view the schools under his command were acting "with excessive tolerance toward events absolutely unlawful and impermissible in any kind of properly organized educational institution." To give pupils and teachers "time to calm down," the curator temporarily suspended classes, with the admonition that the schools were to use the respite to get in touch with parents and solicit their aid in quieting the children.

On October 19, the day after the reception of the news in Moscow of the October manifesto, Schwartz delivered an ultimatum to his directors in flawless bureaucratic style: "If, despite your friendly pressure and that of the pedagogical council, the pupils committed to your care and to that of their parents renew their efforts to create disorders and refuse to submit to your commands given in the name of the pedagogical council, I recommend to you, dear sir, with reference to the circular of February 26, No. 4155, based on the instructions of the special commission organized under the chairmanship of state secretary Ermolov, to declare all such pupils expelled, and to be further guided exactly by the regulations of the same circular. In case of any kind of gross violence on the part of the students, I request you to petition me at once for permission to shut down the school. I have no doubt that the parents, especially at the present time, will dutifully exert their influence on their children and, assuming themselves the concern for desirable improvements in education, will convince the young people that in the school, which cannot tolerate disorder, there is place for only one activity, namely study."[27]

Schwartz's prosaic reminder that school was a haven for scholarship, dropped into the atmosphere of October, exploded. The Moscow union, along with the revived Moscow pedagogical society, parents' meetings, and several pedagogical councils, demanded his resignation, on the grounds that "the circular of the curator of the Moscow school district of October 19, 1905, contradicts the elementary rights of the individual recognized even by the recent manifesto of October 17."[28] In a meeting of the school district on October 23, Schwartz accused the council of the Moscow seventh gymnasium of lying. When the insulted faculty resolved to quit in a body if the curator did not resign, the Moscow union, pressuring the directors when necessary, pushed through the city's pedagogical councils an expression of solidarity and threat of boycott.

Another immediate problem facing the Moscow union was when to resume classes. As long as roaming Black Hundred gangs continued to beat students, the union advised keeping the schools closed. When the streets quieted down at the end of October, the union cautioned each school to decide for itself when to reopen. Closely connected with the question of resuming classes was what to do about students' petitions. On October 29, the union heard student delegates demand the following: removal of Curator Schwartz of the Moscow school district (he soon resigned); freedom of assembly and meetings within the school outside of class time without the mandatory presence of staff members; freedom of organization and student unions; free access for secondary pupils to all public meetings, including zemstvos and courts; abolition of street surveillance for all ages; abolition of persecution for nonfulfillment of religious obligations; and abolition of the obligatory uniform for all students. Approving these solicitations, the union promised to support them in the city's pedagogical councils.[29]

Within a month of its foundation the Moscow union's membership included more than half of the district's 900 secondary school personnel.

Avoiding affiliation with the all-Russian teachers' union because of its openly political character, the nonparty secondary organization actively encouraged close contacts with student and parental groups. In its general assemblies, which met weekly from mid-October until mid-December, the Moscow association not only invited students and parents to send delegates, one from each school, but allowed them to vote along with the teachers. During this period of relative optimism, most of the attention of the members was devoted to schemes for a public secondary school free from social restrictions in fact as well as in theory and independent of the state bureaucracy. By December there were also negotiations in progress between Moscow, St. Petersburg, and the provinces, looking toward the amalgamation of the local unions into a national organization. These plans were delayed by the final upsurge of the general strike movement. On December 8 the Moscow union voted to support the political strike in the city and sent a member of its central bureau to the local strike committee. After the strike became an armed uprising, troops from St. Petersburg crushed it with artillery. The "days of liberty" were over.

In January 1906, when the St. Petersburg and Moscow unions issued a summons for a constitutional congress to establish a nationwide organization of secondary school personnel, frightened faculty were already deserting the local associations. In Moscow two teachers publicly withdrew from the union, although a search of the records failed to verify that they had ever been members. After the first of the year other educators attacked the union for its espousal of direct political action and for its toleration of militant student dissent. University professors wondered whether the union aimed at leveling all educational institutions to one low standard.[30] In St. Petersburg the Ministry of Education ended the rebellion of the first realschule by firing the "progressive eight" faculty members and depriving them of the right to teach anywhere else, even in private schools. It then sent in a new staff, which braved egg-throwing students to restore the bureaucratic regime.

Under these conditions the organizers of the constitutional convention understandably preferred the Grand Duchy of Finland to St. Petersburg as a place for their deliberations. On February 9, 1906, 80 teachers from twenty cities and towns gathered in Imatra to create an all-Russian union of secondary teachers and personnel.[31] The knottiest problem facing the delegates was the structure of the expanded organization. Should the national association be an independent entity or a federation of local groups? Opinion on this question divided between St. Petersburg and the provinces, with Moscow occupying a middle position. The St. Petersburg union presented the case for a strong centralized authority able to bind local groups with its decisions and competent to admit individuals to membership where there was no local receiving body. The provincial groups feared a capital-dominated central bureau dictating tactics to them in the struggle against local officials. At the same time, they needed the support of a strong national organization to survive the pressure of the curators and directors in the outlying cities, where the numbers of secondary personnel were small. Led by the delegates from the Saratov union, the provincial teachers insisted that the local associations have complete discretion on which tactics to employ against local officials as long as they informed the national organization afterward. The Moscow union, in turn, stressed the importance of decisions and resolutions binding all affiliates. It also realized that demoralization was bound to spread through the profession if local groups were unable to implement central policies. It accordingly proposed an arrangement whereby all organizations would accept its six-point program for transforming the "bureaucratic administrative school into a free and autonomous school"* while, at the same time, reserving the right to modify tactics as long as prior notice was given to a general congress.

This solution was well-meaning but too cumbersome. The issue was resolved by accepting the Moscow tactics in principle and leaving their realization to the discretion of each local organization. To further allay the fears that the provincial unions nursed toward the large associations in Moscow and St. Petersburg, the question of the number of delegates that each group would send to the national conventions was decided in favor of regressive proportion. The provinces, however, did not obtain the guarantee they desired, that at least one-third of the seats on the central bureau be reserved for them.

From the consideration of internal structure the founders of the all-Russian union passed to the equally difficult problem of their formal relations with student and parental associations. The most sensitive subject on the agenda of the congress was what stance the teachers should take toward the students, who, like themselves, were rebelling against

---

* For the Moscow program, see above, pp. 185–86.

bureaucratic centralism. Discussion of this issue centered around a number of proposals for neutralizing student spontaneity and bringing it under classroom control. Engaging as the idea was, the realistic appraisal of their vulnerable situation forced the teachers to drop any claim to monopolize the "struggle for academic ideals." Fearful themselves of even meeting in St. Petersburg, they dared not antagonize the students with so much as a hushed disavowal of militant action. After much debate the resolutions, which in their original form were openly critical of some aggressive aspects of student dissent, were softened into a vague recommendation of "support" and "cooperation."

The educational profession had also to define its attitude toward parents' groups. On November 25, 1905, the Ministry of Education had issued regulations for establishing parents' committees at every school. Since the new organs were envisaged as allies of the directors against both students and teachers, St. Petersburg refrained from tying its officials down with detailed instructions beyond the stipulation that the chairman of the local organization would share the rights of the honorary curator in sessions of the pedagogical council. In December, after the state had demonstrated with artillery fire in Moscow that it was capable of restoring order, parents began to lose interest in the limited and formal association permitted them by the November rules. By 1906 indifference was spreading.[32] Its appearance was not altogether unwelcome in progressive teacher circles. In some instances, the delegates to Imatra reported, the family had supported students and teachers against the bureaucracy, but such support could not be taken for granted. On the contrary, the teachers' unions anticipated difficulty spreading "correct views" among the "reactionary and ignorant mass" of parents. After some discussion, the expression "reactionary and ignorant" was deleted from the official resolution of the congress, and the task of faculty members was redefined as enlightening the "remaining mass" of parents.[33]

Besides bringing into existence an all-Russian professional association, the secondary teachers sketched the outlines of a "democratic, autonomous, and free school." In a preliminary statement intended to stimulate discussion, the organizing committee of the congress defined the terms of this common goal. By "democratic" they meant that all social, religious, national, and sexual barriers to admission should be abolished. To ensure accessibility, secondary schools ought to be made available in every district capital and every large village and their program coordinated with that of the lower urban schools. The word "autonomous" stressed the corporate structure of the school. The pedagogical council would select its own members and bear full responsibility for both curriculum and discipline. "Free" denoted the emancipation of the school from the state bureaucracy. Efforts to define these concepts more precisely divided the delegates into two distinct factions. The official protocol of the congress glosses over the political affiliations underlying the differences. But the presence of a "collectivist democratic" Left and an "individualistic liberal" Right within the teachers' liberation movement is evident.

The democratic centralists argued that the school was primarily a social organ and that only society in the broadest sense should have the power to regulate its functions. The younger generation did not belong to its parents but "to itself, the people as a whole, and the future." Once control of the government passed to the representatives of the people, the whole structure of public education must be centralized more than ever. "The ideal school is the state school." Absolute unity of program and structure, they conceded, is impossible in a country as large and as diversified as Russia. Hopefully the advent of parliamentary government would ensure that the "future Ministry of Education will have sufficient flexibility not to level various school types beyond necessity and so restrict the freedom of personal creativity." The danger to the individual was viewed as coming from another direction. Private initiative in education, unless checked by a democratic government, would inevitably give rise to exclusive schools for the privileged few. Such institutions would foster caste instincts and class divisions among the coming generation. The youth must be protected from every effort to shape them into an "antisocial force."

The liberal federalists among the teachers warned the convention that it would be difficult for any Russian government, no matter how democratic, to overcome the habits of history. It was unlikely that after centuries of "slavish centralization" state officials would suddenly display a "free and creative" spirit in education simply because the form of government had been altered. With these reservations in mind, the teaching profession would do well to concentrate on obtaining self-government for the secondary schools. This could best be accomplished by decentralizing the school system. As for democracy, it would be better served by open admission to state schools rather than by recentralization under a government that in February 1906 had not yet revealed how representative it would be. The liberals were prepared to accept a certain lowering of academic standards as the price for mass instruction. This could be partially offset if the government allowed groups and individuals greater freedom to open their own schools. This is what the Ministry of Education was about to do for both financial and political reasons.[34]

Events thrust the teachers toward an early second congress. At the end of April 1906 the first state duma convened. The Constitutional Democratic Party, the tentative political arm of the professional middle class, had emerged from the nation's first electoral campaign as the dominant faction in the legislative assembly. Its leaders intended to exploit their position of leadership to force the autocracy to grant full parliamentary government in which the ministers of state would be responsible to the deputies of the people rather than to the Crown. Nicholas II had other ideas. Fortified by a generous loan from his French ally, secure in the knowledge that the regular army was loyal, and confident that the overwhelming majority of his subjects desired an end to domestic strife, he was ready to adhere to the maxim of his slain uncle Sergei and "stand firm." His civil arm, the bureaucracy, had emerged from the turbulence of 1905 better organized than at any time since its consolidation in 1802. After the October manifesto the central government had been reorganized by Witte as a council of ministers with a prime minister who, if he were a strong and capable man enjoying the confidence of the emperor, might end or at least restrain the traditional rivalry between departments, which had been the bane of the central state bureaucracy.[35] In addition, the monarchy retained the Council of State as an upper house. It had also equipped itself with a number of statutes and fundamental laws defining and constraining the general liberties granted the previous fall.

The state duma, as was predicted, clashed immediately with the tsar's appointed ministers. Behind the rhetoric and maneuvering of May and June was the issue of whether the representatives of the people or state officials would direct the reconstruction of the country after the stalled revolution and the lost war. During the brief stalemate the duma's subcommittees were busy drafting legislation in the event that the contending parties came to a working agreement. Throughout the empire special groups were meeting to formulate their proposals for favorable laws.

The all-Russian union of elementary school teachers announced a convention in June. It was time for the secondary school specialists to put their own conceptions into legal format for presentation to the duma's educational committee. This time they met in St. Petersburg. The first congress had organized the national association. The second of 150 delegates from 51 cities aspired to decentralize the Tolstoy system.[36]

Before taking up the principal business of the convention, the participants disposed of several tactical questions. On March 4, 1906, the government issued temporary rules for societies and unions. Since the regulations required that the constitution of an organization be submitted to the proper authorities for approval, the all-Russian union's central bureau had advised its affiliates "not to pay the slightest attention" to official procedure. If necessary to survive, a local union could camouflage itself as a "pedagogical society." Since February the secondary teachers had stiffened their stance against the bureaucracy. Gone in June was their ambivalence toward the students. They now refused them outright a decisive voice in the administration of the school.

With respect to other related groups the educators had become markedly friendlier. The union of parents of secondary pupils despatched a welcome delegation to the Petersburg gathering. Gymnasium and realschule faculty members were also more anxious than before to cooperate with elementary personnel. On the one hand, they were sincerely interested in meshing the separate levels of education, the urban with the rural, the secondary with the primary. On the other hand, an amalgamation of the 700-member secondary union with the 12,000-member elementary union posed structural problems. There were subtler difficulties as well. In their political sympathies most secondary teachers tended to side with the constitutional democrats. The rural primary teachers were socialistic in temper. The secondary union expressed urban, the primary union rural, aspirations. Further, the all-Russian union of secondary school teachers had grown out of provincial associations. Its structure was federalistic. The all-Russian elementary union drew its strength from the mass of individual members rather than from local groups which were difficult to maintain in isolated areas. Its structure was centralistic. Nevertheless, the second congress of secondary school personnel notified the elementary union that the secondary teachers were ready for consolidation whenever the elementary teachers subordinated political and social to purely professional concerns.

Once they had settled their relations with allied associations, the secondary teachers concentrated on the main purpose of their convocation. No matter what the outcome of the current contest between the bureaucracy and the duma, they wanted to ensure public and professional supremacy within the general educational school. Four projects were presented to the Petersburg congress for reorganizing the administrative structure of the Tolstoy system. All of them reserved pedagogical matters to the teachers alone. Neither the Ministry of Education nor the parents were to interfere in the professional sphere. All of the schemes distributed responsibility for managing the school among the teachers, local government, and the parents. All four projects were in agreement that any limitation of the state's role in education would depend on the outcome of the present duel between the government and the state duma. Supposing the elected deputies won out, should the Ministry of Education be reduced to a mere central agency for gathering statistics and disbursing funds? Would not the transfer of authority from St. Petersburg to the community threaten professional autonomy? A delegate from the teachers' union in Tiflis discussed at length the perils of placing the gymnasiums and the realschulen under the school boards created in 1864 for administering the primary schools. Russia, he observed, was neither England nor the United States, where public life was highly developed. A delegate from the Moscow union praised the merits of a strong Ministry of Education under the control of the state duma. Other delegates stressed the financial facts of life. As long as the state, whether absolute or constitutional, made available the bulk of the funds for secondary education, the schools would remain under central control.

Two of the motions presented to the convention tied school administration directly to local government. The scheme put forward by the St. Petersburg union attached a school council to the zemstvos. This body would include representatives of local government, business, and the educational profession. Ultimate authority over the schools of a given area would rest with the provincial zemstvo assembly. The school councils would function as its "executive organ." Critics were quick to point out the shortcomings of the St. Petersburg scheme. It surrendered the schools completely to the zemstvos, and in areas where the zemstvos were weak this could spell financial ruin. It also left out the parents. Not all the delegates reserved as important a place for the zemstvos as did St. Petersburg. The teachers' union of Nizhni Novgorod introduced a proposal for coordinating the secondary with the primary school system which would seat not only teachers, counselors, and school doctors but representatives from public organizations and parental associations in the pedagogical councils.[37] Only when the elements within the council failed to agree could the school board, composed of public representatives at the provincial level, intervene.

Moscow presented two separate proposals for converting state schools into public schools. One was the product of a teacher who had presented the first sketch of his idea to the Moscow district conference in 1899. His suggestion was to organize society specifically to participate in school policy through expansion of the existing office of honorary curator. Although his scheme was not without originality, it was attacked for being made up of the "debris of the past." More significant because of its prestigious source was the prospectus put forward by the Moscow union, which divided the direction of the secondary school between school council and pedagogical council.[38] The pedagogical council would restrict itself to technical questions concerning curricula and teaching methods. The school council, composed of representatives from the pedagogical council, municipal and county government, and delegates from parents' committees, would be responsible for selecting the faculty. Public representatives were not to make up more than half of the members of the school council. As explained by one of its proponents, the Moscow plan deliberately constructed the school council on a broad basis as a battlefield where "progressive" parents could fight it out with "Black Hundred" parents. The vast majority of politically indifferent parents, it was assumed, would simply stay away. After discussing all four approaches to dismantling bureaucratic centralism, the teachers agreed that a council or board that would bring together the teaching profession, parents, and local officials of town and country would be the best instrument for public control of the school.[39]

The second congress of secondary teachers ended on a cautiously optimistic note. In June the first duma still appeared to be holding its own. There was even talk of forming a ministry that would include constitutionalist opponents of the bureaucracy. Within a month the state demonstrated that it could dismiss an elected national assembly at will. Lesser instruments of public initiative, even "strictly professional" unions, could hardly expect to survive for long.*

* In January 1907 there were 70 groups associated with the all-Russian union of secondary school teachers. Only 40 were active. The life of the association centered in St. Petersburg and Moscow.

PART THREE

Toward Public Enlightenment
1905–1914

A determination to increase the activity of the state and to seek the co-operation of "responsible" representatives of the people in the work of educating the country was an essential part of the broad reform program espoused by the man who became Prime Minister after the dismissal of the first duma in the summer of 1906, Count Petr Stolypin. A graduate in physics and mathematics of St. Petersburg University, this last outstanding practitioner of bureaucratic nationalism never lost sight of the agrarian foundations of tsarist power. His ownership of land in the western provinces acquainted him directly with the social and ethnic complexities of the minority regions. From the governor's palace at Saratov on the Volga he experienced the Revolution of 1905 as the rage of the peasantry at an administrative structure it did not understand. Under his leadership the state bureaucracy not only repressed subversion; it also hastened to reorganize the social foundations of rural life. "You desire a great upheaval. We desire a great Russia," the Prime Minister challenged the belligerent second duma. He then replaced it with the argumentative but less hostile third. Arbitrarily promulgating a new election law, he reduced the representation of the cities and non-Russian territories in order to concentrate the vote in the hands of the Great Russian gentry. The manipulation of the franchise occurred just as the dispirited delegates of the depleted all-Russian union of secondary school teachers were convening for the third and final time to bury their dreams of administrative autonomy for the university preparatory schools.[1]

The coup d'etat of June 3, 1907, branded its mastermind an enemy of public initiative and strangler of the educated class. Stolypin's vigorous pragmatism, which eventually won him as many enemies at court as among the intelligentsia, inaugurated a brief interwar period of internal progress highlighted by phenomenal expansion of educational opportunity. Only the universities failed to prosper. Despite the gift of autonomy to the faculties in 1905, Ministry officials and undergraduates continued their habitual war. Provocations and counterprovocations kept the lecture halls in an uproar, which culminated with the expulsion of 6,000 students in 1911. (After Stolypin's assassination, most were readmitted.) The chronic upset of the state establishments encouraged public support and bureaucratic toleration for the period's most promising adventure in higher schooling, the movement to establish local universities under municipal control. By 1908 there were fifteen organizations at work promoting advanced post-secondary education for working adults. The St. Petersburg society for a people's university maintained ten auditoriums throughout the city. They soon registered an attendance of 20,000 to their lectures on cultural and practical subjects. The generosity of a self-made mining engineer, who had acquired a fortune in Siberia, enabled the city duma of the old capital to open the country's first fully public institution of higher learning in 1908. By 1914 the A. L. Shaniavsky People's University of Moscow had enrolled 1,390 full-time and 3,982 part-time students in its academic sections and special programs. Half of the registrants were women. Most, both men and women, were teachers or officials from the city and provinces taking advantage of the low fees and high quality of the day and night courses (often taught by professors who found working conditions in the state institutions nerve-wracking) to study everything from history and law to pedagogy, library science, and public administration.[2]

The sponsors of the People's University movement were also interested in primary education for the masses. In this vast field the state alone commanded the resources of money and organization to realize significant schemes. The second duma had tried to transfer control over rural enlightenment to the zemstvos and municipal dumas before Stolypin sent its members home. The third duma would have liked to concentrate authority in the central educational bureaucracy in order to promote Russian language preeminence throughout the empire.[3] The Ministry of Education brushed aside efforts of the state duma to participate in elementary school policy. At this stage what was needed was money and staff, not further friction with political minorities. In 1908 the ministry of Aleksandr von Kaufmann presented tsardom with its first systematic legislative program for realizing Tolstoy's dream of universal compulsory elementary schooling. The indispensable prerequisite for the success of this goal (which was projected into the 1920's) was the rapid enlargement of the educated middle class from which the army of teachers would come. And so, within two years of near political collapse, the tsarist state marshaled its resources behind broad-scale expansion of both men's and women's general secondary schools. In this area the bureaucracy accepted ideas from the elected representatives of society. In fact, the upsurge of gymnasium and realschule construction was haphazard until the principal faction in the third state duma prodded the Ministry of Education toward more deliberate and comprehensive planning.

With 154 deputies out of 422, the Union of October 17 was the largest party in the national assembly. Drawing their support from the zemstvos and cities, the Octobrists represented the cautiously progressive vanguard of the Great Russian propertied classes. They owed their position of leadership to an electoral system that guaranteed to 200,000 noblemen 50 per cent of the seats in the state assembly. The Octobrists opposed any form of territorial federalism that might encourage self-determination among the ethnic minorities, but they supported decentralization in the main centers where they favored freedom of action for municipal dumas and country zemstvos. They believed in civil liberties, but not at the expense of property rights. Social change, they were convinced, could best be stabilized by the spread of education under the direction of local leaders of local society. Through their command of key committees, especially education and the budget, they endeavored to guide the growth of schools in a direction that would favor Great Russians in general, and landowning Great Russians in particular.

The first step toward culturally guaranteeing the social hegemony of Great Russian proprietors was to map the existing scholastic topography. Investigating the regional density of the secondary schools for both boys and girls, the budget committee of the state duma made some uncomfortable discoveries. With seven-tenths of the land surface and 11 per cent of the people, eastern Russia was virtually devoid of gymnasiums and realschulen. Except for Irkutsk, with three girls' academies, the Siberian oblasts contained but one boys' and one girls' secondary school apiece. Except for Akmolinsk with its three girls' schools, the central Asian oblasts were equally devoid of secondary schools. As for population ratio, Semirechinsk maintained one secondary school for each half-million people.[4]

The contrast between European and Asian densities was clear and unmistakable. In European Russia, however, the pattern was subtler, since it depended on the historic settlement of the area. As of January 1911 there were 1,725 secondary schools for boys and girls spread through 90 provinces and oblasts for an average of 19.2 schools per administrative region. Six provinces alone—St. Petersburg with 124, Moscow with 116, Kherson with 85, Kiev with 58, Kharkov with 53, Livonia with 52—accounted for 28 per cent of the existing facilities. Not only did the number of schools per province vary widely; there were also considerable differences in the number of inhabitants per student. The province of St. Petersburg, for instance, contained 23,000 persons for each secondary school student, Moscow 27,000, Livonia 28,000, Kiev 76,000, Tula 83,000, and Kursk 99,000.[5] These differences brought out a feature of more immediate interest to the duma than the spotty enlightenment east of the Urals, namely, that outside the cities of St. Petersburg and Moscow secondary schools were more thinly spaced in the central Great Russian provinces than in the non–Great Russian areas.

When the Octobrists began drafting a plan for school construction in 1910, they used their own distribution chart and concentrated on bringing the "neglected" home provinces up to the imperial average. Their hopes for progress in the area of boys' schools were encouraged by the historical record of public support for girls' schools. Since the great reforms of the 1860's, the state had considered secondary education for girls in the same fiscal category as secular primary education for the peasantry, that is, a local responsibility. As early as 1858 the government had declared that girls' schools should have a private character. By this it meant that state funds were unavailable and that the construction and upkeep of the schools would depend on local aid. In 1866 the government had reaffirmed that girls' schools should look for their major support to the community, its social and class groups, and private benefactors. Full state support was restricted to 35 institutions situated in the non-Russian border areas of the empire.[6] Half of these were in Poland alone, with the rest scattered over Lithuania, the Ukraine, Priamur, Turkestan, the Caucasus, and Finland. There were no state-supported gymnasiums for girls in the central Russian provinces. Concurrently with the statute of May 24, 1870, for girls' secondary schools, the state treasury made available 150,000 rubles a year for grants-in-aid. No single gymnasium was to receive more than 2,000 rubles a year and no progymnasium more than 1,000 rubles. From 1884 to 1914 grants-in-aid increased from 618,000 to 1,664,000 rubles. As a percentage of total state funds for education, they steadily declined from 15 per cent in 1884 to 9 per cent in 1902 to less than 6 per cent in 1913.[7] Even at this late date the average amount of state aid to each institution, 1,518 rubles, amounted to less than the food allowance given a director of a state boys' gymnasium.

In 1899, when state funds contributed 8.9 per cent to the total support of girls' secondary schools, 4 per cent of the schools enjoyed an income corresponding to the annual budget of 27,000 rubles of state boys' gymnasiums, 35 per cent had lower but still workable budgets, 64 per cent subsisted on less than 5,000 rubles a year, and 16 per cent were destitute.[8] Salaries were low, often amounting to a half or a quarter of those in boys' schools. In their annual appeals for more state funds, district curators continually reported that women teachers were enthusiastic but poorly trained and that men teachers in the girls' schools preferred regular jobs in boys' establishments, considering their misfortune temporary and leaving at the first opportunity.

Mandatory reliance on local in lieu of state financing hindered academic development. Ninety per cent of local support was in the form of tuition. Better schools required staffs paid the equivalent of teachers in boys' gymnasiums. More adequate salaries could come only from higher payments, which would limit accessibility. Lower fees broadened opportunity but reduced quality by keeping the staffs underpaid. Whatever choice there might have been in theory between accessibility and quality, the decision was made in fact by the state's needs at the moment. After 1905 the projected introduction of universal primary education dominated both official and public thinking. Increasing at the rate of 8,000 units a year, the elementary schools absorbed most of the increases of state funds and made expansion of girls' gymnasiums necessary to relieve the critical shortage of teaching personnel. Official reluctance to let women into the universities was directly connected with official interest in women as more pliable rural instructors than men.

Low cost had the one advantage of stimulating growth. Many communities below the level of district center could afford a girls' school when the state could not finance a regular boys' school in the area. For every boy in general education in 1909 there were 423 males in the empire, whereas for every girl pupil there were 319 women. The reason for this was that there were three girls' schools in the country for every two boys' schools.[9] Observing the numerical preponderance of girls' over boys' schools, the budget committee of the state duma advised the Ministry of Education that if it would relax its administrative stranglehold on men's gymnasiums and realschulen, local communities would be more willing to augment state building grants with public funds.

As long as tsardom was still recovering from the shocks of revolution and war, it relied on public and private agencies to open additional boys' schools. From 1905 to 1908 local sources supplied the main impetus to growth, and the percentage of boys' secondary schools supported exclusively by local accounts increased from 10 to 23 per cent of all gymnasiums and realschulen. Before the Revolution of 1905 there were only

seven private gymnasiums with the right to grant the maturity certificate. Between 1905 and 1908, 60 additional schools of this nature were put
into operation, and between 1908 and the assassination of Stolypin in
1911 another 60.[10] Such institutions depended on high tuition payments
from their clientele. Unlike similar establishments for girls, private boys'
preparatory schools had to compete directly with the Ministry of Education for teaching and administrative staff. Their expensiveness limited
them to affluent metropolitan areas such as St. Petersburg, Moscow, and
Odessa.[11] Local governing bodies also constructed schools entirely on
their own. By 1908 there were 69 *public* gymnasiums deriving their total
support from municipalities and zemstvos. But again, most of them were
concentrated in the same areas where private institutions flourished—
Petersburg and Moscow, Odessa and Kiev.[12] For political reasons the
state bureaucracy had located a number of Russian schools at central
treasury expense among the ethnic minorities. Of the 68 gymnasiums
and realschulen supported exclusively by state funds in 1908, 27 were
located in Poland alone as instruments of Russification.

Prior to the new budget of May 10, 1912, the average boys' secondary
school cost 23,165 rubles a year to run. In 1908 the zemstvos and municipalities contributed on an average 3,431 rubles, that is, approximately a
a seventh of the operating costs.[13] After 1908 the state began to assert
its fiscal power even more. This required a certain amount of courage,
for it was not until 1910 that the country began to come out of the economic doldrums that had set in at the turn of the century. Only then was
there a productive footing under government revenues, which increased
from 3 to 4 per cent annually. Government expenditures also rose—in
five years, from 2.49 billion rubles in 1907 to 3 billion in 1912. During
the same period the budget of the Ministry of Education increased from
45.9 million rubles to 117.3. Primary education absorbed most of the
increase, doubling its share of total outlay from 20 to 40 per cent in five
years. Whereas secondary education's share of the budget dropped from
30 to 21 per cent, the absolute volume of money spent almost doubled,
from 13.8 to 24.6 million rubles during the life of the third duma.[14] The
official investment in middle-class education quickened the pace of new
construction. In 1908 only four gymnasiums and eight realschulen were
opened by state funds. In 1914, 22 gymnasiums and 13 realschulen were
opened with such funds. Construction of additional facilities served partially as a substitute for organizational change. After 1905 the gym-

nasiums and realschulen retained their bureaucratic-police character. But as the number of institutions multiplied, the sense of oppression partially lifted. The term "Tolstoy system" faded from use, although bifurcation, the maturity certificate, and surveillance remained. Indicative of the new mood was the fact that the argument over classicism quietly expired, even though Latin remained an indispensable requirement for entrance to a university.[15]

While welcoming the transfusion of state money into both classical and modern branches of general schooling, the Octobrists and their allies in the duma were fearful that the Ministry, if left to itself, would continue its policy of subordinating Russian to imperial interests. The budget committee of the third duma drew up a chart purporting to show that the central Russian provinces were lagging behind the non-Russian border provinces in the matter of cultural opportunity for males.[16] What the committee left out was as significant as what it included. Missing from its chart were non-Russian border provinces, particularly in Poland and the Caucasus, which were as short of boys' middle institutions as the Asian oblasts.

Through the "persistent representation" of the budget committee, the central authorities gave priority to the erection of new gymnasiums and realschulen in the provinces of central European Russia.[17] During the five-year lifetime of the third national assembly the state with public supplementary aid erected 58 gymnasiums, converted nine progymnasiums into full gymnasiums, opened eight progymnasiums and 49 realschulen. The construction program covered 54 provinces and oblasts. It was concentrated in the Volga-Ural-Dnieper region. In every province within the school districts of Kiev, Kazan, and Orenburg, at least one school was added every year. The 39 areas in which no construction took place belonged preponderantly to the border areas.[18] As a result of this emphasis the central regions of the empire increased their share of the secondary schools from 17.1 per cent in 1905 to 33.7 per cent in 1913. Simultaneously, the portion of the border districts of Vilna, Riga, Warsaw, and Odessa declined from 29.1 to 23.9 per cent.[19]

By their concern for those parts of the country dear to their constituents, the members of the third duma encouraged the state bureaucracy to undertake more comprehensive planning in the placement of new schools. In 1911, besides responding favorably to 44 requests from local areas, the Ministry drew up a list of 163 gymnasiums and realschulen to be opened in the next three years. The list of 1911 was the most ambitious program of central planning since Dmitri Tolstoy established the realschule system, and it definitely subordinated the minority regions to Great Russia.[20] The duma had been dissatisfied with the way the priorities of 1911 had been selected. The central bureaucracy through the district curators, rather than the public through the county zemstvos, had chosen the locations and the chronological order of construction. As the program of 1911 neared completion, the Ministry of Education began gathering statistical information for the next stage of development. In December 1913 it circularized the curators, requesting them to prepare detailed surveys of the educational resources and aspirations of their districts. The central authorities wanted to know the number of secondary schools in each province, where new ones were projected and of what type, what distance the desired buildings would be from a town already favored with schools, and how far the prospective schools would lie from the nearest railroad. St. Petersburg also instructed the districts to report how many rubles the municipalities and zemstvos were prepared to spend for the construction and support of the wanted schools, the extent of public grants-in-aid available to the state treasury, and whether the local communities were at least able to provide an already existing structure, permanent or temporary, for housing classrooms. Only after the compilation of this material did the Ministry intend to instruct the curators to organize county and provincial meetings with representatives of zemstvos, municipalities, other departments of state, and social groups, to work out an all-inclusive scheme.

Despite sharp setbacks in the elections of 1912, the Octobrists still commanded the pivotal position between Right and Left in the fourth duma. In the budget committee they sought to shift the specifics of long-term planning from the state to the public. In its report for 1913 the committee attacked the December circular of 1913 as hopelessly bureaucratic. It dealt in proposals rather than facts, the answers to the questionnaire would be "controversial," resulting only in a "mass of correspondence" which would delay matters. Worst of all, from the national deputies' point of view, differences would inevitably arise between the Ministry's "findings" and local needs locally defined. Any clash between bureaucracy and public would be resolved by the bureaucracy. In opposition to the Ministry's approach, the duma proposed that the public be given a decisive voice at the very start and continue to participate at every stage of planning and implementation. The state would restrict its role to the simple announcement of how much money it proposed to spend on new secondary schools in a given area over the next decade. From that point on, the initiative would rest with local leaders. The elected representatives of the people in the districts and provinces would decide how best to distribute the proposed new schools and would select the type best suited to area needs. By the fall of 1914 the district zemstvos could be discussing school problems on the spot in preparation for provincial assemblies, which could meet by January 1915. In this fashion a plan could be ready by 1916 that would not be a "pile of raw material" but a "detailed program."

The confrontation between the bureaucratic and the public approach to long-range planning was staged in 1914 at a meeting of the budget committee of the fourth duma with officials of the Ministry of Education. The spokesman for local control of education affairs bluntly informed State Councilor Sheviakov: "Neither you nor the curator, not even the Minister, is in a position to work out a plan in the detail in which it can be elaborated at the local level." Unmoved, Sheviakov replied, "The curator has the better grasp."[21] Resolution of the issue of whether public representatives or state officials were best equipped to guide Russia's social development was indefinitely postponed by the outbreak of the First World War.

Upgrading the Urban Schools

During the period in which state and public interests were sparring for control of educational planning, they were also working, more often together than not, to narrow the gap in educational opportunity between town and country. It was generally recognized that the concentration of the secondary schools in the large cities imposed considerable hardship on rural families, especially the small and medium gentry. From the government's point of view the expense of quality schools limited them to the major population centers. As long as a full gymnasium within the revised budget of 1912 cost state and society a minimum of 36,090 rubles a year and a realschule 31,155, any fiscally realistic proposal for "giving the countryside access to the schools" was invariably associated with a reform of the urban schools of 1872. These operated on a modest annual budget of 4,250 rubles.* They had been designed by Dmitri Tolstoy to

---

* The concentration in cities and towns virtually deprived 85 per cent of the population of the opportunity of attending a secondary school. The question was much discussed after

provide the sons of merchants and craftsmen with a six-year program of advanced elementary or "lower" education. Originally intended to funnel their graduates toward the realschulen, the lower schools had become terminal institutions by the mid-1880's. From 1885 to 1905 they had increased in number from 321 to 729, with a corresponding growth in enrollment, from 38,919 to 113,415. Although established originally for the urban population, by 1905 they were operating not only in towns but in villages and suburbs. As a result, peasants constituted a third of the student bodies by 1905.[22]

A study of the town school of Romanovo-Borisogleb in the province of Vladimir within the Moscow district indicates the social currents active in these institutions at the turn of the century.[23] During the sixteen years from 1886 to 1901, 499 boys passed through the establishment. Of this number, 304 were townsmen, 99 were peasants, 87 were sons of officials and noblemen, and nine were children of priests. The pupils were also counted by geographic origin. The 116 who came from the countryside included both peasants and nobles. They were graduates of primary schools and used the lower institution to continue their elementary education. Because of the lack of correlation between the rural primary and the lower urban program, they lost time and money when they transferred. In addition, rural patrons paid from one to ten rubles a

1905. See *Duma Pri.* (1910/1911), IV, No. 347; *Soviet S.O.* (1911/1912), pp. 3782ff (Vserossiiskii sezd po semeinomu vospitaniiu, *Trudy,* St. Petersburg, 1912–13, I, 6). In 1908 Prince Nikolai Volkonsky informed the third duma of the gentry's difficulties: "In the guberniia that I have the honor to represent, 72 per cent of the landowners have less than 100 desiatines. [A desiatine is 2.7 acres.] It is a rare exception when their children get as far as a secondary school. Of all the landlords, 25 per cent have from 100 to 1,000 desiatines and only 3 per cent have more than 1,000 desiatines. The condition of the second group is also extremely difficult: 300 desiatines—that is, the average-sized estate—gives an income of 3,000 rubles, at the most 4,000 rubles in our province. As long as the landlord is active, he makes this much. Then he is faced with the choice of either leaving his children in ignorance or losing his land, his source of income. Gentlemen, the nobility have been accustomed to the idea for a long time that they must get an education. Already Peter I forced them to study. It did not matter what, for state service or something else, but study they must. And so the mass of families leave the countryside. There is a great outcry about absentee landowners, but how can they be anything but absent as long as it is impossible to acquire any culture at home? And so a man moves to the provincial center or capital city and spends his means on education. Very often this is the threshold to ruin. Income declines, because on a small farm it is impossible to make a living without being present. Or staying at home, he surrenders his young children to a distant institution, spending large sums which his estate cannot bear. Mention has been made of the famous circular of Minister Tolstoy or Delianov, the so-called 'cook's son' directive. Of course it is impossible to approve of the circular. But, Gentlemen, I say to you that, because of the expense, it is easier for the son of a cook to get into the university than for the son of the average landowner." (*Duma S.O.,* 11 June 1908, pp. 2812–18.)

month to board their children in town. Minimum expenses were a ruble or two a month for extra food for children staying with relatives and one or two rubles a month for a bed. The urban contingent, on the other hand, composed of 320 sons of townsmen and officials, used the school as it was intended, entering it illiterate. Of all beginners, less than a third finished the full six-year course. Most of those dropping out did so for economic rather than academic reasons.

The rise in the number of townsmen and peasants completing the course after 1893 was due to two circumstances. In the first place, a number of industrious peasants moved into the district from the province of Tver. The Tver immigrants formed associations for buying land from the nobility and sent their sons to school rather than to the fields. In the second place, townsmen were becoming anxious to prepare their sons for positions in the commercial enterprises of Moscow and St. Petersburg. As increasing competition for employment in the capitals made simple literacy no longer adequate qualification for a job, parents saw to it that their children finished the full program. In the view of the investigator, such figures illustrated "the mobilization of peasantry and townspeople on the road to enlightenment."

So much for those flowing into the school. What became of the pupils who completed its full course? How many used the urban school of Romanovo-Borisogleb as a bridge to further opportunity? From 1886 to 1901, of the 156 pupils completing the course, 34, or 21 per cent, continued their education. Fifteen went on to teachers' seminaries to prepare themselves for careers in the primary schools; one continued on to a teachers' institute to become a qualified staff member of an urban school. Five entered realschulen, and thirteen advanced their training in technical, agricultural, and craft schools. Continuing one's education after the town schools appeared difficult in every direction except training in a teachers' seminary for the post of rural schoolmaster. To enter the third year of the realschule, a boy had to spend a year after graduation on modern foreign languages. The one pupil entering the teachers' institute did so only after completing a two-year supplementary course at his urban school, since attendance at a secondary school in a distant provincial town would have entailed an additional expense of up to 1,300 rubles a year for tuition, room, and board.

Because of its legal and academic isolation from elementary and secondary schools, the urban school was the stepchild of the Tolstoy system.

The Ministry of Education was more concerned with the gymnasiums and realschulen. Zemstvos and municipalities were more interested in secondary and, later, in primary schools. Neglected by both state and public authorities, the lower institution of 1872 was more sensitive to the rapidly changing social environment than any other state educational establishment. Without planning, it became the most "public" of all the bureaucratically organized schools. Over the years the central authorities fell into the habit of legally ratifying changes that had already taken place at the local level.

By the turn of the century the demand of a modernizing nation for trained officials and technicians was increasing public interest in the opportunities being opened by all levels of education. In 1902 the press worried over the question of how to attract people with secondary diplomas into the lower civil service. By 1906 government departments were demanding secondary diplomas from applicants, and the press complained of job discrimination against people unable to afford a high school education.[24] By 1903 the Department of Post and Telegraph and the Department of Roads were no longer accepting applications from persons with only primary education. Completion of the urban school was now obligatory. When the secondary technical schools were reorganized, the commission on the development of technical education conducted an inquiry to find where the best applicants for such schools could be obtained. It discovered that the graduates of town schools were the best trained and possessed the proper motivation. In 1902 a secondary technical school in Kostroma opened its preparatory class to urban school graduates for the first time. The response indicated that such persons required only the opportunity to convert their terminal institution into a bridge to further advancement. The 40 vacancies in Kostroma attracted 132 applicants from urban schools in 22 provinces and seven educational regions.[25]

A further source of creative pressure on the structure of the town school of 1872 was the rising quality of elementary education. By the end of the nineteenth century the constitution for primary schools was academically obsolete in many areas despite revisions made in 1874. A survey conducted by the Ministry of Education in 1897 revealed that district school councils were requiring more than the basic program of 1874. Final examinations for the certificate of completion were demanding evidence of the pupils' general intellectual development as well as historical and geographical knowledge not required by the official program. By the beginning of the twentieth century the movement to replace the three-year with a four-year program was well under way. The newspapers reported district zemstvo assemblies active in this area in the autumn of 1902. An exhibit of public education organized by the provincial government of Kursk, which drew exhibitions from fourteen provinces and 33 districts, offered further evidence of progress. From the villages and parishes came a steady influx of graduates into the towns seeking to advance their education. For lack of space in the third year of the urban schools they went back into the first year. The tearful pleas of parents proved stronger than the Ministry's rule not to receive pupils into a class they had already completed elsewhere. Rural families were so anxious to advance their children intellectually that they were willing to pay for the extra years necessitated by the incompatability of rural and town schools. Although some parents were using the town school of 1872 to complete the primary education of their children, others were using it as a convenient progymnasium.[26]

A related phenomenon eroding the officially constituted structure of the lower school of 1872 was the high drop-out rate. In 1890 three times as many pupils dropped out as graduated; in 1905 twice as many (23,729) dropped out as completed the course (13,364). As in the secondary schools there were parents who removed their children for economic reasons before the end of the course. But the principal cause for the lack of pupils in the upper forms was the formal structure of the town school. Isolated by law and curriculum from the secondary school, its graduates could not continue their education except with some difficulty, and hence the ambitious transferred at the first opportunity.

Public pressure on the structure of the urban schools gradually received official recognition. In 1891 N. K. Vessel, the man who had drafted the original constitution of 1872, successfully defended it. Five years later, in 1896, the Council of State permitted the curators to adapt the lower institutions to local needs. Classes were organized by subject rather than by age group, and modern foreign languages were introduced. Most important of all, schools were allowed to drop the first two years. With this concession St. Petersburg in effect granted local authorities the right to create a popular realschule. This would eventually bring secondary education, the key valve in the state's cultural irrigation system, within reach of greater public influence if not public control.

Local changes so disrupted the harmony between general educational and vocational elements in the constitution of 1872 that the Ministry of Education began drafting a new basic law. In 1897 Delianov circulated proposals among the pedagogical councils concerned. On the basis of these discussions the Ministry drafted a statute in 1901, limiting its distribution for comment to superintendents of primary schools and teachers' institutes. The pedagogical councils of the urban schools were consulted only on the question of pay scale. Repeating verbatim three-fifths of Tolstoy's original constitution, the project of 1901 reduced the course from six to four years. The four-year town schools were "to serve as the continuation of the course of public primary schools and have as their purpose to provide children of all classes and creeds with a more complete general education and also to impart to them applied knowledge useful for practical activity."[27] Article 14 spelled out what the Ministry meant by "applied knowledge." With the permission of the Ministry of Education and in accordance with local conditions and needs, municipal schools "can open courses or special supplementary classes in applied knowledge such as pedagogy, drafting, commerce, postal telegraph, horticulture, and truck gardening."[28] The project ignored the crucial social question of the lower school's relation to the secondary level.

Despite the continued isolation from the upper levels of learning, there was considerable support for the Ministry's plan of 1901. The commission of teachers of town schools of 1872 of the section on primary schools of the Moscow University pedagogical society approved it, as did the progressive pedagogical journal, *Russian School*. Opposition to the proposal was made on pedagogical grounds. At the congress of Moscow district teachers of urban schools in 1903 the existing establishment was defended as a model elementary school. Its use as a continuation school was disapproved: the need of the hour was not for an abbreviated lower stage but opportunity for primary school graduates to ascend smoothly into the gymnasiums and realschulen. A spokesman for the original design warned that mutilation of the town school would destroy it as a model six-year institution able to exert an uplifting influence on primary education. Eventually, the Ministry put into effect several concepts from its 1901 project. In 1903 state funds were made available to match local funds to establish and support arts and crafts courses where requested by zemstvos, public organizations, social estates, or private persons. In the same year Treasury rubles were dispensed for the establishment of postal-telegraph courses for urban graduates. Finishers of this special course gained the right to occupy the position of junior mechanic in the civil service. With these measures St. Petersburg appeared to favor conversion of the municipal institutions into vocational schools at the same time that society was trying to strengthen their general educational character.

In their struggle with the educational bureaucracy, the municipal establishments enjoyed a form of public support denied the state gymnasiums. The history of the urban schools in St. Petersburg illustrates the value of such support.[29] On November 6, 1896, in honor of the centennial of Catherine II, the city duma authorized city funds to open a town school "to help the government in spreading enlightenment." It requested the Ministry of Education to permit a change in the constitution of 1872 so as to transfer to the municipal council not only financial responsibility but academic control. After two years a reply came from the Ministry refusing public control but allowing "the duma, if it wants to, to open a school, not with state but with private rights." In 1899 the Petersburg duma opened its first male four-class lower institution with the rights of a private school. This meant that graduates were deprived of an official certificate of completion which carried with it privileges on entering military and civilian service. Even so, the populaton stormed the school. In 1903 in honor of the 200th anniversary of the founding of St. Petersburg, the tuition of twenty rubles a year was abolished. Every year thereafter, except during 1904 and 1905, the city fathers opened one boys' and one girls' town school. By 1911 there were 5,187 children in the system; yet the schools were able to take less than half the applicants. In 1910, 3,910 children applied to enter. Only 45 per cent of them could be taken in. The accepted 1,417 were but 16 per cent of all those completing primary school in the city that year.

Since the public schools employed a staff with the same educational qualifications as those in the city's state establishments, the Petersburg duma requested the curator of the district in 1903 to see that graduates of its schools be given the same rights as pupils completing the ministerial schools. This could be done by having a representative of the Ministry of Education present at final examinations. Meanwhile, duma graduates took final examinations as externs at ministerial schools in order to win a state diploma. The Ministry answered with an attack. It accused the city teachers of substandard qualifications, denounced the academic program for deviating from official norms, charged the city council with opening four additional schools with district but not with central approval, and declared that neither the district nor the Ministry possessed authority to open urban schools for girls.

Chosen in accordance with the ordinance of V. K. Plehve, which allowed only the wealthiest property owners and high officials to participate in local government, the city duma counterattacked the Ministry of Education. Defending the qualifications of its teachers, the duma school committee reported that fourteen were graduates of teachers' institutes or had passed the town teacher examination. Two were university graduates. Three had finished the course of the clerical academy. The staffs in the girls' schools had finished pedagogical courses. As for deviations from the official program, in five years the district inspector had never complained. In the spring of 1906 the Ministry backed down. Henceforth it sent official representatives to the examination committees of the city schools, thus according municipal graduates equal rights with graduates of state schools.

At the turn of the century, the teachers of the lower schools began to organize, adding another form of public initiative to that already being exercised by the local communities. Again, as in the case of the secondary teachers, the impetus to action came from the old capital. In 1900 the pedagogical council of the teachers' institute of Moscow applied to the curator for permission to organize a district-wide congress of urban school teachers. After two years of preparation, 290 staff members met in Moscow from January 2 to 11, 1903.[30] The convention focused its attention on two problems: (1) the relationship of the town school of 1872 to the secondary schools, in view of the Ministry of Education's project for a new type of town school; (2) the economic plight of the teachers. To meet the conditions under which the Ministry permitted the congress, no official resolutions were adopted. In the reports and debates, however, the pedagogical councils made their positions clear on the role their institution should play in the educational system. In the opinion of the teachers, the urban school should be general educational rather than vocational. Vocational courses should remain supplementary. The institution should be reformed so as to make it a four-year higher primary school, intermediate between the elementary and secondary levels of training. Its graduates should be able to continue on to the gymnasiums, the realschulen, or advanced technical schools. The teach-

ers agreed on ending the isolation of the lower school and integrating
it into the general system, but divided into humanists and technicians
on the question of preparing their pupils for entrance either into academic or into practical schools.

In 1909 the teachers of the town schools held their first empire-wide
convention. The initiative originated in St. Petersburg, where graduates
of the teachers' institute had founded a mutual aid society in 1890. In
1906 the society had enrolled 182 members with an aid fund of 4,862
rubles. This group organized the first all-Russian congress of teachers
of urban schools. Almost all of the 521 delegates were faculty members.
Coming from every educational region in the empire, they met in St.
Petersburg from June 7 to June 14, 1909.[31] The first point of discussion
was Russia's need for a unified secondary school. As preparation toward
that end, the teachers wanted the lower school transformed into a progymnasium to replace the present one. The delegates subscribed to a
system of general education with three stages of four years each. This
arrangement would form a connected series running from primary education through the new general progymnasium to a four-year gymnasium with classical and mathematical divisions. On the question of
administration the convention allied itself with the advocates of public
control rather than central control. It recommended transferring all town
schools from the Ministry of Education to the municipal dumas and
district zemstvos, which "can adapt them to the widely different local
conditions characteristic of our fatherland."[32] The state would finance
the schools, but the local communities would control them.

After the revolutionary movement of 1905 subsided, urban school reform offered the state a way out of the impasse it had worked itself into
in 1901 with Vannovsky's project for a unified secondary school. The
imperial rescript to Vannovsky's successor, von Sänger, on June 10, 1902,
had declared that lower general educational institutions occupied an
independent position not connected with the secondary schools.[33] Five
years later Stolypin's most imaginative Minister of Education, Aleksandr
von Kaufmann, combined the two streams of school reform, secondary
and lower, in his project of 1907.[34] This project split the secondary school
in half. The first part was designed for children from eleven to fifteen
years, the second for those from fifteen to eighteen. Each section would
be a self-contained unit. By dividing middle education in this way, von
Kaufmann intended to make schooling less expensive and hence more
accessible to the rural areas. Not only small towns, it was hoped, but

even large villages could support a four-year secondary school. Parents would be able to keep their children at home until their fifteenth year at least. Without the high cost of boarding their children in the large towns and cities for eight years, more families would be able to support the education of their children for the final four.

When in 1911 the Ministry withdrew from the state duma its 1910 project for secondary school reform, the national assembly attempted to realize on its own initiative the upper half of von Kaufmann's earlier proposal. While revising the Ministry's project on "higher elementary" schools, the Octobrist-oriented committee on education recommended the establishment of upper-stage secondary institutions composed of three or four grades for the graduates of the lower schools. The traditional gymnasium was left unmentioned and tacitly intact. In response to the educational committee's recommendations, 116 Octobrists and Constitutional Democrats presented a proposal for reform in March 1911.[35] This bill envisaged a four-year general educational secondary school with two divisions, one stressing classical and the other modern languages. Where practical and in accord with the wishes of the local public, the traditional gymnasium would be transformed into the new type. Approved by the national assembly in June 1912, the project died with the expiration of the third duma. The Ministry of Education informed the fourth duma that its predecessor's unsolicited initiative released the government from the promise made in 1901 to draft a secondary school reform.

As for the lower half of the proposal of 1907, five years later, in 1912, the members of the commission that had drafted von Kaufmann's project still could not agree on the place of the urban school in the plan. One member interpreted the essence of the project as an extension for graduates of the existing lower institution. The chairman of the commission, N. I. Bilibin, insisted that the commission of 1907 had not proposed an "annex" to the urban school of 1872 but a new type of eight-year school with two four-year divisions. Von Kaufmann's project was opposed by A. N. Schwartz, who after a brief term as Moscow's curator in 1905, succeeded him as Minister of Education in 1908. Schwartz proposed separating the two lower grades of the secondary school from the upper six. This would tend to exclude urban school graduates from the secondary school. The basic idea of von Kaufmann's project was borrowed later by the duma. Schwartz by that time was in the State Council and led the attack on it there.

While Bilibin's commission was considering remodeling the secondary school, another ministerial committee was drafting a new type of lower institution. On February 9, 1909, it completed a plan for transforming the urban school of 1872 into a four year "higher elementary" school.[36] In its legislative proposal the Ministry of Education expressly created little that was new; rather, it recognized changes that had taken place over the years and had found support in the reports of the district curators and the conferences of the directors of elementary schools. While modeling the new constitution on the statutes of the secondary schools, the Ministry pointedly ignored the public's demand for integration of the lower level into the secondary system. In substance, its bill of 1909 adhered more closely to the project of 1901 than to that of 1907.

On February 18, 1909, the Ministry's project passed to the state duma's committee on education. Taking their cue from the first all-Russian congress of urban schools held in June of that year, the elected representatives of the nation sought ways to convert the proposed advanced elementary school into a first-stage secondary school for the public at large. Their attention focused on the regulations governing transfer from lower to secondary levels of instruction. According to the existing constitution of 1872, a graduate won the right to enter the first year of the gymnasium. Article 45 of the Ministry's 1909 draft declared that "pupils successfully completing the course of the first two years of the higher elementary schools can enter the third year of secondary general educational institutions of the Ministry of Education in accordance with special rules laid down by the Ministry on this subject."[37] The duma desired to amend this with the stipulation that "people successfully completing the full course of higher elementary schools can enter the fifth year of secondary general educational institutions of the Ministry of Education by passing an examination in foreign languages."[38] The purpose of this revision was "to open first the secondary and then the university-level schools to the broad masses of the population." Further, the duma wanted this channel regulated by specific examination rather than by loose rules that the Petersburg bureaucrats would be free to manipulate.

The antagonism over delay of secondary reform was so intense, the concern for lack of schools in the countryside so pressing, that elements in the State Council supported the duma's views. A group of five led by Professor A. V. Vasilev proposed "welding" the higher elementary school onto the secondary schools, especially in view of the fact that for the countryside the only form of secondary education was the urban school.[39] The majority of the State Council opposed amalgamation on the grounds that the nation needed higher primary school graduates at least as much as, if not more than, more aspirants for the universities. The duma amendments would weaken the character of the higher elementary school as a finishing school and gradually convert it into a second-rate progymnasium. Inevitably, the European standards of general education would be undermined, to the detriment of Russia's social progress. To express this fear, the conservative Aleksandr Schwartz quoted the liberal former rector of Moscow University, Prince S. N. Trubetskoy: "When the philologists, that is, the teachers of critical examination of texts, disappear, if there is no place for them amidst the general democratization of education, then education will go into decline, and no technical successes will replace the oldest and wisest of human arts—the art of intelligent reading."[40]

The educational bureaucracy brought additional pressure to bear during the closing phase of the debate. Meeting in January 1912 at the behest of the curator, the directors of gymnasiums and realschulen in the district of St. Petersburg warned against the creation of "artificial channels" to the universities.[41] While urging the government to make enlightenment more accessible in order to tap the human resources necessary for industrialization, the local heads of general educational schools pointed to the growth of the revolutionary intelligentsia, on the one hand, and, on the other, to the drain of the best talents in the commercial and artisan classes from their fathers' practical professions to the overcrowded free professions, such as journalism and law, as sufficient reason for opposing the trend toward the creation of a unified secondary school out of the urban school of 1872. Providing the awakening masses with easier access to the university preparatory schools through a flexible higher elementary school would serve to "distract them from the vocational schools." These needed support. Between 1905 and 1912 their number had grown but slightly, from 44 to 57. At the present time there were only 10,000 pupils, half of them peasants and one-third of them townsmen, pursuing professional training at the secondary level. In the industrialized area of St. Petersburg, the directors observed for the benefit of the Council of State and the duma, there were only three middle vocational schools for a population that was approaching the two million mark.[42]

The controversy between the deputies of the people, representing local aspirations, and the agents of the government, representing the

central bureaucracy, over the relation between the lower and middle
stages of enlightenment was temporarily resolved by the ratification of
the law of June 25, 1912, which fashioned the higher elementary school
out of the urban school of 1872.[43] On the crucial question of intra-institu-
tional connections, the new constitution followed the Ministry of Education's lead: pupils could transfer from the second year of the higher
elementary school to the third year of the gymnasium or the realschule
on passing examinations in the requisite foreign languages. The duma
won two concessions. The statute of 1912 granted males completing the
higher elementary school the same rights of civil and military service
as graduates of the four-year progymnasium. Article 52 extended the
same legal privileges to externs, that is, to pupils who studied at home
but submitted to state-supervised final examinations. Proposing only to
"stabilize the good features," which were "the result of many years experience," the state, in effect, ratified a step society had taken on its own
toward the unified school, the elusive *école unique* of 1803.[44]

Chapter Eight

Joint Efforts to Raise
Professional Standards

*Special attention will be paid by the Ministry of Education
to the training of teachers for every phase of schooling and
to the improvement of their material condition. . . . The realization of all legislative proposals depends, of course, on
finding the required funds.*

PETR STOLYPIN, *March 1907*

Improving the Teacher's Standard of Living

The teaching profession's economic plight had attracted both official
and public concern since the end of the nineteenth century. Kirill Yanovsky, the curator of the Caucasus, announced to the second congress
on technical education in 1896 that the present rate of pay was particularly hard on teachers with families. Reduced to extreme need, they
tutored privately after school. Straining their strength, they became
"mere teaching machines." In 1898 the Ministry of Education officially
deplored teacher poverty. At the Moscow district conference in 1899
local officials placed the blame for the teacher's lack of moral authority
not on administrative impotence but on material insecurity. Overcrowding of the schools, the shortage of qualified teachers, low pay, the rigidity
of centralized budgets, the law allowing staff padding with locally derived funds, all had created a large unstable market, especially in the
capital cities, where the marginal teacher scrambled for pay by the class
hour. Traveling from school to school, overburdened and insecure, he
dissipated his energy and his influence. The conference endorsed a
maximum teaching burden of eighteen hours a week, classes restricted
to 25 students, and enough pay and security to allow concentration on
a manageable number of pupils in a single school.[1]

In 1899 the pedagogical society of the University of Moscow produced the first detailed study of the salary situation.[2] It found that by the end of the century the secondary teacher was caught in a tightening squeeze between his static and uncertain salary and the rising cost of living. From 1804 to 1828 the value of the ruble declined two and a half times. From 1828 to 1843 it shrank three and a half times, so that in 1843 three and a half paper rubles equaled one silver ruble. By 1898, when the empire went on the gold standard, further inflation had reduced a teacher's fixed salary by over a third of what it had been in 1871. The regular teacher taught twelve obligatory hours a week. Anything above that norm depended on the scheduling of the director. Since 30 lessons a week was the normal load, the teachers were always uncertain of the last eighteen. It was estimated that regular teachers derived one-third of their yearly income from the norm and two-thirds outside of it. The temporary teacher was in an even more precarious position, since none of his hours were guaranteed. The Moscow pedagogical society estimated the average secondary teacher's income at 2,195 rubles a year.[3] It estimated the cost of living for a teacher employed in a large city and supporting a wife and two children at 2,274 rubles annually.[4] A private study placed the cost of living for a married teacher without children in a medium-sized provincial town at 1,100 rubles and for a bachelor at 935 rubles a year.[5]

After ascertaining expenses, the Moscow society recommended a more equitable system of rewards. Educational level rather than the subject or class taught should determine one's salary schedule. Catechists should be given the same rights as other instructors. Graduates of the clerical academy should be treated the same as nonuniversity graduates, and graduates of seminaries the same as nonuniversity personnel. The society also recommended taking into account the higher prices in large cities. This would be done by adding a housing allowance to the base pay. The society further proposed that pay by the hour be abolished. The twelve-hour norm per week was the root of the trouble. It was too low for the good of the school and for the welfare of the teacher. The number of hours for each teacher should be determined by legislation. The norm should be raised from twelve to eighteen hours. Pay scales should be raised so that teachers could support their families on what they received for eighteen hours. The Moscow group based its argument on European practices. In France class hours varied according to subjects taught from twelve to eighteen, and in Sweden and Germany from eighteen to twenty-two without affecting pay. Simply to keep up with the rising cost of living in Russia, a teacher ought to receive a minimum of 1,687 rubles a year, and up to 3,375 rubles depending on length of service and number of weekly class hours.[6]

From 1898 on, the Ministry of Education expressed concern over the deterioration of the teachers' financial position. But the country was in a depression and the state lacked funds. Relief came in sight in 1909, when the Ministry introduced a pay bill into the duma, partly as compensation for failing to fulfill its promise, made in 1901, to draft a new constitution for the secondary schools. Three years later the project became law.[7] The salary schedule of May 10, 1912, for gymnasiums and realschulen fell below the rates recommended by the Moscow pedagogical society and retained many features of the past. The base pay scale for regular science and language teachers with university degrees ran from 900 to 2,500 rubles a year for a twelve-hour week; for those without higher education it reached 750 to 1,550 rubles.[8] For work beyond twelve hours the teacher with an advanced degree received 75 rubles a year per weekly class hour; a teacher without higher education received 60 rubles. Manual arts teachers received the same pay for fifteen hours as those in language and science for twelve. Regardless of educational level they were paid 60 rubles a year per weekly class hour for work in excess of the basic fifteen hours.

Teachers hired by the hour were paid the same as regular faculty for extra classes. Thus they could earn either 75 or 60 rubles a year per weekly class hour. Women language teachers were treated the same as equally qualified men except that they had no right to bureaucratic rank and could not be rewarded with medals. Teachers of the preparatory classes were paid the same for extra hours as regular staff members who lacked a university degree. As a class counselor the teacher was paid 600 rubles a year but limited to teaching eighteen hours a week. All faculty were limited to a maximum of 24 hours a week whether in one or several schools. Thus a teacher with higher education, with an appointment as a class counselor, and with eight years in service could earn 2,350 rubles a year for a full work load.

The law of May 10, 1912, raising teacher salaries added 5,000 rubles, i.e. a fifth, to the cost of an eight-year gymnasium and 3,750 rubles to the cost of a six-year realschule. To cover the pay raise the state spent

3.6 million rubles in 1912 and doubled the appropriation in 1913. This totaled 10.9 million rubles in two years for raising quality, an amount making up almost one-third of the total budget of general secondary schools in 1913.[9]

Although the pay bill brought relief to the teachers, it also created difficulties. The new law restricted the teachers to 24 class hours a week. Since most of them had been working 30, the immediate result of the legislation was a teacher shortage. In the provinces courses were dropped because of the lack of instructors. To make matters worse, the curators issued directives tying the teachers closer to the schools. A circular of the St. Petersburg district directed class counselors to stay at the schools without a break from nine o'clock to four. This measure made it impossible for the teacher to travel to another school to give an extra class for hourly pay.

Another effect of the law of May 10 was the impetus it gave to revisions in other schools. Staffs of the boys' gymnasiums and realschulen were now far better paid than others. There was an exodus of teachers from clerical, commercial, military, and pedagogical institutions. This was severe enough in St. Petersburg to prompt the district curator to summon a meeting of gymnasium directors in the fall of 1912 to discuss remedies.[10] As a result, efforts were made to bring the other schools into line. The War Ministry issued a circular to its teachers promising a new pay scale retroactive to July 1912.[11]

The Ministry of Education's salary increase hit the ecclesiastical schools the hardest of all. There had already been a flight of teachers from the seminaries for internal political reasons.[12] Now, after the pay raise of 1912, salary and pension in secular schools were three times greater than in comparable clerical institutions. Of the 259 vacancies in clerical seminaries and academies for boys in 1912, 28 per cent were due to staff transferring to the Ministry of Education. Administrators were also moving. Of 151 vacancies among inspectors and assistant inspectors in 1912, 28 per cent were caused by personnel leaving for secular schools.[13] In 1909 the state duma had agreed in principle with simultaneous raises for Holy Synod and Ministry of Education employees. At last the law of June 12, 1913, raising religious pay went into effect on September 1, 1913.

The financial and professional condition of urban school teachers was much more depressed than that of secondary school instructors. With good reason, interest had been focused on the problem at the end of the century concomitantly with Bogolepov's "thaw." In 1899 the mutual aid society of the Moscow teachers' institute conducted the first detailed study of the economic position of urban teachers.[14] The results revealed that most faculty members maintained a twenty-hour-a-week schedule, with classes averaging 79 pupils. The official pay scale of 1,124 rubles a year for an eighteen-hour week had been established in 1894. But the teachers were actually earning half that amount in the face of brisk inflation. Since the provinces were divided into three ranks according to degree of urbanization and distance from the Great Russian core of the empire, with a special budget for each group, salaries were not uniform. Allowing for these variations, it was still possible to construct a survey of actual economic conditions.[15] Together with a housing allowance of 6 rubles 25 kopeks a month and a food allowance of 15 rubles 25 kopeks a month, a teacher's total salary generally came to 50 rubles 35 kopeks a month, or 604 rubles and 20 kopeks a year. A graduate fresh from the teachers' institute was customarily hired not as a regular teacher but as an assistant. His total monthly salary of 24 rubles 50 kopeks netted him 294 rubles a year. Including food and housing allowance, the heads of urban schools (called inspectors) earned 62 rubles 45 kopeks a month, for an annual income of 749 rubles and 40 kopeks.

According to figures derived from its survey of 50 completed budgets, the Moscow mutual aid society discovered that the expenses of staff members varied considerably. Inspectors spent anywhere from 53 to 91 rubles a month, teachers and assistants anywhere from 47 to 94 rubles a month. The principal reasons for the differences were individual outlays for education and aid to distressed relatives. Schooling costs for children ranged from 1 to 32 rubles a month, with inspectors spending an average of 13 rubles a month and teachers an average of 6.4 rubles. Aid to relatives varied from 2 to 25 rubles monthly, with inspectors dispensing an average of 9 rubles and teachers 7.75 rubles. The study of 50 budgets also disclosed that urban pedagogues tended to spend more than their salary, that they were slipping into debt at the rate of 12 rubles 10 kopeks a year. The principal reason for this condition was the difference between the amount the state allowed for housing (6 rubles 25 kopeks) and rental costs, which averaged 15 to 20 rubles a month in provincial towns.

Of 99 staff members reporting, 47 per cent earned money outside their regular jobs. The major source of extra income was private tutoring, an activity that added from 30 to 250 rubles a year for an annual average of 119 rubles. Most additional money was earned by weekly lessons, from one to three hours for two or three children for 5 to 15 rubles monthly. Eight teachers reported outside earnings from nonacademic sources, which brought in from 6 to 250 rubles yearly, for an annual average of 137 rubles. Constantly pinched for cash, the teachers could turn to the school for small loans. Of the 99 teachers reporting, 88 over a period of ten years had received some kind of help, amounting on the average to 24 rubles once every three years. Teachers reported that school aid funds were so limited that cash for major catastrophes such as sickness, death, support for relatives, moving, and education for children had to be sought from other sources such as the teachers' mutual aid societies. Their role in the small loan field is illustrated by the mutual aid society of the Moscow teachers' institute. The society's capital in 1903 amounted to 4,543 rubles and 62 kopeks, of which 86 per cent was in the hands of teachers in the form of emergency loans. Basing its recommendations on the study of 1899, the congress of Moscow district town teachers in 1903 recommended a minimum of 50 rubles a year per class hour with a guarantee of eighteen classes a week. Every five years there should be a raise amounting to one-fifth of salary.

After 1905 the faculty's financial position worsened. A study based on 900 answers to questionnaires sent out by the organizing committee of the all-Russian congress of urban teachers in 1908 found that the average pedagogue was earning a base salary of 350 rubles a year. A food allowance of 190 rubles and a housing allowance of 75 rubles brought his annual earnings to 615 rubles a year. The same study showed that unmarried teachers had expenses of 970 rubles a year, and married teachers 1,314 rubles. The gap between income and expenses was covered by performing outside work and by forgoing activities that would have made staff members better teachers.[16]

Adding to his loss of morale, the teacher saw that other people with the same educational qualifications were doing better than he was. Provincial officials of the Ministry of the Interior, Finance Ministry, and Tax Department often had lower educational qualifications or lacked special preparation for their jobs, yet they earned more. Local investigators and judges of the Ministry of Justice were earning up to 2,000 rubles a year. A land captain with military school training received

2,700 rubles. Although junior controllers of the Tax Department were not in the civil service and often lacked educational qualifications, their salary was 1,050 rubles. The majority of lower railroad workers lacked educational qualifications, but free living quarters with firewood made their real income equal to that of the teachers. The town teachers also saw the senior parish schoolmasters enjoying lighter work loads, less responsibility, and comparable remuneration. It was no wonder that the faculty of the urban schools felt themselves despised members of provincial officialdom. A municipal teacher complained that in his uniform people took him for a tax official. "But as soon as they discover my true profession, they begin to treat me like a pariah trying to break into society.... To hide his poverty, a teacher has to crawl into his shell and lead a lonely withdrawn life."[17]

The flight of urban pedagogues from their profession was a recognized social phenomenon. At the first opportunity they transferred to other fields. A favorite step-up was to technical and commercial schools, which offered better salaries. Some teachers even stepped down professionally, taking positions in parish schools where, in addition to regular raises and lighter work, they received furnished quarters. Some younger staff members advanced to places of higher learning such as the agricultural institute. Attention was focused on the mobility of town teachers by a study made of changes in the Moscow school district between 1899 and 1902.[18] It showed that transferring faculty were being replaced with people of less experience and training. The number of those who were graduates of teachers' institutes was diminishing. Recent graduates of the institutes were being appointed immediately as regular teachers rather than as assistants. Because of a large influx of village teachers and people who were appointed teachers by government directive into the lower system, there were few vacancies. A study in 1899 turned up only nine. There was not so much a lack of personnel as deterioration of quality.

In the locally supported urban schools the material position of the teachers was even more precarious than in state institutions. This was illustrated by the vicissitudes of the municipal establishments in St. Petersburg.[19] For urban teachers in the provinces, living expenses were two and three times cheaper than in the capital. Because of the shortage of professional personnel in the outlying areas, it was easier to get extra work. Salaries, in consequence, were rarely below 1,000 rubles a year and often reached 1,500. In St. Petersburg, where three small rooms cost at least 500 rubles a year, there was a rapid turnover of personnel. Four years after its founding, there was only one original teacher left in the first city school. Neither an increase in pensions in 1904 nor a pay raise in 1905 was sufficiently generous to make public employment more attractive than state employment. Teachers continued as before to use the municipal schools as an extra earning source rather than as a permanent profession.

After thorough study of the problem of pay, based on a questionnaire circulated among 4,000 teachers in 1908, the all-Russian congress of urban teachers in 1909 recommended a minimum salary of 1,200 rubles annually for staffs of both state-supported and publicly supported schools, with a 10 per cent raise every four years. It sent its resolutions to the education committee of the third duma and to zemstvo and municipal administrations requesting their support in the duma and State Council at the time when the conversion of the urban schools of 1872 into higher elementary schools was under study. The budget eventually attached to the higher elementary schools granted the teachers a raise in 1912 to 960 rubles a year, or about 300 rubles below their own recommendations. As a result of this action, the St. Petersburg municipal administration granted the staff members in its system a 20 per cent raise, which still left them behind the employees of state schools. Local, public funds could not compete with the central state Treasury.

Refining the Teacher's Skills

The political readjustments of 1905–7 facilitated improvements in the quality of tsarist schooling. At all levels, from the university to the elementary, educators took advantage of the wider opportunities for research, expression, and assembly to strengthen their position as professionals—men and women who were intellectually if not administratively independent of the state bureaucracy. The view that "the teacher is not only an observer and researcher of developing organisms but director and guide of this development"[20] became a goal, if not yet an assumption, of school life. The effort to overcome decades of "pedagogical starvation" was inspired by "a burning faith in the power of exact knowledge to renew teaching."[21] To be effective, empirical methods would have to be given a secure home in the seats of higher learning, from which they might then transform the traditional bureaucratic-religious routines of the secondary, lower, and elementary schools into humane and scientific processes. In time "the power of education based on genuine pedagogical science" might create a "free school—the cradle of a free people."[22]

One of Konstantin Ushinsky's dreams had been to establish pedagogical faculties at the universities. For years the Pirogov society of medical practitioners had urged the government to create independent chairs of psychology within the existing departments of philosophy. At the turn of the century a group of university professors became convinced that it was time to provide the country with pedagogical faculties if educational reform was ever to be placed on a "genuinely rational basis." Drawing on material previously prepared by the curator's office and the pedagogical society of Moscow University, they completed a plan in 1904 in which they observed that while pedagogy itself had gained recognition as a science, classroom teachers did not yet enjoy the status of professionals because of their abysmal ignorance of "the most elementary facts of the human organism."[23] After 1905 the government adopted the position of the Moscow professors that higher education of itself did not necessarily qualify a person to teach effectively. "The university can transmit to young people knowledge in this or that area of science, it can arouse their interest and awaken in them the desire for self-improvement, but it cannot teach them to transmit their special knowledge to others. This must be the responsibility of institutions other than the one that young people enter for the sake of general higher education."* The state did not immediately support its insight with funds. As a result, the actual institutions that shortly came into being owed their existence to organizations other than the Ministry of Education.

Of official agencies, the Ministry of War displayed the liveliest interest in modern theories and arts of teaching. After Dmitri Miliutin's retirement from office in 1881, his liberal spirit continued to inspire enlightenment both within and outside the army through two agencies of the chief administration of military educational institutions—its journal, *Pedagogical Chronicle (Pedagogicheskii Sbornik),* and its pedagogical museum (or institute) in St. Petersburg. With the hope that the collection of "scientifically tested facts" would lay the foundations for the general school reform that national security required, the pedagogical museum established a Konstantin Ushinsky section; and in 1904 the

---

* *Duma Pri.,* IV (1910/1911), No. 382, p. 2. The circular of 28 June 1903 on the restoration of discipline in the schools demanded that the teacher be a "pedagogue."

Ushinsky section conducted for secondary school personnel of the cadet corps and the Ministry of Education the first systematic courses on child psychology in Russian history. In 1907 these year-to-year exercises were converted into a permanent program. The two men who accomplished this task were the former director of the pedagogical museum, General Apollon Makorov, and an instructor at St. Petersburg University, A. P. Nechaev. Nechaev's book on experimental psychology had become a standard text throughout the country since its publication in 1901.[24]

Makarov and Nechaev organized the St. Petersburg pedagogical academy as a public institution, its inner life regulated by the students' own general assembly rather than by the curator. Open to both men and women, the academy offered a two-year course leading to the degree of doctor of pedagogy. In the autumn of 1908 it received its first class of applicants: 85 women, 36 of whom were graduates of higher women's courses; and 68 men, 35 of whom were university students. Secondary school graduates who were already classroom teachers were admitted as auditors. Three-fourths of the initial enrollees were over 30 years of age and a fourth were over 40. In 1909 a younger group of 41 women and twelve men matriculated. In this contingent technical institutes were less well represented, and more students came from the provinces. By 1914 the academy had proved its usefulness, but there was some question whether it could continue without direct government support. The tuition of 100 rubles was expensive for those paying it, but insufficient to attract a qualified permanent staff from the state universities.[25]

A closely related establishment enjoyed sounder financing. V. M. Bekhterev, a professor at the military medical academy in St. Petersburg, had labored for years to promote interest in an agency where pedagogical questions could be studied as aspects of physiology. In 1907 his efforts resulted in the founding of the War Department's psychoneurological institute, where learning was investigated as a function of the nervous system and the brain.[26]

The city of Moscow was the next recipient of advanced facilities for refining learning theory and teaching skills. As early as 1888, in a paper read to the Moscow psychological society, the logician G. I. Chelpanov had pointed out that a number of professors of philosophy were working abroad in psychological laboratories and suggested the need for such facilities at home. While a professor at Kiev in the 1890's, he operated a clandestine empirical laboratory, disguising it as a psychological seminar.

In 1907 Chelpanov was appointed to the prestigious chair of philosophy at Moscow left vacant by the death of the rector, Prince S. N. Trubetskoy. By this time Chelpanov was convinced that the most important practical question of contemporary Russian pedagogy was the organization of the secondary school. "Up to the present time we have not been able to break out of the bounds of such contradictory categories as the classical, modern, and semiclassical. We have not yet made the effort to understand the *psychological* foundations of the concept of general education."[27] In order to create a new framework based on observation and experimentation, he obtained permission from the Ministry of Education to pursue empirical psychology openly. The funds for equipment were the gift of a local businessman. Trips to Germany and the United States provided Chelpanov with organizational models. At last, in 1912, a quarter of a century after his inaugural address on the subject, he opened the institute of psychology affiliated with the University of Moscow, and by 1914 there were over 70 students enrolled in the six-year program.[28]

Like psychology, pedagogy was given a home of its own in the old capital on the eve of the First World War. In 1911 the P. G. Shelaputin pedagogical institute, named after the merchant who donated the land and the buildings to the Ministry of Education, opened its doors with a two-year course for male Russian university graduates of the Orthodox faith. Once accepted by standards set by their wealthy patron, the students pursued introductory courses in logic, psychology, teaching methods, pedagogical theory, and history before concentrating in one of five subject areas: Russian language and literature, physics and mathematics, Russian and world history, natural history, and the classical languages. "Because of the almost complete lack of teachers who at the present time have the necessary scientific preparation in such subjects," the Shelaputin institute did not offer instruction in the teaching of modern languages. After the requisite course work, the students did their practice teaching in a realschule and a gymnasium attached directly to the institute. To attract outstanding aspirants the government made available 40 full scholarships at 900 rubles a year each.*

Efforts were also made to transmit advanced pedagogical knowledge

---

* *Duma Pri.,* IV (1910/1911), No. 382, pp. 1–18. The conventional institutions of higher learning contributed directly to raising the professsional qualifications of the secondary schools. See Sreznevskii.

directly to the teachers already in the field. In 1905 the central bureau of the St. Petersburg union of secondary school teachers drafted a plan for extracurricular courses, which were eventually offered as an adjunct to the second congress of secondary school teachers held in June 1906.[29] The product of cooperation between the recently organized all-Russian union and the freshly autonomous University of St. Petersburg, the program attracted more than 200 persons. For ten days twenty professors from the local university, two from Moscow, and one from Kharkov lectured to secondary teachers on the humanities and the sciences and led discussions on presenting subject matter in the classrooms. In order that more time could be devoted to the problems of practical pedagogy, the following year's program was lengthened to two weeks. Its emphasis on modern history, economics, and chemistry attracted over 500 participants.[30] The third series, projected for two years ahead in order to allow adequate preparation, never took place. By this time the Ministry of Education had seized the initiative with the circular of June 10, 1909, laying down rules for establishing training courses for secondary personnel in all university cities.

The most enthusiastic response to the central directive originated in Moscow. In 1909 and 1910 the curatorship organized half-year courses, which were then lengthened to a full year by government fiat. To support the program, the district provided funds for twenty stipends at 450 rubles a year per trainee. With the assistance of these scholarships 38 men and 59 women from a variety of educational institutions were enrolled in the course in 1911. The teacher trainees were organized into small practice groups according to nine fields of concentration covering ancient and modern languages, mathematics, the social sciences, and the natural sciences.[31] In 1913 the Ministry of Education submitted to the Council of Ministers a proposal for extended courses to train new teachers, along with short-term exercises to refresh veterans. The plan envisaged the expenditure of 100,000 rubles in 1914, 200,000 rubles a year from 1915 to 1918, and 110,000 rubles annually after 1919.

Special courses were augmented by periodic conventions. In this field as in others, the War Department led the way when in 1906 its pedagogical museum staged the first all-Russian congress of pedagogical psychology.[32] A. N. Makarov, A. P. Nechaev, and V. M. Bekhterev were prominent members of an organizing committee that enjoyed the patronage of the chief of military educational institutions, Grand Duke Constantine. The Grand Duke persuaded the Ministry of the Interior to grant the organizers permission to hold the meeting despite the disturbed state of the country. With his help the sponsors also obtained from the Ministry of Education a token of approval in the form of a 500 ruble subsidy. On May 31, 1906, 436 delegates gathered in St. Petersburg. The 294 teachers, 96 medical doctors, and 46 journalists, lawyers, zemstvo and municipal administrators, came from all the school districts of European Russia, with the heaviest concentration from the two capital areas.[33]

In a telegram to the first state duma, the convention emphasized that the road to national education could "be opened only by a ministry enjoying the confidence of the majority of the people's representatives." Their respects paid to the close interdependence of political structure and the organization of schools, the delegates went on to discuss for five days the psychological foundations of learning, teaching, and hygiene. Short courses on psychology were given to demonstrate the experimental method of investigating the psycho-physical nature of children. There was also an exhibition of equipment and diagrams, accompanied by a display of recent literature. Returning to their schools, the delegates inspired the erection of some 50 small psychological laboratories in assorted gymnasiums and realschulen, commercial and cadet corps schools in the provinces.

On the initiative of the organizational committee of the first convention, the second congress on pedagogical psychology met in St. Petersburg from June 1 to June 5, 1909.[34] Since the initial gathering, political hopes had been scaled down, and the sense of reality visibly affected the mood of the meeting. The 304 delegates and 119 guests, mostly teachers from classical gymnasiums, realschulen, girls' gymnasiums, commercial schools, and the teachers' seminaries and institutes, had less faith than before in the power of experimental pychology to solve all the problems of organized learning. They accepted without argument the proposition that the material presently available was too incomplete to serve as a foundation for sweeping reforms.

Four years later, with the help of a subsidy from the Ministry of Education, A. P. Nechaev organized a congress of experimental pedagogy, which met in St. Petersburg from December 26 to December 31, 1913.[35] Aside from 25 medical doctors, it was a convocation of 600 teachers from gymnasiums, realschulen, girls' gymnasiums, commercial and normal schools gathered to hear the Russian pioneers of applied psychology.

A. P. Nechaev, G. I. Chelpanov, P. F. Kapterev, and other professors lectured to attentive audiences on the investigation of intellect in connection with the individual characteristics of students, the advantages of coeducation, a unified plan for systematic investigation of the mental world of schoolchildren, establishment of a central bureau for school statistics, the teaching of psychology and pedagogy in secondary schools, and the reorganization of the school around the findings of experimental science.

By 1912 specialized teacher conventions were the most spectacular public means of improving professional standards. The all-Russian congress of mathematics teachers derived its impulse from international sources. The fourth international congress of mathematicians, held at Rome in 1908, established an international commission on teaching. A section of this commission, associated with the pedagogical museum of the military educational institutions, planned the first all-Russian congress of teachers of mathematics, which met in St. Petersburg from December 27, 1911, to January 2, 1912.[36] The convention attracted 1,216 persons from European Russia, the Caucasus, and Siberia, most of them teachers interested in raising the level of instruction in secondary and urban schools. Two years later, with the support of the Ministry of Education, which made travel grants and subsidies available, the Ministry of Commerce, the Moscow municipal duma, and the Moscow mathematical circle organized the second all-Russian congress, which met in Moscow from December 26, 1913, to January 3, 1914.[37] Besides discussing ways of improving teaching, this gathering was also interested in defining the cultural role of the subject. As seen by the delegates, the aim of mathematics in the curriculum was to "develop strict logical thought," whereas the aim of secondary schooling was to provide "general scientific education."

The humanists were also stirring. In April 1905 a member of the society of classical philology and pedagogy, S. O. Tsybulsky, composed a memorandum that was the starting point for the first all-Russian congress of teachers of ancient languages, held five years later.[38] It was the task of the classical philologist, wrote Tsybulsky, to inform the public that its attack on the teaching of the classics was no longer fully warranted. The study of grammar had been put on a foundation of physiological and psychological laws. Through comparative philology the origins of speech were beginning to be explained and aesthetic analysis was being introduced. Finally, the discoveries of archaeology were enriching the field of classics study beyond the arid grammatical routine of the Tolstoy gymnasium. The Ministry of Education had approved Tsybulsky's suggestion for a conference, but preparations were disrupted by political unrest. Finally, in 1911, the Ministry advanced funds to the classical society to expand the scope of the gathering. At last, 269 delegates from 129 towns met in St. Petersburg in December. The mood of the convention was somber. The members had come to discuss ways of simply preserving in the curriculum a subject that had once dominated it. They had come to bury Katkov and Tolstoy.

In contrast to the classicists, the first all-Russian congress of persons interested in the teaching of new languages, which met in Moscow from December 29, 1912, to January 2, 1913, was a victory rally at the end of a long history of second-class citizenship within the secondary schools.[39] Since many modern language teachers were foreigners who spoke Russian with an accent and lacked a university education, they were often discriminated against. But with the need for more practical language training, their position improved. In 1909 the society of persons interested in the teaching of foreign languages was formed in Moscow in order to publish inexpensive texts for schools and eventually, it was hoped, to unite all co-workers in the empire. In 1910 an independent organization was founded in St. Petersburg, and over the next three years more than 150 associations sprang up in the provinces. During the Easter holidays of 1911 the Moscow group invited provincial members to its meetings. In September 1912 the Moscow and St. Petersburg associations obtained permission to hold an all-Russian congress. The sponsors expected 500 people. To their happy consternation they were deluged with more than 1,000 delegates from every part of the country. On invitation of the convention, distinguished foreign experts participated. Also lending the gathering prestige by their presence were the curator of the Moscow school district, the district inspector of the educational division of the Ministry of Commerce, representatives from the Ministry of Education, and the rectors of Moscow and St. Petersburg universities. The sessions were informal. They were "not a seminar for studying didactics" but an effort to "launch to the mass of workers coming from various ends of Russia new slogans and new ideas."

Even as conservative a body as the Holy Synod took up the idea of professional association. In 1911 its academic committee established a regular commission for preparation of an all-Russian convention of catechism teachers projected for 1914. In pursuit of its task the commission composed a set of questions to be discussed at local conferences on the theme of the teaching of religion in the secular secondary schools.[40] Thus, while the church did not bother to organize pedagogical conferences in its own domain, it mobilized catechism teachers in the secular schools in order to gain the position in secondary education that it was losing in elementary. In 1912 the Holy Synod instructed the bishops to petition the school districts for permission to hold local conferences, and the following year gatherings were held in 24 dioceses. The meeting in Kharkov in the summer of 1913 organized the brotherhood of catechism teachers of the diocese of Kharkov. Farther south the conference in Odessa condemned the evil effects of education. Literacy, it argued, did not prevent crime but only made the criminal more resourceful. The Ekaterinburg gathering denounced "the corrupting influence of free-thinking teachers of secular subjects." The congress at Zhitomir declared that the "teaching of physics, natural science, geography, and history are hardly in agreement with traditional religious-moral training."[41]

While the bishops were rallying the catechists for a last stand against enlightenment, the curator of the St. Petersburg district, Count A. A. Musin-Pushkin, was adopting the technique of periodic professional consultation as a means of local coordination. Inspired by his observations in Germany, he introduced *Direktoren Konferenzen* into his region. The first conference of directors of the secondary schools of the St. Petersburg school district met in January 1912.[42] Its agenda, which had been prepared in consultation with the pedagogical councils of the area, attempted to relate the quest for quality with the need for expansion. It was the sense of the directors that the public would be persuaded to accept vocational schooling for their children only if the quality of the teaching was high. More skillful pedagogy, it was hoped, might offset the snobbism that attracted the lower orders toward academic education at a time when the nation had less use for a restless intelligentsia than for a trained industrial class. To enlist public support for higher elementary and vocational schools, the Ministry of Education should erect pedagogical musems to service a given area.

This suggestion by the directors of gymnasiums and realschulen was but one expression of a growing concern over the primitive character of elementary and lower schooling in general. Logically enough, critical attention focused on the teachers' institutes which had been established in 1872 to prepare candidates of sixteen years and older as urban school teachers. In 1911 there were eleven such installations and plans for five more. At the convention of teachers of urban schools in 1909, the curriculum of the institutes came under fire for its "encyclopedic" character.[48] In response to a questionnaire only 36 out of 548 graduates currently teaching in urban schools expressed satisfaction with their general preparation and only 33 recalled their pedagogical courses with satisfaction. On the basis of these findings the convention's section on experimental psychology characterized the pedagogical training offered by the institutes as inadequate. In a belated response to the appeals of the urban school teachers, 148 members of the third state duma introduced a bill for reform of the teachers' institutes early in 1912. The project was similar to one devised by the Ministry of Education in 1906 except that it also provided the staff with a salary increase. Agreeing with the deputies on the urgent need for a revised pay scale, the Ministry of Education promised that it would not delay reform. Nevertheless the proposal perished in committee.

Before its termination the third duma made one more effort to improve the professional opportunities of urban teachers. In 1912 the duma's special committee on gymnasiums introduced a bill to grant graduates of the existing three-year teachers' institutes the right to enter institutions of higher learning after passing an examination in languages. Graduates of the projected four-year institute would have the same rights as the graduates of the proposed eight-year realschule. The impetus for this legislation originated with the mutual aid societies of the St. Petersburg and Moscow teachers' institutes. They enjoyed the support of professors from the universities of Moscow and St. Petersburg. The faculty of St. Petersburg University was emphatic in its approval, declaring that it considered the program of the St. Petersburg institute adequate preparation for the university with the exception of training in foreign languages.

While the Ministry of Education delayed, the duma debated, and the universities offered moral support, concrete assistance arrived from the commercial institutes of Moscow and Kiev when they began admitting graduates of teachers' institutes on a par with those of gymnasiums and realschulen. In 1910 the Moscow agricultural institute added teachers' institutes to the list of schools whose graduates had the right to matriculate after passing the regular entrance examination in Russian language, mathematics, and physics. The Kiev polytechnical institute had been accepting graduates from teachers' institutes on its own without Ministerial approval. This practice came to a halt in 1910, when the Ministry forbade it despite the fact that, as a group, the more than 50 graduates displayed a finer record than the graduates of gymnasiums and realschulen.* In the same year, however, the St. Petersburg Psychoneurological Institute, recently opened by Bekhterev under the jurisdiction of the War Department, welcomed teachers' institute graduates to its pedagogical department.

From the beginning of the rural elementary school system the obstacles to quality had been the sheer magnitude of the task and the immense costs involved. Although favoring the spread of village schools, Dmitri Tolstoy had considered special institutions for training rural schoolmasters a luxury the state could not afford. "The present situation," he had declared to the Council of State in 1866, "does not call for the establishment of teachers' seminaries. The people need only reasonable literacy; they do not need expensive teachers. Sufficient qualifications can be found among the rural clergy and seminarians."[44] In the 1870's, when revolutionary populism spread to the countryside, he reversed himself and created the basic network of normal schools. Then, following the assassination of Alexander II and the transference of responsibility for schooling the peasants from secular to religious authority, organization in this direction ceased. It was renewed at the end of

* N. Avgustov, "Zakonoproekt o rasshirenii prav okonchivshikh uchitel'skie instituty," *R.U.*, 1912, No. 2, pp. 147–54. Evidence of academic excellence was slow to soften the traditional reserve of the educational bureaucracy toward the teachers' institutes: "As is well known, into the institutes come young men, more or less grown, from social groups that cannot exercise the proper moral influence on their members because of the lack of their own intellectual and moral development. For that reason, among the pupils of the institutes, natures are often found that resist any kind of influence whatever. The bad habits they have picked up at home are often so deeply ingrained that any effort at re-education is sometimes insuperably difficult" (*Otchet MNP*, 1887, p. 170). A study of pupil flow at the Kazan teachers' institute revealed that the candidates for the urban teacher certificate who came to the school between 1876 and 1900 were mostly of peasant and petit bourgeois origins: nobility (2), officials (32), clergy (20), merchants (11), petit bourgeoisie (93), peasants (107), soldiers (28), teachers (2), cossacks (1). Between 1876 and 1900, 1,438 young men applied for entrance, and 396 were accepted. Of this number 41 dropped out—30 for reasons of health, including ten who died, ten for academic failure, and three for improper behavior. Of the 355 who completed the three-year course over the twenty-year period, only twenty took the examination for the urban-school teaching certificate and only nine passed it. Most of the pupils came from urban and district schools. Of the graduates, 149 became urban schoolteachers and 64 urban school inspectors.

the century, when the zemstvos took a strong interest in rural enlightenment as one of their principal contributions to the awakening of public
life. Responding to the requests of local governments, St. Petersburg
opened four new teachers' seminaries on the eve of the Revolution of
1905.

The long moratorium on development of a system of normal schools
left vast areas of the country without a local supply of trained personnel
to staff village schools. Neglected territories included the provinces of
Nizhni Novgorod and Kostroma, the steppe oblasts, and eastern Siberia.
In these places and elsewhere classrooms outnumbered teachers. In
1899, for instance, 7 per cent of the 7,931 vacant posts were left unoccu-
pied and 10 per cent were filled by persons who lacked state certification.[45] The chronic shortage of personnel was further aggravated by the
flight of experienced schoolmasters from the profession at the first opportunity. Thus, when the office of village policeman was introduced,
rural teachers rushed to fill the ranks. In addition, former pedagogues
regularly supplied the need for tax officials in the countryside.[46]

After 1905, the dearth of trained teachers assumed alarming proportions. A study conducted in 1908 reached the conclusion that if the goal
of universal primary education was to be realized in the next ten years,
as anticipated by the Ministry of Education and the state duma, 15,000
men and women would be required every year simply to fill new positions and at least 8,000 annually merely to offset normal attrition. A
survey of the 48 existing facilities revealed that in 1908 they had produced only 1,193 certified elementary teachers. Investigation also showed
that, of the 4,819 applicants for training, a mere 1,421 could be accepted.
At one school alone 240 graduates of primary and lower schools applied
for 27 available seats.[47]

For security reasons the state preferred employing graduates of the
teachers' seminaries in the village schools. This arrangement supposedly
preserved the peasants from direct exposure to urban culture at a time
when the peasants were pouring into the cities on their own. Seventy
per cent of the trainees in the pedagogical seminaries came from the
rural class, and the curriculum stressed traditional moral and religious
values rather than critical thinking. Nevertheless, of necessity a considerable number of those hired to lead the people out of ignorance received their training elsewhere. Many men were graduates of urban
schools and many women were from gymnasiums and progymnasiums.

In order to improve as well as control the quality of these extraneous sources, the Ministry of Education had introduced special courses of one year's duration into some 33 urban schools and girls' secondary schools as part of the educational "thaw" of 1899. The purpose of the program was to train townspeople to teach in rural schools. Its weakness was the lack of funds. At no time did the government spend more than 1,000 rubles annually on the effort. Under Stolypin's administration the program was reorganized as part of the overall campaign to provide tsardom with a literate population. By 1912 the state was spending more than 118,000 rubles annually on 104 postgraduate programs attached to lower and secondary schools; by 1914 it was beginning to lengthen their duration from one to two years.[48]

Although the state was only gradually persuaded to increase the money invested in instructors for the peasants, public organs of local government had long displayed an interest in improving the quality of village teachers. As early as 1873 more than 60 county zemstvos had organized periodic meetings with local schoolmasters to discuss common problems. Shortly thereafter, populist agitation frightened the central authorities. Police officials pointed out the ease with which an innocent gathering of rural pedagogues could be converted into an anti-government meeting, and in 1874 rules were issued prohibiting general convocations but permitting specialized gatherings to discuss strictly technical pedagogical questions. Subsequent meetings were few and far between until the 1890's, when zemstvo assemblies exhumed the rules of 1874 as legal sanction for developing teacher-training courses. Faced with this awakening of public interest in mass enlightenment, the Ministry of Education endeavored to restrict the agenda to prepared lectures on the presentation of authorized subject matter while it discouraged any critical examination of broad or sensitive questions. As expressed in a circular of 1898, "Arousing the participants of the courses to such type of thinking, the leader of the courses only instructs them in immature and unfounded judgments and encourages them to think for themselves, an activity incompatible with the modest position of primary schoolteachers."[49] Despite central admonitions, local officials gradually broadened the scope of the methods courses prescribed by the rules of 1874, until the events of 1904 and 1905 provided the central authorities with a convenient excuse for stifling the program.

As with other facets of education, the postrevolutionary period witnessed a change of attitude toward the training of rural teachers. In 1907 a joint interpretation of the Ministries of Education and Interior ruled that, as long as meetings were not held in school buildings, general educational courses for elementary school instructors did not fall under the restrictive regulations of August 4, 1874, but came within the jurisdiction of the more flexible regulations on meetings and public lectures of March 4, 1906. Upon receipt of this news, privately sponsored organizations in Moscow, St. Petersburg, and Kiev began offering lectures and practice demonstrations in private halls. The most elaborate were presented in St. Petersburg by a group of citizens calling themselves the permanent committee for the establishment of courses for teachers. In 1908 this body offered summer instruction to 575 teachers. In 1911 its program attracted 1,456 schoolteachers from every part of the empire. By 1914 it was offering 140 hours of natural science, 140 hours of humanities, and 122 hours of pedagogy, besides demonstrations on fourteen subjects including experimental psychology and statistics.[50]

The locally organized St. Petersburg enterprise inspired similar public activity throughout the country. By 1911 over twenty district zemstvos were helping to train more than 7,000 secondary graduates in programs that usually took two summers to complete. In St. Petersburg alone the district vacation school attracted 1,456 persons anxious to raise their professional standards. In Moscow enrollment was up to 800, in Saratov and Kharkov to over 700, and in Kiev to more than 500. This burst of local activity was bound to disturb authoritarian circles already alarmed by the explosive pace of enlightenment. And in 1912, an election year, a reaction set in. The moment was the most tense since 1907. The assassination of Stolypin the previous autumn had left the state without a steady helmsman. Once again, as on the eve of 1905, industrial strife, spurred by the Lena goldfields massacre, was attaining comprehensive proportions. The Octobrists, the constructive middle in the third duma, were losing popular support. Public opinion showed symptoms of polarization toward a socialist Left and a nationalist Right. Against this background the central authorities thought it wise to restrict the pedagogical initiatives of the zemstvos. Eleven summer programs were canceled. In St. Petersburg the summer course was banned by the Ministry of the Interior even after the curator of the region and the local police had sanctioned it.[51]

These politically motivated setbacks came at a time when society was increasingly anxious to obtain more state financial support for raising the professional standards of rural elementary teachers. The first all-zemstvo congress on public education, which met in Moscow in 1911, declared that the training of schoolmasters on an adequate scale could be accomplished only through cooperation between central and local governments and by means of state grants to district authorities. It warned that the campaign for universal primary schooling, which the state was promoting out of concern for internal stability and national defense, would stall unless both the number and quality of village teachers were drastically increased.[52] The importance of higher standards was officially recognized in 1912 at the congress of directors of teachers' institutes and seminaries held in the district of St. Petersburg.[53] The curator of the region, Count A. A. Musin-Pushkin, organized the gathering in order to discuss the problems of faculty members within the urban and rural normal schools. Musin-Pushkin maintained that if the level of elementary teaching was to be raised, the quality of teacher training would have to be improved first. In its recommendations to the Minister of Education the Petersburg district conference suggested that the staffs of teachers' institutes, which serviced the urban schools, and those of the teachers' seminaries, which serviced the primary schools, should be graduates of institutions of higher learning. As long as the universities were not equipped with pedagogical faculties, the teachers of the teachers would have to be trained in special advanced courses.

Teacher training was also the principal theme of the first all-Russian congress on public education, which met in St. Petersburg from December 23, 1913, to January 3, 1914—an event that brought together 6,507 primary instructors from every department of government. In 1901 the Ministry of the Interior had refused permission to assemble such a gathering. In 1913 the primary teacher congress opened in the Cathedral of Kazan in the presence of the chairman of the Council of Ministers, who read a telegram of welcome to the delegates from the Tsar.[54] Despite its reluctance to accept political constitutionalism, the state appeared ready to extend guarded recognition to society as co-partner in the campaign for national enlightenment.

Chapter Nine

Tsarist Educational Policy
in Perspective

Between 1700 and 1914 the Russians created for themselves a state system of general education. They equipped it with Western European academic standards, infused it with Orthodox national spirit, and focused it on broad imperial goals. To attract public support, the government endowed state schools with substantial social privileges; to maintain control, it organized them from the top down and the center outward. A bureaucratic framework, it was hoped, would convert a potentially revolutionary force into an instrument for conservatively managed change.

The development of state education from an impromptu vocational agency into a comprehensive political mechanism for guiding the social modernization of a multinational, serf-ridden empire took place over two centuries in three identifiable stages of decreasing length and increasing urgency. For the first, and by far the longest, of the three periods, the state maintained its original educational initiative in the face of popular apathy and aristocratic obstruction. For a century and a half the monarchs themselves, whatever their personal deficiencies, were often responsible for not only broad design but specific impulses of academic policy in the Continental tradition of enlightened despotism. For reasons of state security the autocrats and their advisers concentrated on the highest levels of organized learning. At this level and for minute numbers of people, the privileged class allowed the minimum social democracy necessary to maintain European standards. Closely geared to foreign relations, the official academic pace frequently depended directly on the fortunes of Russian arms. Seeking ready-made and time-tested formulas for improving and maintaining the nation's military position in the world, tsarist statesmen from Peter I to Nicholas I borrowed selectively from the "treasury of European enlightenment." Simultaneously, the land- and labor-owning classes made their own selection with a view to emancipating themselves from academic, technical, and professional service to the state that protected their social, economic, and political privileges.

The pivotal event of the period of enlightened centralism was the refusal of the privileged class to accept the autocracy's offer of academic leadership. From Peter I to Nicholas I the offer was made, repeated, and refused. The deliberateness of the offer and the obduracy of the refusal recast the future of state education. Preferring cultural "bits and pieces" to serious academic work, the nobility forfeited leadership to the bureaucracy. To supply itself with an educated cadre from which to recruit the trained personnel increasingly necessary for the operations of government, the tsarist state stretched the scholastic framework to include the ambitious poor within the professional service class.

In the nineteenth century, when state education served as a substitute for private entrepreneurial enterprise as a means of advancement for the individual subject of the tsar with little but talent and perseverance to compensate for his lack of family connections and funds, the Russian state offered more concrete educational opportunity to the propertyless and the obscure at the university preparatory level and beyond than did any other major European power. If the higher education of the poor undermined the tsarist state, it strengthened Russian society in a unique way for the unforeseen historical future. After the fall of the Romanovs, state education emerged as a major manipulator of social structure in the world at large. A century and a half after Speransky persuaded Alexander I to promulgate the Education Act of 1809, its active principle is increasingly operative in capitalistic, socialistic, and underdeveloped countries, inevitably undermining every elite based on anything but personal competence evaluated academically on a nationwide scale in terms of utility for the outward security and inner stability of the body politic.

In the middle of the nineteenth century, the Russian empire forfeited to a technically superior coalition its military supremacy in Europe. From that moment on, the Industrial Revolution dictated terms the French

Revolution had pressed in vain. Under the gun of this external ultimatum, Alexander II and his closest advisers grappled with the question of how far the social, economic, and cultural innovations necessary for survival as a first-rank power should be allowed to loosen the straps of history. Central authorities responsible for state education experienced the imperial dilemma as an administrative problem. Unless the government abandoned its traditional distrust of public initiative, a distrust nourished by the disruptive record of the aristocracy, Russia might remain incapable of meeting the increasingly complex challenges of her international rivals. At the same time, gestures toward local and professional participation in school policy invariably fed demands for far-reaching political and social changes that were unacceptable to the security-conscious state bureaucracy.

Of all the sectors of academic life caught up in the prolonged debate within the government between official liberals and statists, the one on which attention focused was the secondary school. Circumstances made it appear that the structure of the university preparatory schools would determine not just the scope of individual opportunity but the direction of social change. Viewed in the crosslight of events—the emancipation of the serfs, revolt in Poland, an attempt on the life of the tsar, and the emergence of student nihilism—the secondary schools stood revealed as strategic bridges, either giving central authorities a firm grip on the younger generation at the provincial level and below, or enabling local and professional forces to exert unauthorized influences on the coming generation at the expense of central omnipotence. As Pirogov observed, every educational force, whether public, bureaucratic, or professional, seeks consciously or unconsciously, whatever the language it employs, to mold the younger generation in its own image. Debates over curricula and organization were recognized as struggles for control of society's future as a servant, partner, or even master of the state. Behind the administrative question of the schools lay the constitutional issue of the empire.

When the state paused to share its educational initiative with the local communities and teachers after the Crimean War as part of its scheme for general reform, a minute but virulent protest movement emerged from the very centers of official enlightenment, the recently autonomous state universities. The central authority responded to student nihilism with its most ambitious attempt at institutionalized management of social change—the Tolstoy system. Dmitri Tolstoy's administration of the schools marked the transition from monarchical to ministerial initiative, from emphasis on the universities to emphasis on the secondary schools. To Tolstoy it appeared that the student revolutionaries of the 1860's were following the irresponsible path of the gentry, rejecting serious academic accomplishment for ideological "bits and pieces," clamoring for self-expression when the country desperately needed highly trained service. Welded together by bureaucratic fiat out of European academic traditions and Orthodox moral routines, the "German" gymnasium became the centrally standardized filter of the fourteen-class governing society, set up to ensure that state education would breed not a subversive intelligentsia but a disciplined educated class. What if Tolstoy had borrowed less from abroad and more from domestic sources? The combination of Ushinsky's pragmatism with his own administrative force would have been formidable. The opportunity to innovate was past, the risk and the hope partly canceled by the fear of student radicals.

With the creation of the Tolstoy system, the bureaucracy achieved the supremacy in organized learning that the nobility had earlier enjoyed. Like the nobility, the bureaucracy soon found itself on the defensive. Triggered by the dislocations of the Russo-Turkish War and the shock of organized student nihilism, a crisis of monolithic control set in. Its endurance characterized the second stage in Russian efforts to construct a central mechanism for administration of social change. The attack on academic absolutism came from within the governing apparatus, from the military chiefs of official liberalism at first and eventually from the rank-and-file civil servants, the classroom teachers. Politically an age of centralization, economically an age of investment, in education the last quarter of the nineteenth century witnessed a quiet transformation in the character of the educational bureaucracy—the achievement of professional sophistication at both central and provincial levels.

The most controversial event of this period, and the one most difficult to assess because of the emotional reaction to it, was the effort associated with the names of Delianov and Pobedonostsev at selective deflation of educational opportunity. There are more subtle means of deflation than the social bias expressed in the cook's circular, such as manipulation of standards and economic bias. The tsarist state was not subtle, and it is gone. Its use of education as a political instrument has become routine global procedure behind the universal rhetoric of equal opportunity: the employment of schooling as both an inflationary and a deflationary device, now expanding, now narrowing the conduits of upward mobility for different segments of the population, deliberately fitting the level and direction of national enlightenment to the demands of international security and domestic stability—"tsarist" practice, condemned as reactionary by contemporaries and historians.

Received as an insult to society, the central contraction policy of 1887 was not just a public relations blunder that further alienated educated society from the government. It also revealed a growing awareness on the part of central authorities of the complexities of the drop-out problem, and their recognition of the need for better matching of a complex society to more and different types of schools. It also revealed the growing independence of district authorities from impolitic central commands. The refinement of standards of professional conduct at the district level was followed by the upgrading of the central office. Contemporary publicists and even reputable historians missed the significance of Professor Bogolepov's stewardship as Minister of Education. Called at his initiative in 1899, the Moscow district conference introduced a genuinely representative and highly professional procedure into the formulation of national educational policy. One man gathering ideas from abroad and imposing them by decree from the capital gave way to an orderly flow of ideas from the classroom teachers to St. Petersburg. The "thaw" in academic formalism, following the breakdown of university life at the turn of the century, extended official recognition to the realization that of all the state's bureaucratically structured enterprises, the one most susceptible to public influences was the school. The mediating agent in this case was the professional corps emerging from within the ranks of the classroom teachers. Its dynamism brought the sluggish school question to the brink of rapid change.

Expanded opportunities for action were suddenly possible. In 1905 military disaster in the Orient allowed the liberation movement to challenge authoritarian government at home. The general disorder allowed parents, pupils, teachers, and directors to abandon obedience for politics and to test their talents for organization and alliance. Policy discussions were no longer confined to official committees, expert commissions, and departments of state. In street demonstrations and mass meetings they became matters of passionate public concern. In the ensuing struggle to divide the authority of the Ministry of Education

among themselves, teachers discovered that their interests were no more
strictly identical with those of parents and pupils than they had been
with those of curators and directors. The potential of the schools as a
social control mechanism expanded even as the schools themselves became more difficult to control.

Whatever its limited achievements on the strictly political plane, the
Revolution of 1905 precipitated the third, brief and climactic phase in
Russian development of education as an instrument of national policy.
Under the creative duress of popular upheaval, amidst faltering foreign
affairs, the nation broke through to an enlarged academic future. For
a moment the goal of a "free school in a free society" appeared within
reach. When the restoration of peace prepared the way for the restoration of central authority, an ambiguous constitutional framework afforded official and public forces unprecedented maneuverability at a time
when enducements to work together were compulsively strong. State
officials and representatives of public life agreed that it was time to concentrate on educating the masses and upgrading the teaching profession. Only the compounding of war, revolution, and civil war postponed
the joint commitment to universal compulsory elementary education.[1]
Disaster on the battlefield laid the fulfillment of national enlightenment
in the hands of tsardom's accidental heirs. Anxious to establish their
own questionable legitimacy, the Bolshevik minority industriously hid
their debt to the regime others had overthrown. The evidence remains
impressive, if one takes the trouble to disinter and examine it, that whatever its failings in other areas—and they were massive—in general education tsardom was working hard, productively, and intelligently at
the moment when military disaster retired it from history.

After 1905 the tsarist state extended cautious recognition to "education" as a distinct and autonomous branch of human science with an
internal logic of development of its own. Inspired by foreign and native
publicists and scholars, subsidized by state agencies, and dramatized by
all-Russian pedagogical congresses of wide variety and uniform enthusiasm, an adventurous, empirical spirit was spreading through the
institutions of higher learning, the secondary, urban, and village schools.
For all the difficulties ahead, there was mounting conviction that administrative absolutism had yielded for good to cooperation among
multiple initiatives. The revenues of the state, the participation of the
local public, and the labors of an intellectually independent professional

class were expanding the dimensions of organized learning, making it at one and the same time a more sensitive and less tractable device for directing social development on a grand scale. Aristotle observed in his *Politics* that what "most contributes to the permanence of constitutions is the adaptation of education to the form of government." By 1914 state education in Russia was becoming public education faster than autocracy was becoming constitutional government.

When the tsarist state went down to defeat in 1917, the crash raised the cultural dust of a thousand years, and visions bred in exile became programs for revolution. When order was restored and the population turned from fratricide to reconstruction, the global environment demanded more than ever an educational system capable of harnessing personal tastes and regional and social differences to collective needs. The classical curriculum, student nihilism, and the maturity certificate were gone. Bureaucratic centralism, democratic access, police surveillance, and loyalty to history remained. New leaders out of the old educated class assumed direction of national enlightenment. To a mightily renewed bureaucracy fell the training of Dmitri Tolstoy's "aristocracy of intellect, aristocracy of knowledge, aristocracy of work." Professional educators of independent mind quickly disappeared. A half-century after the revolution that rode to power on the popular desire for emancipation from the state bureaucracy, the educated public, which had gained a voice of its own in the schools after 1905, had yet to recover the influence it was exerting routinely by 1914. A century after Dmitri Tolstoy established his system, the Soviet bureaucracy was not yet ready to acknowledge the hated Minister as a native pioneer of central academic mechanisms for the control of nationwide social stimulation. Soviet authorities have recognized another, more popular civil servant of the tsarist state, Konstantin Ushinsky, as "the man who developed the principles upon which the present-day Soviet school is founded."[2]

The problems of a proud and numerous people thrown on the defensive by the energy of their rivals give rise to universal themes. The weight of an undigested past, the clamor for more educational opportunity amidst resistance to higher academic standards, the hazards of exposing the younger generation to ideas the adult world is not about to realize, the strains inherent in whetting the appetite for spontaneity and self-expression in an environment demanding increasingly higher levels of social conformity and self-control, the difficulty of tuning broad-scale educational systems to the exact specifications of individual children, specific times, and unique places—all these and related questions that occupied Ushinsky, Pirogov, Tolstoy, and other servants of the tsar a century ago have become pressing contemporary concerns, as schooling everywhere becomes less and less a matter of primarily local and parental concern and more and more what it was for the tsarist state: a national issue with international imperatives.

In the rural regions of the earth the tardy students of modernity import foreign schools, as Peter the Great once did, to facilitate their passage from village to urban life. At the same time, plagued by massive leakage of pupils from elaborate systems, explosive student nihilism, and general social uncertainty, the industrial nations of the north shuffle and reshuffle their expensive educational structures. As runaway inflation of scientific and technical knowledge prompts peoples everywhere to create comprehensive school systems as tools for working at their national and international problems, nineteenth-century Russian development of the learning process for political reasons on an ambitious scale assumes more than antiquarian interest. It contains lessons. The tsarist experience suggests that, in the modern world, educational questions are central political issues, that debates over curricula, structure, social complexion, administration, standards, and costs are at bottom power struggles between and within official, professional, and public interest groups with conflicting views of man, differing national priorities, and, often enough, irreconcilable values. The tsarist experience also suggests that educators and statesmen, whatever their ancient or modest academic traditions, will be sorely tried to find a stable working arrangement of central direction with local initiatives and professional enterprise for the school systems that are becoming the major institutional determinants of the modern social order.

APPENDIXES

The Central Contraction of 1887
in Eight School Districts

TABLE 1

NUMBER OF PUPILS IN GYMNASIUMS

Date	Pupils Jan.	Grad- uates June	Drop- outs June	Entrants Sept.	Pupils Jan.	Grad- uates June	Drop- outs June	Entrants Sept.
		MOSCOW	DISTRICT			ST. PETERSBURG	DISTRICT	
1885	10,321	428	1,848	1,991	8,365	373	1,307	1,674
1886	10,036	436	1,671	2,129	8,359	404	1,357	2,045
1887	10,058		1,625	970	8,641		1,168	829
1888	8,669	503	1,533	1,687	7,717	440	1,131	1,533
1889	8,320				7,679			
1890	8,165	534	1,201	1,839	7,704	483	1,072	1,703
1891	8,269				7,856			
		WARSAW	DISTRICT			KIEV	DISTRICT	
1885	11,064	310	2,345	1,250	8,111	381	1,130	1,726
1886	10,659	271	2,252	1,952	8,326	433	1,148	1,792
1887	10,088		2,253	735	8,537		1,320	838
1888	8,290	411	1,635	2,102	7,514	445	1,217	1,391
1889	8,346				7,243			
1890	8,019	421	1,303	1,758	7,152	525	959	1,504
1891	8,053				7,172			
		ODESSA	DISTRICT			KHARKOV	DISTRICT	
1885	7,148	257	1,472	1,592	6,528	229	1,109	1,181
1886	7,011	260	1,291	1,636	6,373	208	1,169	1,220
1887	7,096		1,351	697	6,216			579
1888	5,387	332	1,063	1,110	5,641	285	1,134	938
1889	5,102				5,160			
1890	4,966	364	744	1,201	4,882	356	688	1,193
1891	5,059				5,081			
		VILNA	DISTRICT			CAUCASUS	DISTRICT	
1885	4,975	177	933	920	3,663	116	559	774
1886	4,785	175	838	918	3,762	111	531	705
1887	4,690		804	304	3,825		581	335
1888	4,134	199	629	944	3,429	138	577	683
1889	4,250				3,397			
1890	4,136	196	631	781	3,461	164	705	1,101
1891	4,090				3,693			

TABLE 2

NUMBER OF PUPILS IN EACH CLASS

Date (Jan.)	Prep.	I	II	III	IV	V	VI	VII	VIII	Total
				MOSCOW DISTRICT						
1885	1,402	1,748	1,589	1,439	1,098	845	718	576	528	9,943
1888	304	1,574	1,456	1,372	1,103	746	663	551	491	8,260
1890	287	1,489	1,358	1,287	1,039	698	620	520	458	7,756
			ST. PETERSBURG DISTRICT							
1885	1,058	1,224	1,149	991	819	613	543	467	339	7,203
1888	337	1,126	1,078	945	857	627	506	429	374	6,279
1890	416	1,382	1,328	1,158	1,050	772	618	525	455	7,704
				WARSAW DISTRICT						
1885	1,717	1,916	1,806	1,751	1,507	856	617	446	448	11,064
1888	396	1,577	1,542	1,429	1,338	732	546	389	341	8,290
1890	383	1,525	1,492	1,383	1,294	708	528	376	330	8,019
				KIEV DISTRICT						
1885	1,081	1,252	1,219	1,130	960	784	673	505	507	8,111
1888	258	1,256	1,260	1,156	1,038	762	726	565	493	7,514
1890	245	1,196	1,200	1,101	988	726	692	535	469	7,152
				ODESSA DISTRICT						
1885	1,068	1,295	1,139	976	803	627	479	405	356	7,148
1888	242	1,024	1,016	884	659	543	402	325	292	5,387
1890	223	945	937	815	607	501	370	299	269	4,966
				KHARKOV DISTRICT						
1885		1,370	1,237	1,094	919	621	525	415	347	6,528
1888	253	984	992	931	841	506	468	343	323	5,641
1890	219	851	858	806	728	438	405	297	280	4,882
				VILNA DISTRICT						
1885	708	966	817	762	568	430	287	238	199	4,975
1888	176	791	820	673	628	338	337	190	181	4,134
1890	176	792	820	674	628	338	337	190	181	4,136
				CAUCASUS DISTRICT						
1885	720	582	593	479	428	312	263	147	139	3,663
1888	335	608	568	529	459	336	255	208	131	3,429
1890	338	614	573	534	463	339	258	210	132	3,461

TABLE 3

Number Dropping Out of Each Class

Date (June)	Prep.	I	II	III	IV	V	VI	VII	VIII	Total
MOSCOW DISTRICT										
1885	231	347	279	283	233	204	121	91	59	1,848
1887	165	331	262	259	198	167	98	94	51	1,625
1890	52	205	169	174	144	155	87	83	26	1,095
ST. PETERSBURG DISTRICT										
1885	139	202	183	159	161	97	86	75	18	1,120
1887	111	223	180	197	158	117	81	81	20	1,168
1890	86	176	142	146	108	87	77	50	15	887
WARSAW DISTRICT										
1885	186	330	336	355	435	274	210	131	88	2,345
1887	186	363	302	387	392	292	152	118	61	2,253
1890	177	190	160	180	205	172	89	91	39	1,303
KIEV DISTRICT										
1885	98	185	189	172	163	139	93	73	18	1,130
1887	116	218	202	212	171	161	98	76	66	1,320
1890	57	126	156	157	164	125	79	68	27	959
ODESSA DISTRICT										
1885	156	295	231	249	194	154	91	72	30	1,472
1887	234	242	173	216	154	148	82	71	31	1,351
1890	73	135	115	108	92	100	47	56	18	744
KHARKOV DISTRICT										
1885	92	208	178	159	139	120	79	85	49	1,109
1887										
1890	59	125	101	116	96	75	56	40	20	688
VILNA DISTRICT										
1885	92	133	126	153	180	99	72	53	25	933
1887	64	135	126	123	146	81	67	44	18	804
1890	62	105	91	95	101	71	46	45	15	631
CAUCASUS DISTRICT										
1885	84	93	106	78	60	56	43	30	9	559
1887	67	105	87	88	83	61	44	37	9	581
1890	75	99	109	119	107	82	47	52	15	705

TABLE 4

REASONS FOR DROPPING OUT

Reason	June 1885	June 1890	June 1885	June 1890	June 1885	June 1890	June 1885	June 1890
	MOSCOW DISTRICT		ST. PETERSB. DISTRICT		WARSAW DISTRICT		KIEV DISTRICT	
Transfer to other school	878	650	576	340	812	436	629	452
Enter state or private service	201	220	109	78	233	138	105	99
Failing grades	269	89	145	79	539	123	199	125
Family circumstances	460	112	261	355	725	587	158	252
Death	40	24	29	35	36	19	39	31
Total	1,848	1,095	1,120	887	2,345	1,303	1,130	959
	ODESSA DISTRICT		KHARKOV DISTRICT		VILNA DISTRICT		CAUCASUS DISTRICT	
Transfer to other school	638	403	455	376	400	315	201	416
Enter state or private service	171	145	104	74	104	72	111	83
Failing grades	213	65	172	55	156	61	107	62
Family circumstances	427	120	357	162	263	174	126	122
Death	23	11	21	21	10	9	14	22
Total	1,472	744	1,109	688	933	631	559	705

TABLE 5

NUMBER OF PUPILS IN EACH SOCIAL GROUP

Date (Jan. 1)	Noble-Official	Clergy	Town	Peasant	Other	Total
		MOSCOW DISTRICT				
1886	4,991	540	3,731	511	263	10,036
1887	5,016	558	3,744	499	241	10,058
1888	4,466	432	2,876	381	105	8,260
1889	4,409	422	2,843	405	241	8,320
1890						8,165
1891	4,551	357	2,772	356	233	8,269
		ST. PETERSBURG DISTRICT				
1886	4,743	348	2,662	370	236	8,359
1887	4,925	300	2,693	406	317	8,641
1888	3,860	229	1,797	319	74	6,279
1889	4,586	249	2,257	308	279	7,679
1890						7,704
1891	4,609	244	2,476	274	253	7,856

TABLE 5 (*continued*)

Date (Jan. 1)	Noble-Official	Clergy	Town	Peasant	Other	Total
			WARSAW DISTRICT			
1886	5,269	248	3,948	1,150	44	10,659
1887	5,129	276	3,557	1,083	43	10,088
1888	4,413	241	2,794	813	29	8,290
1889	4,712	263	2,660	675	36	8,346
1890						8,019
1891	4,665	249	2,439	650	50	8,053
			KIEV DISTRICT			
1886	4,538	702	2,328	572	186	8,326
1887	4,626	633	2,605	473	200	8,537
1888	4,183	543	2,149	395	244	7,514
1889	4,116	510	2,014	425	178	7,243
1890						7,152
1891	4,184	448	1,964	349	227	7,172
			ODESSA DISTRICT			
1886	2,491	288	3,763	256	273	7,011
1887	2,540	217	3,670	362	307	7,096
1888	2,096	160	2,729	182	220	5,387
1889	2,169	141	2,397	202	193	5,102
1890						4,966
1891	2,271	133	2,234	199	211	5,059
			KHARKOV DISTRICT			
1886	3,069	406	1,960	833	105	6,373
1887	2,991	384	1,978	770	93	6,216
1888	2,758	340	1,925	514	104	5,641
1889	2,628	282	1,782	370	98	5,160
1890						4,882
1891	2,741	212	1,665	344	119	5,081
			VILNA DISTRICT			
1886	2,702	158	1,509	344	72	4,785
1887	2,677	152	1,440	365	56	4,690
1888	2,462	129	1,206	286	51	4,134
1889	2,675	130	1,143	262	40	4,250
1890						4,136
1891	2,658	110	1,071	208	43	4,090
			CAUCASUS DISTRICT			
1886	2,190	201	1,113	195	63	3,762
1887	2,309	189	1,129	149	49	3,825
1888	2,173	165	939	95	57	3,429
1889						3,397
1890						3,461
1891	2,278	133	1,026	87	169	3,693

TABLE 6

NUMBER OF PUPILS IN EACH RELIGIOUS-NATIONAL GROUP

Date (Jan. 1)	Orthodox	Catholic	Protes-tant	Jewish	Islamic	Other	Total
MOSCOW DISTRICT							
1886	8,575	281	446	517	4	213	10,036
1887	8,510	299	473	559	2	215	10,058
1888	7,265	270	223	445		57	8,260
1889	7,120	288	409	427	2	74	8,320
1890							8,165
1891	7,117	274	409	377	5	87	8,269
ST. PETERSBURG DISTRICT							
1886	6,406	355	1,142	423	4	29	8,359
1887	6,540	353	1,284	425	6	33	8,641
1888	5,211	294	452	290		32	6,279
1889	5,784	322	1,226	311	6	30	7,679
1890							7,704
1891	5,914	359	1,260	271	6	46	7,856
WARSAW DISTRICT							
1886	1,617	7,312	444	1,276	5	5	10,659
1887	1,691	6,796	422	1,171	6	2	10,088
1888	1,452	5,538	352	937		11	8,290
1889	1,473	5,597	394	869	7	6	8,346
1890							8,019
1891	1,547	5,394	386	711	11	4	8,053
KIEV DISTRICT							
1886	5,557	1,612	146	990	2	19	8,326
1887	5,577	1,735	139	1,067		19	8,537
1888	4,910	1,567	138	885		14	7,514
1889	4,704	1,570	143	786	2	38	7,243
1890							7,152
1891	4,677	1,582	144	732	6	31	7,172
ODESSA DISTRICT							
1886	3,984	353	134	2,290	7	243	7,011
1887	4,056	341	136	2,266	21	276	7,096
1888	3,137	272	116	1,622		240	5,387
1889	3,086	299	120	1,358	11	228	5,102
1890							4,966
1891	3,278	317	139	1,090	13	222	5,059

TABLE 6 (*continued*)

Date (Jan. 1)	Orthodox	Catholic	Protes- tant	Jewish	Islamic	Other	Total
			KHARKOV DISTRICT				
1886	5,797	156	152	253		15	6,373
1887	5,635	172	143	247		19	6,216
1888	4,970	169	123	337		42	5,641
1889	4,559	165	121	280		35	5,160
1890							4,882
1891	4,495	168	130	230		58	5,081
			VILNA DISTRICT				
1886	1,752	1,764	199	1,030	36	4	4,785
1887	1,789	1,740	190	939	29	3	4,690
1888	1,610	1,584	160	750		30	4,134
1889	1,749	1,639	173	653	25	11	4,250
1890							4,136
1891	1,771	1,572	174	545	21	7	4,090
			CAUCASUS DISTRICT				
1886	2,455	182	81	112	140	792	3,762
1887	2,494	195	79	133	126	798	3,825
1888	2,242	180	64	113		830	3,429
1889	2,209	183	75	101	101	728	3,397
1890							3,461
1891	2,405	173	60	103	110	842	3,693

Manifesto of the Union of Secondary School Teachers of St. Petersburg, May 1, 1905

A serious situation is coming to a climax in Russian life. Increasing in intensity to the present hour, it exposes to view the hidden weaknesses of Russian life. Following hard upon the catastrophe in the Far East and the upheaval of the workers and peasants, the recent agitation of the students has focused public attention on the violent symptoms of the dangerously sick secondary school. Faced by the complete disorganization and definite collapse of the secondary school, we, its workers and leaders, are faced with an accomplished fact. Were we able to prevent it? What can we do now to find a way out of disaster to reconstruction? An aroused nation, public opinion, and our own conscience demand that we answer these questions.

Whatever our answer, one thing is obvious. Our response must be collective and the effort that we make must be united. The time for individual exertion is past. Experience has shown its futility. Around us, from the ruins of the old order, public groups are beginning to organize and are struggling to create new social forms. To this same challenging work we summon all those to whom the secondary school is precious and for whom its interests are vital. We call upon our colleagues in education, who are the ones directly responsible for its fate. The important role that the school is conceded to play in society's advance defines the enormity of this responsibility.

In our case there is a special difficulty due to the peculiarities of the age group committed to the secondary schools. We are confronted by a human subject who is complex and inconstant, whose care demands tact and intellectual and moral imagination. The secondary school takes into its hands a boy scarcely out of childhood and deposits him on the threshold of young adulthood. It is concerned with him in the most critical period of his life, when his character is being formed, when his elementary passions are in conflict with his higher spiritual aspirations, when his awakening mind seeks serious nourishment, when he is at the same time credulous and extremely skeptical, gregarious and excessively individualistic, conscious of his weakness and energetically confident of his personal dignity. It is the duty of the school to equip this complex subject for life's struggle and for independent mental labor in the full command of his own powers. If he leaves the classroom crippled, having squandered his spiritual inheritance, a heavy responsibility falls upon the school. Claiming to substitute for the slow and haphazard experience of life its own scientifically organized experience, the school assumes a massive responsibility for the future of the country. Under what conditions can it discharge it?

For normal growth, the younger generation needs space and light, an atmosphere of intellectual, moral, and social rights, and mutual trust among teachers, pupils, and family. The organization of the school must be one that preserves respect for the personality of the pupil, where the young, herd-like group becomes aware of itself as a free society of individual children, where the student counselor's authority is recognized freely and willingly, and where not only the individual teacher but the entire class of educators exerts a strong social influence. What alone can give the individual teacher genuine moral authority is the serious scientific level of his teaching and constant precision in his explanation of questions raised. Unless the pupils are convinced that every word of the teacher expresses his convictions as derived from his own experience and thought, rather than notions forcibly imposed, they will not have confidence in him. An absolute condition for a healthy atmosphere in the school, the teacher's credibility is especially vital when the more intimate religious, moral, philosophical, and social questions are raised. But internal conviction and independent thought can only be developed in a social environment where freedom of thought and speech is recognized and secure.

Teachers as a professional class can enjoy public confidence only if they enjoy administrative autonomy. When the school is a tool in the hands of outside political forces, it is completely powerless to affect public opinion and, in the final analysis, the minds of its own pupils. But it can earn public confidence in its work only if it operates in close harmony with local society, in an atmosphere of complete openness.

Finally, the school has the great mission to destroy all the artificial barriers erected around it, to remove the conditions that turn back the mass of children at its door, thereby making education an achievement of an insignificant, privileged minority. The school must remove from itself the stamp of social and class privilege. Each school must be part of a national system organized on the principle of universal free instruction without any national or religious bias. Universal access to the school, its broad democratization, will open to education deep, untouched levels of national life. Bringing together all the children of all the people, democratic access will convert the school into a truly popular institution. Only such a school can fulfill the high national purpose of awakening and renewing the country. As an organization of serious, intellectual talents, enjoying public confidence, it can become a cultural center, spreading its influence far beyond its walls, as an initiator and leader of educational programs that include public lectures, museums, libraries, excursions, and book publication for its locality.

With public support and guidance, educators could devote their professional knowledge and skills to the needs of the community and become an invigorating force in the life of the country. Opening up broad perspectives to the individual teacher would infuse creative energy into the dying system of education. To what extent does reality correspond to this ideal? The contemporary general educational secondary school, both in principle and form, represents the results of the collapse of the school brought on by the influence of Tolstoy under the pressure of certain reactionary forces shaping government policy. At the basis of the Tolstoy System a principle was laid that flowed from the ideal of the police state; it was formulated in the following way: "The school must oppose the development of a material- istic philosophy of life. It must train the youth in the spirit of conservative principles. It must confirm the younger generation in obedience to the law and respect for constituted authority." Developed to its ultimate conclusion in the pet establishment of the reactionary epoch, the classical gymnasium, the conservative system reduced the whole field of education to slavery. The realschule, the commercial school, the clerical seminary, the girls' gymnasium, and the diocesan school, with all their differences in curricula, incorporated in their basic structure one conforming spirit.

After the epoch of emancipation, Russian society, summoned to participate in local government, began to conceive its role more clearly and prepared for a new political mission, for participation in directing the life of the country. The government, aware of the danger to its established forms, mobilized for defense. Our legacy, the secondary school, was first created in this critical moment as a means of preserving the younger generation from the aspirations then gripping society. Later, it was fashioned into an instrument for fighting directly against these ideals. This tactical aim necessarily crippled the school, perverting its salutary mission. The banner of humanitarianism, which the idealists of the 1860's hoisted above the school, was hauled down. Their ideal was to create a harmonious free man, able to confront new truths and be an active force in the unknown future. Instead of these broad ideals, government policy imposed on society and the school the conservative slogan of adherence to the principles of autocracy, orthodoxy, and nationality.

Blocking the road opening toward free development, the state summoned the young generation to retreat. The task of adapting the school to an artifi- cial goal could not be confided to a society that did not acquiesce in the po- litical ideals that fashioned the school. The educated class regarded the school itself with mute or open hostility. The result was the state's avowed mistrust of the public in the school question. The government had to monopolize the school, restricting public and private initiative, imposing the "state program" on private schools, which agreed to sacrifice their academic freedom for the privileges of state educational institutions. The school systematically isolated itself from life. The influence of the family and the cooperation of public bodies such as zemstvo and urban administrations were removed from it. In its internal life it can only express the spirit of bureaucratic absolutism. The school is a creature of the state rather than an active agency of society.

Neutralization of the pedagogical council, the absolute power of the direc- tor over the council, of the curator over the district, of the minister over the whole process of school life, the mechanical transfer of personnel against their will or the consent of the educators involved: these are the basic characteristics of the school. Teachers became passive tools, devoid of creative possibilities. For when human relations become artificial, the personality of the individual suffers.

The sociopolitical atmosphere surrounding the school puts the teacher under severe strain. The vital elements of the school, pupil and teacher, are crushed under the steady pressure of that atmosphere of personal oppression, that lifeless public environment, that oral and written censorship, that universal lack of rights and forced isolation which are the unavoidable concomitants of our political system. While the bureaucratic spirit of the school detracts from the authority of the teacher and conceals his talents, the political system that produced that spirit commits a whole series of encroachments upon his moral integrity. Probably not one element of the intelligentsia suffers so much from the lack of freedom of conscience as the secondary school teacher. Allegedly bound to avoid the slightest hypocrisy, he is obliged to fulfill religious duties publicly, in designated churches on specified days. This obligation becomes especially burdensome and immoral in the border provinces where religion is a controversial issue. Often, while doing violence to his own religious convictions, the teacher must pose as a model of orthodoxy to his pupils and summon them to do the same. The religious question in the school is only one of the aspects of the veto imposed by the political and educational systems on the need of a free, self-respecting person to express his convictions openly. The censorship of the spoken and written word, the ban imposed on all the more controversial questions, the political ideology that imposes secrecy as a means of defense on all who disagree: all these measures seriously affect the school.

Completely lacking confidence in the pedagogical tact of the teacher, the system vetoes informal relations with the pupils, thereby annulling the opportunity for a varied and sophisticated discussion of academic questions and current issues. This political tendency has been especially harmful to the teaching of history and literature, eliminating the vital and serious issues, representing the rest in a false and superficial light. Censorship of the teacher's speech is closely bound to censorship of textbooks, which, while depriving the instructor of the right to select material for reading and study, floods the schools with mediocre, tendentious textbooks. Restricted in his teaching, the teacher is subjected to strict supervision of his life outside the school. Any contribution to the press or even a legal society or union attracts the suspicious attention of his superiors. In this respect, his freedom is even more limited than that of the ordinary Russian citizen, who is restricted enough. Did not the ministry of education just announce that a teacher has the same rights as a zemstvo member, a lawyer, an engineer, or a doctor, and yet were not several secondary school teachers recently fired for attending the congress of teachers of natural science? The possibility constantly hangs over the head of the independent teacher. This sword of Damocles, dispatched invisibly by the school authorities in the form of a circular, is a powerful weapon in the hands of anyone not sickened by the process of anonymous denunciation. Removal takes place without trial and without investigation. Years go by before the ban is removed and the teacher can return to his desk, out of practice, having lost contact with family and friends. Under such conditions is it surprising that everything strong and independent is alien to the teaching profession, that the school is devoid of an intellectually alert staff, that the selection of personnel is pitiful? Is it a wonder that the state school is disintegrating, that society regards it with avowed hostility?

The spiritual development of the younger generation takes place under the protection of the school. Not recognizing the private and public rights of the teachers, the political system has even less respect for the pupils. The mute, growing protest within, the Liberation Movement from without, imposed upon the school a new function: the struggle against social disintegration, the roots of which it must find and destroy. Not content with expelling individuals and whole segments of the population considered actually harmful, the school is striving to rid itself of potential troublemakers as well. The life of the pupils is entangled in petty strictures and regulations and in an atmosphere of excessive reprisal. Exuberant student protest takes on political significance. Exaggerated, treated like a political issue, the revolt of the pupil grew into mammoth disorders, first chronic in the western border areas and now spreading all over Russia, trailing a wake of mass expulsions and sometimes causing the suicide of boys and girls. Not content with the strict regulation of the pupil's life in the school, the system extended its supervision beyond the classroom, following the students onto the street, penetrating into the home, imposing on the teacher repulsive political obligations. When, dissatisfied with the scanty, ill-prepared diet doled out to them in the school, the youth began to seek extracurricular education, the system lowered its heavy hand. It rigorously persecuted the study groups interested in self-education. It restricted the use of public libraries. It established a watch over the private lives of pupils, their amusements, their relatives and friends. It punished children for their parents' political unreliability or encouraged children to spy on their parents, a process that often resulted in breaking up the family.

Leaving school, a youngster found scarcely one kind word to remember it by and, with only a few bright exceptions, bore toward it a smoldering resentment. If the influences of literature, family, or good character saved half, the other half left school ignorant and uneducated, their minds confused, their moral and political comprehension in painful confusion. In the last few years the symptoms have become clearer that the school is suffering from some deep internal disorder. We are witnessing the historic moment of the complete breakdown of the state secondary school and the collapse of the mission entrusted to it. Every means was tried to cut it off from life, but life broke into the school and took the pupils, little more than boys, onto the streets under the cossack whips. Planting religious orthodoxy in the school, the government cultivated it in such gross forms that the harvest was religious indifference. Striving to be an instrument of Russification, the school aroused in the border provinces a deep hatred for the Russian language and culture. Supposedly an arena for inculcating obedience to authority, the school taught the young to protest.

The government itself bankrupted the secondary school. The ministries of Bogolepov and Vannovsky organized commissions to establish the goals of reform. Many valuable comments on the questions of school organization and curricula are preserved in the collected works of the commissions. To this labor were drawn many serious and original pedagogical talents. The public and the pedagogical world placed trust and hope in their efforts. The multivolumed works of the commissions are a monument to the great intellectual exertion and at the same time an eloquent witness to the sterility of public passion confined to a bureaucratic frame. The school could not be remodeled in an immobile political and social atmosphere. The ministerial commissions could not heal the disease. They only deceived the hopes of the public one time too many, inflicting a new, final disappointment. It became all the more obvious that the renewal of education could not be expected from a dying institution, the educational bureaucracy.

In the last few years public awareness has grown with increasing intensity. In the last few months most of the fundamental questions of national life have been posed with firmness and distinctness. The history of education in recent times has demonstrated that it cannot develop without broad public initiative, without the regular influence of social forces on the school. Only a popularly representative administration, organized on the broadest possible democratic base, can create and secure the conditions necessary for popular support of education. If the official policy of sacrificing the cultural needs of the country to reactionary purposes created the school crisis, no less responsible is the inertness of society, which, in a state of disorganization, did not raise a decisive voice in defense of its principles. This disorganization, this silence, was a form of public participation in the bureaucracy's crimes against the school.

Now this period is passed. A feeling of solidarity has seized the various elements of Russian society. We, who up to this time were condemned to bear in isolation the heavy labor in the stifling atmosphere of the secondary school, strongly feel this solidarity and community of interests. The call to unity and union must resound in our midst. A union of teachers is an important and urgent task. It must seize the initiative for the creation of a school based on the cooperation of the public with the teaching profession. Unless society and the educators can provide the country with a school that produces citizens who can think for themselves, the cultural renewal of Russia is impossible.

Let our union be the union for the struggle for genuinely public education. To the measures restricting academic freedom, annihilating the personalities of teachers and pupils, turning the school into a tool of reaction, let it register a strong collective protest. Let it be the pledge of open debate in school questions. Let it organize public opinion, which, together with the united action of the teachers, will defend the pupils from arbitrary force. The union of student counselors must take from the weak and inexperienced hands of the pupils the struggle for the school.

Union has a more immediate significance for us, the teachers. The teacher is so forgotten, so alone in the contemporary school system, that at every step he feels the impotence of his individual efforts to vindicate his pedagogical ideals and to resist the pressures of the political system. Organized association must replace this isolation with the awareness of common interests and collective work for the good of the school. It gives the opportunity to each to appeal to a large group of people who think the same way and to find among them moral and material help in the difficult conditions often created for a teacher who does not compromise his convictions. Such are the goals of the Union of Secondary School Teachers. The urgent necessity of its creation is demanded by the interests of the school and the severity of the crisis into which the bureaucratic system has plunged it. We cannot and must not remain observers of the feverish process in which old structures disintegrate and life creates new forms. There is no return to dead forms. We openly strike out on a new road. We realize what conditions are necessary to create a new school. In the fight against the old for the creation of new forms we pledge our united strength. To this same end we summon our teaching comrades.

NOTES

Notes

Complete authors' names, titles, and publication data will be found in the Bibliography, pp. 295–312. The following abbreviations used in the Notes are listed in alphabetical order in the Bibliography in the form of cross-references to formal Bibliography entries:

DSZ	*Obraz. Zhenshchin*	*R.U.*
Duma B.K.	*Obzor Dumy*	*Sbornik post. MNP*
Duma Pri.	*Obzor MNP*	*Sbornik ras. MNP*
Duma S.O.	*Otchet MNP*	*SMS*
EVR	*PSU*	*Soviet S.O.*
GUM	*PSZ*	*VEP*
MVD	*R.S.*	*V.V.*
		ZMNP

Chapter One

Epigraph: N. K. Shilder, *Imperator Aleksandr Pervyi* (St. Petersburg, 1904), II, 372.

1. Walter Mediger, *Moskaus Weg nach Europa* (Braunschweig, 1952), p. 7.
2. Pushkin, p. 1380.
3. S. M. Soloviev, *Istoriia Rossii s drevneishikh vremen* (Moscow, 1962), VII, 77.
4. Andreev, p. 90.
5. B. H. Sumner, *Peter the Great and the Emergence of Russia* (New York, 1962), p. 136.
6. *Sbornik imperatorskogo russkogo istoricheskogo obshchestva* (St. Petersburg, 1867–1917), LVI, 320–21.
7. Ostrovitianov, I, 430.
8. Kliuchevsky, V, 177.
9. *Obzor MNP*, p. 7.
10. M. N. Tikhomirov, I, 38.

11. *Ibid.*

12. For a positive treatment of eighteenth-century gentry self-education, see Marc Raeff, *Origins of the Russian Intelligentsia* (New York, 1966).

13. Kliuchevsky, V, 191.

14. I. I. Betskoi (*Uchrezhdeniia i ustavy, kasaiushchiesia do vospitaniia i obucheniia v Rossii iunoshestva oboego pola*, 2 vols., St. Petersburg, 1774), quoted in S. F. Platonov, *Lektsii po russkoi istorii* (St. Petersburg, 1909, 6th ed.), p. 607.

15. A. P. Piatkovskii, "S-Peterburgskii vospitatel'nyi dom pod upravleniem I. I. Betskago," *Russkaia starina*, XII (1875), 146–59, 359–80, 665–80.

16. Diderot, p. 441.

17. Miliukov, "Shkola," p. 756; the instructional aids are in Dmitri Tolstoy, pp. 210ff.

18. Muzhuev, p. 384.   19. *Stroganov*, II, 111.

20. Hans, pp. 41–51.   21. *Obzor MNP*, p. 76.

22. *PSZ*, 1803, item 20597. Original italics.

23. *Ibid.*, item 20598.

24. Nicholas Hans, *Comparative Education* (London, 1958), p. 309.

25. *Stroganov*, II, 211.

26. *PSZ*, 1809, item 23771.

27. Richard Pipes, *Karamzin's Memoir on Ancient and Modern Russia* (Cambridge, Mass., 1959), p. 162.

28. Marc Raeff, *Michael Speransky* (The Hague, 1957), pp. 65ff, 193.

29. *PSZ*, 1809, item 23771.   30. Miliukov, "Shkola," p. 779.

31. Shchebal'skii, p. 199.   32. Granovsky, p. 152.

33. *Chteniia v imperatorskom obshchestve istorii i drevnostei rossiiskikh pri moskovskom universitete* (1861), IV, 160–61.

34. *PSZ*, 1826, item 464. Original italics.

35. Pushkin, p. 1293.

36. *PSZ*, 1826, item 338.

37. N. K. Shilder, *Imperator Nikolai Pervyi* (St. Petersburg, 1903), II, 287.

38. *PSZ*, 1827, item 1308.

39. *Ibid.*

40. Granovsky, pp. 152ff.

41. *Sbornik ras. MNP* (legislation cited 1833), No. 423.

42. *PSZ*, 1835, item 2.

43. *PSZ*, 1826, item 338.

44. Nicholas Riasanovsky, *Nicholas I and Official Nationality in Russia, 1825–1855* (Berkeley, Calif., 1959), pp. 213–14.

45. Muzhuev, p. 386.

46. *Sbornik ras. MNP* (1840), No. 436.

47. Muzhuev, p. 386; *Sbornik ras. MNP* (1845), Nos. 720, 721.

48. *Sbornik ras. MNP* (1845), No. 759.

49. Cyon, p. 82.

50. Martin Malia, "What Is the Intelligentsia?" in Richard Pipes, ed., *The Russian Intelligentsia* (New York, 1961), p. 14.

51. Ostrovitianov, I, 117.

52. Belinsky, I, 87.

53. Herbert Bowman, *Vissarion Belinsky* (Cambridge, Mass., 1954), pp. 143–44.

54. Belinsky, III, 708.

55. Aksakov, III, 281. Original italics.
56. Miliukov, "Shkola," p. 795. Original italics.
57. Granovsky, p. 152.

Chapter Two

Epigraph: Chicherin, *Vospominaniia,* pp. 32–33.
   1. Nikitenko, II, 20–21. Original italics.
   2. *EVR,* p. 561.
   3. V. A. Zhukovsky, "Pis'ma k Ego Imperatorskomu Vysochestvu Velikomu Kniaziu Konstantinu Nikolaevichu," *Russkii arkhiv,* 1867, pp. 1406–7, 1437–38. Original italics.
   4. Nikitenko, II, 339.
   5. N. P. Pavlov-Silvanskii, *Ocherki po russkoi istorii xviii–xix vv.* (St. Petersburg, 1910), p. 312.
   6. *EVR,* p. 223.
   7. Venturi, p. 221.
   8. Chicherin, *Vospominaniia,* p. 16.
   9. "Pis'mo I. S. Turgeneva k K. K. Sluchevskomu (Paris, 14 April 1862)," in I. S. Turgenev, *Otsy i deti* (Moscow, 1950), p. 211.
   10. Pirogov, p. 520.   11. Nikitenko, II, 371.
   12. Pisarev, p. 368.   13. M. N. Tikhomirov, I, 267.
   14. See Pisarev, p. 302.   15. Nikitenko, II, 52.
   16. Chicherin, *Vospominaniia,* p. 33; Herzen, XV, 179.
   17. Chicherin, *Vospominaniia,* pp. 32–33.
   18. Venturi, p. 227.
   19. Herzen, XV, 186. Original italics.
   20. Spasovich, pp. xx–xxi.
   21. *Ibid.*
   22. For the figures, see Peter Lyashchenko, *History of the National Economy of Russia to the 1917 Revolution,* translated by L. M. Herman (New York, 1949, p. 393). On hearing the "frightening, holy word" of emancipation, Sergei Aksakov expressed the apprehension of educated society in verse (*Sobranie sochinenii,* Moscow, 1909, I, 485–86):

> How will the people awaken?
> How will the nightmare turn?
> Will freedom slip in softly
> And the law remain firm?
>
> Will you go to church with thanksgiving,
> Or head for the nearest bar,
> Afterward grab your axes
> And head for the landlord's barn?

   23. The tsarist police counted 1,176 rebellious villages in 1861. Soviet scholars count 91 peasant outbreaks in 1859 and 1,259 in 1861. S. V. Tokarev, "O chislennosti krest'ianskikh vystuplenii v Rossii v gody pervoi revoliutsionnoi situatsii," *Revoliutsionnaia situatsiia v Rossii v 1859–1861 gg.* (Moscow, 1960), p. 125.
   24. Chicherin, *Vospominaniia,* p. 217.
   25. Nikitenko, II, 49.

26. *Zhurnaly zasedaniia uchenago komiteta glavnogo upravleniia uchilishch po proektu obshchago ustava rossiiskikh universitetov* (St. Petersburg, 1862), pp. 3–16.

27. Ostrovitianov, I, 429.

28. Pirogov, p. 406.

29. *Ibid.*, p. 389.

30. Chicherin, *Vospominaniia*, pp. 56–57.

31. Pirogov, p. 411.

32. *Ibid.*, pp. 402–4.

33. V. I. Ger'e, "Svet i teni universitetskogo byta," *Vestnik Evropy*, 1876, p. 694.

34. Baddeley, p. 176.

35. Chicherin, *Vospominaniia*, p. 43.

36. Spasovich, p. xxii.

37. R. E. Zelnik, "The Sunday-School Movement in Russia, 1859–1862," *The Journal of Modern History*, June 1965, pp. 151–70.

38. Pirogov, pp. 464–74.

39. Zelnik, pp. 151–70.

40. M. Dragomanov, ed., *Pis'ma K. Dm. Kavelina*, pp. 160–61.

41. *Ibid.* The description is Turgenev's.

42. Tatishchev, II, 255ff.

43. *Obzor MNP*, p. 397.

44. Cyon, p. 93.

45. A work by Tolstoy on the economic history of Russia, *Istoriia finansovykh uchrezhdenii v Rossii so vremeni osnovaniia gosudarstva do konchiny imperatritsy Ekateriny II*, appeared in 1848. For other works see p. 274, note 64.

46. Tatishchev, II, 259–61.

47. Chicherin, *Vospominaniia*, p. 29.

48. Pirogov, p. 65. Original italics.

49. The essays in Hans Walter Bähr, *Erziehung zur Menschlichkeit, Die Bildung im Umbruch der Zeit, Festschrift für Eduard Spranger* (Tübingen, 1957), analyze classical education in modern times.

50. Ushinsky, *Izbrannye*, II, 268.

51. Pirogov, p. 307.

52. Matthew Arnold, *Schools and Universities on the Continent* (London, 1868), pp. 94–95 *passim*.

53. Gessen, pp. 322ff.

54. Belinsky, I, 58.

55. Pirogov, p. 609, original italics; Dmitri Tolstoy quoted "bits and pieces" in Odessa, *ZMNP*, November 1875, p. 67.

56. *Obzor MNP*, p. 514.

57. Pirogov, p. 24. The description is Ushinsky's.

58. *Ibid.*, pp. 55, 76.

59. *Ibid.*, p. 577.

60. "Dnevnik Grafa Petra Aleksandrovich Valueva," *Russkaia starina*, LXX (1891), 341.

61. Pirogov, pp. 583, 637; Lemke, p. 82.

62. Tatishchev, II, 235.

63. Pisarev, p. 313.

64. *MVD*, pp. 244–45. The adjective "colorful" was used by the censor.

65. *Ibid.*, p. 216.

66. *Ibid.,* pp. 216–17.
67. Zaionchkovskii, p. 329.
68. Pisarev, pp. 122, 313–14 *passim;* for another revolutionary's positive view of his gymnasium experience, see Dragomanov, "Avtobiografiia."
69. Pisarev, pp. 372–77.
70. *MVD,* p. 264.
71. Pirogov, p. 239.
72. *Ibid.,* p. 233.
73. Ushinsky, *Izbrannye,* II, 252–53.
74. Pirogov, p. 234.
75. Lemke, p. 82.
76. Pirogov, pp. 230ff.
77. *Svod zakonov,* XI (1912), No. 1, art. 1463.
78. For salary scales, 1828–59, see William H. E. Johnson, *Russia's Educational Heritage,* (Pittsburgh, 1950), p. 279.
79. Muzhuev, p. 388.

Chapter Three

Epigraph: Baddeley, p. 186.
1. Ushinsky, *Izbrannye,* II, 267.
2. Nikitenko, II, 51.
3. A. Leroy-Beaulieu, p. 159.
4. Zaionchkovskii, p. 335.
5. Tatishchev, II, 583.
6. Lemke, p. 66; Chicherin, *Vospominaniia,* p. 192.
7. Cyon, p. 99.
8. Tatishchev, II, 260.
9. Lemke, pp. 84–85.
10. Nikitenko, II, 287. Original italics.
11. Tatishchev, II, 236.
12. Chicherin, *Vospominaniia,* p. 192.
13. *Ibid.,* p. 194; V. N. Lamzdorf, *Dnevnik* (Moscow, 1926), pp. 194–95.
14. Cyon, p. 115.
15. Nikitenko, II, 307–8; for Katkov's view of his relationship with Tolstoy, see Martin Katz, *Mikhail N. Katkov* (The Hague, 1966).
16. Cyon, p. 114.
17. Granovsky, p. 152.
18. *SMS,* II, Prilozhenie, p. 15.
19. Pirogov, p. 244.
20. I. V. Shelgunov, *Izbrannye pedagogicheskie sochineniia* (Moscow, 1954), p. 319.
21. Zaionchkovskii, pp. 329–30.
22. Baddeley, p. 187.
23. Pirogov, pp. 453–54.
24. Stepniak, pp. 392–93.
25. *Obzor MNP,* p. 520.
26. Ushinsky, *Izbrannye,* II, 266.
27. Katkov, pp. 70–71, 78–79, 83.
28. With the university statute of 1863, the state committed itself to spend 1,872,-000 rubles a year on the universities instead of the previous outlay of 988,000 rubles. The secondary statute of 1864 raised the state funds for general educational schools from 1,045,000 rubles to 1,808,000 rubles. Tolstoy continued the expansion begun under Golovnin and centered it around secondary schools. Between 1866 and 1879 the budget of the Ministry of Education rose from 6,769,000 rubles to 16,407,000 rubles. Of this latter amount 2,484,000 rubles went for universities, 5,275,000 for gymnasiums and progymnasiums, 1,558,000 for realschulen, 1,245,000 for urban and district schools, 1,507,000 for elementary schools, and 229,000 for parish schools (Tatishchev, II, 249, 251, 282).
29. *ZMNP,* December 1875, p. 132. The phrase is Tolstoy's.

30. B. G. Kuznetsov, *Lomonosov, Lobachevskii, Mendeleev* (Moscow, 1945), pp. 233, 246.
31. Nikitenko, II, 500.
32. Baddeley, p. 176.
33. Stepniak, pp. 392–93; A. Yarmolinsky, *Road to Revolution* (New York, 1962), pp. 313–14.
34. Gessen, p. 322.
35. Ushinsky's major essays on the subject appeared between 1862 and 1868. Before 1866 his anti-classical views were published in the *Journal of the Ministry of Education*; after 1866 they appeared in *Voice* and *St. Petersburg News*.

36. Ushinsky, *Izbrannye*, II, 276.   37. *Ibid.*, p. 278. Ushinsky's italics.
38. Cyon, p. 115.   39. Katkov, p. 85.
40. Lemke, p. 85.   41. Katkov, pp. 72–74.
42. Nikitenko, II, 407ff.   43. Spasovich, p. xxviii.

44. N. Smirnov-Sokol'skii, *Russkie literaturnye al'manakhi i sborniki xviii–xix vv.* (Moscow, 1965), pp. 301–2.
45. "Aleksandr Vasil'evich Golovnin," *Russkaia starina*, LV (1887), 663–66.

46. *EVR*, p. 496.   47. *Ibid.*, p. 491.
48. *Ibid.*, pp. 485–86.   49. *Ibid.*, p. 501, note 20.

50. *Obzor MNP*, p. 524.
51. *Svod zakonov*, 1912, XI, No. 1, art. 1464–1586.
52. *Ibid.*, art. 1688–1778.
53. *Sbornik ras. MNP* (1872), No. 206.
54. *Ibid.*, No. 245.
55. Baddeley, p. 186.
56. *Sbornik ras. MNP* (1872), No. 211.
57. *Sbornik ras. MNP* (1866), No. 107.
58. *Sbornik post. MNP*, 1871, July 19.
59. *Obzor MNP*, pp. 482–83.
60. *Sbornik ras. MNP* (1874), No. 83.
61. *SMS*, I–VI, *passim*.
62. *ZMNP*, May 1865, p. 4.
63. Pirogov, pp. 230ff.
64. Tolstoy, *Die Stadtschulen während der Regierung der Kaiserin Katharina II.* Tolstoy examined eighteenth-century Russian education in two other works: *Akademicheskaia gimnaziia v xviii stoletii po rukopisnym dokumentam arkhiva akademii nauk* and *Akademicheskii universitet v xviii stoletii po rukopisnym dokumentam arkhiva akademii nauk, vzgliad na uchebnuiu chast' v Rossii v xviii stoletii do 1782 goda.*
65. Miliukov, "Shkola," p. 765.
66. M. P. Makarov, "Activities of I. N. Ulyanov in Behalf of the Education of the Chuvash People," *Soviet Education*, 1958, No. 1, pp. 43–48. For a judicious assessment of Tolstoy's policy see Allen Sinel, "Educating the Russian Peasantry: The Elementary School Reforms of Count Dmitrii Tolstoy," *Slavic Review*, March 1968, pp. 49–70.

Chapter Four

Epigraph: *Obzor MNP*, p. 485.
1. On official and public hatred of "German" institutions, see Max Weber, "Zur

Lage der bürgerlichen Demokratie in Russland," *Archiv für Sozialwissenschaft und Sozialpolitik,* XXII, 1906, 235–36, note 2. After a historical survey of Germano-phobia ("In the 1880's Dragomanov labeled the Petersburg bureaucracy simply 'the German party' "), Weber concluded: "At least this much is certain, that the Russian democracy hates us as much as the Russian bureaucracy has hated us since the Congress of Berlin. It is also certain that this hatred will endure, for Germany's outward might will continue to irritate bureaucratic nationalism and Germany's territorial possessions will continue to antagonize democratic federalists."

2. Venturi, p. 596.
3. George Fischer, *Russian Liberalism* (Cambridge, Mass., 1958), pp. 34–35.
4. Tatishchev, II, 606.   5. *Obzor MNP,* pp. 530–31.
6. *Sbornik ras. MNP* (1877), No. 130.   7. Tatishchev, II, 610–11.
8. Kizevetter, p. 95.   9. *Obzor MNP,* p. 485.
10. Venturi, p. 653.
11. Tatishchev, II, 613. In 1864 the student population of the universities was 4,323. In 1875 it was 5,679; in 1880, 8,193. Muzhuev, p. 388.
12. *Obzor MNP,* p. 486.
13. *EVR,* p. 572.
14. Venturi, p. 695.
15. Kizevetter, p. 95.
16. D. S. Mirsky, *A History of Russian Literature* (New York, 1958), p. 338.
17. Pobedonostsev, *Reflections of a Russian Statesman,* p. 75.
18. *Otchet MNP,* 1887, pp. 97–98.
19. *Duma S. O.,* 11 June 1908, pp. 2812–18.
20. *Otchet MNP,* 1887, pp. 134–35.
21. *Otchet MNP,* 1885, pp. 64–65.
22. *Ibid.*
23. *Ibid.,* p. 80.
24. *Sbornik ras. MNP* (1872), No. 205.
25. In 1887 there were 103 realschulen with 20,716 pupils. *Otchet MNP,* 1887, Appendix, p. 114. The gymnasiums rather than the realschulen ("camps for academic refugees from the gymnasiums," *SMS,* IV, 81) were serving as preparatory schools for a number of higher technical institutions. Of the 225 students entering the Kharkov veterinary institute in 1890, one came from an agricultural school, one from a military gymnasium, 28 were graduates of realschulen, and 195 were holders of maturity certificates from gymnasiums. Of 36 young men entering the Kazan veterinary institute in 1890, 30 were graduates of university preparatory schools (*Otchet MNP,* 1890, p. 52). Only persons completing the full course of a gymnasium could enter the Riga polytechnicum without an entrance examination (*Otchet MNP,* 1887, p. 69). Standards were lower in Warsaw, where persons with at least six years of work at a classical gymnasium could enter the veterinary institute if their academic record was satisfactory (*Otchet MNP,* 1888/1889, p. 55).
26. The Council of State aired relations between general education and vocational training (*Soviet S.O.,* 1887, pp. 396–428). The Ministry of Education issued urgent instructions to the districts to open vocational schools in 1900 (*Sbornik ras. MNP,* 1900, No. 907). The state duma discussed transferring responsibility for vocational training from the Ministry of Education to the Ministry of Commerce and Industry (*Duma S.O.,* 16 April 1912, pp. 2403ff. For a historical survey of commercial instruction in Ministry of Education schools, see Sakharov, pp. 216–36. The state stressed its interest in technical instruction for women in 1900 by organizing a

special section on female vocational training within the Ministry of Education (*Sbornik ras. MNP* (1900), No. 901).

27. On January 1, 1886, the gymnasium population stood at 70,651, the realschulen at 20,577, and the urban schools at 40,734. This meant that the lower and middle practical schools together (61,311) instructed 9,340 fewer boys than the university preparatory schools. On January 1, 1899, the gymnasiums were instructing 77,041 boys, the realschulen 34,495, and the urban schools 78,024. The public acceptance of the urban schools was officially noted in 1885 when one-fourth of the 406 boys who passed the entrance examination for the urban schools of Kazan province were turned away for lack of space. The conversion of the district schools of 1828 (2,500 rubles annual cost) into the urban schools (4,000 rubles yearly operating budget) was hampered by lack of local funds (*Otchet MNP,* 1886, pp. 293–94). On the borders of the empire, where the urban school "besides its pedagogical significance has political importance" (*Otchet MNP,* 1886, pp. 294–95), state funds were applied to facilitate the conversion of native language district schools into Russian-speaking urban schools. The Germans of the Dorpat (later, Riga) region were no more amenable to Russian schools than the Poles of the Vilna district, and both races clung to the inferior district schools for that reason (*Otchet MNP,* 1885, pp. 206–7, 211–12; 1886, p. 294; 1887, p. 236). The state was also interested in the spread of urban schools in connection with universal military service. A Ministry of Education circular of June 18, 1889, instructed the pupils of teachers' institutes to master basic infantry drills so that later in their capacity as teachers in urban schools they could instruct their students in military gymnastics.

28. K. Pobedonostsev, "Otryvok iz neizdannogo sochineniia o Rossii," in *K. P. Pobedonostsev i ego korrespondenty,* I, 30.

29. It was a characteristic of tsarist educational policy that the men who were responsible for the schools were also deep in internal security and foreign affairs. "A more complicated chapter of diplomacy than that dealing with the year 1887 could hardly be found in the history of European international relations... the clouds of war lowered on all horizons" (William L. Langer, *European Alliances and Alignments 1871–1890,* New York, 1964, Vintage ed., p. 451). In 1887 Katkov, Tolstoy, Delianov, and Pobedonostsev, the "Prussianizers" of the Russian school system, were working to change the official policy of friendship with Bismarck's Germany for an open hand toward France. They were also preoccupied with the attempt on the Tsar's life organized by students of St. Petersburg University to mark the anniversary of Alexander II's assassination (Cyon, p. 99). For an interpretation of educational policy within the political context of 1887, see the despatch of the *New York Times* correspondent quoted in the footnote on pp. 129–30.

30. Of 9,386 pupils in the preparatory classes of the gymnasiums in 1884, 3,122 belonged to the lower orders of society. In 1887 the state was paying 201,699 rubles to support the preparatory classes. Local funds amounted to but 25,648 rubles. On May 30, 1888, in response to a request from the Ministry of Education made on April 11, 1887, the Council of State withdrew state funds for support of preparatory classes in "predominantly Russian-speaking areas" (*Obzor MNP,* pp. 641–42). For the regional effects of this order, see Appendix A, Table 2, for each school district. In some schools in the large cities townspeople had actually gained numerical ascendancy over the privileged class. The breakthrough came in 1876, when a change in the rules permitted children in the preparatory classes to pass directly into the gymnasium proper without an entrance examination. Often there was simply no

room in the first Latin year for the upper-class products of home-tutoring once the preparatory pupils from the lower orders had taken their places. The effects of the rules change in 1876 and the withdrawal of funds from the preparatory classes in 1887 on the social composition of the gymnasium were shown in a study of the student body of the Moscow fourth gymnasium (*SMS*, I, 16–17):

Year	No. of Pupils from the Gentry and Official Estates	No. of Pupils from the Urban and Rural Estates
1877	136	156
1882	173	270
1887	171	198
1889	220	136
1892	244	152

31. *Obzor MNP*, p. 641.

32. The statute of 1871 absorbed Par. 23 of the statute of 1864 without change.

33. Greenberg, I, 35.

34. See Appendix A for type and quality of figures with which the Ministry of Education was working. Table 1 in Appendix A correlates with Table 2 except in the cases of the St. Petersburg and Moscow districts. In these two regions the difference between the number of pupils in Table 1 and the total number of pupils in each class in Table 2 is explained by the fact that, in counting the number of pupils in the gymnasiums and progymnasiums of St. Petersburg and Moscow, the Ministry of Education included the five German Lutheran gymnasiums in St. Petersburg and the two private gymnasiums in Moscow that enjoyed full state rights; in counting the number of pupils in each class, however, only state schools were taken into account. For detailed information on the church and private gymnasiums, see *Otchet MNP*, 1887, pp. 86–87. The principal charts for constructing Table 2 were found in *Otchet MNP*, 1887, pp. 91, 98–101; for constructing Table 3, *Otchet MNP*, 1885, pp. 77–79; 1887, p. 96; 1890, pp. 96–97. Table 4 was derived from the same documents as Table 3 except that extra material (such as *Otchet MNP*, 1885, p. 71) was used to break "other reasons" down further into academic failures and family circumstances. Various difficulties arose from the happenstance that the Ministry produced a combined report for the years 1888/1889 rather than individual reports, that not all districts were included in every statistical compilation, that sometimes percentages were given and sometimes numbers of social groups, those dropping out, and pupils in a class. Finally, numbers given in the Appendixes to the annual reports did not always agree with numbers appearing in the text; numbers given in one volume did not always agree with those offered in another. Discrepancies and omissions could not obscure the main features of the provincial responses to central directions.

35. The government had fiscal as well as political reasons for wanting to shut down progymnasiums. Because of the smaller number of pupils in a given four-year or six-year school, the cost per pupil to the state of a progymnasium was as much as double that of the cost per pupil in a full eight-year gymnasium (*Otchet MNP*, 1890, p. 67).

36. In the fall of 1899 the Ministry of Education made it easier for the schools to open parallel classes with the use of tuition funds. As long as no state aid was re-

quired, district curators had the authority to allow expansion on local income. By the following spring Petersburg was warning the regions of the seriousness of the situation, particularly in the two capital cities, where many gymnasiums, their populations swollen by parallel classes, were actually two full-scale schools trying to operate in a building designed for one. The price for this inexpensive form of internal expansion was a lowering of scholastic performance and a rise in disciplinary problems. On April 20, 1900, the Ministry recommended restricting the entrance of additional numbers of students into the existing gymnasiums until new facilities could be opened. Simultaneously, norms were imposed on the institutions of higher learning, both technical schools and universities, limiting the rise in new registrations to a 10 per cent increment over the previous year. None of these central regulations was strictly enforced.

37. The percentage of a class dropping out tended to be relatively low for the preparatory class (10 per cent annually), high for the first year (17 per cent), a high plateau for the second, third, and fourth years (14/15 per cent), and sharply declining from the fifth to the eighth year (11, 6, 5, .66 per cent). *Otchet MNP*, 1887, p. 96. See Appendix A, Table 3, for individual school districts.

38. Of the total number of academic failures, 1,054 owed their defeat to Latin, 908 to mathematics, 565 to Greek, 440 to history and geography, 419 to modern languages, 101 to catechism, and 36 to physics. Of those failing, 75 per cent failed in more than one subject (*Otchet MNP*, 1885, p. 71). See Appendix A, Table 4, for individual school districts.

39. See Appendix A, Table 1 for each district. Note the correlation between the reduction of entrants in September and the increase of graduates in June. The figures for 1887 and 1890 have been italicized to highlight the principal positive feature of the central contraction policy of 1887.

40. The curator continued: "The agitation from various sides against the ancient languages, which has turned into an out-and-out attack against classicism, threatening to end with the complete breakdown of serious education in the secondary school, cannot but have a dire influence on the normal course of study and training in the gymnasiums, undermining the teachers' confidence in a stable order and arousing in the pupils senseless hopes of achieving good results without hard work" (*Otchet MNP*, 1888/1889, p. 79). The curator's attitude echoes what Matthew Arnold found in Western Europe 20 years earlier: "Authority does all that can be done in favour of the old classical training; ministers of state sing its praises . . . Still in the body of society there spreads a growing disbelief in Greek and Latin, at any rate as at present taught; a growing disposition to make modern languages and the natural sciences take their place." In the 1860's this was the case in Germany as well as in France. And "in Germany too, as in France, the movement is in no wise due to the school authorities, but is rather in their despite, and against their advice and testimony" (*Schools and Universities on the Continent*, London, 1868, pp. 94–95).

41. On October 12, 1889, military gymnastics were made obligatory in the general educational secondary schools. Instructors were drawn from officers of local military forces. Soldiers from the ranks served as assistants (*Otchet MNP*, 1890, p. 89). In 1890 St. Petersburg was not as insistent on administrative and academic uniformity as in 1871. Gymnasiums in areas of large non-Russian population were instructed to increase the number of hours devoted to Russian language; pay increases of 50 per cent were offered to attract European Russians to Turkestan and eastern Siberia (*Otchet MNP*, 1890, pp. 75–76).

42. "In order to give the universities a rational administration it is first of all necessary to put people in charge of them who understand both universities and the condition of society. For the past 13 years, we have not had one minister or one curator who understood anything of this kind. Imagine the condition of the army if for a decade diplomats or postal officials were appointed generals and ministers of war" (Chicherin, *Vospominaniia*, p. 38).

43. *ZMNP*, December 1875, p. 135.

44. "Ianovsky, Kirill Petrovich, 1822–1902—zamechatel'nyi pedagog-administrator," *Entsiklopedicheskii slovar*, Vol. 82 (St. Petersburg: Brockhaus-Efron, 1904).

45. The school districts of the Russian Empire with their total population and their urban population, according to the imperial census of 1897:

District	Total	Urban
Moscow	17,970,749	2,638,974
Kiev	14,722,167	1,394,130
Kharkov	14,235,129	1,391,224
Kazan	13,001,444	1,005,856
Vilna	10,126,295	1,194,742
Caucasus	9,620,888	1,053,046
Warsaw	9,465,943	2,055,892
Odessa	8,222,485	1,636,206
Orenburg	7,930,217	532,756
St. Petersburg	6,716,975	1,703,484
West Siberia	5,721,837	406,905
Turkestan	3,898,106	628,258
East Siberia	2,359,514	256,872

46. Percentages of townsmen in the gymnasiums in 1886 and 1894:

	1886	1894	Difference
In the whole empire	35.8	31.6	−4.2
In the districts more democratic than the empire as a whole in 1886:			
Odessa	51.7	38.3	−13.4
Riga	43.7	40.3	−3.4
In the districts as democratic as the empire as a whole in 1886:			
Moscow	37.2	32.7	−4.5
Warsaw	35.2	30.1	−5.1
Kazan	33.7	30.2	−3.5
In the districts less democratic than the empire as a whole in 1886:			
Kharkov	31.8	34.6	+2.8
Petersburg	31.1	29.5	−1.6
Kiev	30.5	28.5	−2.0
Vilna	30.7	23.6	−7.1
Caucasus	29.3	30.7	+1.4

Riga, which by 1894 contained the most democratically textured gymnasiums, took the most urgent steps to curb academic drop-out. In 1890 St. Petersburg noted that "half of the district's gymnasiums did not practice this harsh measure [expulsion for academic failure] in accordance with the provisions of Par. 34 of the Statute of 1871, but by every means available the school authorities strove to continue the education of children committed to their care" (*Otchet MNP*, 1890, p. 87).

47. *Otchet MNP*, 1890, p. 86.
48. Percentages of Jews in the gymnasiums in 1886 and 1894:

	1886	1894	Difference
In the whole empire	10.7	6.2	−4.5
In districts more Jewish than the empire as a whole in 1886:			
Odessa	31.9	14.8	−17.1
Vilna	20	11.7	−8.3
In districts as Jewish as the empire as a whole in 1886:			
Kiev	12.5	9.3	−3.2
Warsaw	11.6	7.7	−3.9
Riga	10.7	7.3	−3.4
In districts less Jewish than the empire as a whole in 1886:			
Moscow	5.5	2.6	−2.9
Petersburg	4.9	2.6	−2.3
Kharkov	3.9	4.1	+0.2
Caucasus	3.4	2.3	−1.1
Kazan	2.9	2.1	−0.8

There was also modification from above. "Even the minister of education, Delianov, who inaugurated the restrictions and instructed the administrators to enforce them strictly, made many exceptions. Of the 82 Jewish students who were admitted in 1897 to the University of Odessa, 71 were registered above the quota at the personal instructions of Delianov" (Greenberg, I, 85).

Chapter Five

Epigraph: *Sbornik ras. MNP*, 1899, No. 528.
1. The title of the classic contemporary work on this period stresses the public theme: Martov and others, *Obshchestvennoe*.
2. Kireev, p. 317.
3. Nekrasov, pp. 576–77.
4. For an analysis of these principles, see Robert F. Byrnes, "Pobedonostsev on the Instruments of Russian Government," in Cyril E. Black, ed., *The Transformation of Russian Society* (Cambridge, Mass., 1960), pp. 113–28.
5. T. H. von Laue, "The State and the Economy," in Cyril E. Black, ed., *The Transformation of Russian Society* (Cambridge, Mass., 1960), pp. 216–17.
6. The Russian empire's first comprehensive census numbered almost half a million persons in the professional middle class and a quarter million in the imperial bureaucracy. The somewhat vague figures are in N. Troinitsky, *Obshchii svod po*

Imperii rezultatov razrabotki dannykh pervoi vseobshchei perepisi naseleniia, proizvedennoi 28 ianvaria 1897 goda (2 vols., St. Petersburg, 1905).

7. On economic grounds alone, aside from political, Witte argued that Russia must have schools of European quality (*Soviet S.O.* [1911/1912], pp. 3799–3800).

8. Max Weber, "Zur Lage der bürgerlichen Demokratie in Russland," *Archiv für Sozialwissenschaft und Sozialpolitik,* XXII (1906), 237, note 3.

9. George Fischer, *Russian Liberalism* (Cambridge, Mass., 1958), pp. 57–59.

10. Martov and others, I, 341–48.

11. "Chelovek v futliare," in *Rasskazy* (Moscow, 1951), pp. 346, 355. Paul Miliukov used the phrase "man in the instrument case" in an attack on the Ministry of Education (*Duma S.O.*, 16 April 1912, pp. 2396–98).

12. *Russkaia Shkola* was published in St. Petersburg and developed close relations with the independent-minded secondary teachers in the capital. *Vestnik Vospitaniia* originated in Moscow and was closely associated with the pedagogical society of Moscow University. In the 1890's the number of imaginative teachers was growing: Baltalon, a realschule teacher, published articles on better ways to develop students' critical judgment through compositions on literary themes (*SMS*, III, Prilozhenie, pp. 217ff); Kasatkin, teacher of manual arts in the Moscow Teachers' Institute, was concerned with the pedagogical implications of manual dexterity (*SMS*, V, Prilozhenie, pp. 117ff); Nedachin, of Moscow's fifth gymnasium, pondered the effects on children of lifeless Latin programs. These teachers and others like them were working for "a new school, better adapted to the pedagogy and social conditions" of the twentieth century (*SMS*, V, p. 6).

13. Society tends to view the state school as "an alien force intruding into the family, not to help it but with completely different aims" (V. O. Einhorn, teacher, Moscow first gymnasium, *SMS*, I, Prilozhenie, p. 125).

14. *Ibid.*, I, p. 51.

15. V. P. Nedachin, teacher, Moscow fifth gymnasium, *SMS*, I, Prilozhenie, pp. 3–14.

16. A. V. Adolf, director, Moscow fifth gymnasium, *ibid.*, I, Prilozhenie, p. 224.

17. "In the secondary school, as in the kingdom of its creator, the law is constantly violated and counts for less than the 'discretion' of those in power. The superior presses down hard upon his subordinate, squeezing out his individual personality and transforming him into an automaton. The volume of work is distributed in inverse proportion to service rights and salary paid to the mere cog in the machine. Whoever is paid less, has fewer employment rights and privileges, while he is obligated to work harder. In this realm one is not rewarded equally for equal work but according to his service rank, a system that justifies higher salaries for those in power than for those doing more and better work. The ideal superior in this system is not the outstanding performer who issues orders without shirking his own tasks, but the person who only knows how to echo commands that uphold the prestige of the establishment" (Senex, pp. 136–37).

18. *Ibid.*, p. 136.

19. *SMS*, I, 11–13, 121–25, 184–94; Prilozhenie, pp. 3–14, 15–25.

20. *Ibid.*, Prilozhenie, pp. 59–64.

21. A. I. Kirpichnikov, dean of the historical-philological faculty, Moscow University, *ibid.*, Prilozhenie, p. 46.

22. *Tsirkuliar po s-peterburgskomu okrugu,* 1896, No. 6.

23. *SMS*, I, Prilozhenie, pp. 41–50.

24. Resolution adopted by the Moscow district conference in 1899, *ibid.*, I, 235.

25. *Ibid.*, I, 45.

26. *Ibid.*, I, 198–99, Prilozhenie, pp. 263–76.

27. A. A. Tikhomirov, the rector of Moscow University, had figures to show that "the best gymnasium pupils [the gold and silver medalists] are completely successful at the beginning of their university studies" (*SMS*, I, 23–26).

28. *Ibid.*, pp. 196, 207.

29. *Otchet MNP*, 1885, pp. 83–84.

30. *SMS*, I, 202–20, Prilozhenie, pp. 125–35; Count P. A. Kapnist, curator of the Moscow district in the reign of Alexander III, served as chairman of a commission studying the maturity examination in 1891. He came to the conclusion that "examinations are an evil, but a necessary one" (*SMS*, I, 196).

31. Nekrasov, p. 577.

32. Martov and others, I, 273–83.

33. "I, the undersigned, promise and swear before Almighty God and His Holy Gospel that I will and must, truly and sincerely, serve His Imperial Highness, the true and legitimate Most Gracious Supreme Sovereign Emperorer Nicholas Alexandrovitch, Autocrat of All the Russias and the legitimate Heir of His Imperial Highness's All-Russian Throne, and that I will obey in all things, not sparing my body to the last drop of blood, and that I will guard and defend to the limits of my intelligence, strength, and possibilities all the rights and privileges, stipulated and unstipulated, inherent in the absolute power and authority of His Imperial Highness; furthermore, that I will strive to promote as far as possible everything that in every instance redounds to the true service and state utility of His Imperial Highness; I will notify the proper authorities as quickly as possible of any threatened injury, harm, or loss to His Majesty's interests, and I will not only notify the authorities in good time but endeavor to ward off and guard against such injuries, and I will faithfully preserve all secret information entrusted to my care; ... I will conscientiously carry out the instructions, regulations, and directives of the superiors placed over me; and I will not admit of any profit, relationship, friendship, or enmity contrary to my duty and oath, and in this way I will conduct myself as behooves a true and faithful subject of His Imperial Highness, so as to be able always to render an account before God's terrible judgment, so help me, Lord God, body and soul. To seal my oath I kiss the words and cross of my Savior, Amen." *Sbornik ras. MNP* (1899), No. 575.

34. *Sbornik ras. MNP* (1898), No. 17.

35. Vodovozov, p. 351.

36. *SMS*, I, v–vii.

37. *Ibid.*, p. 11.

38. *Sbornik ras. MNP* (1900), No. 973.

39. *Ibid.*, No. 972.

40. *Ibid.*, No. 974.

41. *Ibid.*, No. 972.

42. *Obzor MNP*, p. 714.

43. Witte, I, 179.

44. *Obzor MNP*, pp. 701–2.

45. *Sbornik ras. MNP* (1901), No. 95.

46. *Sbornik ras. MNP* (1901), Prilozhenie k 188.

47. *Sbornik ras. MNP* (1901), No. 189.

48. *Ibid.*, No. 208.

49. *Ibid.*, No. 247.

50. *Ibid.*, No. 208.

51. Kireev, *passim.*

52. *Sbornik ras. MNP* (1902), No. 777.

53. *Obzor MNP*, pp. 703–4.

54. *Ibid.*, p. 719.
55. *Sbornik ras. MNP* (1902), No. 630.
56. Miliukov, *Russia and Its Crisis*, pp. 163–64.
57. *Ibid.*, pp. 371–72.
58. *Tsirkuliar po moskovskomu uchebnomu okrugu*, 1904, No. 10.
59. Selenkin, pp. 81–118.
60. *Sbornik ras. MNP* (1903), No. 1028.
61. *Ibid.*, 1900, No. 973.
62. *Ibid.*, No. 1067.
63. *Sbornik ras. MNP* (1903), No. 1074.
64. *Ibid.*, 1902, No. 616. 65. *Ibid.*, 1903, No. 1028.
66. *Ibid.* 67. *SMS*, I, 22.
68. *Sbornik ras. MNP* (1903), No. 1028.

69. Martov and others, I, 290. Between 1897 and 1909 the incidence of child mortality was increasing. In 1897, 28.5 per cent of all children born died within one year; in 1909, 32.7 per cent. During the same period 45 per cent of all children born in the country died before reaching the age of five (*Vserossiiskii sezd po semeinomu vospitaniiu. Trudy*, St. Petersburg, 1914, p. 6).

Chapter Six

Epigraph: *Pravo*, No. 6, 1905, pp. 424–25.
1. Ivar Spector, *The First Russian Revolution. Its Impact on Asia* (Englewood Cliffs, N.J., 1962), Appendix One, p. 120.
2. Senex, p. 136. 3. *R.S.*, May/June 1905, pp. 108–9.
4. *Ibid.* 5. *V.V.*, December 1905, p. 119.
6. *Ibid.*, pp. 143–44. 7. *Ibid.*, pp. 121–24.
8. For the reaction in the Caucasus, see *V.V.*, December 1905, pp. 112–13. For events in Samara, see *R.S.*, March 1905, p. 108; in Kazan, *ibid.*, September 1905, pp. 64–65.
9. *V.V.*, December 1905, p. 111.
10. On the origins of the manifesto, see Witte, I, 339.
11. *R.S.*, April 1905, pp. 92–95.
12. *Ibid.*, p. 91; in the district of Riga the curator organized parent-teacher circles to discuss mutual problems (*S-Peterburgskiia vedomosti*, 20 January 1905, p. 5).
13. *R.S.*, March 1905, pp. 103–6, and September 1905, pp. 63–64. Parents' committees had been serving as public agencies within the decentralized commercial schools of the Ministry of Finance since 1897 (Fisher, p. 11). For the social influence of parents' committees in the loosely organized girls' schools, see Agraev, pp. 160–218.
14. *Pravo*, No. 6, 1905, pp. 424–25. In 1913 the manifesto was quoted at the first all-Russian congress on women's education (*I-go vserossiiskago sezda po obrazovaniiu zhenshchin*, St. Petersburg, 1915, II, 240).
15. "Trudy kommissii po voprosu o zhelatel'nykh preobrazovaniiakh srednei shkoly," *Trudy moskovskago pedagogicheskago obshchestva*, I (Moscow, 1899); see also Vetukhov, pp. 261–73. The Moscow society devoted its February meetings to the question of organizing an all-Russian union of pedagogues (*V.V.*, March 1905, p. 111).
16. *R.S.*, April 1905, p. 87.
17. Kizevetter, p. 375.

18. *R.S.,* May/June 1905, pp. 104–6; *Pravo,* No. 17, 1905, p. 1393. The university students and dropouts who tutored secondary students for examinations were the first members of the teaching fraternity to organize. They demanded a minimum wage of one ruble an hour. *S-Peterburgskiia vedomosti,* 25 January 1905, p. 6.

19. *R.S.,* May/June 1905, p. 104. On November 10, 1905, over 1,000 rural school-teachers met in Riga. All but seven voted to support the political program of the Social Democratic Party. Martov and others, II, 122.

20. "Moskva, 18 oktiabria," *Russkiia vedomosti,* 18 October 1905, p. 1.

21. See Isaac Babel, "The Story of My Dovecot," in Douglas Angus, ed., *The Best Short Stories of the Modern Age* (Greenwich, Conn., 1962), pp. 196–97, the auto-biographical tale of a Jewish boy who won admittance to a state gymnasium in 1905.

22. *PSU,* p. 24.

23. *Ibid.*

24. *R.S.,* December 1905, pp. 87–88.

25. *PSU, passim,* surveys provincial activities.

26. *Ibid.,* pp. 57–65.

27. *Russkiia vedomosti,* 20 October 1905, p. 3.

28. *V.V.,* January 1906, p. 106.

29. *Ibid.,* p. 107.   30. *Ibid.,* p. 114.

31. *PSU,* pp. 30–34, discusses organizational structure; and *PSU,* pp. 35–45, discusses teacher-student relations.

32. Agraev, pp. 42–57. In 1912 the parents' committees were practically defunct. Working parents could not attend meetings. The poor and uneducated stayed away. Public reluctance played into the hands of hostile officials. N. P. Ursin, *Vserossiiskii sezd po semeinomu vospitaniiu. Trudy* (St. Petersburg, 1914), pp. 199–200.

33. *PSU,* p. 45; *V.V.,* April 1906, p. 137.

34. On the question of public vs private schools, see *R.S.,* July/August 1905, pp. 90–91.

35. "Everyone can see at once what has been created here: the definitive bureaucratic rationalization of the autocracy throughout the entire range of its internal politics. This reorganization leaves the direction of affairs in the hands of the expert specialist, and in Russia, where there is so little self-government, that means *exclusively* the bureaucrats." Max Weber, "Russlands Übergang zum Scheinkonstitutionalismus," *Arkhiv für Sozialwissenschaft und Sozialpolitik,* XXIII (1906), 228. Original italics.

36. The work of the second congress was recorded in *Sezd uchitelei i deiatelei srednei shkoly v Peterburge iiun' 1906 goda* (St. Petersburg, 1906), published by the journal *Russkaia Shkola.*

37. *Ibid.,* p. 50.

38. The Moscow Plan appears in *PSU.*

39. Members of the central bureau of the all-Russian union of secondary school teachers took part in the work of the committee on public education of the second duma (*Trudy kursov dlia uchitelia srednei shkoly,* St. Petersburg, 1907, p. vii). See below, Chapter Seven, note 3.

Chapter Seven

Epigraph: *Duma S.O.* (6 March 1907), pp. 39–40; for Stolypin's long-range plans for national enlightenment, see Zenkovskii, pp. 92–96.

1. *V.V.*, December 1907, pp. 118–46.

2. *Trudy pervago vserossiiskago sezda deiatelei obshchstv narodnykh universitetov i drugikh prosvetitel'nykh uchrezhdenii chastnoi initsiativy S-Peterburga 3–7 ianvaria 1908 g.* (St. Petersburg, 1908); *Otchet moskovskago gorodskago narodnago universiteta imeni A. L. Shaniavskago za 1911–1916 akademicheskii god* (Moscow, 1912–16).

3. "Proekt osnovnykh polozhenii gosudarstvennago organicheskago zakona po narodnomu obrazovaniiu," *Zakonodatel'nyia zaiavleniia, vnesennyia na osnovanii st. 55 uchrezhdeniia gosudarstvennoi dumy* (St. Petersburg, 1907), pp. 233–37.

4. *Duma B. K.*, 1909/1910, p. 16.

5. *Ibid.*, II (1911/1912), No. 57, p. 27.

6. Kliuzhev ("Voprosy," p. 141) presented an abbreviated version of a table devised by the Ministry of Education at the behest of the state duma illustrating the neglect of the Great Russian center (Moscow) relative to western (Livland) and southern (Kherson) provinces, as of January 1, 1910:

	Moscow	Petersburg	Kherson
Women per province	1,402,400	1,330,200	1,641,500
Gymnasiums	43	24	31
Progymnasiums	7	2	2
Women secondary students	12,492	7,312	11,207
Women per school	28,048	51,161	49,742
Women per secondary student	312	181	146

	Kiev	Livland	Astrakhan
Women per province	2,176,500	735,300	593,500
Gymnasiums	26	14	1
Progymnasiums	1	2	0
Women secondary students	6,941	4,121	479
Women per school	80,611	45,956	593,500
Women per secondary student	313	178	1,239

7. Malinovskii, pp. 145–51. Students' tuition fees contributed more than half of the total support of girls' schools. Sources of support for girls' gymnasiums and progymnasiums in 1908 were as follows:

Source	Amount	Source	Amount
State treasury	1,561,241	Gifts	82,361
Boarders	520,299	Cossacks	48,945
Tuition	9,879,336	Jews	2,932
Gentry	45,735	Ministry of Education	613,290
Municipalities	1,013,263	Other	374,660
Zemstvos	931,730	Total	15,245,922
Interest on gifts	172,130	(*Otchet MNP* [1908] gives as the total 15,245,926.)	

8. *Obzor MNP*, p. 720.

9. *Duma B. K.*, 1909/1910, p. 16. Following is a comparison of the number of boys' and girls' secondary schools as of January 1, 1909:

District	Boys	Girls	District	Boys	Girls
Petersburg	77	98	Warsaw	37	23
Moscow	118	193	Riga	33	43
Kazan	40	63	Caucasus	45	45
Orenburg	22	41	West Siberia	9	20
Kharkov	71	106	Turkestan	7	9
Odessa	75	114	Irkutsk	8	18
Kiev	60	88	Priamur	5	7
Vilna	50	90	Total 657		958

10. For a survey of the rapid growth of secondary schools in the wake of the revolution of 1905, see *Duma Pri.*, IV (1910/1911), No. 347, pp. 3–8.

11. *Duma B. K.*, 1909/1910, p. 20.

12. *Ibid.*

13. Sources of support for boys' gymnasiums and progymnasiums (based on *Otchet MNP*) follow. The totals are not those given in *Otchet MNP* but the sums derived by adding the sources of funds.

Source of Funds	1900	1904	1913
State treasury	5,541,647	6,475,533	14,064,034
Student fees	3,822,921	4,919,371	8,212,192
Boarders' fees	1,422,359	1,469,934	936,396
Municipalities	461,988	515,801	877,154
Zemstvos	254,082	271,306	476,010
Gentry	13,462	12,240	271,006
Gifts	841,944	969,404	110,259
Interest on gifts	355,223	427,016	317,466
Cossacks	41,431	44,328	65,385
Jews	1,825	1,655	1,500
Ministry of Education	23,596	13,564	776,358
Other	262,809	275,536	333,134
Total 13,043,287		15,395,688	26,440,894

14. The figure given in *Obzor Dumy*, III, 282–83 (24.1 million rubles) has been adjusted to 24.6 million rubles in accordance with the extra funds listed in *Smeta dokhodov, raskhodov i spetsialnykh sredstv ministerstva narodnago prosveshcheniia na 1913 god.* (St. Petersburg, 1912), pp. 22–24. After 1905 state expenditure on education increased not only in absolute sums but as a proportion of total state outlay. The Ministry of Education bore direct fiscal responsibility for approximately 60 per cent of the national scholastic effort. Kliuzhev, "Voprosy," calculated a doubling of that effort on the eve of the First World War:

Year	Total State Budget	Amount Granted MNP	Percentage Granted MNP
1872	495,814,000	11,285,687	2.3
1882	703,505,000	18,056,393	2.6
1902	1,775,914,000	36,624,312	2.1
1912	3,001,919,261	117,377,000	3.9
1913	3,208,406,961	136,734,000	4.2

15. Intermittent restoration of Tolstoyan discipline after 1905 was described by a teacher in a letter to his brother, which was read in 1913 at the first all-Russian congress on women's education: "The new director has tightened up the discipline of the realschule and has unloaded onto the teachers the duties of surveillance outside school hours. Before, this was mostly the job of the inspector and prefects, but now the teachers are supposed to do it—the class counselors—and the inspector checks up on them; isn't that a mess? Every week your job is to check the cinematograph twice in the evening and the main street two times from 7:00 to 9:00, since the students are allowed to promenade only to 7:00 o'clock; after that the teachers are supposed to write them up and chase them home. Nice, isn't it? This really upsets me—until 3:00 o'clock busy in school, then home to prepare the next day's lessons, and, in addition, busy almost the whole evening checking up on students! Add to that, that the director expressed the desire for all teachers to be present at all church services—judge for yourself, what's left over for yourself and your family?" *Obraz. Zhenshchin*, II, 221–22.

16. The number of males in a province for each secondary pupil on January 1, 1909 (*Duma B. K.*, 1909/1910, p. 18), was as follows:

St. Petersburg	99	Bessarabia	464
Livonia	139	Vladimir	472
Moscow	146	Kazan	636
Tiflis	159	Tula	765
Kurland	186	Tomsk	1,090
Kherson	237	Samara	1,212
Warsaw	250	Ufa	1,513
Kiev	296	Fergana	3,617

17. The Octobrist representatives in the third duma took credit for guiding the Ministry of Education away from an imperialist policy and toward a Great Russian policy (*Obzor Dumy*, III, 292).

18. Provinces and oblasts in which no state gymnasium or realschule was added from 1908 to 1912 (derived from *Podrobnaia obiasnitel'naia zapiska k proektu smety MNP na 1913 god*. St. Petersburg, 1913, p. 9); St. Petersburg, Kaluga, Yaroslavl, Penza, Tauride, Kurland, Samarkand, Semipalatinks, Syr-Daria, Fergana; all areas of the Caucasus except Baku, Stavropol, and Kuban; all of Siberia except Irkutsk, Tobolsk, Tomsk, and Priamur; and all areas of Poland except Suwalki.

19. The vitality of local initiative and state priorities combined to produce varying district growth rates for the period from January 1, 1908, to January 1, 1913, when the empire-wide increase in the number of gymnasiums and realschulen reached 43 per cent:

European Russia	Uralia	Border	Asia
Moscow 63%	Kazan 66%	Vilna 33%	E. Siberia .. —
Kharkov 48%	Orenburg ...94%	Riga 10%	Turkestan . —
Kiev 46%	W. Siberia 100%	Warsaw 36%	Priamur ..13.5%
Petersburg ..23%		Caucasus ...58%	
		Odessa 14%	

The unequal growth rates induced shifts in the geographical distribution of the schools. Following are percentages of total boys' gymnasiums and realschulen in each school district:

School District	Percentage		
	1905	*1908*	*1913*
Petersburg	14.0	12.0	10.5
Moscow	16.0	17.5	19.5
Kharkov	10.0	9.3	9.6
Odessa	10.8	11.7	9.3
Kiev	9.2	9.7	10.0
Vilna	5.3	4.8	4.5
Kazan	6.5	6.5	7.5
Orenburg	2.7	3.2	4.5
Caucasus	6.5	8.2	9.1
Riga	4.2	4.2	3.2
Warsaw	8.8	7.2	6.9
W. Siberia	2.0	1.8	2.2
E. Siberia	4.0	3.6	3.0

20. The list of 1911 appears in *Duma B.K.*, IIk (1911/1912), No. 57, pp. 97–100. Its realization can be derived from *Smeta dokhodov, raskhodov i spetsial'nykh sredstv MNP na 1913 god.* (St. Petersburg, 1913), pp. 22–23.

21. *Duma B.K.*, IIk (1913/1914), No. 18, pp. 26–27.

22. The social complexion of the Urban Schools in 1906 (based on *Otchet MNP 1905*) was as follows:

Estate	No. of Pupils
Hereditary nobility	3,030
Personal nobility and officials	6,635
Clergy	1,465
Honored citizens and merchants	6,654
Townsmen	60,597
Cossacks	4,513
Peasants	46,572
Native peoples	486
Others	1,957
Total	131,909

23. *GUM*, pp. 155–61.

24. *S-Peterburgskiia vedomosti*, No. 250, 1906, p. 2.

25. *GUM*, pp. 47–50, 261.

26. *S-Peterburgskiia vedomosti*, No. 17, 1905, p. 2.

27. *GUM*, p. 192.

28. *Ibid.* pp. 192–93.

29. Velikosel'skii, Nos. 4, 5, 10.

30. *Otchet o sezde uchitelei gorodskikh po polozheniiu 1872 g. uchilishch moskovskago uchebnago okruga 2–11 ianvaria 1903 g.*, cited as *GUM*.

31. *Trudy pervago vserossiiskago sezda uchitelei gorodskikh po polozheniiu 1872 g. uchilishch 7–14 iunia 1909 g.*, 2 vols. (St. Petersburg, 1910).

32. *Ibid.*, I, 547.

33. *Obzor MNP*, pp. 703–4.

34. *Duma Pri.*, IV (1910/1911), No. 347, pp. 9–10.

35. *Ibid.*, pp. 1–19.
36. *Duma Pri.*, IV (1910/1911), No. 381.
37. *Predstavlenie M-a N-ago P-iia po departamentu narodnago prosveshcheniia, ot 9 fevralia 1909 g. No. 2963.*
38. *Duma Pri.*, IV (1910/1911), No. 381, Prilozhenie No. 5.
39. In his address to the Council of State, Professor Vasilev traced the idea of the unified school back to Catherine II (*Soviet S.O.*, 1911/1912, pp. 3808–9).
40. *Soviet S.O.*, 1911/1912, p. 3796.
41. *DSZ*, pp. 177–97.
42. *Ibid.*, pp. 207–8.
43. *Svod zakonov*, XI (1912), No. 1, pp. 449–59.
44. Growth and reform increased the tempo of the democratic trend, which had been rising since the breakdown of the central contraction policy of 1887. The following tabulation shows the numbers of the different social groups as of January 1, 1913, according to *Otchet MNP*, 1912.

Estate	Boys' Gymnasiums	Realschulen	Girls' Gymnasiums	Urban
Nobility	12,294	4,705	16,788	3,546
Officials	34,537	12,545	49,990	5,025
Clergy	7,969	2,137	14,715	1,640
Merchants	14,749	7,621	29,707	3,898
Townsmen	38,743	23,612	108,320	59,139
Cossacks	2,753	3,532	5,720	7,163
Peasants	26,700	20,172	67,210	79,996
Foreigners	1,444	1,158	2,531	516
Others	3,676	1,489	8,709	1,935
Total	142,935	76,971	303,690	162,858

Chapter Eight

Epigraph: *Duma S.O.*, 6 March 1907, pp. 39–40.
1. *SMS*, I, Prilozhenie, pp. 3–18.
2. *Trudy pedagogicheskago obshchestva sostoiashchago pri imperatorskom moskovskom universitete* (Moscow, 1900), I, 15–90.
3. Estimate of an average teacher's income by the Moscow pedagogical society: 12 lessons a week at 75 rubles a year per weekly hour (900 rubles a year), 18 lessons a week at 60 rubles a year per weekly hour (1,080 rubles a year), 160 rubles a year as class counselor, 100 rubles a year for correcting papers, minus 2 per cent for pension (45 rubles), for a total of 2,195 rubles a year.
4. The Moscow pedagogical society estimated the cost of living per year (in rubles) for a teacher and his family in the city as follows:

	Number of Children				
	0	1–2	3–4	5–6	7+
Living quarters	400	500	600	600	700
Firewood	96	144	144	144	192
Light	24	30	36	42	48

| | Number of Children | | | | |
	0	*1–2*	*3–4*	*5–6*	*7+*
Floor polisher	12	18	24	24	24
Housing tax	7	11	11	11	14
Servants	72	156	156	156	228
Servants' board	72	144	144	144	180
Food	540	600	720	840	960
Clothes, boots	200	250	300	350	400
Laundry	96	108	120	132	144
Tobacco	36	36	36	36	36
Water	12	18	24	30	42
Books, paper	50	50	50	50	50
Medical	30	50	70	90	100
Recreation	63	44	7	0	0
Other	78	115	132	125	144
Total rubles	1,800	2,274	2,574	2,774	3,262

5. *St. Petersburger Zeitung* (15 November 1898, pp. 5–6) estimated the cost of living per year for a married and an unmarried teacher in a provincial town:

Married Teacher Without Children	Rubles
Rooms	180
Firewood	60
Maid	60
Food and gifts for maid	70
Clothing	130
Food	360
Water	12
Laundry	12
Light	26
Medical	20
Books, paper	20
Vacation	100
Tobacco	20
Other	30
Total	1,100

Bachelor Teacher	Rubles
Rooms	120
Food	360
Clothes	100
Laundry	15
Books, paper	25
Tobacco	20
Medical	10
Recreation	250
Other	35
Total	935

6. The Moscow society recommended the following scale:

| | Pay for Twelve Hours | |
Years of Service	Present	Recommended
1– 5	750	1,125
6–10	900	1,350
11–15	1,050	1,575
16–20	1,250	1,875
21–25	1,500	2,250

7. *Duma S.O.*, 2 November 1911, pp. 1071–82.
8. Base pay (twelve-hour week) for regular science and language teachers, in rubles per year:

Years of Service	With University Degree	Without Degree
1– 5	900	750
6–10	1,300	950
11–15	1,700	1,150
16–20	2,100	1,350
21–25	2,500	1,550

9. *Podrobnaia obiasnitel'naia zapiska k proektu smety MNP na 1913 god.* (St. Petersburg, 1913), p. 11.
10. *Russkii uchitel'*, No. 11, 1912, pp. 780–82.
11. *Ibid.*, No. 6/9, 1912, pp. 585–87.
12. *Ibid.*, No. 3, 1913, pp. 261–66.
13. *Tserkovnyia vedomosti*, No. 7/8, 1913, pp. 359–60.
14. *GUM*, pp. 266–76.
15. *Voprosy i nuzhdy uchitel'stva*, III (1910), 54–71.
16. Married urban teachers doing without cultural aids have the following breakdown (source: *ibid.*):

Activity	Percentage Doing Without
Social life	35
Theaters and concerts	25
Magazines and papers	14
Books	26
Vacation trips	37

17. *Voprosy i nuzhdy uchitel'stva*, III (1910), 70.
18. *GUM*, pp. 266–76.
19. Velikosel'skii, Nos. 4, 5, 10.
20. Kapterev, "Chto est' pedagogika?" p. 34.
21. Nechaev, "K voprosu o reforme nashei shkoly," p. 227.
22. *Ibid.*, p. 228.
23. "Proekt ustroistva pedagogicheskago facul'teta pri universitetakh," *Nauchnoe slovo*, Book 5, 1905, pp. 109–16.
24. Nechaev, *Sovremennaia eksperimental'naia psikhologiia v eia otnoshenii k voprosam shkol'nago obucheniia* (Contemporary Experimental Psychology in Its Relation to the Questions of School Teaching).
25. *Trudy s-peterburgskoi pedagogicheskoi akademii*, I (St. Petersburg, 1910).
26. *Sbornik posviashchennyi Vladimiru Mikhailovichu Bekhterevu k 40-letiiu professorskoi deiatel'nosti, 1885–1925* (Leningrad, 1926).
27. Chelpanov, "Sovremennaia," p. 16. Original italics.
28. Chelpanov, "Zadachi," pp. 135–38.
29. *Trudy kursov dlia uchitelia srednei shkoly* (St. Petersburg, 1907), pp. i–xlii.
30. *Ibid.*, pp. xxxii–xxxvi.
31. *Pedagogicheskii vestnik moskovskago uchebnago okruga. Sredniaia i nizshaia shkola*, No. 5/6, 1911, pp. 136–38.
32. *Trudy pervago vserossiiskago sezda po pedagogicheskoi psikhologii v S-Peterburge v 1906 g.* (St. Petersburg, 1906).

33. The women's medical institute, the technological institute, the page corps, the institute for retarded children, the St. Petersburg historical-philological institute, the cadet corps, the military medical academy, the academy of science, the Moscow clerical academy, the all-Russian union of primary education, the Russian society of normal and pathological psychology, the Bogatyr society, and the league of public education sent delegates. Also present were the curator of the Riga school district, the editor of *Pedagogical Chronicle,* the chairman of the league of public education, the director of military educational institutions, the director of educational institutions for the Ministry of Roads, the secretary of the school council of the Holy Synod, and the provincial inspector of the St. Petersburg school district. The universities of Moscow, St. Petersburg, Kiev, Kharkov, Jurev, Kazan, and Odessa sent delegates, as did fourteen gymnasiums, twelve realschulen, 27 girls' gymnasiums, 33 commercial schools, 24 ecclesiastical schools, two schools for the blind, two for the deaf, and one railroad school.

34. *Trudy vtorogo vserossiiskago sezda po pedagogicheskoi psikhologii* (St. Petersburg, 1910).

35. *Trudy vtorogo vserossiiskago sezda po eksperimental'noi pedagogike v Petrograde* (Petrograd, 1914).

36. *Shkola i zhizn',* 30 January 1912, pp. 2–3.

37. *Doklady chitannye na 2-m vserossiiskom sezde prepodavatelei matematiki v Moskve* (Moscow, 1915).

38. *Trudy pervago vserossiiskago sezda prepodavatelei drevnikh iazykov 28–31 dekabria 1911 g.* (St. Petersburg, 1912).

39. *Trudy pervago vserossiiskago sezda lits interesuiushchikhsia prepodavaniem novykh iazykov* (Moscow, 1913).

40. *Tserkovnyia vedomosti,* 1913, No. 3, pp. 152–53.

41. *Ibid.,* Nos. 37, 39, 48; *Russkii uchitel,* 1913, No. 3, pp. 261–66, and No. 6/9, Khronika, pp. 653–64.

42. *Trudy pervago sezda direktorov sredneuchebnykh zavedenii s-peterburgskago uchebnago okruga s 7–11 ianvaria 1912 g.* (St. Petersburg, 1912). Cited as DSZ.

43. See above, Chapter Seven, note 31.

44. *Obzor MNP,* p. 749.

45. *Ibid.,* p. 723.

46. *Ibid.,* p. 725.

47. *Voprosy i nuzhdy uchitel'stva,* II (1909), 16.

48. *Obzor MNP,* p. 724.

49. *Zemskie obshcheobrazovatel'nye kursy dlia narodnykh uchitelei,* p. 35.

50. *R.U.,* 1912, No. 1, pp. 42–56; and No. 2, pp. 115–26; *Voprosy i nuzhdy uchitel'stva,* I (1909), 17–32.

51. *Otchet postoiannoi komissii po ustroistvu kursov dlia uchitelei za 1912 god.* (St. Petersburg, 1913); *Russkiia vedomosti,* No. 127, 1912; *R.U.,* 1913, No. 5, pp. 553–66.

52. *R.U.,* 1912, No. 3, pp. 281–98.

53. *Ibid.,* No. 10, pp. 669–74.

54. *Trudy pervago vserossiiskago sezda po voprosam narodnago obrazovaniia,* 2 vols. (Petrograd, 1915).

Chapter Nine

1. See D. M. Odinetz and P. J. Novgorotsev, *Russian Schools and Universities During the War* (New Haven, 1929).

2. *USSR Soviet Life Today,* March 1964, p. 7. None of the English language textbooks currently offered for use in college and university courses on Russian history so much as mentions the name of the man whom the Soviet government recognized in its official exchange magazine as the native theoretician of the Soviet school system.

Bibliography

This study is based on both official and public sources. The annual reports of the Ministry of Education and the collections of central regulations issued to the provinces contain a mass of statistical and administrative material that is useful for a balanced view of social transformation and political policy in the Russian empire. This investigation also utilized but by no means exhausted the voluminous but scattered works of the numerous pedagogical congresses, official and professional. Contemporary memoirs, journals, and newspapers are likewise rich in empire-wide and local educational material. There is no pioneering bibliography of national enlightenment as practiced under the tsars. There is not even a serious study of such a central figure as Dmitri Tolstoy. This list, reflecting the perspective of this work, is one man's foray over a number of years into a little explored sector of the Russian past.

Agraev, G. V. *Roditeli, uchitelia, ucheniki. Zhizn' srednei shkoly za poslednie gody. Roditel'skie komitety i organizatsii*. St. Petersburg, 1907.

Akademiia Nauk SSSR, Institut Istorii. *Revoliutsionnaia situatsiia v Rossii v 1859–1861 gg*. Moscow, 1960.

Aksakov, I. S. *Ivan Sergeevich Aksakov v ego pis'makh*. Moscow, 1892. 3 vols.

Aleshintsev, I. *Istoriia gimnazicheskago obrazovaniia v Rossii*. St. Petersburg, 1912.

Ananin, S. A. *Pedagogicheskii kalendar'-spravochnik na 1910–1911*. Kiev, 1910.

Andreev, A. N. "Petr I v Anglii v 1698 g.," in *Petr Velikii, sbornik statei*. Moscow, 1947. Vol. I.

Anopov, I. A. *Opyt sistematicheskago obozreniia materialov k izucheniiu sovremennago sostoianiia sredniago i nizshago tekhnicheskago i remeslennago obrazovaniia v Rossii.* St. Petersburg, 1889.

Antonov, N. "Klassitsizm v tsifrakh," in *Sbornik pedagogicheskikh statei v chest' redaktora zhurnala "Pedagogicheskii Sbornik" A. N. Ostrogorskago po sluchaiu dvadtsatipiatiletiia po ego redaktorskoi deiatel'nosti.* St. Petersburg, 1907, pp. 307–20.

Baddeley, John F. *Russia in the 'Eighties.* London, 1921.

Bekhterev, V. M. "Ob uchrezhdenii psikhologich. soiuza, dlia organizatsii period. psikhologich. sezdov i ob ustroistve osobago psikhonevrologich. ili psikhologicheskago instituta," *Trudy pervago vserossiiskago sezda po pedagogicheskoi psikhologii v S-Peterburge v 1906 g.,* pp. 238–46.

Belinsky, V. G. *Sobranie sochinenii.* Moscow, 1948. 3 vols.

Bobylev, D. M. *Kakaia shkola nuzhna derevne (otzyvy krest'ian o shkole).* Perm, 1908.

Boch, G. N. "Dannyia o sovmestnom obrazovanii v Rossii," *Trudy 1-go vserossiiskago sezda po obrazovaniiu zhenshchin,* II, 24–28.

Bogdanov, I. M. *Gramatnost' i obrazovanie v dorevoliutsionnoi Rossii i v SSSR.* Moscow, 1964.

"Bogolepov, N. P.," in *Entsiklopedicheskii slovar.* St. Petersburg: Brockhaus-Efron, 1891.

Charnoluskii, V. I. *Ezhegodnik narodnago obrazovaniia. God pervyi. Vypusk I. Sezdy po narodnomu obrazovaniiu. Sbornik postanovlenii i rezoliutsii vserossiiskikh i oblastnykh sezdov po voprosam narodnago obrazovaniia (shkol'nago, vneshkol'nago i doshkol'nago) s podrobnym svodnym alfavitnym ukazatelem soderzhaniia.* Petrograd, 1915.

——— *Osnovnye voprosy organizatsii shkoly v Rossii.* St. Petersburg, 1909.

——— "Spisok [125] uchitel'skikh obshchestv, sobranii i klubov, uchrezhdennykh do 1907 goda," *Russkii uchitel',* 1912, No. 4, pp. 411–16, No. 5, pp. 503–6, Nos. 6/9, pp. 599–606, No. 10, pp. 702–25.

Chelpanov, G. I. "O postanovke prepodavaniia psikhologii v srednei shkole," *Trudy pervago vserossiiskago sezda po pedagogicheskoi psikhologii v S-Peterburge v 1906 g.,* pp. 80–86.

——— "Sovremennaia psikhologiia myshleniia i eia znachenie dlia pedagogiki," *Trudy vtorogo vserossiiskago sezda po eksperimental'noi pedagogike v Petrograde s 26 po 31 dek. 1913 g.,* pp. 9–18.

——— "Zadachi i organizatsiia moskovskago psikhologicheskago instituta," *Trudy vtorogo vserossiiskago sezda po eksperimental'noi pedagogike v Petrograde s 26 po 31 dek. 1913 g.,* pp. 135–38.

Chicherin, Boris. *Vospominaniia, moskovskii universitet.* Moscow, 1929.

——— "Zadachi novogo tsarstvovaniia," in *K. P. Pobedonostsev i ego korrespondenty* (Moscow, 1923), I, 104–20.

Cyon, Elie de. *Histoire de l'Entente Franco-Russe, 1886–1894, Documents et Souvenirs.* 3d ed. Paris, 1895.

Demkov, M. I. *Istoriia russkoi pedagogii.* Moscow, 1909.

——— *Nachal'naia narodnaia shkola, eia istoriia, didaktika i metodika.* 2d ed. Moscow, 1916.

Diderot, Denis. "Plan d'une université pour le gouvernement de Russie ou d'une éducation publique dans toutes les sciences," in *Oeuvres complètes de Diderot* (Paris, 1875), III, 409–534.

Didrikhson, A. *Istoricheskii obzor deiatel'nosti khar'kovskago obshchestva rasprostraneiia v narod gramotnosti. 1868–1909.* Moscow, 1911.

"Die pekuniäre Lage der Lehrer unserer Lehranstalten. Offener Brief eines Schulmannes," *St. Petersburger Zeitung*, November 15, 1898, pp. 5–6.

Dmitriev, S. A. "K voprosu o material'nom polozhenii uchitelei gorodskikh po polozheniiu 1872 goda, uchilishch," *Otchet o sezde uchitelei gorodskikh, po polozheniiu 1872 g., uchilishch moskovskago uchebnago okruga 2–11 ianvaria 1903 g.*, pp. 266–76.

——— "Proekt polozheniia o chetyreklassnykh i trekhklassnykh gorodskikh uchilishchakh," *Otchet o sezde uchitelei gorodskikh, po polozheniiu 1872 g., uchilishch moskovskago uchebnago okruga 2–11 ianvaria 1903 g.*, pp. 189–201.

Dorofeev, G. K. *K voprosu o reforme srednei shkoly.* Warsaw, 1904.

Dragomanov, M. P. "Avtobiografiia," *Byloe* (1906), I, No. 6, pp. 182–213.

Dragomanov, M. P., ed. *Pis'ma K. Dm. Kavelina i Iv. S. Turgeneva k Al. Iv. Gertsenu.* Geneva, 1892.

DSZ. See Trudy.

Duma B.K. See Gosudarstvennaia duma, *Biudzhetnaia komissiia.*

Duma Pri. See Gosudarstvennaia duma, *Prilozheniia.*

Duma S.O. See Gosudarstvennaia duma, *Stenograficheskie otchety.*

Dushkevich, Ia. I. "Kratkosrochnye uchitel'skie kursy," *Izvestiia postoiannoi komissii.* 1911, No. 1.

Dzhanshiev, G. *Iz epokhi velikikh reform.* 5th ed. Moscow, 1894.

EVR. See Dzhanshiev.

Falbork, G. A., and V. I. Charnoluskii, eds. *Nachal'noe narodnoe obrazovanie v Rossii.* St. Petersburg, 1900. 4 vols.

——— *Narodnoe obrazovanie v Rossii.* St. Petersburg, 1899.

Fisher, M. O. *O roditel'skikh komitetakh pri srednikh uchebnykh zavedeniiakh v Rossii.* St. Petersburg, 1912.

Ganelin, S. I. *Ocherki po istorii srednei shkoly v Rossii vtoroi poloviny XIX veka.* 2d ed. Moscow, 1954.

Gardenin, S. "Voprosy statistiki narodnago obrazovaniia na sezdakh i soveshchaniiakh russkikh statistikov," *Pervyi obshchezemskii sezd po statistike narodnago obrazovaniia 1913 goda. Doklady.* Kharkov, 1913, pp. 1–14.

Georgievskii, A. K. *Predpolozhennaia reforma nashei srednei shkoly.* St. Petersburg, 1901.

Gessen, S. I. *Osnovy pedagogiki.* Berlin, 1923.

Gorodenskii, N. I. "Otchet o trudakh komissii tiflisskikh prepodavatelei po voprosam postanovki prepodavaniia filosofskoi propedevtiki v srednei shkole," *Trudy vtorogo vserossiiskago sezda po pedagogicheskoi psikhologii*, pp. 134–47.

Gosudarstvennaia duma. *Biudzhetnaia komissiia. Doklady.* St. Petersburg, 1907–16.

―――― *Obzor deiatel'nosti gosudarstvennoi dumy tret'iago sozyva 1907– 1912 gg.* St. Petersburg, 1912. 3 vols.

―――― *Prilozheniia k stenograficheskim otchetam gosudarstvennoi dumy.* St. Petersburg, 1907–16. 40 vols.

―――― *Stenograficheskie otchety.* St. Petersburg, 1906–17. 36 vols.

―――― *Zakonodatel'nyia zaiavleniia, vnesennyia na osnovanii st. 55 uchrezhdeniia gosudarstvennoi dumy.* St. Petersburg, 1907.

Gosudarstvennyi soviet. *Stenograficheskie otchety.* St. Petersburg, 1906–17. 13 vols.

Granovsky, T. N. "Oslablenie klassicheskago prepodavaniia v gimnaziiakh i neizbezhnyia posledstviia etoi sistemy," in M. N. Katkov, *Nasha uchebnaia reforma* (Moscow, 1890), pp. 151–62.

Greenberg, Louis. *The Jews in Russia.* New Haven, 1951. 2 vols.

Grigorev, V. V. *Istoricheskii ocherk russkoi shkoly.* Moscow, 1900.

Grushevskii, S. F. *Sbornik zakonopolozhenii i pravitel'stvennykh rasporiazhenii.* Stavropol, 1876.

GUM. See Otchet.

Hans, Nicholas. *History of Russian Educational Policy.* London, 1931.

Herzen, A. I. *Sobranie sochinenii v tridtsati tomakh.* 30 vols. Moscow, 1954– 64.

Iakushevich, P. G. *Nedugi shkol'nago klassitsizma i mery dlia bor'by s nimi.* Vitebsk, 1896.

"Ianovsky, K. P.—zamechatel'ny pedagog-administrator," *Entsiklopedicheskii slovar.* St. Petersburg: Brockhaus-Efron, 1904.

Ianzhul, I. "Statisticheskaia otsenka dobrykh i durnykh uchitel'skikh vliianii v stenakh shkoly," in *Trudy pedagogicheskago otdela khar'kovskago istoriko-filologicheskago obshchestva* (Kharkov, 1900), VI, 39–57.

Iarotskii, A. I. *Kakova dolzhna byt' sredniaia shkola?* Iurev, 1914.

Ignatev, N. I. *Sbornik podrobnykh pravil i programm dlia postupleniia vo vse uchebnyia zavedeniia (iskliuch. vysshikh) muzhskiia i zhenskiia, s kharakteristikami uchebnykh zavedenii, na 1890–1891 gg.* St. Petersburg, 1890.

Imperatorskaia nikolaevskaia tsarskosel'skaia gimnaziia. *Kratkii istoricheskii ocherk imperatorskoi nikolaevskoi tsarskosel'skoi gimnazii za xxv let (1870–1895).* N.p., n.d.

Imperatorskii s-peterburgskii istoriko-filologicheskii institut. *Pamiatnaia knizhka imperatorskago s-peterburgskago istoriko-filologicheskago instituta i gimnazii pri onom.* St. Petersburg, 1887–1902. 3 vols.

Imperatorskoe moskovskoe obshchestvo sel'skago khoziaistva. *Otchet o deiatel'nosti komiteta gramotnosti pri imperatorskom moskovskom obshchestve sel'skago khoziaistva za 1893 g. i zhurnaly zasedanii 27 oktiabria 1893 g.–19 maia 1894 g.* Moscow, 1894.

Imperatorskoe russkoe tekhnicheskoe obshchestvo. *Trudy komissii po tekhnicheskomu obrazovaniiu i otchet o shkolakh dlia rabochikh i ikh detei, uchrezhdennykh imperatorskim russkim tekhnicheskim obshchestvom pri sodeistvii G. G. fabrikantov i zavodchikov g. S-Peterburga.* St. Petersburg, 1880–88.

Imperatorskoe vol'noe ekonomicheskoe obshchestvo. *Otchet o deiatel'nosti byvshego s-peterburgskogo komiteta gramotnosti imperatorskogo vol'nogo ekonomicheskogo obshchestva za 1895 god.* St. Petersburg, 1896.

——— *Trudy komissii po sostavleniiu proekta polozheniia nizshikh sel'skokhoziaistvennykh shkolakh.* St. Petersburg, 1879.

Iunitskii, P. *Spravochnik po organizatsii nizshago promyshlennago obrazovaniia v Rossii.* Moscow, 1912.

Iur'evskii universitet. *K voprosu kachestvennago pod'ema srednei shkoly. Revizionnye otchety gg. professorov imperatorskago iur'eskago universiteta.* Riga, 1912.

Iuzefovich, B. M. *Politicheskiia, ekonomicheskiia, sotsial'nyia i pedagogicheskiia osnovy dlia reformy russkoi gosudarstvennoi shkoly.* St. Petersburg, 1910.

Ivanovich, V. *Rossiiskiia partii, soiuzy i ligi.* St. Petersburg, 1906.

Kalantarov, G. S. "K voprosu o sovremennom polozhenii prepodavaniia gigieny v srednikh uchebnykh zavedeniiakh," *Materialy k voprosu o prepodavanii gigieny v srednei shkole,* II, 54–59.

Kapnist, P. *K voprosu o reorganizatsii sredniago obrazovaniia.* St. Petersburg, 1909.

Kapterev, P. F. "Analogiia v razvitii cheloveka i chelovechestva," *Trudy pervago vserossiiskago sezda po pedagogicheskoi psikhologii v S-Peterburge v 1906 g.,* pp. 135–40.

——— "Chto est' pedagogika?" *Trudy vtorogo vserossiiskago sezda po eksperimental'noi pedagogike v Petrograde s 26 po 31 dek. 1913 g.,* pp. 33–35.

Kareev, N. *Zametki o prepodavanii istorii v srednei shkole.* St. Petersburg, 1900.

Kasatkin, S. F. "Material'noe polozhenie uchashchikh v gorodskikh, po polozheniiu 1872 g., uchilishchakh," *Otchet o sezde uchitelei gorodskikh, po polozheniiu 1872 g., uchilishch moskovskago uchebnago okruga 2–11 ianvaria 1903 g.,* pp. 227–80.

Katkov, M. N. *Nasha uchebnaia reforma.* Moscow, 1890.

Kavelin, K. D. "Nashi nedorazumeniia" (1878), in *Sobranie sochinenii* (St. Petersburg, [1898?]), II, 1055.

——— "Zapiska o bezporiadkakh v s-peterburgskom universitete, osen'iu 1861 goda," in *Sobranie sochinenii* (St. Petersburg, [1898?]), II, 1191–1206.

Kavkazskii uchebnyi okrug. *Sbornik rasporiazhenii napechatannykh v tsir-*

kuliarakh po upravleniiu kavkazskim uchebnym okrugom. Tiflis, 1903. 10 vols.

———— *Svod mnenii pedagogicheskikh sovetov gimnazii i real'nykh uchilishch po voprosu o preobrazovanii nashei srednei shkoly.* N.p., n.d.

Kazanskii uchitel'skii institut. *Dvadtsatipiatiletie kazanskago uchitel'skago instituta 1876–1901.* Kazan, 1901.

Kazanskii universitet. *Trudy i protokoly. Pedagogicheskoe obshchestvo sostoiashchee pri imperatorskom kazanskom universitete.* Kazan, 1901–16. 4 vols.

Kennard, Howard P., ed. *The Russian Year Book.* London, 1911–16. 6 vols.

"Khar'kovskii eparkhial'nyi sezd o. o. zakonouchitelei svetskikh srednikh uchebnykh zavedenii," *Tserkovnyia vedomosti,* 1913, No. 37, pp. 1680–83.

Khar'kovskoe istoriko-filologicheskoe obshchestvo. *Trudy pedagogicheskago otdela khar'kovskago istoriko-filologicheskago obshchestva.* Kharkov, 1896–1902. 7 vols.

Kholpin, G. V. *Samoubiistva, pokusheniia na samoubiistvo i neschastnye sluchai sredi uchashchikhsia uchebnykh zavedenii M. N. P-ia, v 1909 gody.* St. Petersburg, 1911.

Kievskii uchebnyi okrug. *Otchet popechitelia kievskago uchebnago okruga o sostoianii uchebnykh zavedenii okruga za 1894 god.* Kiev, 1895.

———— *Otzyvy professorov universiteta sv. Vladimira o pis'mennykh otvetakh lits podvergavshikhsia ispytaniiu zrelosti v gimnaziiakh i okonchatel'nym ispytaniiam v real'nykh uchilishchakh kievskago uchebnago okruga za 1893–94 god.* Kiev, 1895.

———— *Trudy kievskago pedagogicheskago sezda. 12–19 aprelia 1916 goda.* Kiev, 1916.

Kireev, A. "O predstoiashchei reforme nashego obrazovaniia," *Russkii vestnik,* January 1902, pp. 303–31.

Kizevetter, A. A. *Na rubezhe dvukh stoletii. Vospominaniia 1881–1914.* Prague, 1929.

Kliuchevsky, V. O. *Kurs russkoi istorii.* Moscow, 1937. 5 vols.

Kliuzhev, I. S. *O podgotovke uchitelei i uchitel'nits nachal'nykh shkol.* [St. Petersburg? 1913?]

———— "Voprosy sredniago zhenskago obrazovaniia v obsuzhdenii ikh v gosudarstvennoi dume. Raskhody min. nar. pr. na zhenskoe obrazovanie," *Trudy 1-go vserossiiskago sezda po obrazovaniiu zhenshchin,* II, 132–45.

Komissiia "Po obshchim voprosam shkol'noi reformy" pri moskovskom soiuze deiatelei srednikh shkol. "Proekt normal'nago ustava gosudarstvennykh obshcheobrazovatel'nykh srednikh zavedenii," *Protokoly 1-go vserossiiskago sezda uchitelei i deiatelei srednei shkoly na Imatre 9–11 fevralia 1906 g.,* pp. 57-65.

Komissiia po ustroistvu kursov dlia uchitelei. *Otchet postoiannoi komissii po ustroistvu kursov dlia uchitelei za 1912 god.* St. Petersburg, 1913.

Komissiia po voprosu ob uluchsheniiakh v srednei obshcheobrazovatel'noi shkole. *Trudy vysochaishe uchrezhdennoi komissii po voprosu ob uluch-sheniiakh v sredneobrazovatel'noi shkole ministerstva narodnago pros-veshcheniia.* St. Petersburg, 1900. 8 vols.

Komissiia po vyiasneniiu pravogo polozheniia uchitelei. "Doklad komissii po vyiasneniiu pravogo polozheniia uchitelei, dolozhennyi v zasedanii 1-oi sektsii sezda delegatov obshchestva vzaimopomoshchi uchitelei 4 ianvaria 1903," in V. Vasilevich, *Moskovskii sezd predstavitelei uchitel'skikh ob-shchestv vzaimopomoshchi,* pp. 157-70.

Kononenko, A. A. "Uchitel', kak vospitatel' i ego pravovoe polozhenie," *Trudy kievskago pedagogicheskago sezda. 12–19 aprelia 1916 goda,* pp. 161–70.

K.-ov, V. "Gruppa, kak uchitel'skaia organizatsiia," *Russkii uchitel'.* 1913. No. 3, pp. 211–18.

Kovalevskii, E., ed. *Narodnoe obrazovanie na vserossiiskoi vystavke v N.-Novgorode v 1896 g.* St. Petersburg, 1897.

Kulomzin, A. A. *Opytnyi podshchet sovremennago sostoianiia nashego na-rodnago obrazovaniia.* St. Petersburg, 1912.

Kuskova, E. D. "O vneshkol'nom nadzore za uchashchimisia," *Trudy 1-go vserossiiskago sezda po obrazovaniiu zhenshchin,* II, 215–42.

Kuzmenko, D., ed. *Sbornik postanovlenii i rasporiazhenii po zhenskim gim-naziiam i progimnaziiam ministerstva narodnago prosveshcheniia za 1870–1912 gody.* 3d ed. Moscow, 1912.

Kuznetsov, A. "K voprosu ob otnoshenii gorodskikh uchilishch, po polo-zheniiu 1872 goda, k srednim i nachal'nym uchebnym za vedeniiam," *Otchet o sezde uchitelei gorodskikh, po polozheniiu 1872 g., uchilishch moskovskago uchebnago okruga 2–11 ianvaria 1903 g.,* pp. 155–61.

Laurson, A. M., ed. *Sobranie deistvuiushchikh zakonopolozhenii i raspor-iazhenii o chastnykh uchebnykh zavedeniiakh i o domashnem obuchenii.* St. Petersburg, 1912.

———— *Spravochnaia kniga dlia uchebnykh zavedenii i uchrezhdenii vedom-stva ministerstva narodnago prosveshcheniia.* St. Petersburg, 1911. 2 ed., 1916.

———— *Svod noveishikh zakonopolozhenii o material'nom obezpechenii slu-zhashchikh v direktsiiakh narodynkh uchilishch i v srednikh obshcheobra-zovatel'nykh muzhskikh uchebnykh zavedeniiakh vedomstva M.N.P.-iia.* St. Petersburg, 1912.

Lavrovskii, N. "Po voprosu ob ustroistve gimnazii," *Zhurnal ministerstva narodnago prosveshcheniia,* October 1867, pp. 115–92.

Lazurskii, A. *Shkol'nyia kharakteristiki.* 2d ed. St. Petersburg, 1913.

Lemke, M. *Ocherki po istorii russkoi tsenzury i zhurnalistiki xix stoletiia.* St. Petersburg, 1904.

Lenin, V. I. "Ot kakogo nasledstva my otkazyvaemsia," in *Polnoe sobranie sochinenii* (5th ed., Moscow, 1958), II, 505–50.

Leroy-Beaulieu, A. *Un homme d'état russe, Nicolas Milutine.* Paris, 1884.

"Letnie uchitel'skie kursy," *Voprosy i nuzhdy uchitel'stva,* I (1909), 17–32.

Liiutsh, A. "Ekonomicheskaia zavisimost' prepodavatelei v kazennykh i chastnykh uchebnykh zavedeniiakh," *Russkii uchitel',* 1912, No. 2, 105–16.

Magnitsky, M. "Rech' k imperatorskomu kazanskomu universtitetu 15 sentiabria 1825 goda," in *Chteniia v imperatorskom obshchestve istorii i drevnostei rossiiskikh pri moskovskom universitete* (1861), Book IV, pp. 160–61.

Malinovskii, N. P. "Finansovoe polozhenie zhenskikh srednikh uchebnykh zavedenii m-va nar. prosv. v Rossii," *Trudy 1-go vserossiiskago sezda po obrazovaniiu zhenshchin,* II, (1915), 145–51.

Markov, E. *Grekhi i nuzhdy nashei srednei shkoly.* St. Petersburg, 1900.

Martov, L., and others, eds. *Obshchestvennoe dvizhenie v Rossii v nachale xx-go veka.* 4 vols. St. Petersburg, 1909–14.

Mavritskii, V. A. *Pravila i programmy real'nykh uchilishch vedomstva M. N. P-iia.* 8th ed. Moscow, 1900.

—— *Sbornik pravil i podrobnykh programm dlia postupleniia vo vse uchebnyia zavedeniia, na 1887–1888 g.* Voronezh, 1887.

Medynskii, E. N., *Istoriia russkoi pedagogiki.* 2d ed. Moscow, 1938.

—— *Istoriia russkoi pedagogiki do velikoi oktiabr'skoi sotsialisticheskoi revoliutsii.* 2d ed. Moscow, 1938.

Miliukov, P. N. *Russia and Its Crisis.* New York, Collier ed., 1962.

—— "Shkola i Prosveshchenie," *Ocherki po istorii russkoi kul'tury.* Paris, 1931, Vol. II.

Ministerstvo finansov. *Sezd direktorov i predstavitelei popechitel'nykh sovetov v ianvare mesiatse 1902 goda, v gor. S-Peterburge. Vypusk II. Kommercheskiia uchilishcha.* St. Petersburg, 1902.

—— *Sezd direktorov i predstavitelei popechitel'nykh sovetov v iiune mesiatse 1901 goda v g. S-Peterburge. Vypusk I. Materialy po kommercheskomu obrazovaniiu.* St. Petersburg, 1901.

—— *Sostav sluzhashchikh v promyshlennykh zavedeniiakh v otnoshenii poddanstva, iazyka i obrazovatel'nago tsenza.* St. Petersburg, 1904.

Ministerstvo narodnago prosveshcheniia. *Izvlechenie iz vsepoddaneishago otcheta ministra narodnago prosveshcheniia.* St. Petersburg, 1851–1915.

—— *Kratkii obzor deiatel'nosti MNP za vremia upravleniia pokoinago ministra N. P. Bogolepova.* St. Petersburg, 1901.

—— *Materialy po reforme srednei shkoly. Primernyia programmy i obiasnitel'nyia zapiski, izdannyia po rasporiazheniiu g. ministra narodnago prosveshcheniia.* Petrograd, 1915.

—— *Opyt kataloga uchenicheskikh bibliotek srednikh uchebnykh zavedenii vedomstva ministerstva narodnago prosveshcheniia.* 2d ed. St. Petersburg, 1896.

—— *Podrobnaia ob'iasnitel'naia zapiska k proektu smety ministerstva narodnago prosveshcheniia na 1913 god.* St. Petersburg, 1913.

—— *Sbornik postanovlenii i rasporiazhenii po gimnaziiam i progimnaziiam vedomstva ministerstva narodnago prosveshcheniia.* St. Petersburg, 1874.

—— *Sbornik postanovlenii i rasporiazhenii po uchitel'skim institutam, uchitel'skim seminariiam, gorodskim uchilishcham i nachal'nym narodnym uchilishcham vedomstva ministerstva narodnago prosveshcheniia 1859–1875.*

—— *Sbornik postanovlenii po ministerstvu narodnago prosveshcheniia.* St. Petersburg, 1864–1904. 17 vols.

—— *Sbornik rasporiazhenii po ministerstvu narodnago prosveshcheniia.* St. Petersburg, 1866–1905. 17 vols.

—— *Smeta dokhodov, raskhodov i spetsial'nykh sredstv ministerstva narodnago prosveshcheniia.* St. Petersburg, 1911–13. 3 vols.

—— *Vsepoddaneishii otchet ministra narodnago prosveshcheniia.* St. Petersburg, 1851–1915.

——, —— Otdelenie promyshlennykh uchilishch, *Materialy i trudy komissii po voprosam zhenskago professional'nago obrazovaniia.* St. Petersburg, 1904.

——, —— *Po voprosu o srednei obshcheobrazovatel'noi shkole, s primeneniem eia k zaprosam i nuzhdam sovremennoi zhizni nekotorykh mestnostei Rossii. (Otchet o komandirovke upravliaiushchago otdeleniem promyshlennykh uchilishch ministerstva narodnago prosveshcheniia tainago sovetnika Anopova).* St. Petersburg, 1900.

——, —— *Sbornik materialov po tekhnicheskomu i professional'nomu obrazovaniiu.* St. Petersburg, 1900–1902. 3 vols.

——, —— *Trudy soveshchaniia direktorov i lits pedagogicheskago personala srednikh tekhnicheskikh uchilishch dlia vyrabotki mer k vozstanovleniiu v etikh zavedeniiakh normal'nago techeniia zaniatii.* St. Petersburg, 1907.

Ministerstvo vnutrennikh del. *Sobranie materialov o napravlenii razlichnykh otraslei russkoi slovesnosti za poslednee desiatiletie i otechestvennoi zhurnalistiki za 1863 i 1864 g.* St. Petersburg, 1865.

Moskovskaia prakticheskaia akademiia kommercheskikh nauk. *Otchet moskovskoi prakticheskoi akademii kommercheskikh nauk za 1901 god.* Moscow, 1901.

Moskovskii uchebnyi okrug. *Otchet o pis'mennykh ispytaniiakh zrelosti, proizvedennykh v gimnaziiakh moskovskago uchebnago okruga.* Moscow, 1887–99. 12 vols.

—— *Otchet o sezde uchitelei gorodskikh, po polozheniiu 1872 g., uchilishch moskovskago uchebnago okruga 2–11 ianvaria 1903 g.* Moscow, 1904.

—— *Pedagogicheskii vestnik moskovskago uchebnago okruga. Sredniaia i nizshaia shkola,* Moscow, 1911. Nos. 1–9.

―――― *Prilozheniia ḳ sborniḳu postanovlenii i rasporiazhenii po gimnaziiam i progimnaziiam mosḳovsḳago uchebnago oḳruga za 1872–1888 gody.* Moscow, 1889.

―――― *Sborniḳ postanovlenii i rasporiazhenii po uchitel'sḳomu institutu, uchitel'sḳim seminariiam i nizshim uchebnym zavedeniiam mosḳovsḳago uchebnago oḳruga.* Part 1, Moscow, 1895. Part 2, Moscow, 1896.

―――― *Soveshchaniia proisḳhodivshiia v 1899 godu v mosḳovsḳom uchebnom oḳruge po voprosam o srednei shḳole v sviazi s tsirḳuliarom g. ministra narodnago prosveshcheniia ot 8 iiulia g. za No. 16212.* Moscow, 1899. 6 vols. Prilozhenie.

―――― *Trudy soveshchaniia inspeḳtorov, zaḳonouchitelei i uchashchiḳh vysshiḳh nachal'nyḳh uchilishch nizhegorodsḳoi gubernii. 3–9 iiunia 1914 goda.* Nizhnii Novgorod, 1915.

Mosḳovsḳii universitet. *Otchet o sostoianii i deistviiaḳh imperatorsḳago mosḳovsḳago universiteta za 1898–1916.* Moscow, 1900–1917. 19 vols.

―――― *Pedagogichesḳoe obshchestvo pri imperatorsḳom mosḳovsḳom universitete—muzei pedagogichesḳago obshchestva v 1903 godu. God pervyi.* Moscow, 1904.

―――― *Trudy pedagogichesḳago obshchestva sostoiashchago pri imperatorsḳom mosḳovsḳom universitete.* Moscow, 1900. 3 vols.

Musin-Pushkin, A. A. *K voprosu o vsaimnyḳh otnosheniiaḳh sem'i i shḳoly v pedagogichesḳoi literature i shḳol'noi praḳtiḳe u nas i na zapade.* St. Petersburg, 1914.

―――― *Sbnorniḳ statei po voprosam shḳol'nago obrazovaniia na zapade i v Rossii.* St. Petersburg, 1912. 2 vols.

―――― *Sredneobrazovatel'naia shḳola v Rossii i eia znachenie.* Petrograd, 1915.

Muzhuev, P. "Prosveshchenie," in vol. 54, "Rossiia," *Entsiḳlopedicheskii slovar.* St. Petersburg: Brockhaus-Efron, 1899.

MVD. See Ministerstvo vnutrennikh del.

Nechaev, A. P. "K voprosu o reforme nashei shkoly," in *Trudy ruḳovoditelei i slushatelei pedagogichesḳiḳh ḳursov voenno-uchebnyḳh zavedenii* (St. Petersburg, 1906), pp. 217–28.

―――― "Psikhologiia i istoriia pedagogiki, kak predmety chtenii na kursakh dlia narodnykh uchitelei," *Zemsḳie obshcheobrazovatel'nye ḳursy dlia narodnyḳh uchitelei. Sborniḳ statei,* pp. 53–60.

―――― "Sostoianie pedagogicheskoi psikhologii za poslednie tri goda." *Trudy vtorogo vserossiisḳago sezda po pedagogichesḳoi psiḳhologii,* pp. 31–32.

―――― "Sovmestnoe obuchenie s tochki zreniia pedagogicheskoi psikhologii," *Trudy vtorogo vserossiisḳago sezda po eḳsperimental'noi pedagogiḳe v Petrograde s 26 po 31 deḳ. 1913 g.,* pp. 103–15.

―――― *Sovremennaia eḳsperimental'naia psiḳhologiia v eia otnoshenii ḳ voprosam shḳol'nago obucheniia.* St. Petersburg, 1901.

Nekrasov, P. A. "Nikolai Pavlovich Bogolepov," *Russkii vestnik,* February 1902, pp. 564–79.

Nicholas, Grand Duke of Russia. *Graf Pavel Aleksandrovich Stroganov.* St. Petersburg, 1903. 3 vols.

—— *L' Empereur Alexandre I.* St. Petersburg, 1912. 2 vols.

Nikitenko, A. *Moia povest' o samom sebe i o tom "chemu svidetel' v zhizni byl."* *Zapiski i dnevnik.* 2d ed. St. Petersburg, 1905. 2 vols.

Obchinnikov, M. V. *Ezhegodnik dlia uchitelei nachal'nykh uchilishch, tserkovnoprikhodskikh shkol. God pervyi.* Moscow, 1889.

Obraz. Zhenshchin. See Rossiiskaia liga.

Obshchestvo eksperimental'noi pedagogiki, *Trudy pervago vserossiiskago sezda po eksperimental'noi pedagogike v 1910 godu.* St. Petersburg, 1911.

—— *Trudy vtorogo vserossiiskago sezda po eksperimental'noi pedagogike v Petrograde s 26 po 31 dek. 1913 g.* St. Petersburg, 1914.

Obshchestvo rasprostraneniia kommercheskago obrazovaniia v g. Kieve. *Otchet po uchebno-vospitatel'noi chasti torgovykh shkol i klassov obshchestva. Za 1900–1901 uch. god.* Kiev, 1901.

Obshchestvo rasprostraneniia nachal'nago obrazovaniia v Nizhegorodskoi gubernii. *Otchet soveta obshchestva rasprostraneniia nachal'nago obrazovaniia v Nizhegorodskoi gubernii za 1903 god.* Nizhnii Novgorod, 1904.

Obshchestvo rasprostraneniia tekhnicheskikh znanii. *Godichnyi otchet o deiatel'nosti obshchestva rasprostraneniia tekhnicheskikh znanii za dvadtsat' pervyi (1889/90) god.* Moscow, 1891.

—— *Otchet o deiatel'nosti uchebnago otdela obshchestva rasprostraneniia tekhnicheskikh znanii za 1908 i 1909.* Moscow, 1911.

Obshchestvo russkikh vrachei v pamiat' N. I. Pirogova. Komissiia po rasprostraneniiu gigienicheskikh znanii, *Materialy k voprosu o prepodavanii gigieny v srednei shkole.* Moscow, 1908–12. 2 vols.

Obshchestvo vspomoshchestvovaniia litsam uchitel'skago zvaniia. *Dnevnik sezda predstavitelei obshchestv vspomoshchestvovaniia litsam uchitel'skago zvaniia.* Moscow, 1903. 10 vols.

—— *Trudy 1-go vserossiiskago sezda predstavitelei obshchestv vspomoshchestvovaniia litsam uchitel'skago zvaniia (1902–1903).* Moscow, 1907. 2 vols. (For the second congress see *S-Peterburgskoe pedagogicheskoe obshchestvo vzaimnoi pomoshchi.*)

Obshchezemskii sezd po narodnomu obrazovaniiu. *Pervyi obshchezemskii sezd po narodnomu obrazovaniiu 1911 goda.* Moscow, 1911–12. 9 vols.

Obshchezemskii sezd po statistike narodnago obrazovaniia. *Pervyi obshchezemskii sezd po statistike narodnago obrazovaniia 1913 goda. Doklady.* Kharkov, 1913.

Obukhov, M. "O zhelatel'nykh izmeneniiakh v organizatsii uchitel'skikh obshchestv, na osnovanii vzaimnykh otnoshenii tsentra i filial'nykh otdelenii," *Russkii uchitel',* 1913, No. 12, pp. 905–16.

Obzor Dumy. See Gosudarstvennaia duma, *Obzor.*

Obzor MNP. See Rozhdestvenskii.

"O dorogovizne sredniago obrazovaniia," *Russkaia shkola*, 1905, No. 12, pp. 126–41.

"O nekotorykh prichinakh vrazhebnago otnosheniia obshchestva k pedagogam," *Russkaia shkola*, 1905, No. 1, pp. 98–108.

Ostrogorskii, A. N. "O sovesti, strakhe nakazaniia i proch.," *Trudy rukovoditelei i slushatelei pedagogicheskikh kursov voenno-uchebnykh zavedenii*, pp. 1–17.

Ostrovitianov, K. V., ed. *Istoriia akademii nauk SSSR*. Moscow, 1958. 3 vols.

Otchet MNP. See Ministerstvo narodnago prosveshcheniia, *Vsepoddaneishii otchet.*

Otchet o sezde uchitelei gorodskikh, po polozheniiu 1872 g., uchilishch moskovskago uchebnago okruga 2–11 ianvaria 1903 g. Moscow, 1904.

Pavlov, A. P. *Reforma sredniago obrazovaniia*. 2d ed. Moscow, 1908.

Pedagogicheskii muzei voenno-uchebnikh zavedenii, *Dvadtsatipiatiletie pedagogicheskago muzeia voenno-uchebnykh zavedenii. 1864–1889.* St. Petersburg, 1889.

——— *Trudy rukovoditelei i slushatelei pedagogicheskikh kursov voenno-uchebnykh zavedenii.* St. Petersburg, 1906.

Petrov, P. V., ed. *Sbornik pedagogicheskikh statei v chest' redaktora zhurnala "Pedagogicheskii sbornik" A. N. Ostrogorskago po sluchaiu dvadtsatipiatiletiia po ego redaktorskoi deiatel'nosti.* St. Petersburg, 1907.

Pirogov, N. I. *Izbrannye pedagogicheskie sochineniia*. Moscow, 1952.

Pisarev, D. I. *Izbrannye pedagogicheskie vyskazyvaniia*. Moscow, 1938.

Plesterer, A. "O zhelatel'nom voznagrazhdenii prepodavatelei srednikh uchebnykh zavedenii," *Trudy pedagogicheskago obshchestva sostoiashchago pri imperatorskom moskovskom universitete*, II, 15–90.

Pobedonostsev, K. P. *K. P. Pobedonostsev i ego korrespondenty.* Moscow, 1923. 3 vols.

——— *Reflections of a Russian Statesman.* London, 1898.

——— "Russia and Popular Education (A Reply to Prince Kropotkin)," *North American Review*, CLXXIII (1901), 349–54.

Pokrovskii, V. I. "O shkol'noi perepisi 1911 goda," *Pervyi obshchezemskii sezd po statistike narodnago obrazovaniia 1913 goda*, pp. 691–94.

Polnoe sobranie zakonov rossiiskoi imperii . . . , 1649–1913. Petrograd, 1830–1916.

Pravila i programmy dlia postupleniia v vysshiia i sredniia uchebnyia zavedeniia grazhdanskago, voennago, morskago i dukhovnago vedomstv na 1874–75 uchebnyi g. 7th ed. St. Petersburg, 1874.

"Proekt ustroistva pedagogicheskago fakul'teta pri universitetakh," *Nauchnoe slovo*. V (1905), 109–16.

Professional'nyia uchitel'skiia organizatsii na zapade i v Rossii. Sbornik statei. Petrograd, 1915. 2 vols.

Protopopov, D. D. *Istoriia s-peterburgskogo komiteta gramotnosti sostoiav-*

shego pri imperatorskom vol'nom ekonomicheskom obshchestve, 1861–1895. St. Petersburg, 1898.

PSU. See Vserossiiskii soiuz uchitelei, *Protokoly 1-go vserossiiskago sezda uchitelei.*

PSZ. See Polnoe.

Pushkin, A. S. *Polnoe sobranie sochinenii v odnom tome.* Moscow, 1949.

Radonezhkii, A. *Osnovy russkoi shkoly i sovremennaia gimnaziia.* St. Petersburg, 1901.

Rizhskii uchebnyi okrug. *Materialy po voprosu o povyshenii kachestva srednei shkoly.* Riga, 1910. 3 vols.

Ropp, A. N. *Chto sdelala tret'ia gosudarstvennaia duma dlia narodnago obrazovaniia?* St. Petersburg, 1912.

Rossiiskaia liga ravnopraviia zhenshchin. *Trudy 1-go vserossiiskago sezda po obrazovaniiu zhenshchin (1912–1913).* Petrograd, 1914–15. 2 vols.

Rozhdestvenskii, S. V. *Istoricheskii obzor deiatel'nosti ministerstva narodnago prosveshcheniia 1802–1902.* St. Petersburg, 1902.

R.S. See Russkaia shkola.

R.U. See Russkii uchitel'.

Russkaia shkola. Obshchepedagogicheskii zhurnal dlia shkoly i sem'i. St. Petersburg, 1890–1917.

Russkii uchitel'. Ezhemesiachnyi professional'nyi organ uchitel'stva nachal'-noi i srednei shkoly. St. Petersburg, 1912–[1917?].

Sakharov, A. "Kommercheskoe obrazovanie v shkolakh ministerstva narodnago prosveshcheniia," *Russkaia shkola.* July/August 1905, pp. 216–36.

Saltykov, N. N. "Ob organizatsii podgotovki prepodavatelei srednei shkoly," *Doklady chitannye na 2-m vserossiiskom sezde prepodavatelei matematiki v Moskve,* pp. 29–42.

Sbornik post. MNP. See Ministerstvo narodnago prosveshcheniia, *Sbornik postanovlenii po ministerstvu narodnago prosveshcheniia.*

Sbornik ras. MNP. See Ministerstvo narodnago prosveshcheniia, *Sbornik rasporiazhenii.*

Selenkin, V. "Sredniaia shkola v bor'be s prostupkami uchenikov," *Vestnik vospitaniia,* January 1905, pp. 81–118.

Semeino-pedagogicheskii kruzhok. *Sbornik semeino-pedagogicheskago kruzhka v gor. Kazani.* No. 2. Kazan, 1902.

Senex [pseudonym]. "K defektam srednei shkoly," *Russkaia shkola,* December 1905, pp. 126–41.

"Sezdy zakonouchitelei srednikh uchebnykh zavedenii," *Tserkovnyia vedomosti,* 1913, No. 39, 1780–83; No. 43, 1984–87; No. 46, 2128–32; No. 48, 2236–40.

Shaposhnikov, I. N. "Novyi tip gorodskikh uchilishch bez mladshikh otdelenii i otnosheniia gorodskikh uchilishch k nachal'nym uchilishcham," *Otchet o sezde uchitelei gorodskikh, po polozheniiu 1872 g., uchilishch moskovskago uchebnago okruga 2–11 ianvaria 1903 g.,* pp. 162–89.

Shchebal'skii, P. "A. S. Shishkov, ego soiuzniki i protivniki," *Russkii vestnik*, 90 (1870), 192–254.

Shcherbin, K. M. *Matematika v russkoi srednei shkole. Obzor trudov i mnenii po voprosu ob uluchshenii programm matematiki v srednei shkole za poslednie deviat' let. (1899–1907).* Kiev, 1908.

Shevyrev, S. *Istoriia imperatorskogo moskovskogo universiteta, napisannaia k stoletnemu ego iubileiu. 1755–1855.* Moscow, 1955.

Shilovoi, N. I. "Zhenshchiny v russkikh universitetakh i tekhnicheskikh vysshikh uchebnykh zavedeniiakh v 1906–1912 g.," *Trudy 1-go vserossiiskago sezda po obrazovaniiu zhenshchin*, I, 31–34.

Shokhol', K. P. *Vysshee zhenskoe obrazovanie v Rossii (istoriko-iiuridicheskii ocherk).* St. Petersburg, 1910.

"Shuvalov, Ivan Ivanovich." *Russkii biograficheskii slovar.* St. Petersburg, 1911. Vol. XXIII.

Simashkevich, N. V. "Uchitel', kak vospitatel', i ego pravovoe polozhenie," *Trudy kievskago pedagogicheskago sezda. 12–19 aprelia 1916 goda*, pp. 161–70.

Sintsov, D. M. "Doklad o mezhdunarodnoi komissii po prepodavaniiu matematiki," *Doklady chitannye na 2-m vserossiiskom sezde prepodavatelei matematiki v Moskve*, pp. 4–20.

Skortsov, N. E. "Organicheskii nedug sovremennoi gimnazii," *Zhurnal ministerstva narodnago prosveshcheniia*, May 1895, pp. 1–36.

SMS. See Moskovskii uchebnyi okrug, *Soveshchaniia proiskhodivshiia.*

"Soiuz uchitelei srednei shkoly (Spb)," *Pravo*, 1905, No. 17, pp. 1385–92.

Sokolov, N. M., ed. *Sovmestnoe obrazovanie. Sbornik statei.* St. Petersburg, 1914.

Sokolovskii, P. *Russkaia shkola v vostochnoi Sibiri i priamurskom krae.* Kharkov, 1914.

Soloviev, S. M. *Istoriia Rossii s drevneishikh vremen.* Moscow, 1959–62.

Soviet S. O. See Gosudarstvennyi soviet.

Sozonov, S. *Sud'by srednei shkoly.* Moscow, 1907.

Spasovich, B. D. "Vospominaniia o K. D. Kaveline," *Sobranie sochinenii K. D. Kavelina.* St. Petersburg, [1898?], II, vii–xxxi.

S-Peterburgskaia pedagogicheskaia akademiia. *Trudy s-peterburgskoi pedagogicheskoi akademii.* St. Petersburg, 1910.

S-Peterburgskii uchebnyi okrug. *Otchet o sostoianii shestoi s-peterburgskoi gimnazii za 1910–1911.* St. Petersburg, 1911.

———— *Programmy dlia narodnykh uchilishch s-peterburgskago uchebnago okruga.* 3d ed. St. Petersburg, 1896.

———— *Sbornik alfavitny zakonopolozhenii i rasporiazhenii po s-pet. uchebnomu okrugu za 1858–1876, 1876–1882, 1883–1893.* 3 vols. N.p., n.d.

———— *Trudy pervago sezda direktorov sredneuchebnykh zavedenii s-peterburgskago uchebnago okruga (s 7–11 ianvaria 1912 g.).* St. Petersburg, 1912.

S-Peterburgskoe obshchestvo narodnykh universitetov. *Otchet o deiatel'nosti s-peterburgskago obshchestva narodnykh universitetov za 1909 g.* St. Petersburg, 1910.

S-Peterburgskoe pedagogicheskoe obshchestvo vzaimnoi pomoshchi. *Dnevnik II vserossiiskago imeni K.D. Ushinskago sezda predstavitelei obshchestv vspomoshchestvovaniia litsam uchitel'skago zvaniia. 29 dek. 1913 g.–5 ianv. 1914 g.* St. Petersburg, 1914. 6 vols.

——— *Spravochnyi listok s-peterburgskago pedagogicheskago obshchestva vzaimnoi pomoshchi. Oktiabr'–Mart 1904–1905.* St. Petersburg, 1905.

——— *Trudy vtorogo vserossiiskago sezda imeni K. D. Ushinskago. 29 dek. 1913 g.–5 ianv. 1914 g.* Petrograd, 1914–16. 3 vols.

Spravochnaia kniga po voprosam obrazovaniia evreev. St. Petersburg, 1901.

Sreznevskii, B. I. "Otchet prof. B. I. Sreznevskago po revizii prepodavaniia geografii v srednikh uchebnykh zavedeniiakh rizhskago uchebnago okruga," *K voprosu kachestvennago pod'ema srednei shkoly. Revizionnye otchety gg. professorov imperatorskago iur'evskago universiteta.* Riga, 1912, pp. 191–370.

Stepanov, S. L. "K voprosu o pedagogicheskoi podgotovke prepodavatelei srednei shkoly v Rossii," *Zhurnal ministerstva narodnago prosveshcheniia.* March 1909, pp. 1–35.

——— "Ob ustanovlenii sviazi mezhdu nizshei i srednei obshcheobrazovatel'- noi shkoloi," *Trudy pervago sezda direktorov sredneuchebnykh zavedenii s-peterburgskago uchebnago okruga (s 7–11 ianvaria 1912 g.),* pp. 177–97.

Stepniak [S. M. Kravchinskii]. *Russia under the Tsars.* London, 1894. [2d?] ed.

Stroganov. See Nicholas, Grand Duke of Russia, *Graf Pavel Aleksandrovich Stroganov.*

Studitskii, F. *Zadachi russkoi zhizni.* St. Petersburg, 1881.

"Svedeniia o chisle uchivshikhsia v nashikh gimnaziiakh s 1857 po 1866 god," *Zhurnal ministerstva narodnago prosveshcheniia.* August and October, 1868.

Tatishchev, S. S. *Imperator Aleksandr II. Ego zhizn' i tsarstvovanie.* St. Petersburg, 1903. 2 vols.

Tikhomirov, D. I. *O reforme dukhovnoi shkoly.* St. Petersburg, 1905.

Tikhomirov, M. N., ed. *Istoriia moskovskogo universiteta.* Moscow, 1955. 2 vols.

Timashev, N. S. "Overcoming Illiteracy. Public Education in Russia, 1880– 1940," *Russian Review, Autumn* 1942, pp. 80–88.

Tolstoy, D. A. *Die Stadtschulen während der Regierung der Kaiserin Katharina II, Beiträge zur Kenntniss des Russischen Reiches.* St. Petersburg, 1887. 3d Series, Vol. II.

Trudy pervago sezda direktorov sredneuchebnykh zavedenii s-peterburgskago uchebnago okruga s 7–11 ianvaria 1912 g. St. Petersburg, 1912.

Tsirul', K. *Ruchnoi trud v obshcheobrazovatel'noi shkole.* St. Petersburg, 1894.

Tsypovich, E. P. "O reforme real'nykh uchilishch," *Trudy pervago sezda direktorov sredneuchebnykh zavedenii s-peterburgskago uchebnago okruga (s 7–11 ianvaria 1912 g.),* pp. 224–49.

Uchitel'. Pedagogicheskii i literaturno-nauchnyi zhurnal. Nos. 1–9. St. Petersburg, 1907.

Ulianov, G. "Ob organizatsii v Rossii zhenskago professional'nago obrazovaniia. Skhema," in *Trudy 1-go vserossiiskago sezda po obrazovaniiu zhenshchin,* II, 520.

Urusov, V. M. *Izledovanie nastoiashchago polozheniia shkol'nago dela v dorogobuzhskom uezde i proekt plana dal'neishago ego razvitiia.* Smolensk, 1897.

Ushinsky, K. D. *Chelovek kak predmet vospitaniia. Opyt pedagogicheskoi antropologii.* (Original publication 1868–69.) 11th ed. St. Petersburg, 1903.

——— *Izbrannye pedagogicheskie sochineniia.* Moscow, 1952. 2 vols.

——— "Trud v ego psikhicheskom i vospitatel'nom znachenii," *Zhurnal ministerstva narodnogo prosveshcheniia,* July 1860.

Uspenskii, V. V., and others. *Ocherki po istorii pedagogicheskikh uchenii.* Moscow, 1911.

Vasilevich, V. *Moskovskii sezd predstavitelei uchitel'skikh obshchestv vzaimopomoshchi. 28 dek. 1902–6 ianv. 1903.* Moscow, 1905. (*See* Obshchestvo vspomoshchestvovaniia litsam uchitel'skago zvaniia.)

V–ch, "Professional'nyia nuzhdy moskovskago uchitel'stva," *Russkii uchitel'.* 1912. No. 3, pp. 281–98.

Velikoselskii, N. "Dumskiia 4-kh-klassnyia uchilishcha v Spb.," *Russkii uchitel',* 1913, No. 4, pp. 319–34; No. 5, pp. 503–16; No. 10, pp. 679–94.

Venturi, Franco. *Roots of Revolution.* New York, 1960.

VEP. See Obshchestvo eksperimental'noi pedagogiki, *Trudy vtorogo vserossiiskago sezda.*

Vestnik vospitaniia. Nauchno-populiarnyi zhurnal. Moscow, 1890–1917.

Vetukhov, A. "Trudy pedagogicheskago obshchestva, sostoiashchago pri imperatorskom moskovskom universitete," *Trudy pedagogicheskago otdela khar'kovskago istoriko-filologicheskago obshchestva.* Kharkov, 1900, VI, 261–73.

Vilenskii uchebnyi okrug. *Sezd prepodavatelei russkago iazyka i istorii srednikh uchebnykh zavedenii vilenskago uchebnago okruga v marte 1907 goda. Sektsiia russkago iazyka.* Vilna, 1908.

Vinogradov, N. D. "Blizhaishiia zadachi eksperimental'noi pedagogiki," *Trudy vtorogo vserossiiskago sezda po pedagogicheskoi psikhologii,* pp. 32–40.

Vladimirskii, A., A. Orshanskii, and G. Falbork, eds. *Voprosy pedagogicheskoi patologii.* St. Petersburg, 1912. 2 vols.

Vlasov, A. K. "Kakiia storony elementarnoi matematiki predstavliaiut tsennost' dlia obshchago obrazovaniia?," *Doklad chitannyi na 2-m vserossiiskom sezde prepodavatelei matematiki v Moskve,* pp. 20–29.

Vodovozov, V. I. *Izbrannye pedagogicheskie sochineniia.* Moscow, 1953.

Volkovich, V. A. *Pedagogika-nauka pered sudom eia protivnikov.* 2d ed. St. Petersburg, 1909.

Voprosy i nuzhdy uchitel'stva. Sbornik Vol. I–X. Moscow, 1909–11.

Voskoboinikov, I., "Glavnye itogi sezda gorodskikh uchitelei v S-Peterburge 7–14 iiunia 1909 g.," *Voprosy i nuzhdy uchitel'stva,* 1910, No. 3, pp. 54–71.

Vserossiiskii sezd deiatelei obshchestv narodnykh universitetov. *Dnevnik.* Nos. 1, 2, 3. St. Petersburg, 1908.

——— *Trudy pervago vserossiiskago sezda deiatelei obshchestv narodnykh universitetov i drugikh prosvetitel'nykh uchrezhdenii chastnoi initsiativy. 3–7 ianvaria 1908 g.* St. Petersburg, 1908.

Vserossiiskii sezd lits interesuiushchikhsia prepodavaniem novykh iazykov. *Trudy pervago vserossiiskago sezda lits interesuiushchikhsia prepodavaniem novykh iazykov. 29-go dek. 1912 po 3 ianv. 1913 goda.* Moscow, [1913?].

Vserossiiskii sezd po pedagogicheskoi psikhologii. *Trudy pervago vserossiiskago sezda po pedagogicheskoi psikhologii v S-Peterburge v 1906 g.* St. Petersburg, 1906.

——— *Trudy vtorogo vserossiiskago sezda po pedagogicheskoi psikhologii.* St. Petersburg, 1910.

Vserossiiskii sezd po semeinomu vospitaniiu. *Trudy.* St. Petersburg, 1914.

Vserossiiskii sezd po voprosam narodnago obrazovaniia. *Trudy pervago vserossiiskago sezda po voprosam narodnago obrazovaniia 23 dek. 1913– 3 ianv. 1914.* Petrograd, 1915. 2 vols.

Vserossiiskii sezd prepodavatelei drevnikh iazykov. *Trudy pervago vserossiiskago sezda prepodavatelei drevnikh iazykov.* St. Petersburg, 1912.

Vserossiiskii sezd prepodavatelei matematiki. *Doklady chitannye na 2-m vserossiiskom sezde prepodavatelei matematiki v Moskve.* Moscow, 1915.

——— *Trudy 1-go vserossiiskago sezda prepodavatelei matematiki 27 dek. 1911–3 ianv. 1912.* St. Petersburg, 1913. 2 vols.

Vserossiiskii sezd uchitelei gorodskikh po polozheniiu 1872 g. uchilishch. *Trudy pervago vserossiiskago sezda uchitelei gorodskikh po polozheniiu 1872 g. uchilishch 7–14 iiunia 1909 g.* St. Petersburg, 1909–10. 3 vols.

Vserossiiskii soiuz uchitelei i deiatelei srednei shkoly. *Protokoly 1-go vserossiiskago sezda uchitelei i deiatelei srednei shkoly na Imatre 9–11 fevralia 1906 g.* Moscow, 1906.

——— *Sezd uchitelei i deiatelei srednei shkoly v Peterburge iiun' 1906 goda.* St. Petersburg, 1906.

——— *Trudy kursov dlia uchitelei srednei shkoly 5–25 iiunia 1907 g.,* A. Zaks, ed. St. Petersburg, 1907.

V. V. See Vestnik vospitaniia.

Witte, Sergei. *Vospominaniia. Tsarstvovanie Nikolaia II.* Berlin, 1922–23. 2 vols.

Zaionchkovskii, P. A. "Zapiska K. D. Kavelina o nigilizme," *Istoricheskii arkhiv,* V (1950), 323–41.

Zakharchenko, M. M. *Kommercheskoe i tekhnicheskoe zhenskoe obrazovanie v Avstrii, Frantsii, Germanii, i Rossii.* St. Petersburg, 1900.

"Zapiska prepodavatelei moskovskikh srednikh uchebnykh zavedenii," *Pravo* 1905, No. 6, pp. 424–25.

"Zavadovskii, Petr Vasilevich," *Russkii biograficheskii slovar.* St. Petersburg, 1911. Vol. VII.

Zemskie obshcheobrazovatel'nye kursy dlia narodnykh uchitelei. Sbornik statei. St. Petersburg, 1906.

Zenkovskii, A. V. *Pravda o Stolypine.* New York, 1956.

Zhebelev, S. A. "Sredniaia shkola i istoriko-filologicheskii fakul'tet," *Trudy pervago vserossiiskago sezda prepodavatelei drevnikh iazykov,* pp. 162–71.

Zhurnal ministerstva narodnago prosveshcheniia. St. Petersburg, 1834–1917.

ZMNP. See Zhurnal.

Znamenskii, S. *Sredniaia shkola za poslednie gody. Uchenicheskiia volneniia 1905–1906 g. i ikh znachenie. Obshchii ocherk i materialy.* St. Petersburg, 1909.

INDEX

Index